Douglas

John Home's
Douglas: A Tragedy

WITH CONTEMPORARY COMMENTARIES

edited by Ralph McLean

humming earth

Published by

Humming Earth
an imprint of
Zeticula
57 St Vincent Crescent
Glasgow
G3 8NQ
Scotland.

http://www.hummingearth.com
admin@hummingearth.com

First published in 1757.
This edition first published 2010
Copyright © Zeticula 2010
Introduction © Ralph McLean 2010

Cover illustration reproduced by kind permission of
The Mitchell Library, Glasgow.

ISBN-13 978-1-84622-034-0 Paperback

Acknowledgements

I would like to thank Andrew Hook for his role in the production of this book, and in particular for his comments on the introduction and the pamphlet commentaries. Of course, any mistakes that remain are my own.

Rick Sher provided useful information on the location of pamphlet materials, for which I am very grateful.

I would also like to thank Gerard Carruthers for the conversations that we have had on eighteenth century Scottish literature in general, and Professor Colin Kidd who first introduced me to the world of Douglas during his Scottish Enlightenment course at the University of Glasgow.

I should also like to thank the librarians and staff at the following institutions who provided help and assistance with materials:

Glasgow University Library, and in particular its Special Collections department,

the Mitchell Library,

the National Library of Scotland, and

the British Library.

Ralph McLean,
Glasgow,
September 2010

Contents

Introduction

When John Home (1722-1808) finally saw his play *Douglas* performed in Edinburgh on December the 14th 1756, he could scarcely have imagined the controversy that would erupt around it. For although the intention of his work was to stake a claim for the cultural vibrancy of Scotland, the production itself occasioned a fierce and passionate pamphlet war which raged over the relationship of the stage and the church, the concept of taste, and the state of literary production in Scotland.[1] Indeed, part of the reason why *Douglas* remained a staple of the British and American stage for almost a hundred years, was the intense debate that surrounded the early life of the play. Born in Leith to a town clerk, the young Home was educated at Leith grammar school before attending the University of Edinburgh where he met such influential figures as William Robertson, Alexander Carlyle, and John Witherspoon, who would all go on to play a part in the *Douglas* controversy. Just like his colleagues, Home would be ordained as a minister in the Church of Scotland (1745), taking up a position at Athelstanesford in East Lothian, before quitting his job in the aftermath of the controversy.

Previous editions of *Douglas*, including Gerald D. Parker's 1972 version, have made allusions to the importance of this controversy, and the rich pamphlet war that erupted around the play and its production. This edition, rather than simply acknowledging these pamphlets, seeks to make available, along with the play itself, a representative selection of this material, demonstrating the range and variety of contributions to the debate. As well as the major contributions of such figures as Witherspoon, Carlyle, Adam Ferguson and David Hume, examples of the extensive religious responses to *Douglas*, and the intense literary debate that ensued over the quality of the work, are also included. These responses extend from the sophisticated, in-depth arguments proffered by the literati of Scotland, to the harangues of anonymous critics in the forms of bawdy verse and angry broadsides. In some cases, pamphlets initiated a chain of publications, refuting, qualifying or agreeing upon issues raised in the controversy. I have tried to preserve this pattern of chain reaction wherever it has been possible to do so. However, as this has not always been feasible, I have included, as an appendix, a list of the materials used in this edition, along with their publication dates, in the cases where this information has been available.

History of the Play

Douglas was not Home's first play. His previous effort, *Agis*, which recounts the life of a Spartan king, was turned down for the London stage by the actor David Garrick in 1749. Undeterred, Home returned to compose another piece, this time drawing on Scottish, rather than classical tradition. He borrowed considerably from the ballad 'Gil Morrice' to form the core of his new play. Alexander Carlyle remarked that it was after Home heard the ballad sung, that he began to formulate his idea for *Douglas*, although it took him five years to offer it for stage production as he was 'but an idle composer'.[2] 'Gil Morrice' recounts the tragic tale of a youth, murdered by a jealous stepfather, who believes him to be his wife's lover. However, Home sanitised parts of the ballad to make it more acceptable to his eighteenth-century audience: for example, making Norval the legitimate offspring of Lady Randolph, where before, Gil Morrice was the illegitimate son of Lady Barnard. Another source frequently cited as an influence upon *Douglas* is Voltaire's *Mérope* (1743). It has a similar militaristic setting, and a hero whose true identity is shrouded in mystery, but there are significant differences between the two pieces. Indeed, contemporary reviewers noted that although there were similarities the differences were so great that Home could not be accused of plagiarism.[3]

On completion of his first draft around February 1755, Home travelled to London where he presented it to Garrick for his approval. Rejection was once again Garrick's response. Another round of revisions followed and by April 1756 the latest version of *Douglas* was complete. Home sent a draft of the fourth Act to the Earl of Bute, the Scotsman who would go on to become George III's Prime Minister, as well as Home's patron.[4] Bute attempted to exert his influence over Garrick in order to convince him to stage the production, but once again the actor-manager refused. In a letter to Bute, Garrick outlined his reasons in no uncertain terms: 'Had I thought yt the Tragedy could possibly have appear'd', he argued, 'I would have submitted some Alterations to ye Author; But upon my Word & honor, I think ye Tragedy radically defective, & in Every Act incapable of raising the Passions, or comanding Attention.'[5] Despite his subsequent friendly association with Home, which would see him stage his future plays, Garrick at this point would not yield over *Douglas*. While Home undoubtedly viewed this as a setback, the enlightened literati of Scotland considered it an opportunity to bring the play closer to perfection. Hugh Blair, who would be instrumental in establishing modes of literary critical thinking in Scotland and the Atlantic world, offered his advice, as did William Robertson, the future moderator of the General Assembly and Principal of Edinburgh University.[6] In the milieu of enlightened Scotland, Home benefited from the revisions and criticisms suggested by his fellows in the Edinburgh Select Society, a body designed to act as a stimulus for polite debate and the pursuit of eloquence. Carlyle copied *Douglas* several times over for Home, adding his own criticisms along the way, although he cites Gilbert

Elliot as the man who made the most decisive critical contribution to the final acting version.[7] As Garrick refused to put the play on in London, the literati took the opportunity to launch it in Edinburgh, believing that if it succeeded there, London could not refuse to put it on. Supposedly, leading figures among the Edinburgh literati attended the rehearsals and even acted out some of the parts. Home took the plum role of Young Norval, David Hume, ironically, portrayed the villain of the piece, Glenalvon. Robertson was Lord Randolph, while Adam Ferguson was Lady Randolph. Carlyle acted the part of Old Norval, with Blair as Anna the maid.[8] The audience for this rehearsal was just as eminent as the cast itself, since it included the Lords Elibank, Kames, Milton and Monboddo. Milton's involvement in the play was crucial, for it was his patron, the Duke of Argyll, who held enough political sway in the city to ensure that the play was staged. This was a fact not lost on Carlyle, who noted, 'The Duke's good opinion, made Milton adhere more firmly to him [Home], and assist in bringing on his play in the end of that season.'[9]

The manager of the Canongate theatre, West Digges, staged the play, starring as young Norval. Sarah Ward took the role of Lady Randolph.[10] By all accounts Ward was a triumph as the tragic heroine, although her performances were later eclipsed by the formidable talents of Sarah Siddons. In order to promote the opening night of the play a circular was distributed which specifically stated that space would be available for members of the clergy who wished to attend. The notice also advised that anyone who wished for tickets should visit 'the lodgings of D----- H----- Esq.', which is almost certainly a reference to David Hume, a friend of the author and a fervent supporter of the play.[11] *Douglas* was an immediate hit with audiences, and there are accounts of disappointed theatre-goers being turned away at the door. In the patriotic fervour that ensued, one zealous audience member on opening night is reported to have uttered the famous words, 'Whaur's yer Wully Shakspere noo', although the authenticity of this statement has been difficult to confirm.[12] The performance ran six nights in the capital, making it a resounding success. However, as interest began to wane, Digges asked for Carlyle's help in teasing out a few more dates. His response was to write the broadside, *A Full and True History of the Bloody Tragedy of Douglas*, which was designed to appeal to the lower orders in Edinburgh. Carlyle believed that his effort had added two further days to the run. Following *Douglas's* success in Edinburgh, London's interest had now been piqued. John Rich saw the potential to capitalise on the controversy and staged his version of the play at Covent Garden theatre on March 14th 1757. With the attention generated by the Edinburgh production, in addition to the intoxicating whiff of controversy which began to emanate from the printing presses, the play enjoyed a run of nine nights in the British capital. Although *Douglas* had acquitted itself well on the London stage, it was not until Mrs. Siddons dazzled audiences with her interpretation of Lady Randolph that it established itself as a staple of the Anglo-American theatre for almost a century.

Controversy and Pamphlet War

The controversy that surrounds *Douglas* is twofold. There was both a literary and religious backlash after the play was released. The staging of *Douglas* would inevitably have garnered some attention from press reviews, but the grandiloquent patronage of David Hume enshrined in the dedication to his friend published in his *Four Dissertations* ensured that sustained and virulent criticism was focused on the play. Hume located *Douglas* at the apex of taste and polite culture. In the Scottish playwright he saw, 'the true theatric genius of *Shakespear* and Otway, refined from the unhappy barbarism of the one, and licentiousness of the other.'[13] As Ernest Campbell Mossner has asserted, Hume's position as the pre-eminent man of letters in Britain, forced Scottish and English critics to address the work.[14] However, Hume's cultural agenda rather than his critical acumen is betrayed in his dedication, for he was mainly concerned with the creation of a Scottish literary canon built upon conventional neo-classical foundations. He enthused over the now forgotten poetry of Thomas Blacklock and William Wilkie, whose *Epigoniad*, he believed, could provide Scotland with the great epic poem its literary tradition lacked. It was in *Douglas*, however, that Hume saw the greatest opportunity to cement his claim that Scots were 'the People most distinguish'd for Literature in Europe.'[15] Hume was aware of the function he was performing and was prepared to risk a degree of critical ridicule for the reward of critical attention. Writing to the Abbé Le Blanc, he boasted that, 'In order to raise it [*Douglas*] from Obscurity, I wrote to the Author the Dedication, prefix'd to the Four Disserations, which had so good an Effect, that the Tragedy was brought on in Covent Garden, and extremely well received by the Public.'[16] Although the Moderates were on friendly terms with Hume, his dedication, which appeared in a collection of essays including the skeptical 'The Natural History of Religion', was yet another point which opponents of the play could use to their advantage. The dedication induced a tempest of responses, some outraged at the aesthetic claims Hume made for *Douglas*, others critical of his brand of cultural nationalism. Of the more restrained responses to the play the *Critical Review* offered a stern critique of *Douglas's* flaws, but concluded that, 'We should not indeed have dwelt so long on the little obvious faults to be found in this tragedy, had not Mr David Hume, whose name is certainly respectable in the republic of letters, made it absolutely necessary.'[17]

In addition to the literary controversy, *Douglas* also attracted the Church's wrath. The Scottish stage had a fractious association with the Church in the eighteenth century, but the relationship had been contentious ever since the Reformation.[18] Before the controversy over *Douglas* emerged, the Church had frequently railed against the stage.[19] The English actor Anthony Aston, initially welcomed to Edinburgh, formed a theatrical company in 1726, but was forced out in 1727 by the local council and a legal battle ensued. Although Aston appealed to the Court of Session, and won, the council fought back by issuing another writ, claiming that allowing him to perform would set an immoral precedent. The Scottish poet and playwright, Allan Ramsay, whose pastoral themed *Gentle Shepherd* also enjoyed a degree of popularity, similarly attracted the ire of the Edinburgh Presbytery when he set up a theatre in 1736. This time, following the government's Licensing Act of 1737, the Presbytery had the law on its side. The Act stated that in order to stage a performance, a theatre must first obtain a royal Patent, which itself required an Act of Parliament. The result was the closure of almost all theatres. Nevertheless, ingenious managers circumvented the Act by performing for free, and sandwiching plays between two pieces of music.

As a consequence of the cultural ascendancy of the Moderate clergy in the Church of Scotland, there is a tendency to make a sharp delineation between the enlightened Moderates, acting as the arbiters of taste and manners in Scottish culture, and the more evangelical and religiously orthodox Popular party[20] and their followers, who believed the pursuit of polite literature to be a luxury which infringed upon man's real business of glorifying God.[21] While it is certainly true that the Moderates dominated their Popular counterparts in the publication of materials relating to taste and composition, it is inaccurate to write off the literary efforts of their opponents as simply the extremist ideas of religious fundamentalists.[22] Nowhere is this clash of opposing styles more pronounced, or more misunderstood, than in the *Douglas* controversy which pitted the two sides against each other over the role of the stage and the value of literary production. The opponents of the Moderates seized upon the fact that a member of the clergy had the audacity to write a play, and then compounded his sin by encouraging his parishioners to attend. This was a fact not lost on the Presbytery of Edinburgh, who reacted swiftly to the production, and began proceedings to punish those ministers connected with the play. To this end they issued an, *Admonition and Exhortation*, which was to be read from pulpits, and then published to reach the widest audience possible. This backfired to a great extent, because it only focused more attention on the play, and initiated a raft of print retaliation. As Henry Mackenzie noted, 'This step of the Presbytery, like all other overstrained proceedings of that nature provoked resistance and ridicule on the part of the public. The wags poured forth parodies, epigrams, and songs. These were, in general not remarkable for their wit or pleasantry, though some of them were the productions of young men, afterwards eminent in letters or in station.'[23]

The Presbytery of Edinburgh was unrepentant however. The first minister to be punished was Thomas Whyte, the minister of Liberton in Edinburgh, who was hauled before the Presbytery to account for his actions. Whyte humbly submitted that as he was so far from his parish he did not think he would be recognised. Furthermore, he added that he had only attended the theatre once, and that he had endeavoured to conceal himself in a corner to avoid giving any offence.[24] Whyte was given a three-week suspension from his parish – a sentence reduced as an acknowledgement of his contrition. Of the other ministers who attended the play, George Steele of Stair was called before the Presbytery of Ayr, and rebuked for his attendance, as was the Reverend George Cupples who was likewise reprimanded by the Presbytery of Chirnside in Berwickshire. Not all the Presbyteries spoke with a unified voice over the issue however. Both William Home of Polwarth and Francis Scott of Westruther were defended in a letter from the Presbytery of Dunse to the Presbytery of Edinburgh. Furious that the Edinburgh Presbytery had infringed upon a matter that did not concern them, the authors James Laurie and Alexander Hume questioned the furore that had erupted stating, 'We cannot allow ourselves to think, that a thing really criminal in itself, and morally evil, in Scotland, is innocent or indifferent on the other side of the Tweed.'[25] Ironically, the author of the play himself managed to escape relatively unscathed. Summoned to the Presbytery of Haddington on April 5th to answer the charges brought against him, Home replied that as he was in London he would not be able to attend until May 1st.[26] He had still not returned by this date, and on the 10th of May the matter was referred to the Presbytery. The Moderates had strong representation in Haddington, especially in the form of Robertson and Hugh Bannatine, and they along with other Moderates were able to delay any decisive action against Home. Home resolved the matter himself when he resigned from his position at Athelstanesford on 7th June.

While Home had escaped relatively untouched, Alexander Carlyle, one of the play's staunchest defenders, endured an altogether more harrowing ordeal. Since he would admit to doing no wrong, the Presbytery of Dalkeith sought to make an example of him. After a bullish display before the Presbytery on March 1st, his opponents issued a libel, charging him with three transgressions. Firstly, that he kept company with the actors themselves, who in the eye of the law, 'are of bad fame'. Secondly, that he attended the rehearsal of the tragedy, and thirdly, that he attended the opening night.[27] The matter was ultimately referred to the Synod of Lothian and Tweeddale, where under the influence of the Moderates, Carlyle was given a lenient sentence.[28] John Home, who had returned from London to help his friend, addressed the Synod to announce that it was he and not Carlyle who was to blame for the situation.[29] The Presbytery of Edinburgh lamented that there was no act in place which prevented churchmen from visiting the theatre. The hardliners wanted legislation that would prohibit both church and lay figures from attending all future productions, but the Moderates defeated the proposal. However, Robert Dundas, Lord Arniston, proposed a measure that would exclude ministers only, and to this, the Moderates submitted. Nevertheless, this was not enforced, and as Carlyle famously recalled, was flouted openly by the 1780s. 'It is remarkable, that in the year 1784, when the Great Actress Mrs Siddons 1st appeared in Edinburgh during the sitting of the General Assembly, That Court was obliged to fix all its important Business for the Alternate Days when she Did not Act, as all the Younger Members Clergy as well as Laity, took their Stations in the Theatre on Those Days by three in the afternoon.'[30]

In certain quarters there was an outpouring of religious bile which on one level attacked the quality of the production, but on another was deployed specifically to denigrate the Moderates themselves. A typical example of this is John Haldane's, *The Players Scourge* (1757), which describes actors as 'the filth and garbage of the earth, the scum and stain of human nature, the excrements and refuse of all mankind, the pests and plagues of human society, the debauchers of mens minds and morals, unclean beasts, idolatrous Papists or atheists, and the most horrid and abandoned villains that ever the sun shone upon'.[31] When one is faced with this type of response it is understandable why historians have tended to view the writers against *Douglas* as representing an anti-cultural movement, but this is to deny the literary qualities, and the powerful rhetoric of key figures in the Popular party. The most notable of these men is John Witherspoon. His work, *A Serious Enquiry into the Nature and Effects of Stage Plays* is a sophisticated and measured anti-theatrical response to *Douglas*, which concedes that plays may contain admirable sentiments and morals, but owing to their fictive construction, are not capable of disseminating truth in an appropriate manner. To reinforce his argument, Witherspoon sought the authority of scriptural evidence, and used examples of the impropriety of the stage in early Christianity. Although the Moderates secured a victory of sorts in this cultural battle, the outcome was not as inevitable as John Jackson, writing his history of the Scottish stage in the 1790s, imagined it to be. The tribulations which the theatre-going ministers suffered, and the onslaught of 'popular' opposition to *Douglas*, coupled with the more articulate evangelical response of men such as Witherspoon all indicate that the cultural and literary victory of Moderates, though secured, was not decisive.

Versions of the Play

There is no surviving manuscript copy of the first Edinburgh performance of *Douglas*. There are however two 'first' editions of the play printed in 1757. The Scottish printer Andrew Millar was the first to publish his version, based on the performance at Covent Garden. The *Public Advertiser* of March 18th announced that the tragedy would be published the following day. This predates the Edinburgh edition of the play by around ten days, for the *Edinburgh Evening Courant* announced that the play would be available on March 29th 1757, published by G. Hamilton, J. Balfour, W. Gray and W. Peter, for a price of one shilling and sixpence.

The major difference between the London (henceforth L1) and Edinburgh (henceforth E1) editions of the play is that L1 is shorter. One of the reasons for this is that E1 carries two different prologues, whereas L1 omits the Edinburgh prologue. The Edinburgh prologue has a strong nationalistic flavour, which represents Home's cultural agenda. There is an unmistakable attempt to link ancient Athens to contemporary Scotland, a bond made stronger by Edinburgh's claims to be an 'Athens of the North'. As well as an emphasis on the neo-classical elements, which saturate Home's play, there is more than a hint of resentment at Garrick's refusal to stage it. There is also a potent political message in the prologue. For while *Douglas* has rightly been identified as portraying something of the stereotypical martial prowess of Scotland's past, that aspect of the play would have struck a chord with Scots theatre goers who were caught up in the debate over the 'militia issue'. Indeed, on the very day that *Douglas* was first performed, Pitt the Elder introduced his militia bill to parliament.[32] The Edinburgh prologue therefore deals specifically with Scottish issues, while simultaneously attempting to blend the literary sphere with the civic sphere.[33]

As well as the prologues, E1 also has more lines than L1, particularly in Act I. Most of the lines that are cut from this act in the London version, 33-41, 43, 45-70, 79-92, are dialogue between Lord and Lady Randolph. The reason for these cuts is most likely to remove scene setting, which is not necessary to the overall comprehension of the play. Elsewhere, line 89 from Act II is missing from L1, and the words, 'O, my mother' from line 244 in Act V are also omitted. All the cuts from L1 can be attributed to the necessity of trimming a production for the purposes of the stage. In addition to these alterations, E1 is superior to its London counterpart typographically, for it contains fewer errors, and is more consistent with the contemporary practice of capitalising nouns.

Harder to detect are the changes that occurred between the first Edinburgh performances in 1756 and the publication of the play in its alternate versions. Some alterations are obvious. For example, Lord and Lady Randolph were initially called Lord and Lady Barnet, but Home believed that this would cause unintended hilarity because it was also the name of a village near London. Another prominent example of script alteration is the profane language to which a number of the pamphlets make reference. In his *Apology for the Writers Against the Tragedy of Douglas* (1757), John Maclaurin, an arch-critic of the play stated that, 'Though the friends of the author had puffed it away as a perfect tragedy, yet the very first night convinced them, and every body else, that it was cross'd and divided with strange-coloured absurdities; many of which were struck out of it then, and more afterwards, when it was re-formed at London.'[34] The satirical pamphlet, *An Epilogue to the Tragedy of Douglas* (1756), provides in a footnote two of the potentially incendiary lines that were removed: first when a character swears, 'by him that died on the accursed tree to save mankind', and secondly when another character utters the words, 'I'll risk eternal fire', moments from death.[35] As Richard Sher has pointed out, the printed versions of both texts still contain phrases such as 'Despiteful Fate' and 'O God of heaven', which the religious opponents of play could argue were blasphemous.[36]

Owing to the existence of the two versions, much ink has been spilt in an attempt to assess which is more authoritative.[37] For the purposes of reissuing editions of the play, because E1 contains everything that L1 has, plus the extra lines aforementioned, it has generally been selected as the copy text by editors. Indeed, Kevin McGinley has recently questioned the validity of assigning one version precedence over the other, precisely because Home himself would have been aware of both of them, and may well have sanctioned the two versions. As a result of these considerations, I have chosen to use the Edinburgh edition of the play as the foundation text for this volume.

Ralph McLean
Glasgow, August 2010

1   Harold Wilson Thompson went as far as to say that *Douglas* was 'the Scottish Declaration of Literary Independence', because what began life as a reworked Scottish ballad captured the literary attention of the whole of Britain on its artistic merit. Harold Wilson Thompson, *A Scottish Man of Feeling; Some Account of Henry Mackenzie, Esq.* (London, 1931), p. 37

2   Alexander Carlyle, *Autobiography of the Reverend Dr. Alexander Carlyle Minister of Inveresk* (Edinburgh, 1861), p. 233

3   Home was in London when Aaron Hill's adaptation of *Mérope* (1749) was on the stage. This version of the play is closer to Home's *Douglas* than Voltaire's original.

4   Richard B. Sher, *Church and University in the Scottish Enlightenment* (Edinburgh, 1985), p. 76

5   David Garrick, *The Letters of David Garrick*, eds., David M. Little & George M. Kahrl (3 vols, London, 1963), I, p. 245

6   Hugh Blair taught a course on polite taste and composition, which eventually formed the basis for his influential work, *Lectures on Rhetoric and Belles Lettres* (1783). Some of these lectures touch upon the style and composition of Home's tragedy.

7   Carlyle, *Autobiography*, p. 234

8   Henry Peter Brougham, *The Life and Times of Henry, Lord Brougham* (3vols., Edinburgh, 1871), I, pp. 540-542

9   Carlyle, *Autobiography*, p. 310

10 George R. Bushnell, 'The Original Lady Randolph', in, *Theatre Notebook* 13 (1959), pp. 119-123. For more on the relationship between Digges and Ward see: *Letters which passed between Mr. West Digges, comedian, and Mrs. Sarah Ward, 1752-1759*, eds., James Maidment and William Hugh Logan (Edinburgh, 1833)

11 Anon., *Theatre: As the manager has been informed…* (Edinburgh, 1756), p. 1

12 Macdonald Emslie, 'Home's *Douglas* and Wully Shakespeare', in, *Studies in Scottish Literature* 2 (1964), pp. 128-129

13 David Hume, *Four Dissertations* (London, 1757), pp. v-vi

14 Ernest Campbell Mossner, 'Hume and the Scottish Shakespeare', in, *The Huntington Library Quarterly* 4 (1940), p. 423

15 David Hume, *The Letters of David Hume*, ed., J. Y. T. Greig (2 vols., Oxford, 1932), I, p. 255

16 *Ibid.*, p. 261

17 *Critical Review* May 1757, p. 75

18 Despite the Church's animosity to the stage, in the period before the Reformation Protestants were supportive of plays that attacked Catholics, and even after 1560 plays that demonstrated a moral or a sacred purpose

were often condoned. In 1571 John Knox attended a play performed at St Andrews, written by John Davidson who was a regent at the university. Bill Findlay, 'Introduction', in, Bill Findlay, ed., *A History of the Scottish Theatre* (Edinburgh, 1998), p. 18

19 For more on the Scottish stage in the eighteenth century see: Terence Tobin, *Plays by Scots 1660-1800* (Iowa, 1964); Alasdair Cameron, 'Theatre in Scotland 1660-1800', in, Andrew Hook, ed., *The History of Scottish Literature Volume 2 1660-1800* (Aberdeen, 1987), pp. 191-208; Adrienne Scullion, 'The Eighteenth Century', in, Bill Findlay, ed., *A History of the Scottish Theatre* (Edinburgh, 1998), pp. 80-136

20 As John MacIntosh has suggested, the term Popular party is an imprecise appellation attributed to a large group opposed to the Moderates in the General Assembly, particularly over the issue of Patronage but which nevertheless was not a coherent organization. However, in this introduction I will deploy the term to mean those in the Church of Scotland writing against the Moderates in the sphere of polite literature. For more on the problems of labeling the Popular party see, John R. MacIntosh, *Church and Theology in Enlightenment Scotland: The Popular Party, 1740-1800* (East Linton, 1998)

21 The belief that the popular party stood for a narrow-minded anti-culturalist agenda has long been promulgated by Scottish historians: W.L. Mathieson, *The Awakening of Scotland: A History from 1747 to 1797* (Glasgow, 1910) pp. 197-99, 229-30; J. H. S. Burleigh, *A Church History of Scotland* (Edinburgh, 1983) pp. 304-5; A. L. Drummond and J. Bulloch, *The Scottish Church 1688-1843: The Age of the Moderates* (Edinburgh, 1973) pp. 76-8; and Anand Chitnis, *Scottish Enlightenment* (London, 1976), pp. 54-5

22 MacIntosh estimates that there were around twelve times as many Moderate publications in the literary field as Popular ones. However the Popular party produced far more analyses of scriptural passages and commentaries of the bible than the Moderates. John R. MacIntosh, 'The Popular party in the Church of Scotland, 1740-1800', (Glasgow University PhD. Thesis, 1989), Appendix E

23 Henry Mackenzie, *Account of the Life and Writings of John Home* (Edinburgh, 1822), p. 43

24 *Ibid.*, p. 44

25 *Scots Magazine* April 1757, p. 215

26 *Scots Magazine* March 1757, p. 158

27 *Ibid.*, p. 159

28 For more details on Carlyle's case see: Sher, *Church and University*, pp. 79-82

29 John Jackson, *The History of the Scottish Stage* (Edinburgh, 1793), p. 317

30 Carlyle, *Autobiography*, pp. 322-3

31 Anon. [?John Haldane], *The Players Scourge* (?, 1757), p. 1

32 Scots were up in arms over the issue because the Militia Act would allow citizens to form militias, but not in Scotland. Not only was this an affront to Scots as British citizens, but it was a slight against the Scots' martial

heritage. For more on this, see: John Robertson, *The Scottish Enlightenment and the Militia Issue* (Edinburgh, 1985)

33 Yoon sun Lee, 'Giants in the North: *Douglas*, the Scottish Enlightenment, and Scott's *Redguantlet*', in, *Studies in Romanticism* 40 (2001), pp. 109-121

34 John Maclaurin, *An Apology for the Writers against the Tragedy of Douglas* (Edinburgh, 1757), pp. 6-7

35 Anon., *An Epilogue to the Tragedy of Douglas, spoke by the Author* [Edinburgh, 1756]

36 Sher, *Church and University*, p. 81

37 For examples of this see: Alice Edna Gipson, *John Home: His Life and Works* (Idaho, 1917); Dougald MacMillan, 'The first Editions of Home's *Douglas*', in, *Studies in Philology* 26 (1929), pp. 401-409; Kevin J. McGinley, 'The first Edinburgh and London editions of John Home's *Douglas* and the play's early stage history', in, *Theatre Notebook* 60 (2006), pp. 134-146

DOUGLAS
A TRAGEDY

Prologue

Spoken by Mr. SPARKS

IN antient times, when Britain's *trade was arms,*
   And the lov'd music of her youth, alarms;
A god-like race sustain'd fair England's *fame:*
Who has not heard of gallant PIERCY's *name?*
Ay, and of DOUGLAS? *Such illustrious foes*
In rival Rome *and* Carthage *never rose!*
From age to age bright shone the British *fire,*
And every hero was a hero's sire.
When powerful fate decreed one warrior's doom,
Up sprung the Phoenix from his parent's tomb.
But whilst these generous rivals fought and fell,
Those generous rivals lov'd each other well:
Tho' many a bloody field was lost and won,
Nothing in hate, in honour all was done.
When PIERCY *wrong'd defy'd his prince or peers,*
Fast came the DOUGLAS, *with his Scottish spears;*
And, when proud DOUGLAS *made his King his foe,*
For DOUGLAS, PIERCY *bent his English bow.*
Expell'd their native homes by adverse fate,
They knock'd alternate at each other's gate:
Then blaz'd the castle, at the midnight hour,
For him whose arms had shook its firmest tow'r.

This night a DOUGLAS *your protection claims;*
A wife! a mother! Pity's softest names:
The story of her woes indulgent hear,
 And grant your suppliant all she begs, a tear.
In confidence she begs, and hopes to find
Each English breast, like noble PIERCY's, *kind.*

DRAMATIS PERSONAE,

As represented at LONDON

Lord RANDOLPH,	Mr. RIDOUT
GLENALVON,	Mr. SMITH
NORVAL, DOUGLAS,	Mr. BARRY
STRANGER,	Mr. SPARKS
SERVANTS	

WOMEN

MATILDA, LADY RANDOLPH,	Mrs. WOFFINGTON
ANNA,	Mrs. VINCENT

Prologue

Spoken at EDINBURGH

IN days of classic fame, when Persia's Lord
  Oppos'd his millions to the Grecian *sword,*
Flourish'd the state of Athens, small her store,
Rugged her soil, and rocky was her shore,
Like Caledonia's: *yet she gain'd a name*
That stands unrivall'd in the rolls of fame.
  Such proud pre-eminence not valour gave,
(For who than Sparta's dauntless sons more brave?)
But learning, and the love of every art,
That Virgin Pallas *and the Muse impart.*
  Above the rest the Tragic Muse *admir'd*
Each Attic *breast, with noblest passions fir'd.*
In peace their poets with their heroes shar'd
Glory, the hero's, and the bard's reward.
The Tragic Muse *each glorious record kept,*
  And, o'er the kings she conquer'd, Athens *wept.*[1]
  Here let me cease, impatient for the scene,
To you I need not praise the Tragic Queen:
Oft has this audience soft compassion shown
To woes of heroes, heroes not their own.
This night our scenes no common tear demand,
He comes, the hero of your native land!
Douglas, *a name thro' all the world renown'd,*
A name that rouses like the trumpet's sound!
Oft have your fathers, prodigal of life,
A Douglas *follow'd thro' the bloody strife;*
Hosts have been known at that dread name to yield,
And, Douglas *dead, his name hath won the field.*
  Listen attentive to the various tale,
Mark if the author's kindred feelings fail;
Sway'd by alternate hopes, alternate fears,
He waits the test of your congenial tears.
If they shall flow, back to the Muse he flies,
And bids your heroes in succession rise;
Collects the wand'ring warriors as they roam,
Douglas *assures them of a welcome-home.*

[1] See the *Persai* of Aeschylus.

DRAMATIS PERSONAE

As represented at EDINBURGH

Lord Randolph,	Mr. Younger
Glenalvon,	Mr. Love
Norval, Douglas,	Mr. Diggs
Stranger,	Mr. Hayman

Servants, &c.

WOMEN

Matilda, Lady Randolph,	Mrs. Ward
Anna,	Mrs. Hopkins

Douglas: A Tragedy

ACT I

The court of a castle surrounded by woods.
Enter Lady Randolph.

Lady RANDOLPH. Ye wood and wilds, whose melancholy gloom
  Accords with my soul's sadness, and draws forth
  The voice of sorrow from my bursting heart,
  Farewel a while: I will not leave you long;
  For in your shades I deem some spirit dwells,
  Who from the chiding stream, or groaning oak,
  Still hears, and answers to Matilda's moan.
  O Douglas! Douglas! if departed ghosts
  Are e'er permitted to review this world,
  Within the circle of that wood thou art,
  And with the passion of immortals hear'st
  My lamentation: hear'st thy wretched wife
  Weep for her husband slain, her infant lost.
  My brother's timeless death I seem to mourn;
  Who perish'd with thee on this fatal day.
  To thee I lift my voice; to thee address
  The plaint which mortal ear has never heard.
  O disregard me not; tho' I am call'd
  Another's now, my heart is wholly thine.
  Incapable of change, affection lies
  Buried, my Douglas, in thy bloody grave.
  But Randolph comes, whom fate has made my Lord,
  To chide my anguish, and defraud the dead.

Enter Lord Randolph.

Lord RANDOLPH. Again these weeds of woe! say, do'st thou well
  To feed a passion which consumes thy life?
  The living claim some duty; vainly thou
  Bestow'st thy cares upon the silent dead.

Lady RANDOLPH. Silent, alas! is he for whom I mourn:
  Childless, without memorial of his name,
  He only now in my remembrance lives.
  This fatal day stirs my time-settled sorrow,
  Troubles afresh the fountain of my heart.

Lord RANDOLPH. When was it pure of sadness? These black weeds
  Express the wonted colour of thy mind,

For ever dark and dismal. Seven long years
Are pass'd, since we were join'd by sacred ties:
Clouds, all the while have hung upon thy brow,
Nor broke, nor parted by one gleam of joy.
Time, that wears out the trace of deepest anguish,
As the sea smooths the prints made in the sand,
Has past o'er thee in vain.
Lady RANDOLPH.   If time to come
Should prove as ineffectual, yet, my Lord,
Thou canst not blame me. When our Scottish youth
Vy'd with each other for my luckless love,
Oft I besought them, I implor'd them all
Not to assail me with my father's aid,
Nor blend their better destiny with mine.
For melancholy had congeal'd my blood,
And froze affection in my chilly breast.
At last my Sire, rous'd with the base attempt
To force me from him, which thou rend'red'st vain,
To his own daughter bow'd his hoary head,
Besought me to commiserate his age,
And vow'd he should not, could not die in peace,
Unless he saw me wedded, and secur'd
From violence and outrage. Then, my Lord!
In my extreme distress I call'd on thee,
Thee I bespake, profess'd my strong desire
To lead a single, solitary life,
And begg'd thy Nobleness, not to demand
Her for a wife whose heart was dead to love.
How thou persisted'st after this, thou know'st,
And must confess that I am not unjust,
Nor more to thee than to myself injurious.
Lord RANDOLPH. That I confess; yet ever must regret
The grief I cannot cure. Would thou wert not
Compos'd of grief and tenderness alone,
But had'st a spark of other passions in thee,
Pride, anger, vanity, the strong desire
Of admiration, dear to woman kind;
These might contend with, and allay thy grief,
As meeting tides and currents smooth our firth.
Lady RANDOLPH. To such a cause the human mind oft owes

Its transient calm, a calm I envy not.

Lord RANDOLPH. Sure thou art not the daughter of Sir Malcolm:
  Strong was his rage, eternal his resentment:
  For when thy brother fell, he smil'd to hear
  That Douglas' son in the same field was slain.

Lady RANDOLPH. Oh! rake not up the ashes of my fathers:
  Implacable resentment was their crime,
  And grievous has the expiation been.
  Contending with the Douglas, gallant lives
  Of either house were lost; my ancestors
  Compell'd, at last, to leave their ancient seat
  On Tiviot's pleasant banks; and now, of them
  No heir is left. Had they not been so stern,
  I had not been the last of all my race.

Lord RANDOLPH. Thy grief wrests to its purposes my words.
  I never ask'd of thee that ardent love,
  Which in the breasts of fancy's children burns.
  Decent affection and complacent kindness
  Were all I wish'd for; but I wish'd in vain.
  Hence with the less regret my eyes behold
  The storm of war that gathers o'er this land:
  If I should perish by the Danish sword,
  Matilda would not shed one tear the more.

Lady RANDOLPH. Thou do'st not think so: woeful as I am
  I love thy merit, and esteem thy virtues.
  But wither go'st thou now?

Lord RANDOLPH.   Straight to the camp,
  Where every warrior on the tip-toe stands
  Of expectation, and impatient asks
  Each who arrives, if he is come to tell
  The Danes are landed.

Lady RANDOLPH.   O, may adverse winds,
  Far from the coast of Scotland, drive their fleet!
  And every soldier of both hosts return
  In peace and safety to his pleasant home!

Lord RANDOLPH. Thou speak'st a woman's, hear a warrior's wish:
  Right from their native land, the stormy north,
  May the wind blow, till every keel is fix'd
  Immoveable in Caledonia's strand!
  Then shall our foes repent their bold invasion,

And roving armies shun the fatal shore.

Lady RANDOLPH. War I detest: but war with foreign foes,
  Whose manners, language, and whose looks are strange,
  Is not so horrid, nor to me so hateful,
  As that which with our neighbours oft we wage.
  A river here, there an ideal line,
  By fancy drawn, divides the sister kingdoms.
  On each side dwells a people similar,
  As twins are to each other; valiant both;
  Both for their valour famous thro' the world.
  Yet will they not unite their kindred arms,
  And, if they must have war, wage distant war,
  But with each other fight in cruel conflict.
  Gallant in strife, and noble in their ire,
  The battle is their pastime. They go forth
  Gay in the morning, as to summer sport;
  When ev'ning comes, the glory of the morn,
  The youthful warrior is a clod of clay.
  Thus fall the prime of either hapless land;
  And such the fruit of Scotch and English wars.

Lord RANDOLPH. I'll hear no more: this melody would make
  A soldier drop his sword, and doff his arms,
  Sit down and weep the conquests he has made;
  Yea, (like a monk), sing rest and peace in heav'n
  To souls of warriors in his battles slain.
  Lady, farewel: I leave thee not alone;
  Yonder comes one whose love makes duty light.

                                 Exit.

Enter ANNA.

ANNA. Forgive the rashness of your Anna's love:
  Urg'd by affection, I have thus presum'd
  To interrupt your solitary thoughts;
  And warn you of the hours that you neglect,
  And lose in sadness.

Lady RANDOLPH.   So to lose my hours
  Is all the use I wish to make of time.

ANNA. To blame thee, Lady, suits not with my state:
  But sure I am, since death first prey'd on man,
  Never did sister thus a brother mourn.
  What had your sorrows been if you had lost,

In early youth, the husband of your heart?

Lady RANDOLPH.   Oh!

ANNA. Have I distress'd you with officious love,
    And ill-tim'd mention of your brother's fate?
    Forgive me, Lady: humble tho' I am,
    The mind I bear partakes not of my fortune:
    So fervently I love you, that to dry
    These piteous tears, I'd throw my life away.

Lady RANDOLPH. What power directed thy unconscious tongue
    To speak as thou hast done ? to name —

ANNA.   I know not:
    But since my words have made my mistress tremble,
    I will speak so no more; but silent mix
    My tears with her's.

Lady RANDOLPH.   No, thou shalt not be silent.
    I'll trust thy faithful love, and thou shalt be
    Henceforth th'instructed partner of my woes.
    But what avails it ? Can thy feeble pity
    Roll back the flood of never-ebbing time ?
    Compel the earth and ocean to give up
    Their dead alive?

ANNA.   What means my noble mistress ?

Lady Randolph. Didst thou not ask what had my sorrows been ? —
    If I in early youth had lost a husband ? —
    In the cold bosom of the earth is lodg'd,
    Mangl'd with wounds, the husband of my youth;
    And in some cavern of the ocean lies
    My child and his. —

ANNA.   O! Lady, most rever'd!
    The tale wrapt up in your amazing words
    Deign to unfold.

Lady RANDOLPH. Alas! an antient feud,
    Hereditary evil, was the source
    Of my misfortunes. Ruling fate decreed,
    That my brave brother should in battle save
    The life of Douglas' son, our house's foe:
    The youthful warriors vow'd eternal friendship.
    To see the vaunted sister of his friend
    Impatient, Douglas to Balarmo came,
    Under a borrow'd name. — My heart he gain'd;

Nor did I long refuse the hand he begg'd:
My brother's presence authoris'd our marriage.
Three weeks, three little weeks, with wings of down,
Had o'er us flown, when my lov'd Lord was call'd
To fight his father's battles; and with him,
In spite of all my tears, did Malcolm go.
Scarce were they gone, when my stern Sire was told
That the false stranger was Lord Douglas' son.
Frantic with rage, the Baron drew his sword,
And question'd me. Alone, forsaken, faint,
Kneeling beneath his sword, fault'ring I took
An oath equivocal, that I ne'er would
Wed one of Douglas' name. Sincerity,
Thou first of virtues, let no mortal leave
Thy onward path! altho' the earth should gape,
And from the gulph of hell destruction cry
To take dissimulation's winding way.
ANNA. Alas! how few of woman's fearful kind
  Durst own a truth so hardy!
Lady RANDOLPH.   The first truth
  Is easiest to avow. This moral learn,
  This precious moral, from my tragic tale. —
  In a few days the dreadful tidings came
  That Douglas and my brother both were slain.
  My Lord! my life! my husband! — mighty God!
  What had I done to merit such affliction?
ANNA. My dearest Lady! many a tale of tears
  I've listen'd to; but never did I hear
  A tale so sad as this.
Lady RANDOLPH.   In the first days
  Of my distracting grief, I found myself —
  As women wish to be who love their Lords.
  But who durst tell my father ? The good priest
  Who join'd our hands, my brother's antient tutor,
  With his lov'd Malcolm, in the battle fell:
  They two alone were privy to the marriage.
  On silence and concealment I resolv'd,
  Till time should make my father's fortune mine.
  That very night on which my son was born,
  My nurse, the only confident I had,

Set out with him to reach her sister's house:
But nurse, nor infant, have I ever seen
Or heard of, Anna, since that fatal hour.
My murder'd child! — had thy fond mother fear'd
The loss of thee, she had loud fame defy'd,
Despis'd her father's rage, her father's grief,
And wander'd with thee thro' the scorning world.
ANNA. Not seen nor heard of! then perhaps he lives.
Lady RANDOLPH. No. It was dark December: wind and rain
   Had beat all night. Across the Carron lay
   The destin'd road; and in its swelling flood
   My faithful servant perish'd with my child.
   O hapless son! of a most hapless sire! —
   But they are both at rest; and I alone
   Dwell in this world of woe, condemn'd to walk,
   Like a guilt-troubl'd ghost, my painful rounds:
   Nor has despiteful fate permitted me
   The comfort of a solitary sorrow.
   Tho' dead to love, I was compell'd to wed
   Randolph, who snatch'd me from a villain's arms;
   And Randolph now possesses the domains,
   That by Sir Malcolm's death on me devolv'd;
   Domains, that should to Douglas' son have giv'n
   A Baron's title, and a Baron's power.
   Such were my soothing thoughts, while I bewail'd
   The slaughter'd father of a son unborn.
   And when that son came, like a ray from heav'n,
   Which shines and disappears; alas! my child!
   How long did thy fond mother grasp the hope
   Of having thee, she knew not how, restor'd.
   Year after year hath worn her hope away;
   But left still undiminish'd her desire.
ANNA. The hand, that spins th'uneven thread of life,
   May smooth the length that's yet to come of yours.
Lady RANDOLPH. Not in this world: I have consider'd well
   Its various evils, and on whom they fall.
   Alas! how oft does goodness wound itself?
   And sweet affection prove the spring of woe.
   O! had I died when my lov'd husband fell!
   Had some good angel op'd to me the book

Of providence, and let me read my life,
My heart had broke when I beheld the sum
Of ills, which one by one I have endur'd.
ANNA. That God, whose ministers good angels are,
Hath shut the book in mercy to mankind.
But we must leave this theme: Glenalvon comes:
I saw him bend on you his thoughtful eyes,
And hitherwards he slowly stalks his way.
Lady RANDOLPH. I will avoid him. An ungracious person
Is doubly irksome in an hour like this.
ANNA. Why speaks my Lady thus of Randolph's heir?
Lady RANDOLPH. Because he's not the heir of Randolph's virtues.
Subtle and shrewd, he offers to mankind
An artificial image of himself:
And he with ease can vary to the taste
Of different men, its features. Self-deny'd,
And master of his appetites he seems:
But his fierce nature, like a fox chain'd up,
Watches to seize unseen the wish'd-for prey.
Never were vice and virtue pois'd so ill,
As in GLENALVON'S unrelenting mind.
Yet is he brave and politic in war,
And stands aloft in these unruly times.
Why I describe him thus I'll tell hereafter:
Stay and detain him till I reach the castle.

Exit Lady RANDOLPH.

ANNA. O happiness! where art thou to be found?
I see thou dwellest not with birth and beauty,
Tho' grac'd with grandeur, and in wealth array'd:
Nor dost thou, it would seem, with virtue dwell;
Else had this gentle Lady miss'd thee not.
Enter GLENALVON.
GLENALVON. What dost thou muse on, meditating maid?
Like some entranc'd and visionary seer
On earth thou stand'st, thy thoughts ascend to heaven.
ANNA. Wou'd that I were, e'en as thou say'st, a seer,
To have my doubts by heav'nly vision clear'd!
GLENALVON. What dost thou doubt of? what has thou to do
With subjects intricate ? Thy youth, thy beauty,
Cannot be question'd: think of these good gifts;

And then thy contemplations will be pleasing.
ANNA. Let women view yon monument of woe,
   Then boast of beauty: who so fair as she?
   But I must follow: this revolving day
   Awakes the memory of her antient woes.

                                    Exit Anna.

GLENALVON *solus.* So! — Lady RANDOLPH shuns me; by and by
   I'll woo her as the lion wooes his brides.
   The deed's a-doing now, that makes me lord
   Of these rich valleys, and a chief of power.
   The season is most apt; my sounding steps
   Will not be heard amidst the din of arms.
    RANDOLPH has liv'd too long: his better fate
   Had the ascendant once, and kept me down:
   When I had seiz'd the dame, by chance he came,
   Rescu'd, and had the Lady for his labour;
   I 'scap'd unknown: a slender consolation!
   Heaven is my witness that I do not love
   To sow in peril, and let others reap
   The jocund harvest. Yet I am not safe:
   By love, or something like it, stung, inflam'd,
   Madly I blabb'd my passion to his wife,
   And she has threaten'd to acquaint him of it.
   The way of woman's will I do not know:
   But well I know the Baron's wrath is deadly.
   I will not live in fear: the man I dread
   Is as a Dane to me; ay, and the man
   Who stands betwixt me and my chief desire.
   No bar but he; she has no kinsman near;
   No brother in his sister's quarrel bold;
   And for the righteous cause, a stranger's cause,
    I know no chief that will defy GLENALVON.

End of the First Act.

ACT II
A Court, &c.

Enter Servants and a Stranger at one door, and Lady RANDOLPH,
ANNA *at another.*

Lady RANDOLPH. WHAT means this clamour? Stranger! speak secure;
   Hast thou been wrong'd? have these rude men presum'd
   To vex the weary traveller on his way?

First SERVANT. By us no stranger ever suffer'd wrong:
   This man with outcry wild has call'd us forth;
   So sore afraid he cannot speak his fears.

Enter Lord RANDOLPH *and young man, with their swords drawn and bloody.*

Lady RANDOLPH. Not vain the Stranger's fears! how fares my Lord?

Lord RANDOLPH. That it fares well, thanks to this gallant youth,
   Whose valour sav'd me from a wretched death!
   As down the winding dale I walk'd alone,
   At the cross way four armed men attack'd me:
   Rovers, I judge, from the licentious camp,
   Who would have quickly laid Lord RANDOLPH low,
   Had not this brave and generous Stranger come,
   Like my good angel in the hour of fate,
   And, mocking danger, made my foes his own.
   They turn'd upon him: but his active arm
   Struck to the ground, from whence they rose no more,
   The fiercest two; the others fled amain,
   And left him master of the bloody field.
   Speak, Lady RANDOLPH: upon Beauty's tongue
   Dwell accents pleasing to the brave and bold.
   Speak, noble Dame, and thank him for thy Lord.

Lady RANDOLPH. My Lord, I cannot speak what now I feel.
   My heart o'erflows with gratitude to heav'n,
   And to this noble youth, who all unknown
   To you and yours, deliberated not,
   Nor paus'd at peril, but humanely brave
   Fought on your side, against such fearful odds.
   Have you yet learn'd of him whom we should thank?
   Whom call the saviour of Lord RANDOLPH's life?

Lord RANDOLPH. I ask'd that question, and he answer'd not:
   But I must know who my deliverer is.
(to the Stranger)

STRANGER. A low born man, of parentage obscure,
  Who nought can boast but his desire to be
  A soldier, and to gain a name in arms.
Lord RANDOLPH. Whoe'er thou art, thy spirit is ennobl'd
  By the great King of Kings! thou art ordain'd
  And stamp'd a hero by the sovereign hand
  Of Nature! blush not, flower of modesty
  As well as valour, to declare thy birth.
STRANGER. My name is NORVAL: on the Grampian hills
  My father feeds his flocks; a frugal swain,
  Whose constant cares were to increase his store,
  And keep his only son, myself, at home.
  For I had heard of battles, and I long'd
  To follow to the field some warlike Lord:
  And heaven soon granted what my Sire deny'd.
  This moon which rose last night, round as my shield,
  Had not yet fill'd her horns, when, by her light,
  A band of fierce Barbarians, from the hills,
  Rush'd like a torret down upon the vale,
  Sweeping our flocks and herds. The shepherds fled
  For safety, and for succour. I alone,
  With bended bow, and quiver full of arrows,
  Hover'd about the enemy, and mark'd
  The road he took, then hasted to my friends;
  Whom, with a troop of fifty chosen men,
  I met advancing. The pursuit I led,
  Till we o'ertook the spoil-encumber'd foe.
  We fought and conquer'd. E're a sword was drawn,
  An arrow from my bow had pierc'd their chief,
  Who wore that day the arms which now I wear.
  Returning home in triumph, I disdain'd
  The shepherd's slothful life: and having heard
  That our good King had summon'd his bold Peers
  To lead their warriors to the Carron side,
  I left my father's house, and took with me
  A chosen servant to conduct my steps;—
  Yon trembling coward who forsook his master.
  Journeying with this intent, I past these towers,
  And, heaven-directed, came this day to do
  The happy deed that gilds my humble name.

Lord RANDOLPH. He is as wise as brave. Was ever tale
   With such a gallant modesty rehears'd?
   My brave deliverer! thou shalt enter now
   A nobler list, and in a monarch's fight
   Contend with princes for the prize of fame.
   I will present thee to our Scottish King,
   Whose valiant spirit ever valour lov'd.
   Ha! my MATILDA! wherefore starts that tear?
Lady RANDOLPH. I cannot say: for various affections,
   And strangely mingled, in my bosom swell;
   Yet each of them may well command a tear.
   I joy that thou art safe, and I admire
   Him and his fortune who hath wrought thy safety;
   Yea, as my mind predicts, with thine his own.
   Obscure and friendliness, he the army sought,
   Bent upon peril, in the range of death
   Resolv'd to hunt for fame, and with his sword
   To gain distinction which his birth deny'd.
   In this attempt unknown he might have perish'd,
   And gain'd, with all his valour, but oblivion.
   Now grac'd by thee, his virtue serves no more
   Beneath despair. The soldier now of hope
   He stands conspicuous; fame and great renown
   Are brought within the compass of his sword.
   On this my mind reflected, whilst you spoke,
   And bless'd the wonder-working Lord of heaven.
Lord RANDOLPH. Pious and grateful ever are thy thoughts!
   My deeds shall follow where thou point'st the way.
   Next to myself, and equal to GLENALVON,
   In honour and command shall NORVAL be.
NORVAL. I know not how to thank you. Rude I am
   In speech and manners: never till this hour
   Stood I in such a presence: yet, my Lord,
   There's something in my breast which makes me bold
   To say, that NORVAL ne'er will shame thy favour.
Lady RANDOLPH. I will be sworn thou wilt not. Thou shalt be
   My knight; and ever, as thou didst to-day,
   With happy valour guard the life of RANDOLPH.
Lord RANDOLPH.   *To* NORVAL.
   Well hast thou spoke. Let me forbid reply.

We are thy debtors still; thy high desert
O'ertops our gratitude. I must proceed,
As was at first intended, to the camp.
Some of my train I see are speeding hither,
Impatient doubtless of their Lord's delay.
Go with me, NORVAL, and thine eyes shall see
The chosen warriors of thy native land,
Who languish for the fight, and beat the air
With brandish'd swords.
NORVAL.   Let us begone, my Lord.
Lord RANDOLPH.   *To Lady* RANDOLPH.
About the time that the declining sun
Shall his broad orbit o'er yon hill suspend,
Expect us to return. This night once more
Within these walls I rest; my tent I pitch
To-morrow in the field. Prepare the feast.
Free is his heart who for his country fights:
He in the eve of battle may resign
Himself to social pleasure; sweetest then,
When danger to a soldier's soul endears
The human joy that never may return.
                         Exeunt RANDOLPH AND NORVAL.

Lady RANDOLPH and ANNA.
Lady RANDOLPH. His parting words have struck a fatal truth.
O DOUGLAS! DOUGLAS! tender was the time
When we two parted, ne'er to meet again!
How many years of anguish and despair
Has heav'n annex'd to those swift passing hours
Of love and fondness! Then my bosom's flame
Oft, as blown back by the rude breath of fear,
Return'd, and with redoubled ardour blaz'd.
ANNA. May gracious heav'n pour the sweet balm of peace
Into the wounds that fester in your breast!
For earthly consolation cannot cure them.
Lady RANDOLPH. One only cure can heav'n itself bestow;—
A grave—that bed in which the weary rest.
Wretch that I am! Alas! why am I so?
At every happy parent I repine!
How blest the mother of yon gallant NORVAL!

She for a living husband bore her pains,
And heard him bless her when a man was born:
She nurs'd her smiling infant on her breast;
Tended the child, and rear'd the pleasing boy:
She, with affection's triumph, saw the youth
In grace and comeliness surpass his peers:
Whilst I to a dead husband bore a son,
And to the roaring waters gave my child.

ANNA. Alas! alas! why will you thus resume
Your grief afresh? I thought that gallant youth
Would for a while have won you from your woe.
On him intent you gazed, with a look
Much more delighted, than your pensive eye
Has deign'd on other objects to bestow.

Lady RANDOLPH. Delighted, say'st thou? Oh! even there mine eye
Found fuel for my life-consuming sorrow.
I thought, that had the son of DOUGLAS liv'd,
He might have been like this young gallant stranger,
And pair'd with him in features and in shape;
In all endowments, as in years, I deem,
My boy with blooming NORVAL might have number'd.
Whilst thus I mus'd, a spark from fancy fell
On my sad heart, and kindled up a fondness
For this young stranger, wand'ring from his home,
And like an orphan cast upon my care.
I will protect thee, (said I to myself)
With all my power, and grace with all my favour.

ANNA. Sure heav'n will bless so generous a resolve.
You must, my noble Dame, exert your power:
You must awake: devices will be fram'd,
And arrows pointed at the breast of NORVAL.

Lady RANDOLPH. GLENALVON'S false and crafty head will work
Against a rival in his kinsman's love,
If I deter him not: I only can.
Bold as he is, GLENALVON will beware
How he pulls down the fabric that I raise.
I'll be the artist of young NORVAL'S fortune.
'Tis pleasing to admire! most apt was I
To this affection in my better days;
Tho' now I seem to you shrunk up, retir'd

Within the narrow compass of my woe.
Have you not sometimes seen an early flower
Open its bud, and spread its silken leaves,
To catch sweet airs, and odours to bestow;
Then, by the keen blast nipt, pull in its leaves,
And, tho' still living, die to scent and beauty?
Emblem of me: affliction, like a storm,
Hath kill'd the forward blossom of my heart.

Enter GLENALVON.

GLENALVON. Where is my dearest kinsman, noble RANDOLPH?

Lady RANDOLPH. Have you not heard, GLENALVON, of the base —

GLENALVON. I have: and that the villains may not 'scape,
  With a strong band I have begirt the wood.
  If they lurk there, alive they shall be taken,
  And torture force from them th'important secret,
  Whether some foe of RANDOLPH hir'd their swords, Or if —

Lady RANDOLPH. That care becomes a kinsman's love
  I have a counsel for GLENALVON's ear.

                                        Exit Anna.

GLENALVON. To him your counsels always are commands.

Lady RANDOLPH. I have not found so: thou art known to me.

GLENALVON. Known!

Lady RANDOLPH. And most certain is my cause of knowledge,

GLENALVON. What do you know? By the most blessed cross,
  You much amaze me. No created being,
  Yourself except, durst thus accost GLENALVON.

Lady RANDOLPH. Is guilt so bold? and dost thou make a merit
  Of thy pretended meekness ? This to me,
  Who, with a gentleness which thy duty blames,
  Hath hitherto conceal'd what, if divulg'd,
  Would make thee nothing; or, what's worse than that,
  An outcast beggar, and unpitied too!
  For mortals shudder at a crime like thine.

GLENALVON. Thy virtue awes me. First of womankind!
  Permit me yet to say, that the fond man,
  Whom love transports beyond strict virtue's bounds,
  If he is brought by love to misery,
  In fortune ruin'd, as in mind forlorn,
  Unpitied cannot be. Pity's the alms
  Which on such beggars freely is bestow'd:

For mortals know that love is still their lord,
And o'er their vain resolves advances still:
As fire, when kindled by our shepherds, moves
Thro' the dry heath before the fanning wind.
Lady RANDOLPH. Reserve these accents for some other ear.
To love's apology I listen not.
Mark thou my words; for it is meet thou should'st.
His brave deliverer RANDOLPH here retains.
Perhaps his presence may not please thee well:
But, at thy peril, practice ought against him:
Let not thy jealousy attempt to shake
And loosen the good root he has in RANDOLPH;
Whose favourites I know thou hast supplanted.
Thou look'st at me, as if thou fain would'st pry
Into my heart. 'Tis open as my speech.
I give this early caution, and put on
The curb, before thy temper breaks away.
The friendless Stranger my protection claims:
His friend I am, and be not thou his foe.

Exit.

Manet GLENALVON.

Child that I was, to start at my own shadow,
And be the shallow fool of coward conscience!
I am not what I have been; what I should be.
The darts of destiny have almost pierc'd
My marble heart. Had I one grain of faith
In holy legends, and religious tales,
I should conclude there was an arm above,
That fought against me, and malignant turn'd,
To catch myself, the subtle snare I set.
Why, rape and murder are not simple means!
Th' imperfect rape to RANDOLPH gave a spouse;
And the intended murder introduc'd
A favourite to hide the sun from me;
And worst of all, a rival. Burning hell!
This were thy centre, if I thought she lov'd him!
Tis certain she contemns me; nay commands me,
And waves the flag of her displeasure o'er me,
In his behalf. And shall I thus be brav'd?

Curb'd, as she calls it, by dame chastity?
Infernal fiends, if any fiends there are
More fierce than hate, ambition, and revenge,
Rise up and fill my bosom with your fires,
And policy remorseless! Chance may spoil
A single aim; but perseverance must
Prosper at last. For chance and fate are words:
Persistive wisdom is the fate of man.
Darkly a project peers upon my mind,
Like the red moon when rising in the east,
Cross'd and divided by strange-colour'd clouds.
I'll seek the slave who came with NORVAL hither,
And for his cowardice was spurned from him.
I've known a follower's rankled bosom breed
Venom most fatal to his heedless Lord.

Exit.

End of the Second Act.

ACT III

A Court, &c. as before.

Enter ANNA.

ANNA. THY vassals, Grief! great Nature's order break,
  And change the noon-tide to the midnight hour.
  Whilst Lady RANDOLPH sleeps, I will walk forth,
  And taste the air that breathes on yonder bank.
  Sweet may her slumbers be! Ye ministers
  Of gracious heaven who love the human race,
  Angels and seraphs who delight in goodness!
  Forsake your skies, and to her couch descend!
  There from her fancy chace those dismal forms
  That haunt her waking; her sad spirit charm
  With images celestial, such as please
  The bless'd above upon their golden beds.

Enter SERVANT.

SERVANT. One of the vile assassins is secur'd.
  We found the villain lurking in the wood:
  With dreadful imprecations he denies
  All knowledge of the crime. But this is not
  His first essay: these jewels were conceal'd
  In the most secret places of his garment;
  Belike the spoils of some that he has murder'd.

ANNA. Let me look on them. Ha! here is a heart,
  The chosen crest of DOUGLAS' valiant name!
  These are no vulgar jewels. Guard the wretch.

                                        Exit Anna.

Enter Servants with a Prisoner.

PRISONER. I know no more than does the child unborn
  Of what you charge me with.

First SERVANT.   You say so, Sir!
  But torture soon shall make you speak the truth.
  Behold the Lady of Lord RANDOLPH comes:
  Prepare yourself to meet her just revenge.

Enter Lady RANDOLPH *and* ANNA.

ANNA. Summon your utmost fortitude, before
  You speak with him. Your dignity, your fame,
  Are now at stake. Think of the fatal secret,
  Which in a moment from your lips may fly.

Lady RANDOLPH. Thou shalt behold me, with a desperate heart,
   Hear how my infant perish'd. See he kneels.
                              The Prisoner kneels.
PRISONER. Heav'n bless that countenance, so sweet and mild!
   A judge like thee makes innocence more bold.
   O save me, Lady! from these cruel men,
   Who have attack'd and seiz'd me; who accuse
   Me of intended murder. As I hope
   For mercy at the judgment seat of God,
   The tender lamb, that never nipt the grass,
   Is not more innocent than I of murder.
Lady RANDOLPH. Of this man's guilt what proof can ye produce ?
First SERVANT. We found him lurking in the hollow Glynn.
   When view'd and call'd upon, amaz'd, he fled.
   We overtook him, and inquir'd from whence
   And what he was: he said, he came from far,
   And was upon his journey to the camp.
   Not satisfy'd with this, we search'd his cloaths,
   And found these jewels; whose rich value plead
   Most powerfully against him. Hard he seems
   And old in villainy. Permit us try
   His stubbornness against the torture's force.
PRISONER. O gentle Lady! by your Lord's dear life!
   Which these weak hands, I swear, did ne'er assail;
   And by your children's welfare, spare my age!
   Let not the iron tear my antient joints,
   And my grey hairs bring to the grave with pain.
Lady RANDOLPH. Account for these: thine own they cannot be:
   For these, I say: be stedfast to the truth;
   Detected falsehood is most certain death.
                    ANNA *removes the Servants and returns.*
PRISONER. Alas! I'm sore beset! let never man,
   For sake of lucre, sin against his soul!
   Eternal justice is in this most just!
   I, guiltless now, must former guilt reveal.
Lady RANDOLPH. O! ANNA hear!—once more I charge thee speak
   The truth direct: for these to me foretel
   And certify a part of thy narration;
   With which if the remainder tallies not,
   An instant and a dreadful death abides thee.
PRISONER. Then, thus adjur'd, I'll speak to you as just
   As if you were the minister of heaven,
   Sent down to search the secret sins of men.
     SOME eighteen years ago, I rented land
   Of brave Sir MALCOLM, then BALARMO'S Lord;

But falling to decay, his servants seiz'd
All that I had, and then turn'd me and mine,
(Four helpless infants and their weeping mother)
Out to the mercy of the winter winds.
A little hovel by the river's side
Receiv'd us: there hard labour, and the skill
In fishing, which was formerly my sport,
Supported life. Whilst thus we poorly liv'd,
One stormy night, as I remember well,
The wind and rain beat hard upon our roof:
Red came the river down, and loud and oft
The angry spirit of the water shriek'd.
At the dead hour of night was heard the cry
Of one in jeopardy. I rose, and ran
To where the circling eddy of a pool,
Beneath the ford, us'd oft to bring within
My reach whatever floating thing the stream
Had caught. The voice was ceas'd; the person lost:
But looking sad and earnest on the waters,
By the moon's light I saw, whirl'd round and round,
A basket: soon I drew it to the bank,
And nestled curious there an infant lay.
Lady RANDOLPH. Was he alive?
PRISONER. He was.
Lady RANDOLPH. Inhuman that thou art!
  How could'st thou kill what waves and tempests spar'd ?
PRISONER. I am not so inhuman.
Lady RANDOLPH.   Didst thou not?
ANNA. My noble Mistress, you are mov'd too much:
  This man has not the aspect of stern murder;
  Let him go on, and you, I hope ,will hear
  Good tidings of your kinsman's long lost child.
PRISONER. The needy man, who has known better days,
  One whom distress has spited at the world,
  Is he whom tempting fiends would pitch upon
  To do such deeds, as make the prosperous men
  Lift up their hands and wonder who could do them.
  And such a man was I; a man declin'd,
  Who saw no end of black adversity:
  Yet for the wealth of kingdoms, I would not
  Have touch'd that infant, with a hand of harm.

Lady RANDOLPH. Ha! dost thou say so? Then perhaps he lives!
PRISONER. Not many days ago he was alive.
Lady RANDOLPH. O! God of heav'n! Did he then die so lately?
PRISONER. I did not say he died; I hope he lives.
   Not many days ago these eyes beheld
   Him, flourishing in youth, and health, and beauty.
Lady RANDOLPH. Where is he now?
PRISONER.   Alas! I know not where.
Lady RANDOLPH. Oh fate! I fear thee still. Thou riddler, speak
   Direct and clear; else I will search thy soul.
ANNA. Permit me, ever honour'd! Keen impatience,
   Tho' hard to be restrain'd, defeats itself. —
   Pursue thy story with a faithful tongue,
   To the last hour that thou didst keep the child.
PRISONER. Fear not my faith, tho' I must speak my shame.
   Within the cradle, where the infant lay,
   Was stow'd a mighty store of gold and jewels:
   Tempted by which we did resolve to hide,
   From all the world, this wonderful event,
   And like a peasant breed the noble child.
   That none might mark the change of our estate,
   We left the country, travell'd to the North,
   Bought flocks and herds, and gradually brought forth
   Our secret wealth. But God's all-seeing eye
   Beheld our avarice, and smote us sore.
   For one by one all our own children died,
   And he, the Stranger, sole remain'd the heir
   Of what indeed was his. Fain then would I,
   Who with a father's fondness lov'd the boy,
   Have trusted him, now in the dawn of youth,
   With his own secret: but my anxious wife,
   Foreboding evil, never would consent.
   Mean while the stripling grew in years and beauty;
   And, as we oft observ'd, he bore himself,
   Not as the offspring of our cottage blood;
   For nature will break out: mild with the mild,
   But with the froward he was fierce as fire,
   And night and day he talk'd of war and arms.
   I set myself against his warlike bent;
   But all in vain: for when a desperate band

Of robbers from the savage mountains came —
Lady RANDOLPH. Eternal Providence! what is thy name?
PRISONER. My name is NORVAL; and my name he bears.
Lady RANDOLPH. 'Tis he; 'tis he himself! It is my son!
  O sovereign mercy! 'Twas my child I saw!
  No wonder, ANNA, that my bosom burn'd.
ANNA. Just are your transports: ne'er was woman's heart
  Prov'd with such fierce extremes. High fated Dame!
  But yet remember that you are beheld
  By servile eyes; your gestures may be seen
  Impassion'd, strange; perhaps your words o'erheard.
Lady RANDOLPH. Well dost thou counsel, ANNA: heaven bestow
  On me that wisdom which my state requires!
ANNA. The moments of deliberation pass,
  And soon you must resolve. This useful man
  Must be dismiss'd in safety, 'ere my Lord
  Shall with his brave deliverer return.
PRISONER. If I, amidst astonishment and fear,
  Have of your words and gestures rightly judg'd,
  Thou art the daughter of my antient master;
  The child I rescu'd from the flood is thine.
Lady RANDOLPH. With thee dissimulation now were vain.
  I am indeed the daughter of Sir MALCOLM;
  The child thou rescu'd from the flood is mine.
PRISONER. Bless'd be the hour that made me a poor man!
  My poverty hath sav'd my master's house!
Lady RANDOLPH. Thy words surprize me: sure thou dost not feign:
  The tear stands in thine eye: such love from thee
  Sir MALCOLM's house deserv'd not; if aright
  Thou told'st the story of thy own distress.
PRISONER. Sir MALCOLM of our Barons was the flower;
  The fastest friend, the best, the kindest master:
  But ah! he knew not of my sad estate.
  After the battle, where his gallant son,
  Your own brave brother, fell, the good old Lord
  Grew desperate and reckless of the world;
  And never, as he erst was wont, went forth
  To overlook the conduct of his servants.
  By them I was thrust out, and them I blame:
  May heav'n so judge me as I judg'd my master!

And God so love me as I love his race!

Lady RANDOLPH. His race shall yet reward thee. On thy faith
  Depends the fate of thy lov'd master's house.
  Rememb'rest thou a little lonely hut,
  That like a holy hermitage appears
  Among the clifts of Carron?

PRISONER. I remember
  The cottage of the clifts.

Lady RANDOLPH. 'Tis that I mean:
  There dwells a man of venerable age,
  Who in my father's service spent his youth:
  Tell him I sent thee, and with him remain,
  Till I shall call upon thee to declare,
  Before the King and Nobles, what thou now
  To me hast told. No more but this, and thou
  Shalt live in honour all thy future days:
  Thy son so long shall call thee father still,
  And all the land shall bless the man, who sav'd
  The son of DOUGLAS, and Sir MALCOLM's heir.
  Remember well my words: if thou should'st meet
  Him whom thou call'st thy son, still call him so;
  And mention nothing of his nobler father.

PRISONER. Fear not that I shall mar so fair an harvest,
  By putting in my sickle 'ere 'tis ripe.
  Why did I leave my home and antient dame?
  To find the youth to tell him all I knew,
  And make him wear these jewels in his arms;
  Which might, I thought, be challeng'd, and so bring
  To light the secret of his noble birth.

Lady RANDOLPH *goes towards the Servants.*

Lady RANDOLPH. This man is not th'assassin you suspected,
  Tho' chance combin'd some likelihoods against him.
  He is the faithful bearer of the jewels
  To their right owner, whom in haste he seeks.
  'Tis meet that you should put him on his way,
  Since your mistaken zeal hath dragg'd him hither.

Exeunt Stranger and Servants.

Lady RANDOLPH and ANNA.

Lady RANDOLPH. My faithful ANNA! dost thou share my joy?
  I know thou dost. Unparallel'd event!

Reaching from heav'n to earth, Jehovah's arm
Snatch'd from the waves, and brings to me my son!
Judge of the widow, and the orphan's father!
Accept a widow's, and a mother's thanks
For such a gift! What does my Anna think
Of the young eaglet of a valiant nest?
How soon he gaz'd on bright and burning arms,
Spurn'd the low dunghill where his fate had thrown him,
And tower'd up to the region of his sire!
Anna. How fondly did your eyes devour the boy!
  Mysterious nature, with the unseen cord
  Of powerful instinct, drew you to your own.
Lady Randolph. The ready story of his birth believ'd
  Supprest my fancy quite; nor did he owe
  To any likeness my so sudden favour:
  But now I long to see his face again,
  Examine every feature, and find out
  The lineaments of Douglas, or my own.
  But most of all I long to let him know
  Who his true parents are, to clasp his neck,
  And tell him all the story of his father.
Anna. With wary caution you must bear yourself
  In public, lest your tenderness break forth,
  And in observers stir conjectures strange.
  For, if a cherub in the shape of woman
  Should walk this world, yet defamation would,
  Like a vile cur, bark at the angel's train —
  To-day the Baron started at your tears.
Lady Randolph. He did so, Anna! well thy Mistress knows,
  If the least circumstance, mote of offence,
  Should touch the Baron's eye, his sight would be
  With jealousy disorder'd. But the more
  It does behove me instant to declare
  The birth of Douglas, and assert his rights.
  This night I purpose with my son to meet,
  Reveal the secret, and consult with him:
  For wise he is, or my fond judgment errs.
  As he does now, so look'd his noble father,
  Array'd in nature's ease: his mien, his speech,
  Were sweetly simple, and full oft deceiv'd

Those trivial mortals who seem always wise.
But, when the matter match'd his mighty mind,
Up rose the Hero: on his piercing eye
Sat Observation: on each glance of thought
Decision follow'd, as the thunder-bolt
Pursues the flash.

ANNA.   That demon haunts you still:
Behold Glenalvon.

Lady RANDOLPH.   Now I shun him not.
This day I brav'd him in behalf of NORVAL;
Perhaps too far: at least my nicer fears
For DOUGLAS thus interpret.

Enter Glenalvon.

GLENALVON.   Noble Dame!
The hov'ring Dane at last his men hath landed:
No band of pirates; but a mighty host,
That come to settle where their valour conquers;
To win a country, or to lose themselves.

Lady RANDOLPH. But whence comes this intelligence,
   GLENALVON?

GLENALVON. A nimble courier sent from yonder camp,
To hasten up the chieftains of the north,
Inform'd me, as he past, that the fierce Dane
Had on the eastern coast of Lothian landed,
Near to that place where the sea-rock immense,
Amazing Bass, looks o'er a fertile land.

Lady RANDOLPH. Then must this western army march to join
The warlike troops that guard Edina's tow'rs.

GLENALVON. Beyond all question. If impairing time
Has not effac'd the image of a place,
Once perfect in my breast, there is a wild
Which lies to westward of that mighty rock,
And seems by nature formed for the camp
Of water-wafted armies, whose chief strength
Lies in firm foot, unflank'd with warlike horse:
If martial skill directs the Danish lords,
There inaccessible their army lies
To our swift scow'ring horse, the bloody field
Must man to man, and foot to foot, be fought.

Lady RANDOLPH. How many mothers shall bewail their sons!
How many widows weep their husband's slain!

Ye dames of Denmark! ev'n for you I feel,
Who sadly sitting on the sea-beat shore,
Long look for lords that never shall return.
GLENALVON. Oft has th'unconquer'd Caledonian sword
    Widow'd the north. The children of the slain
    Come, as I hope, to meet their father's fate.
    The monster war, with her infernal brood,
    Loud yelling fury, and life-ending pain,
    Are objects suited to GLENALVON's soul.
    Scorn is more grievous than the pains of death:
    Reproach more piercing than the pointed sword.
Lady RANDOLPH. I scorn thee not, but when I ought to scorn;
    Nor e'er reproach, but when insulted virtue
    Against audacious vice asserts herself.
     I own thy worth, GLENALVON; none more apt
    Than I to praise thine eminence in arms,
    And be the echo of thy martial fame.
    No longer vainly feed a guilty passion:
    Go and pursue a lawful mistress, glory.
    Upon the Danish crests redeem thy fault,
    And let thy valour be the shield of RANDOLPH.
GLENALVON. One instant stay, and hear an alter'd man.
    When beauty pleads for virtue, vice abash'd
    Flies its own colours, and goes o'er to virtue.
    I am your convert; time will shew how truly:
    Yet one immediate proof I mean to give.
    That youth, for whom your ardent zeal to-day,
    Somewhat too haughtily, defy'd your slave,
    Amidst the shock of armies I'll defend,
    And turn death from him, with a guardian arm.
    Sedate by use, my bosom maddens not
    At the tumultuous uproar of the field.
Lady RANDOLPH. Act thus, GLENALVON, and I am thy friend:
    But that's thy least reward. Believe me, Sir,
    The truly generous is the truly wise;
    And he who loves not others, lives unblest.
                                Exit Lady Randolph
GLENALVON *solus.*
    Amen! and virtue is its own reward! —
    I think that I have hit the very tone
    In which she loves to speak. Honey'd assent,

How pleasing art thou to the taste of man,
And woman also! flattery direct
Rarely disgusts. They little know mankind
Who doubt its operation: 'tis my key,
And opes the wicket of the human heart.
How far I have succeeded now I know not.
Yet I incline to think her stormy virtue
Is lull'd a while: 'tis her alone I fear:
Whilst she and RANDOLPH live, and live in faith
And amity, uncertain is my tenure.
Fate o'er my head suspends disgrace and death,
By that weak hair, a peevish female's will.
I am not idle: but the ebbs and flows
Of fortune's tide cannot be calculated.
That slave of NORVAL'S I have found most apt:
I shew'd him gold, and he has pawn'd his soul
To say and swear whatever I suggest.
 NORVAL, I'm told, has that alluring look,
'Twixt man and woman, which I have observ'd
To charm the nicer and fantastic dames,
Who are, like Lady RANDOLPH, full of virtue.
In raising RANDOLPH'S jealousy I may
But point him to the truth. He seldom errs
Who thinks the worst he can of womankind.

The End of the THIRD ACT.

ACT IV

Flourish of Trumpets.

Enter Lord RANDOLPH *attended.*

Lord RANDOLPH. Summon an hundred horse, by break of day;
  To wait our pleasure at the castle gate.

Enter Lady RANDOLPH.

  Alas! my Lord! I've heard unwelcome news;
  The Danes are landed

Lord RANDOLPH.   Ay, no inroad this
  Of the Northumbrian bent to take a spoil:
  No sportive war, no tournament essay,
  Of some young knight resolv'd to break a spear,
  And stain with hostile blood his maiden arms.
  The Danes are landed: we must beat them back,
  Or live the slaves of Denmark.

Lady RANDOLPH.   Dreadful times!

Lord RANDOLPH. The fenceless villages are all forsaken;
  The trembling mothers and their children lodg'd
  In wall-girt towers and castles; whilst the men
  Retire indignant. Yet, like broken waves,
  They but retire more awful to return.

Lady RANDOLPH. Immense, as fame reports, the Danish host—

Lord RANDOLPH. Were it as numerous as loud fame reports,
  An army knit like ours wou'd pierce it thro':
  Brothers, that shrink not from each other's side,
  And fond companions, fill our warlike files:
  For his dear offspring, and the wife he loves,
  The husband, and the fearless father arm.
  In vulgar breasts heroic ardor burns,
  And the poor peasant mates his daring lord.

Lady RANDOLPH. Men's minds are temper'd, like their swords, for war;
  Lovers of danger, on destruction's brink
  They joy to rear erect their daring forms.
  Hence, early graves; hence, the lone widow's life;
  And the sad mother's grief-embitter'd age.
  Where is our gallant guest?

Lord RANDOLPH.   Down in the vale
  I left him, managing a fiery steed,
  Whose stubbornness had foil'd the strength and skill

Of every rider. But behold he comes,
In earnest conversation with GLENALVON.
Enter NORVAL *and* GLENALVON.
  GLENALVON! with the lark arise; go forth,
And lead my troops that ly in yonder vale:
Private I travel to the royal camp:
  NORVAL, thou goest with me. But say, young man!
Where didst thou learn so to discourse of war,
And in such terms as I o'erheard to-day?
War is no village science, nor its phrase
A language taught amongst the shepherd swains.
NORVAL. Small is the skill my Lord delights to praise
In him he favours. — Hear from whence it came.
Beneath a mountain's brow, the most remote
And inaccessible by shepherds trod,
In a deep cave, dug by no mortal hand,
A hermit liv'd; a melancholy man,
Who was the wonder of our wand'ring swains.
Austere and lonely, cruel to himself,
Did they report him; the cold earth his bed,
Water his drink, his food the shepherd's alms.
I went to see him, and my heart was touch'd
With rev'rence and with pity. Mild he spake,
And, entring on discourse, such stories told
As made me oft revisit his sad cell.
For he had been a soldier in his youth;
And fought in famous battles, when the Peers
Of Europe, by the bold GODFREDO led,
Against th'usurping Infidel display'd
The cross of Christ, and won the Holy Land.
Pleas'd with my admiration, and the fire
His speech struck from me, the old man wou'd shake
His years away, and act his young encounters:
Then, having shew'd his wounds, he'd sit him down,
And all the live-long day discourse of war.
To help my fancy, in the smooth green turf
He cut the figures of the marshall'd hosts;
Describ'd the motions, and explain'd the use
Of the deep column, and the lengthen'd line,
The square, the crescent, and the phalanx firm.

For all that Saracen or Christian knew
Of war's vast art, was to this hermit known.
Lord RANDOLPH. Why did this soldier in a desert hide
Those qualities that should have grac'd a camp?
NORVAL. That too at last I learn'd. Unhappy man!
Returning homewards by Messina's port,
Loaded with wealth and honours bravely won,
A rude and boist'rous captain of the sea
Fasten'd a quarrel on him. Fierce they fought:
The stranger fell, and with his dying breath
Declar'd his name and lineage! Mighty God!
The soldier cried, my brother! Oh! my brother!
Lady RANDOLPH. His brother!
NORVAL.   Yes; of the same parents born;
His only brother. They exchang'd forgiveness:
And happy, in my mind, was he that died:
For many deaths has the survivor suffer'd.
In the wild desert on a rock he sits,
Or on some nameless streams untrodden banks,
And ruminates all day his dreadful fate.
At times, alas! not in his perfect mind!
Holds dialogues with his lov'd brother's ghost;
And oft each night forsakes his sullen couch,
To make sad orisons for him he slew.
Lady RANDOLPH. To what mysterious woes are mortals born!
In this dire tragedy were there no more
Unhappy persons? did the parents live?
NORVAL. No; they were dead: kind heav'n had clos'd their eyes
Before their son had shed his brother's blood.
Lord RANDOLPH. Hard is his fate; for he was not to blame!
There is a destiny in this strange world,
Which oft decrees an undeserved doom:
Let schoolmen tell us why. — From whence these sounds?
                                        Trumpets at a distance.
Enter an Officer.
OFFICER. My Lord, the trumpets of the troops of Lorn:
The valiant leader hails the noble RANDOLPH.
Lord RANDOLPH. Mine antient guest! does he the warriors lead?
Has Denmark rous'd the brave old Knight to arms?
OFFICER. No; worn with warfare, he resigns the sword.

His eldest hope, the valiant JOHN of Lorn,
Now leads his kindred bands.
Lord RANDOLPH. GLENALVON, go.
  With hospitality's most strong request
  Intreat the chief.

                                Exit GLENALVON.

OFFICER.   My Lord, requests are vain.
  He urges on, impatient of delay,
  Stung with the tidings of the foe's approach.
Lord RANDOLPH. May victory sit on the warrior's plume!
  Bravest of men! his flocks and herds are safe;
  Remote from war's alarms his pastures lie,
  By mountains inaccessible secur'd:
  Yet foremost he into the plain descends,
  Eager to bleed in battles not his own.
  Such were the heroes of the antient world:
  Contemners they of indolence and gain;
  But still for love of glory, and of arms,
  Prone to encounter peril, and to lift
  Against each strong antagonist the spear.
  I'll go and press the hero to my breast.

                                Exit Randolph.

Manet Lady Randolph and Norval.
Lady RANDOLPH. The soldier's loftiness, the pride and pomp
  Investing awful war, NORVAL, I see,
  Transport thy youthful mind.
NORVAL.   Ah! should they not?
  Bless'd be the hour I left my father's house!
  I might have been a shepherd all my days,
  And stole obscurely to a peasant's grave.
  Now, if I live, with mighty chiefs I stand;
  And, if I fall, with noble dust I lie.
Lady RANDOLPH. There is a gen'rous spirit in thy breast,
  That could have well sustain'd a prouder fortune.
  This way with me; under yon spreading beech,
  Unseen, unheard, by human eye or ear,
  I will amaze thee with a wond'rous tale.
NORVAL. Let there be danger, Lady, with the secret,
  That I may hug it to my grateful heart,
  And prove my faith. Command my sword, my life:

35

These are the sole possessions of poor NORVAL.

Lady RANDOLPH. Know'st thou these gems?

NORVAL.   Durst I believe mine eyes
I'd say I knew them, and they were my father's.

Lady RANDOLPH. Thy father's, say'st thou! ah! they were thy father's!

NORVAL. I saw them once, and curiously inquir'd
Of both my parents, whence such splendor came?
But I was check'd, and more could never learn.

Lady RANDOLPH. Then learn of me, thou art not NORVAL's son.

NORVAL. Not NORVAL's son!

Lady RANDOLPH.   Nor of a shepherd sprung.

NORVAL. Lady, who am I then ?

Lady RANDOLPH.   Noble thou art;
For noble was thy Sire!

NORVAL.   I will believe —
O! tell me farther! Say who was my father?

Lady RANDOLPH. DOUGLAS!

NORVAL.   Lord DOUGLAS, whom to-day I saw?

Lady RANDOLPH. His younger brother.

NORVAL.   And in yonder camp ?

Lady RANDOLPH. Alas!

NORVAL. You make me tremble — Sighs and tears!
Lives my brave father?

Lady RANDOLPH. Ah! too brave indeed!
He fell in battle 'ere thyself was born.

NORVAL. Ah me unhappy! 'ere I saw the light?
But does my mother live ? I may conclude,
From my own fate, her portion has been sorrow.

Lady RANDOLPH. She lives; but wastes her life in constant woe,
Weeping her husband slain, her infant lost.

NORVAL. You that are skill'd so well in the sad story
Of my unhappy parents, and with tears
Bewail her destiny, now have compassion
Upon the offspring of the friends you lov'd!
O! tell me who, and where my mother is!
Oppress'd by a base world, perhaps she bends
Beneath the weight of other ills than grief;
And desolate, implores of heav'n the aid
Her son should give. It is, it must be so —
Your countenance confesses that she's wretched.

O! tell me her condition! Can the sword—
Who shall resist me in a parent's cause?
Lady RANDOLPH. Thy virtue ends her woe.— My son, my son!
   I am thy mother, and the wife of DOUGLAS!

                                        Falls upon his neck.
NORVAL. O heav'n and earth, how wondrous is my fate!
   Art thou my mother? Ever let me kneel!
Lady RANDOLPH. Image of DOUGLAS! Fruit of fatal love!
   All that I owe thy Sire, I pay to thee.
NORVAL. Respect and admiration still possess me,
   Checking the love and fondness of a son.
   Yet I was filial to my humble parents.
   But did my Sire surpass the rest of men,
   As thou excellest all of womankind?
Lady RANDOLPH. Arise, my son! In me thou dost behold
   The poor remains of beauty once admir'd:
   The autumn of my days is come already;
   For sorrow made my summer haste away.
   Yet in my prime I equal'd not thy father:
   His eyes were like the eagle's, yet sometimes
   Liker the dove's; and, as he pleas'd, he won
   All hearts with softness, or with spirit aw'd.
NORVAL. How did he fall? Sure 'twas a bloody field
   When DOUGLAS died. O I have much to ask!
Lady RANDOLPH. Hereafter thou shalt hear the lengthen'd tale
   Of all thy father's and thy mother's woes.
   At present this: thou art the rightful heir
   Of yonder castle, and the wide domains
   Which now Lord RANDOLPH, as my husband, holds.
   But thou shalt not be wrong'd; I have the power
   To right thee still: before the King I'll kneel,
   And call Lord DOUGLAS to protect his blood.
NORVAL. The blood of DOUGLAS will protect itself.
Lady RANDOLPH. But we shall need both friends and favour, boy,
   To wrest thy lands and lordship from the gripe
   Of RANDOLPH and his kinsman. Yet I think
   My tale will move each gentle heart to pity,
   My life incline the virtuous to believe.
NORVAL. To be the son of DOUGLAS is to me
   Inheritance enough. Declare my birth,

And in the field I'll seek for fame and fortune.
Lady RANDOLPH. Thou dost not know what perils and injustice
   Await the poor man's valour. O! my son!
   The noblest blood in all the land's abash'd,
   Having no lacquey but pale poverty.
   Too long hast thou been thus attended, DOUGLAS!
   Too long hast thou been deem'd a peasant's child.
   The wanton heir of some inglorious chief
   Perhaps has scorn'd thee, in the youthful sports;
   Whilst thy indignant spirit swell'd in vain!
   Such contumely thou no more shalt bear:
   But how I purpose to redress thy wrongs
   Must be hereafter told. Prudence directs
   That we should part before yon chiefs return.
   Retire, and from thy rustic follower's hand
   Receive a billet, which thy mother's care,
   Anxious to see thee, dictated before
   This casual opportunity arose
   Of private conference. Its purport mark;
   For as I there appoint we meet again.
   Leave me, my son! and frame thy manners still
   To NORVAL'S, not to noble DOUGLAS' state.
NORVAL. I will remember. Where is NORVAL now?
   That good old man.
Lady RANDOLPH.   At hand conceal'd he lies,
   An useful witness. But beware, my son,
   Of yon GLENALVON; in his guilty breast
   Resides a villain's shrewdness, ever prone
   To false conjecture. He hath griev'd my heart.
NORVAL. Has he indeed? Then let yon false GLENALVON
   Beware of me.

                                        Exit DOUGLAS.

              Manet Lady RANDOLPH.
                    There burst the smother'd flame!
   O! thou all righteous and eternal King!
   Who father of the fatherless art call'd,
   Protect my son! — Thy inspiration, Lord!
   Hath fill'd his bosom with that sacred fire,
   Which in the breasts of his forefathers burn'd:
   Set him on high like them, that he may shine

The star and glory of his native land!
Then let the minister of death descend,
And bear my willing spirit to its place.
Yonder they come. How do bad women find
Unchanging aspects to conceal their guilt?
When I, by reason, and by justice urg'd,
Full hardly can dissemble with these men
In nature's pious cause.

Enter Lord RANDOLPH *and* GLENALVON.

Lord RANDOLPH.   Yon gallant chief,
Of arms enamour'd, all repose disclaims.

Lady RANDOLPH. Be not, my Lord, by his example sway'd:
Arrange the business of to-morrow now,
And, when you enter, speak of war no more.

                              Exit Lady RANDOLPH.
        Manet Lord RANDOLPH *and* GLENALVON.

Lord RANDOLPH. 'Tis so, by heav'n! her mien, her voice, her eye,
And her impatience to be gone, confirm it.

GLENALVON. He parted from her now: behind the mount,
Amongst the trees, I saw him glide along.

Lord RANDOLPH. For sad, sequester'd virtue she's renown'd!

GLENALVON. Most true, my Lord.

Lord RANDOLPH. Yet this distinguish'd Dame
Invites a youth, the acquaintance of a day,
Alone to meet her at the midnight hour.
This assignation, [*shews a letter*] the assassin freed,
Her manifest affection for the youth,
Might breed suspicion in a husband's brain,
Whose gentle consort all for love had wedded;
Much more in mine. MATILDA never lov'd me.
Let no man, after me, a woman wed,
Whose heart he knows he has not; tho' she brings
A mine of gold, a kingdom for her dowry,
For let her seem, like the night's shadowy queen,
Cold and contemplative;—He cannot trust her:
She may, she will, bring shame and sorrow on him;
The worst of sorrows, and the worst of shames!

GLENALVON. Yield not, my Lord, to such afflicting thoughts;
But let the spirit of an husband sleep,
Till your own senses make a sure conclusion.

This billet must to blooming NORVAL go:
At the next turn awaits my trusty spy;
I'll give it him refitted for his master.
In the close thicket take your secret stand;
The moon shines bright, and your own eyes may judge
Of their behaviour.
Lord RANDOLPH.   Thou dost counsel well.
GLENALVON. Permit me now to make one slight essay.
Of all the trophies which vain mortals boast,
By wit, by valour, or by wisdom won,
The first and fairest, in a young man's eye,
Is woman's captive heart. Successful love
With glorious fumes intoxicates the mind;
And the proud conqueror in triumph moves
Air-born, exalted above vulgar men.
Lord RANDOLPH. And what avails this maxim?
GLENALVON.   Much, my Lord!
Withdraw a little: I'll accost young NORVAL,
And with ironical derisive counsel
Explore his spirit. If he is no more
Than humble NORVAL, by thy favour rais'd,
Brave as he is, he'll shrink astonish'd from me:
But if he be the fav'rite of the fair,
Lov'd by the first of Caledonia's dames,
He'll turn upon me, as the lion turns
Upon the hunter's spear.
Lord RANDOLPH.   'Tis shrewdly thought.
GLENALVON. When we grow loud, draw near. But let my Lord
His rising wrath restrain.   *Exit* RANDOLPH.
                    Manet GLENALVON.
                              'Tis strange, by heav'n!
That she should run full tilt her fond career,
To one so little known. She too that seem'd
Pure as the winter stream, when ice emboss'd
Whitens its course. Even I did think her chaste,
Whose charity exceeds not. Precious sex!
Whose deeds lascivious pass GLENALVON's thoughts!
                                        NORVAL *appears*

His port I love; he's in a proper mood
To chide the thunder, if at him it roar'd.
Has NORVAL seen the troops?

NORVAL.   The setting sun,
   With yellow radiance lighten'd all the vale,
   And as the warriors mov'd, each polish'd helm,
   Corslet, or spear, glanc'd back his gilded beams.
   The hill they climb'd, and halting at its top,
   Of more than mortal size, tow'ring, they seem'd,
   An host angelic, clad in burning arms.
GLENALVON. Thou talk'st it well; no leader of our host,
   In sounds more lofty, speaks of glorious war.
NORVAL. If I shall e'er acquire a leader's name,
   My speech will be less ardent. Novelty
   Now prompts my tongue, and youthful admiration
   Vents itself freely; since no part is mine
   Of praise pertaining to the great in arms.
GLENALVON. You wrong yourself, brave Sir; your martial deeds
   Have rank'd you with the great: but mark me NORVAL;
   Lord RANDOLPH's favour now exalts your youth
   Above his veterans of famous service.
   Let me who know these soldiers, counsel you.
   Give them all honour; seem not to command:
   Else they will scarcely brook your late sprung power,
   Which nor alliance props, nor birth adorns.
NORVAL. Sir, I have been accustom'd all my days
   To hear and speak the plain and simple truth:
   And tho' I have been told, that there are men
   Who borrow friendship's tongue to speak their scorn,
   Yet in such language I am little skill'd.
   Therefore I thank GLENALVON for his counsel,
   Altho' it sounded harshly. Why remind
   Me of my birth obscure? Why slur my power
   With such contemptuous terms?
GLENALVON.   I did not mean
   To gall your pride, which now I see is great.
NORVAL. My pride!
GLENALVON.   Suppress it as you wish to prosper.
   Your pride's excessive. Yet for RANDOLPH's sake
   I will not leave you to its rash direction.
   If thus you swell, and frown at high-born men,
   Will high-born men endure a shepherd's scorn?
NORVAL.   A shepherd's scorn?

GLENALVON.   Yes, if you presume
  To bend on soldiers these disdainful eyes,
  As if you took the measure of their minds,
  And said in secret, you're no match for me;
  What will become of you?
NORVAL.   If this were told—*Aside.*
  Has thou no fears for thy presumptuous self?
GLENALVON. Ha! dost thou threaten me?
NORVAL.   Didst thou not hear?
GLENALVON. Unwillingly I did; a nobler foe
  Had not been question'd thus. But such as thee—
NORVAL. Whom dost thou think me?
Glenalvon. *Norval.*
NORVAL.   So I am—
  And who is NORVAL in GLENALVON's eyes?
GLENALVON. A peasant's son, a wand'ring beggar-boy;
  At best no more, even if he speaks the truth.
NORVAL. False as thou art, dost thou suspect my truth?
GLENALVON. Thy truth! thou'rt all a lie; and false as hell
  Is the vain-glorious tale thou told'st to RANDOLPH.
NORVAL. If I were chain'd, unarm'd, and bedrid old,
  Perhaps I should revile: But as I am
  I have no tongue to rail. The humble NORVAL
  Is of a race who strive not but with deeds.
  Did I not fear to freeze thy shallow valour,
  And make thee sink too soon beneath my sword,
  I'd tell thee—what thou art. I know thee well.
GLENALVON. Dost thou not know GLENALVON, born to command
  Ten thousand slaves like thee?
NORVAL.   Villain, no more:
  Draw and defend thy life. I did design
  To have defy'd thee in another cause:
  But heaven accelerates its vengeance on thee.
  Now for my own and Lady RANDOLPH's wrongs.
Enter Lord RANDOLPH.
Lord RANDOLPH. Hold, I command you both. The man that stirs
  Makes me his foe.
NORVAL.   Another voice than thine
  That threat had vainly sounded, noble RANDOLPH.
GLENALVON. Hear him, my Lord; he's wondrous condescending!

Mark the humility of shepherd NORVAL!

NORVAL. Now you may scoff in safety. *Sheaths his sword.*

Lord RANDOLPH. Speak not thus,
Taunting each other; but unfold to me
The cause of quarrel, then I judge betwixt you.

NORVAL. Nay, my good Lord, tho' I revere you much,
My cause I plead not, nor demand your judgment.
I blush to speak; I will not, cannot speak
Th' opprobrious words that I from him have borne.
To the liege-lord of my dear native land
I owe a subject's homage; but even him
And his high arbitration I'd reject.
Within my bosom reigns another lord;
Honour, sole judge and umpire of itself.
If my free speech offend you, noble RANDOLPH,
Revoke your favours, and let NORVAL go
Hence as he came, alone, but not dishonour'd.

Lord RANDOLPH. Thus far I'll mediate with impartial voice:
The antient foe of Caledonia's land
Now waves his banners o'er her frighted fields.
Suspend your purpose, till your country's arms
Repel the bold invader; then decide
The private quarrel.

GLENALVON. I agree to this.

NORVAL. And I.

Enter Servant.

SERVANT. The banquet waits.

Lord RANDOLPH. We come.

Exit Randolph.

GLENALVON. Norval,
Let not our variance mar the social hour,
Nor wrong the hospitality of RANDOLPH.
Nor frowning anger, nor yet wrinkl'd hate,
Shall stain my countenance. Smooth thou thy brow;
Nor let our strife disturb the gentle Dame.

NORVAL. Think not so lightly, Sir, of my resentment;
When we contend again, our strife is mortal.

The End of the FOURTH ACT.

ACT V
The Wood

Enter DOUGLAS.

THIS is the place, the centre of the grove.
Here stands the oak, the monarch of the wood.
How sweet and solemn is this mid-night scene!
The silver moon, unclouded, holds her way
Thro' skies where I could count each little star.
The fanning west wind scarcely stirs the leaves;
The river, rushing o'er its pebbled bed,
Imposes silence with a stilly sound.
In such a place as this, at such an hour,
If ancestry can be in ought believ'd,
Descending spirits have convers'd with man,
And told the secrets of the world unknown.

Enter Old NORVAL.

Old NORVAL. 'Tis he. But what if he should chide me hence?
His just reproach I fear.

                         DOUGLAS *turns and sees him.*
                   Forgive, forgive,
Canst thou forgive the man, the selfish man,
Who bred Sir MALCOLM's heir a shepherd's son?

DOUGLAS. Kneel not to me: thou art my father still:
Thy wish'd-for presence now compleats my joy.
Welcome to me, my fortunes thou shalt share,
And ever honour'd with thy DOUGLAS live.

Old NORVAL. And thou call me father? O my son!
I think that I could die to make amends
For the great wrong I did thee. 'Twas my crime
Which in the wilderness so long conceal'd
The blossom of thy youth.

DOUGLAS.   Not worse the fruit,
That in the wilderness the blossom blow'd.
Amongst the shepherds, in the humble cote,
I learn'd some lessons, which I'll not forget
When I inhabit yonder lofty towers.
I, who was once a swain, will ever prove
The poor man's friend; and, when my vassals bow,
NORVAL shall smooth the crested pride of DOUGLAS.

Old NORVAL. Let me but live to see thine exaltation!
  Yet grievous are my fears. O leave this place,
  And those unfriendly towers.
DOUGLAS.   Why should I leave them?
Old NORVAL. Lord RANDOLPH and his kinsman seek your life.
DOUGLAS. How know'st thou that?
Old NORVAL.   I will inform you how.
  When evening came, I left the secret place
  Appointed for me by your mother's care,
  And fondly trod in each accustom'd path
  That to the castle leads. Whilst thus I rang'd,
  I was alarm'd with unexpected sounds
  Of earnest voices. On the persons came;
  Unseen I lurk'd, and overheard them name
  Each other as they talk'd, Lord RANDOLPH this,
  And that GLENALVON: still of you they spoke,
  And of the Lady: threat'ning was their speech,
  Tho' but imperfectly my ear could hear it.
  'Twas strange, they said, a wonderful discov'ry;
  And ever and anon they vow'd revenge.
DOUGLAS. Revenge! for what?
Old NORVAL.   For being what you are;
  Sir MALCOLM'S heir: how else have you offended?
  When they were gone, I hied me to my cottage,
  And there sat musing how I best might find
  Means to inform you of their wicked purpose.
  But I could think of none: at last perplex'd
  I issued forth, encompassing the tower
  With many a weary step and wishful look.
  Now Providence hath brought you to my sight,
  Let not your too couragious spirit scorn
  The caution which I give.
DOUGLAS. I scorn it not.
  My mother warn'd me of GLENALVON'S baseness:
  But I will not suspect the noble RANDOLPH.
  In our encounter with the vile assassins,
  I mark'd his brave demeanor: him I'll trust.
Old NORVAL. I fear you will too far.
DOUGLAS. Here in this place
  I wait my mother's coming: she shall know

What thou hast told: her counsel I will follow:
And cautious ever are a mother's counsels.
You must depart; your presence may prevent
Our interview.

Old NORVAL. My blessing rest upon thee!
O may heav'n's hand, which sav'd thee from the wave,
And from the sword of foes, be near thee still;
Turning mischance, if ought hangs o'er thy head,
All upon mine!

Exit OLD Norval.

DOUGLAS.   He loves me like a parent;
And must not, shall not lose the son he loves,
Altho' his son has found a nobler father.
Eventful day! how hast thou chang'd my state!
Once on the cold, and winter shaded side
Of a bleak hill, mischance had rooted me,
Never to thrive, child of another soil:
Transplanted now to the gay sunny vale,
Like the green thorn of May my fortune flowers.
Ye glorious stars! high heav'n's resplendent host!
To whom I oft have of my lot complain'd,
Hear and record my soul's unalter'd wish!
Dead or alive, let me but be renown'd!
May heav'n inspire some fierce gigantic Dane,
To give a gold defiance to our host!
Before he speaks it out I will accept;
Like DOUGLAS conquer, or like DOUGLAS die.

Enter Lady RANDOLPH.

Lady RANDOLPH. My son! I heard a voice—

DOUGLAS.   —The voice was mine.

Lady RANDOLPH. Didst thou complain aloud to nature's ear,
That thus in dusky shades, at mid-night hours,
By stealth the mother and the son should meet?

Embracing him.

DOUGLAS. No; on this happy day, this better birth-day,
My thoughts and words are all of hope and joy.

Lady RANDOLPH. Sad fear and melancholy still divide
The empire of my breast with hope and joy.
Now hear what I advise.

DOUGLAS.   First, let me tell

What may the tenor of your counsel change.

Lady RANDOLPH. My heart forebodes some evil!

DOUGLAS. 'Tis not good. —
  At eve, unseen by RANDOLPH and GLENALVON,
  The good old NORVAL in the grove o'erheard
  Their conversation: oft they mention'd me
  With dreadful threatnings; you they sometimes nam'd.
  'Twas strange, they said, a wonderful discov'ry;
  And ever and anon they vow'd revenge.

Lady RANDOLPH. Defend us gracious God! we are betray'd:
  They have found out the secret of thy birth;
  It must be so. That is the great discovery.
  Sir MALCOLM's heir is come to claim his own;
  And he will be reveng'd. Perhaps even now,
  Arm'd and prepar'd for murder, they but wait
  A darker and more silent hour, to break
  Into the chamber where they think thou sleep'st.
  This moment, this, heav'n hath ordained to save thee!
  Fly to the camp, my son!

DOUGLAS.   And leave you here?
  No: to the castle let us go together,
  Call up the antient servants of your house,
  Who in their youth did eat your father's bread.
  Then tell them loudly that I am your son.
  If in the breasts of men one spark remains
  Of sacred love, fidelity, or pity,
  Some in your cause will arm. I ask but few
  To drive those spoilers from my father's house.

Lady RANDOLPH. O Nature, Nature! what can check thy force?
  Thou genuine offspring of the daring DOUGLAS!
  But rush not on destruction: save thyself,
  And I am safe. To me they mean no harm.
  Thy stay but risks thy precious life in vain.
  That winding path conducts thee to the river.
  Cross where thou seest a broad and beaten way,
  Which running eastward leads thee to the camp.
  Instant demand admittance to Lord DOUGLAS.
  Shew him these jewels, which his brother wore.
  Thy look, thy voice, will make him feel the truth,
  Which I by certain proof will soon confirm.

DOUGLAS. I yield me and obey: but yet my heart
  Bleeds at this parting. Something bids me stay
  And guard a mother's life. Oft have I read
  Of wondrous deeds by one bold arm atchiev'd.
  Our foes are two: no more: let me go forth,
  And see if any shield can guard GLENALVON.
Lady RANDOLPH. If thou regard'st thy mother, or rever'st
  Thy father's mem'ry, think of this no more.
  One thing I have to say before we part;
  Long wert thou lost; and thou art found, my child,
  In a most fearful season. War and battle
  I have great cause to dread. Too well I see
  Which way the current of thy temper sets:
  To-day I've found thee. Oh! my long lost hope!
  If thou to giddy valour giv'st the rein,
  To-morrow I may lose my son for ever.
  The love of thee, before thou saw'st the light,
  Sustain'd my life when thy brave father fell.
  If thou shalt fall, I have nor love nor hope
  In this waste world! my son, remember me!
DOUGLAS. What shall I say? how can I give you comfort?
  The God of battles of my life dispose
  As may be best for you! for whose dear sake
  I will not bear myself as I resolv'd.
  But yet consider, as no vulgar name
  That which I boast sounds amongst martial men.
  How will inglorious caution suit my claim ?
  The post of fate unshrinking I maintain.
  My country's foes must witness who I am.
  On the invaders heads I'll prove my birth,
  'Till friends and foes confess the genuine strain.
  If in this strife I fall, blame not your son,
  Who if he lives not honour'd, must not live.
Lady RANDOLPH. I will not utter what my bosom feels.
  Too well I love that valour which I warn.
  Farewel, my son! my counsels are but vain.   *Embracing.*
  And as high heav'n hath will'd it all must be.   *Separate.*
Lady RANDOLPH. Gaze not on me, thou wilt mistake the path;
  I'll point it out again.
Just as they are separating, enter from the wood Lord RANDOLPH *and* GLENALVON.

Lord RANDOLPH. Not in her presence.

 Now —

GLENALVON. I'm prepar'd.

Lord RANDOLPH.   No: I command thee stay.

 I go alone: it never shall be said

 That I took odds to combat mortal man.

 The noblest vengeance is the most compleat.

Exit Lord RANDOLPH.

GLENALVON *makes some steps to the same side of the stage, listens and speaks.*

GLENALVON. Demons of death come settle on my sword,

 And to a double slaughter guide it home!

 The lover and the husband both must die.

Lord RANDOLPH *behind the scenes.*

Lord RANDOLPH. Draw, villain! draw.

DOUGLAS. Assail me not, Lord RANDOLPH;

 Not as thou lov'st thyself.

Clashing of swords.

GLENALVON *running out.*

 Now is the time.

Enter Lady RANDOLPH *at the opposite side of the stage, faint and breathless.*

Lady RANDOLPH. Lord RANDOLPH, hear me; all shall be thine own:

 But spare! Oh spare my son!

Enter DOUGLAS *with a sword in each hand.*

 My mother's voice!

 I can protect thee still.

Lady RANDOLPH. He lives, he lives:

 For this, for this to heaven eternal praise!

 But sure I saw thee fall.

DOUGLAS. It was GLENALVON.

 Just as my arm had master'd RANDOLPH's sword,

 The villain came behind me; but I slew him.

Lady RANDOLPH. Behind thee! Ah; thou'rt wounded! O my child,

 How pale thou look'st! and shall I lose thee now?

DOUGLAS. Do not despair: I feel a little faintness;

 I hope it will not last.

Leans upon his sword.

Lady RANDOLPH.   There is no hope!

 And we must part! the hand of death is on thee!

  O my beloved child! O DOUGLAS, DOUGLAS!

DOUGLAS. Too soon we part; I have not long been DOUGLAS,

O destiny! hardly thou deal'st with me:
Clouded and hid, a stranger to myself,
In low and poor obscurity I liv'd.
Lady RANDOLPH. Has heav'n preserved thee for an end like this?
DOUGLAS. O had I fallen as my brave fathers fell,
Turning with great effort the tide of battle!
Like them I should have smil'd and welcom'd death.
But thus to perish by a villain's hand!
Cut off from nature's and from glory's course,
Which never mortal was so fond to run.
Lady RANDOLPH. Hear justice! hear! stretch thy avenging arm.
DOUGLAS *falls*.
DOUGLAS. Unknown I die; no tongue shall speak of me. —
Some noble spirits, judging by themselves,
May yet conjecture what I might have prov'd,
And think life only wanting to my fame:
But who shall comfort thee?
Lady RANDOLPH.   Despair! despair!
DOUGLAS. O had it pleas'd high heaven to let me live
A little while! — my eyes that gaze on thee
Grow dim apace! my mother — O! my mother. Dies.
Enter Lord RANDOLPH *and* ANNA.
Lord RANDOLPH. Thy words, the words of truth, have pierc'd my heart.
I am the stain of knighthood and of arms.
Oh! if my brave deliverer survives
The traitor's sword —
ANNA.   Alas! look there, my Lord.
Lord RANDOLPH. The mother and her son! How curst I am!
Was I the cause? No: I was not the cause.
Yon matchless villain did seduce my soul
To frantic jealousy.
ANNA.   My Lady lives:
The agony of grief hath but supprest
A while her powers.
Lord RANDOLPH.   But my deliverer's dead!
The world did once esteem Lord Randolph well,
Sincere of heart, for spotless honour fam'd:
And, in my early days, glory I gain'd
Beneath the holy banner of the cross.
Now past the noon of life, shame comes upon me;

Reproach, and infamy, and public hate,
Are near at hand: for all mankind will think
That Randolph basely stab'd Sir Malcolm's heir.

Lady RANDOLPH *recovering*.

Lady RANDOLPH. Where am I now? still in this wretched world!
  Grief cannot break a heart so hard as mine,
  My youth was worn in anguish: but youth's strength,
  With hope's assistance, bore the brunt of sorrow;
  And train'd me on to be the object now,
  On which Omnipotence displays itself,
  Making a spectacle, a tale of me,
  To awe its vassal, man.
Lord RANDOLPH.   O misery!
  Amidst thy raging grief I must proclaim
  My innocence.
Lady RANDOLPH. Thy innocence?
Lord RANDOLPH.   My guilt
  Is innocence compar'd with what thou think'st it.
Lady RANDOLPH. Of thee I think not: what have I to do
  With thee or any thing? My son! my son!
  My beautiful! my brave! how proud was I
  Of thee, and of thy valour! My fond heart
  O'erflow'd this day with transport, when I thought
  Of growing old amidst a race of thine,
  Who might make up to me their father's childhood,
  And bear my brother's and my husband's name:
  Now all my hopes are dead! A little while
  Was I a wife! a mother not so long!
  What am I now ?—I know.— But I shall be
  That only whilst I please; for such a son
  And such a husband make a woman bold.

Runs out.

Lord RANDOLPH. Follow her, Anna: I myself would follow,
  But in this rage she must abhor my presence.

Exit ANNA

Enter OLD NORVAL.
OLD NORVAL. I hear the voice of woe; heaven guard my child!
Lord RANDOLPH. Already is the idle gaping crowd,
  The spiteful vulgar come to gaze on Randolph.
  Begone.

Old NORVAL. I fear thee not. I will not go.
  Here I'll remain. I'm an accomplice, Lord.
  With thee in murder. Yes, my sins did help
  To crush down to the ground this lovely plant.
  O noblest youth that ever yet was born!
  Sweetest and best, gentlest and bravest spirit,
  That ever bless'd the world! Wretch that I am,
  Who saw that noble spirit swell and rise
  Above the narrow limits that confin'd it!
  Yet never was by all thy virtues won
  To do thee justice, and reveal the secret,
  Which timely known, had rais'd thee far above
  The villain's snare! Oh! I am punish'd now!
  These are the hairs that should have strew'd the ground,
  And not the locks of Douglas.
Tears his hair, and throws himself upon the body of Douglas.
Lord RANDOLPH. I know thee now: thy boldness I forgive;
  My crest is fallen. For thee I will appoint
  A place of rest, if grief will let thee rest.
  I will reward, altho' I cannot punish.
  Curst, curst Glenalvon, he escap'd too well,
  Tho' slain and baffled by the hand he hated.
  Foaming with rage and fury to the last,
  Cursing his conqueror, the felon dy'd.
Enter ANNA.
  My Lord, my Lord!
Lord RANDOLPH.   Speak: I can hear of horror.
ANNA. Horror indeed!
Lord RANDOLPH.   Matilda?
ANNA.   Is no more;
  She ran, she flew like light'ning up the hill,
  Nor halted till the precipice she gain'd,
  Beneath whose low'ring top the river falls
  Ingulph'd in rifted rocks: thither she came,
  As fearless as the eagle lights upon it,
  And headlong down. —
Lord RANDOLPH.   'Twas I! alas! 'twas I
  That fill'd her breast with fury; drove her down
  The precipice of death! Wretch that I am!
ANNA. O had you seen her last despairing look!

Upon the brink she stood, and cast her eyes
Down on the deep: then lifting up her head
And her white hands to heaven, seeming to say,
Why am I forc'd to this? she plung'd herself
Into the empty air.
Lord RANDOLPH.   I will not vent,
In vain complaints, the passion of my soul.
Peace in this world I never can enjoy.
These wounds the gratitude of Randolph gave.
They speak aloud, and with the voice of fate
Denounce my doom. I am resolv'd. I'll go
Straight to the battle, where the man that makes
Me turn aside must threaten worse than death.
Thou, faithful to thy mistress, take this ring,
Full warrant of my power. Let every rite
With cost and pomp upon their funerals wait:
For Randolph hopes he never shall return.

FINIS

EPILOGUE

An Epilogue I ask'd; but not one word
* Our bard will write. He vows, 'tis most absurd*
With comic wit to contradict the strain
Of tragedy, and make your sorrows vain.
Sadly he says, that pity is the best,
The noblest passion of the human breast:
For when its sacred streams the heart o'erflow,
In gushes pleasure with the tide of woe;
And when its waves retire, like those of Nile,
They leave behind them such a golden soil,
That there the virtues without culture grow,
There the sweet blossoms of affection blow.
These were his words: – void of delusive art
I felt them; for he spoke them from his heart.
Nor will I now attempt, with witty folly,
To chase away celestial melancholy.

ADVERTISEMENTS FOR THE PLAY

1 Advertisement for Douglas

Written in December 1756 before the premier on 14th of the month, this pamphlet announces the upcoming tragedy in the Canongate theatre. It alludes to the clerical presence expected to attend by West Digges (the theatre manager), but insists that plenty of space will be available for others who wish to go. Tickets for the event are to be had from the lodgings of D--- H--- Esq. almost certainly David Hume, who had attended rehearsals of the play, and was a staunch friend of the author.

THEATRE.

AS the MANAGER has been informed, That a Report prevails, that no Perfons will be admitted into the Theatre on *Tuefday* the 14th inftant, but CLERGYMEN, at which Rumour many other Perfons are offended; He thinks it his Duty to acquaint the Public, That the PIT ALONE IS PARTICULARLY kept BY ORDER for the FRATERNITY. The Boxes are already let to Ladies (except the Box prepared for the MODERATOR) and there will be feveral vacant Places in them, which will no doubt be filled by Gentlemen who do not belong to that ANCIENT and VENERABLE SOCIETY.

AS the Novelty of the Sight, and Grandeur of the Preparations for their Reception in the THEATRE, may reafonably be prefum'd to excite an extraordinary Curiofity, to prevent the leaft Offence at any Diftinction or Preference, the whole Houfe is laid at ONE PRICE; and the two Galleries will be elegantly illuminated with Sconces, &c. and hung with BLACK. It is to accommodate the PUBLIC, and particularly fuch BROTHERS as may, in cafe of a great Throng, not find Admittance below Stairs, or in the FIRST GALLERY, that the UPPER GALLERY is new benched, and ornamented in an elegant Manner, and is perfectly cleared from every Diforder and Indecorum it was formerly fubject to; and is rendered as warm, as decent, and as commodious as any Part of the Houfe, no Expence being fpared for the MOURNFUL OCCASION.

The two Galleries will be opened for CLERGYMEN, CHURCH-WARDENS, and OTHERS, exactly at Half an Hour after Four o' Clock: The PIT will be referv'd, by ORDER, ready for the Reception of the Brethren who fhall have the diftinguifhed Honour to accompany the MODERATOR. LADIES are defired to fend Servants to keep their Boxes, punctually at Three: And it is moft humbly requefted, that no Offence will be taken by any GENTLEMAN, fince the Decency, Decorum and Conduct of the DRAMA requires, That

No Perfon whatever (*THE AUTHOR EXCEPTED*) can be admitted behind the Scenes.

The whole to be concluded with a SOLEMN FARCE, called the ADDRESS, never before acted; where the FIVE principal CHARACTERS will be exhibited in their true Colours.

Tickets printed for the Occafion to be had at the Lodgings of D----- H------ Efq; and no other Tickets will be received at the Door, nor will any Money be taken there.

Guards will be placed about the Houfe, and a fufficient Number of BEADLES, with Flambeaus will attend the Avenues for the Conveniency of the Brethren.

2 A Full and True History of the Bloody Tragedy of Douglas

Alexander Carlyle penned this advertisement in response to a request from the theatre manager at the Canongate, West Digges, who was also performing the role of Douglas. Although Carlyle wrote a larger piece which attempted an ironical defence of the play, he valued this sheet as a greater service to the production. As the initial numbers began to drop away from the theatre, Home hoped that something could be done to attract the 'lower orders of tradesmen and apprentices' to attend. Focusing on the play's militarism, and the promise of blood, jealousy, revenge and battle, Carlyle believed that he had succeeded in securing its run for two more nights.

A FULL AND TRUE

HISTORY

Of the BLOODY TRAGEDY of

DOUGLAS,

As it is now to be feen acting at the THEATRE in the Canongate.

IN the days of good king Alexander III. the ninety-fifth king of Scotland, there lived a valiant and wealthy knight, called Sir Malcolm of Rockcastle in Teviotdale. It is his daughter, and her fon, the noble DOUGLAS, that are the chief perfons of this deep tragedy. For this lady being privately joined in wedlock to a fon of lord Douglas, who dying foon thereafter in battle, together with her brother, and fhe proving with child, durft not tell her father, becaufe he was a great enemy of the Douglas; wherefore, fo foon as her fon is born, fhe lays him in a bafket, with much gold and jewels, and commits him to the care of her nurfe: the nurfe fets out at the dead of night, and having a river to crofs, it is believed fhe perifhed, as alfo the child; for the lady heareth no more of them. Whereupon, pining away with grief, fhe refufes all offers of marriage, till at laft her aged father befeeching her upon his knees, fhe gives her hand to lord Barnet, who had lately faved her from ravifhers. With him fhe lives many years a pattern and mirror of virtue, though grief is all the while inwardly preying upon her heart, till at length, by God's providence, her fon is miraculoufly reftored.

For at this time the Danes land a vaft army below Gularnefs to conquer Scotland. King Alexander fummons an army to meet near Barnet's caftle. My lord, as he is riding one day towards that camp, is attack'd by four arm'd ruffians, who would have foon finifh'd his days; but at that inftant a young ftranger compleatly arm'd with bow, and quiver, fword and target, rufhes from a thicket, and having kill'd two of the ruffians with his trufty broad fword, puts the reft to flight. Lord Barnet comes back, and having prefented his deliverer to his beautiful and virtuous wife, he raifes him to high command, and takes him with him to the camp. Immediately hereafter is to be feen, the furprifing and wonderful manner in which lady Barnet finds out that this young ftranger is her own fon by the valiant Douglas; and how he was faved in Carron water, and educated by a fhepherd: together with other accidents that befel him. The heart of that good lady is overjoyed at this unexpected bleffing; neverthelefs fearing that lord Barnet might defraud her fon of his rights, or caufe him to be murdered, fhe refolves to conceal the fecret in her own breaft till the hour of midnight, when fhe propofes to meet her fon in the middle of the wood, and advife him in what manner to conduct himfelf. But Glenalvon, lord Barnet's coufin and heir, a falfe and bloody minded man, whofe horrid actions are painted in their true colours in this drama, being himfelf a lover of lady Barnet, tho' fcorned by that chafte and virtuous dame, partly through jealoufy, and partly to compafs his lewd defires, lays a plot to obtain both the lady and the eftate: for intercepting the letter which lady Barnet had wrote young Douglas to meet her in the wood, by that means, and others more fly, he impofes on the fimple Barnet, and by kindling the fire of jealoufy in his bofom, makes him to believe that his honourable lady is in love with the ftranger: whereupon, fealing the letter again, he fends it to Douglas, who comes as appointed to meet his mother, but the moon being then at the full, lord Barnet and Glenalvon come forth alfo, and watch them at a diftance; and beholding the fond careffes that are given by the mother and the fon, Barnet burns with a defire of revenge; and no fooner are the lady and Douglas parted, than he makes furioufly upon the youth, who when he is valiantly defending his life, is ftabbed behind his back by the traitor Glenalvon; yet turning upon him, he at one blow gives him death as the reward of his treachery. Thus perifhes the valiant Douglas, in the 19th year of his age, the delight of Scotland, and the wonder of his time. His wretched mother foon throws herfelf frantic over a precipice into Carron water, and lord Barnet, when he knows it was his dear and virtuous lady's fon he had killed, repents of his bloody deed, and rufhes foon after into the thickeft of the battle, and is flain.

FINIS.

OFFICIAL CHURCH RESPONSE AND WITHERSPOON'S ARGUMENT AGAINST THE STAGE

3 Admonition and Exhortation by the Presbytery of Edinburgh

The Admonition and Exhortation was to be read from pulpits on Sunday 30th January, and subsequently published in order to reach as wide an audience as possible. Although it was addressed to 'all within their bounds', the Presbytery's handling of the ministers who attended the play was attacked by the Presbytery of Dunse which rebuked Edinburgh for overstepping its bounds. The Admonition cites both religious and legal precedents against the stage, referring to Anthony Aston's attempts to set up a theatre company in 1726-1727, and the Licensing Act of 1737 which was enacted in response to Henry Fielding's satire Tom Thumb which had bitterly assaulted the Walpole government. Under the act, any theatre wishing to perform a play had to obtain a royal patent first. In addition, all texts of a performance had to be submitted to the office of the Lord Chamberlain at least fourteen days in advance. In Scotland it was the Court of Session that enforced the Act. The Presbytery also laments that the censuring of the theatre has been circumvented by sandwiching a play between two pieces of music, allowing the venue to be termed a concert-hall and thus avoid the jurisdiction of the Licensing Act.

ADMONITION and EXHORTATION

BY THE

Reverend Presbytery of *EDINBURGH*

To all within their Bounds.

At Edinburgh, *the fifth Day of* January, *One thousand seven hundred and fifty-seven Years.*

THE Presbytery taking into their serious Consideration, the declining State of Religion, the open Profanation of the Lord's Day, the Contempt of public Worship, the growing Luxury and Levity of the present Age; in which so many seem Lovers of Pleasure, more than Lovers of God: And being particularly affected with the UNPRECEDENTED COUNTENANCE given of late to the Playhouse in this Place, when the State of the Nation, and the Circumstances of the Poor, make such hurtful Entertainments still more pernicious; judged it their indispensable Duty to express, in the most open and solemn Manner, the deep Concern they feel on this Occasion.

THE Opinion which the Christian Church has always entertained of Stage Plays and Players, as prejudicial to the Interests of Religion and Morality, is well known; and the fatal Influence which they commonly have on the far greater Part of Mankind, particularly the younger Sort, is too obvious to be called in question.

To enumerate how many Servants, Apprentices, and Students in different Branches of Literature, in this City and Suburbs, have been seduced from their proper Business, by attending the Stage, would be a painful, disagreeable Task.

THE Presbytery, in the Year 1727, when consisting of many pious, prudent, and learned Ministers, whose Praise is in all the Churches, being aware of these Evils, did prepare a Paper, which was read from the several Pulpits within their Bounds, warning their People against the dangerous Infection of the Theatre then erected here.

IN the Year 1737, the Legislature, in their great Wisdom, did, by an Act of the 1oth of *George* II. enact and declare, " That every Person who should, for Hire or " Reward, act, or cause to be acted, any Play, or other Entertainment of the Stage, " without the special Licence and Authority mentioned in the said Act, should be " deemed a Rogue and a Vagabond, and for every such Offence should forfeit the " Sum of *L.* 50 *Sterling.*"

AT that Time a Project was set on Foot to obtain a licensed Theatre in this City; but the Masters and Professors of the University, supported by the Magistrates, having prepared a Petition, setting forth the dangerous Tendency of a Playhouse here, with respect to the important Interests of Virtue and Learning, the Project was laid aside.

THE Players, however, being so audacious as to continue to act in defiance of the Law, the Presbytery did, at their own Charge, prosecute them before the Court of Session; and prevailed in the Process. The Players were fined in terms of Law; and Warrants being issued for apprehending them, they fled from Justice. But others came in their place; who since that Time have attempted to elude the Law, by changing the Name of the PLAYHOUSE into that of the CONCERT-HALL.

As

63

As such a slight Evasion, the mere Change of a Name, could not make the smallest Variation in the Nature of the Thing, the Presbytery continued to do all in their Power, and in their Sphere, to prevent the growing Evil; and think themselves at this Time loudly called upon, in ONE BODY, and with ONE VOICE, to expostulate, in the Bowels of Love and Compassion, with all under their Care and Inspection.

WHEN our gracious Sovereign, attentive to the Voice of Providence, is calling from the Throne to Humiliation and Prayer, how unseemly is it for his Subjects to give themselves up to Mirth and Jollity? When the War in which we are engaged, and many awful Tokens of the divine Displeasure, bespeak us, in the Language of an inspired Writer, to *redeem the time because the days are evil*, should that Time be squandered away in running the constant Round of foolish, not to say sinful Amusements? When the Wants and Cries of the numerous Poor require extraordinary Supplies, how unaccountable is it to lavish away vast Sums for such vain and idle Purposes? When the Wisdom of the Nation has guarded the Inhabitants of this City and Suburbs from the Infection of the Stage, by a plain and express Statute; is it not a high Instance of Folly, to break down that Barrier, and open a Door with their own Hands for theatrical Representations? which are in many Respects no less inconsistent with good Policy, than unfriendly to Religion; and will be found, sooner or later, to affect their temporal as well as spiritual Interests.

ON these Accounts, and for many other obvious and weighty Considerations, the Presbytery, warmed with just Concern for the Good of Souls, do, in the Fear of God, WARN, EXHORT, and OBTEST, all within their Bounds, as they regard the Glory of God, the Credit of our holy Religion, and their own Welfare, to walk worthy of the Vocation wherewith they are called, by shewing a sacred Regard to the Lord's Day, and all the Ordinances of divine Institution; and by discouraging, in their respective Spheres, the illegal and dangerous Entertainments of the Stage.

THE Presbytery would plead with ALL in Authority, with TEACHERS of Youth, PARENTS, and MASTERS of Families, to restrain, by every habile Method, such as are under their Influence, from frequenting these Seminaries of Folly and Vice. They would particularly beseech the younger Part of their Flock, to beware, lest, by Example, or from a foolish Desire of appearing in the fashionable World, they be misled into such pernicious Snares; Snares which must necessarily retard, if not entirely mar that Progress in the respective Parts of their Education, on which their future Usefulness and Success depends. And, lastly, they would intreat and obtest Persons of all Ranks and Conditions, that, instead of contributing to the growing Licentiousness of the Age, they may distinguish themselves by shining as Lights in the World, being blameless and harmless, the Sons of God, without Rebuke, in the midst of a crooked and perverse Nation; OCCUPYING, for the great Purposes of the Honour of God and the Good of Mankind, that Time, that Substance, and those other Talents which they have received from their Lord and Master.

ON the whole, The Presbytery do, in the most earnest Manner, call upon all who have the Interest of Religion at Heart, to plead fervently at the Throne of Grace, in the prevailing Name of the great Mediator, *until the spirit be poured upon us from on high, and the wilderness be a fruitful field, and the fruitful field be counted for a forest: then judgment shall dwell in the wilderness, and righteousness remain in the fruitful field; and the work of righteousness shall be peace, and the effect of righteousness, quietness and assurance for ever.*

THE Presbytery appoint this ADMONITION and EXHORTATION to be read from all the Pulpits within their Bounds, on the last Sabbath, being the thirtieth Day of this Month, immediately after divine Service before Noon.

Extracted from the Records of Presbytery, by

JAMES CRAIG, *Presb. Clerk.*

4 Serious Enquiry into the Nature and Effects of the Stage

John Witherspoon's measured and considered response to theatrical representation is the most sophisticated critical weapon in the arsenal of the anti-*Douglas* faction. Although a large number of the pamphlets were written anonymously, Witherspoon acknowledged his authorship and dedicated the work to the Earl of Gifford. In subsequent years Witherspoon would go on to become the President of the College of New Jersey, later Princeton, and a signatory of the Declaration of Independence. However in Scotland he had already established himself as a minister of formidable intellect and a competent opponent of the Moderate literati in the Church of Scotland. His earlier pamphlet, *Ecclesiastical Characteristics* (1753) was a searing and witty critique of the Moderates' attitudes to religion and culture. However, in the *Serious Enquiry*, he abandoned his humorous tone believing it to be inappropriate for so grave a subject, despite the fact that in his own times he considered that, 'very few persons of fashion will read or consider anything that is written in a grave or serious stile'. Witherspoon's target is not so much the play itself, but is instead an investigation into the stage on which any play might be performed. In his only real direct reference to Home's tragedy, he dismisses it as 'a work of very little merit'. Witherspoon firmly believes that a minister who writes a play commits a sinful act, but refrains from providing extensive investigatory material in this area because the case he is making is a self evident one. Instead, the core of the pamphlet's argument centres on the premise that plays lack a necessary sanction from God that would permit them to provide moral instruction. In attempting to transmit a moral message a play had to be as realistic as possible, and given the current state of the world according to Witherspoon, it would have to include more of what is evil than good. The consequences of such a representation would, as a result, either bring reassurance to the sinners, or despair to the virtuous. The depiction of love on the stage is of particular concern to Witherspoon because he judges it to be the most dangerous human passion, and one which, in its most virulent form, can lead to crimes of the worst kind. This position is further complicated by Witherspoon's assertion that a play's primary function is to entertain the spectator, which makes a performance a pleasurable indulgence only, and therefore, merely a luxury. Even if a playwright sacrificed realism to produce a wholly moral work, he would still be employing a code of virtue different from that of the Christian moral system. Unlike most of his fellow anti-*Douglas* pamphleteers however, Witherspoon conceded that some plays had both literary and artistic merit, but insisted that these were ultimately the most dangerous of the breed, for they possessed a powerful rhetorical persuasion emanating from a degenerate practice.

SERIOUS ENQUIRY

INTO THE

NATURE AND EFFECTS

OF THE

STAGE.

Being an Attempt to fhow,

That contributing to the Support of a PUB-
LIC THEATRE, is inconfiftent with
the Character of a Chriftian.

By *JOHN WITHERSPOON*, M. A.

Minifter of the Gofpel in *Beith*.

GLASGOW:

Printed by J. BRYCE and D. PATERSON.
M DCC LVII.

TO

THE MOST HONOURABLE

JOHN Marquis of TWEEDALE,

Earl of GIFFORD,

Vifcount of WALDEN,

Lord HAY of YESTER,

The following TREATISE is humbly infcribed by

His LORDSHIP's

moft obedient, and

moft humble Servant,

JOHN WITHERSPOON.

A

S-ERIOUS ENQUIRY

INTO THE

NATURE and EFFECTS of the STAGE.

THE Reader will probably conjecture, and therefore, I. do readily acknowledge, that what gave occasion both to the writing, and publishing the ensuing treatise, was the new Tragedy of Douglass lately acted in the theatre at Edinburgh. This, universal uncontradicted fame says, is the work of a minister of the church of Scotland. One of that character and office employing his time in writing for the stage, every body will allow, is a very new and extraordinary event. In one respect neither author nor actors have suffered any thing from this circumstance : for doubtless, it contributed its share in procuring that run upon the representation, which continued for several days. Natural curiosity prompted many to make trial, whether there was any difference between a play wrote by a clergyman, and one of another author. And a concern for the fate of such a person excited the zeal and diligence of friends, to do all in their power to procure a full house, that the bold adventurer might be treated with respect and honour.

Some resolutions of the presbytery of Edinburgh seem to threaten, that public notice will be taken of this author and his associates by their superiors in the church. Whether this will be carried on, and, if it be, whether they will be approven or censured; and, if the last, to what degree, I pretend not to foretell. But one thing is certain, that it hath been and will be the subject of much thought and conversation among the laity of all ranks, and that it must have a very great influence upon the state of religion among us, in this part of the nation. That

A   this

this influence will be for the better, tho' I resolve to examine the subject with all impartiality, I confess, I see little ground to hope. There is no doubt that it will be condemned by the great plurality of those who go by the appellation of the stricter sort. With them, it will bring a great reproach upon the church of Scotland, as containing one minister who writes for the stage, and many who think it no crime to attend the representation. It is true no other consequences are to be apprehended from their displeasure, than the weakest of them being provoked to unchristian resentment, or tempted to draw rash and general conclusions from the conduct of a few to the character of the whole, or perhaps some of them separating from the established church, none of which effects of late have been much either feared or shunned. However, even upon this account, it were to be wished, either that it had never happened, or that it could be shewn, to the conviction of unprejudiced minds, that it was a just and commendable action.

But, to be sure, the chief danger is, that, in case it be really a bad thing, it must give very great offence, in the Scripture sense of that word, to those who are most apt to take it, *viz.* such as have least religion or none at all. An offence is a stumbling block over which the weak and unstedfast are in danger of falling ; that is to say, It emboldens them to commit, and hardens them in the practice of sin. Now, if the stage is unlawful or dangerous to a Christian, those who are by inclination so addicted to it that it is already difficult to convince them of their error, must be greatly confirmed in this error, by the example and countenance of such as call themselves ministers of Christ. It has accordingly already occasioned more discourse among the gay part of the world in defence or commendation of the stage than past, perhaps, for some years preceeding this event.

Nothing therefore can be more seasonable at this time, or necessary for the publick good, than a careful and accurate discussion of this question, Whether supporting and encouraging stage-
plays

plays by writing, acting or attending them, is confiftent or inconfiftent with the character of a Chriftian. It is to no purpofe to
confine the enquiry to this, Whether a minifter is not appearing in an improper light, and mifapplying his time and talents
when he dedicates them to the fervice of the ftage. That point
would probably be given up by moft, and thofe who would deny it, do not merit a confutation. But if the matter is refted
here, it will be confidered only as a fmaller mifdemeanour, and
though treated or even condemned as fuch, it will ftill have the
bad effect, (upon fuppofition of theatrical amufements being
wrong and finful), of greatly promoting them, tho' we feem to
be already as much given to them as even worldly confiderations
will allow.

The felf-denying Apologies common with authors, of their
being fenfible of their unfitnefs for the tafk they undertake, their
doing it to ftir up a better hand, and fo on, I wholly pafs, having never read any of them with approbation. Prudence is good,
and I would not willingly lofe fight of it, but zeal and concern
for the glory of God, and faithfulnefs to the fouls of others, are
duties equally neceffary in their place, but much more rare.
How far I am fenfible of my own unfitnefs, for treating this fubject, and of the reputation that is rifked by attempting it, the
world is not obliged to believe upon my own teftimony; but in
whatever degree it be, it is greatly overballanced at prefent by a
view of the declining ftate of religion among us, the prevalence
of national fins, and the danger of defolating judgments.

It is fome difcouragement in this attempt that it is very uncertain, whether many of thofe, for whofe fakes it is chiefly intended, and who ftand moft in need of information upon the
fubject, will take the pains to look into it. Such a levity of
fpirit prevails in this age, that very few perfons of fafhion will
read or confider any thing that is written in a grave or ferious
ftile. Whoever will look into the monthly catalogues of books
publifhed in Britain for fome years paft, may be convinced of

A 2   this

this at one glance. What an immense proportion do Romances under the titles of Lives, Adventures, Memoirs, Histories, &c. bear to any other sort of production in this age? Perhaps, therefore, it may be thought that it would have been more proper to have gratified the public taste, by raising up some allegorical structure, and handling this subject in the way of wit and humour; especially, as it seems to be a modern principle, that ridicule is the test of truth, and as there seems to be so large a fund for mirth in the character of a stage-playing priest. But tho' I deny not the lawfulness of using ridicule in some cases, or even its propriety here, yet I am far from thinking it is the test of truth. It seems to be more proper for correction than for instruction, and, tho' it be fit enough to whip an offender, it is not unusual, nor unsuitable, first to expostulate a little with him, and shew him that he deserves it. Besides, every man's talent is not equally fit for it, and indeed, now the matter seems to have been carried beyond a jest, and to require a very serious consideration.

There is also, besides some discouragement, a real difficulty in entering upon this disquisition. It will be hard to know in what manner to reason, or upon what principles to build. It were easy to shew the unlawfulness of stage-plays, by such arguments as would appear conclusive to those who already hate both them and their supporters: But it is not so easy to make it appear to those who chiefly frequent them, because they will both applaud and justify some of the very things that others look upon as the worst effects of the practice, and will deny the very principles upon which they are condemned. The truth is, it is our having different views of the nature of religion, that causes different opinions upon this subject. For many ages there was no debate upon it at all. There were players, but they did not pretend to be Christians themselves, and they had neither countenance nor support from any who did. Whereas now, there are abundance of advocates for the lawfulness, some for the usefulness fulnefs of plays ; not that the ftage is become more pure, but that Chriftians are become lefs fo, and have lowered the ftandard or meafure requifite to attain and preferve that character.

_ But there is ftill another difficulty, that, whoever undertakes to write againft plays, though the provocation is given by what they are, is yet always called upon to attack them, not as they are, but as they might be. A writer on this fubject is actually reduced to the neceffity of fighting with a fhadow, of maintaining a combat with an ideal or imaginary fort of Drama, which never yet exifted, but which the defenders of the caufe form by way of fuppofition, and which fhall appear in fact in that happy future age, which fhall fee, what thefe gentlemen are pleafed to ftile, a well regulated ftage.   However little fupport may feem to be given by this to a vitious and corrupted ftage, there is no attender of plays, but, when he hears this chimæra defended, imagines it is his own caufe that is efpoufed, and, with great compofure and felf-fatisfaction, continues his practice. A conduct not lefs abfurd, than if one who was exprefly affured a certain difh of meat before him was poifoned, fhould anfwer thus, All meat is not poifoned, and therefore I may eat this with fafety.

It is very plain, that were men but ferioufly difpofed, and without prejudice defiring the knowledge of their duty, it would not be neceffary, in order to fhew the unlawfulnefs of the ftage as it now is, to combat it in its imaginary reformed ftate. Such a reformation, were not men by the prevalence of vitious and corrupt affections, in love with it, even in its prefent condition, would have been long ago given up as a hopelefs and vifionary project, and the whole trade or employment detefted, on account of the abufes that had always adhered to it. But fince all advocates for the ftage have, and do ftill defend it in this manner, by forming an idea of it feparate from its evil qualities ; fince they defend it fo far with fuccefs, that many who would otherwife abftain, do, upon this very account, allow themfelves in attending the theatre fometimes, to their own hurt and that

of

of others; and, as I am convinced upon the moft mature deliberation, that the reafon why there never was a well regulated ftage in fact is becaufe it cannot be, the nature of the thing not admitting of it, I will endeavour to fhew, that PUBLIC THEATRICAL REPRESENTATIONS either tragedy or comedy are, in their general nature, or in their beft poffible ftate, unlawful, contrary to the purity of our religion; and that writing, acting or attending them, is inconfiftent with the character of a Chriftian. If this be done with fuccefs, it will give great weight to the reflections which fhall be added upon the aggravation of the crime, confidering the circumftances that at prefent attend the practice.

But, though I have thus far complied with the unreafonable terms impofed by the advocates for this amufement, they muft not proceed to any higher demand, nor expect, becaufe they have prevailed to have plays confidered in the way that they themfelves defire, that therefore the fame thing muft be done by religion, and that it muft be lowered down to the defcriptions they are fometimes pleafed to give of it. I will by no means attack plays upon the principles of modern relaxed morality. In that cafe, to be fure, it would be a loft caufe. If fome late writers on the fubject of morals be permitted to determine what are the ingredients that muft enter into the compofition of a good man, that good man, it is agreed, may much more probably be found in the play-houfe than in any other place. But what belongs to the character of a Chriftian muft be taken from the holy Scriptures, the word of the living God. Notwithftanding therefore, that through the great degeneracy of the age, and very culpable relaxation of difcipline, not a few continue to be called Chriftians, who are a reproach to the name, and fupport and countenance one another in many practices contrary to the purity of the Chriftian profeffion, I fhall beg leave ftill to recur to the unerring ftandard, and to confider, not what many nominal Chriftians are, but what every real Chriftian ought to be.

In fo doing I think I fhall reafon juftly; and at the fame time

it

it is my refolution, not only to fpeak the fenfe, but as often as poffible the very language and phrafes of the Scripture, and of our pious fathers. Thefe are either become venerable to me for their antiquity or they are much fitter for expreffing the truths of the gofpel and delineating the character and duty of a difciple of Chrift, than any that have been invented in latter times. As the growth or decay of vegetable nature is often fo gradual as to be infenfible; fo in the moral world, verbal alterations, which are counted as nothing, do often introduce real changes, which are firmly eftablished before their approach is fo much as fufpected. Were the ftile, not only of fome modern effays, but of fome modern fermons to be introduced upon this fubject, it would greatly weaken the argument, though no other alteration fhould be made. Should we every where put virtue for holinefs, honour, or even moral fenfe for confcience, improvement of the heart for fanctification, the oppofition between fuch things and theatrical entertainments would not appear half fo fenfible.

By taking up the argument in the light now propofed, I am faved, in a great meafure, from the repetition of what has been written by other authors upon the fubject. But let it be remembered, that they have clearly and copioufly fhown the corruption and impurity of the ftage, and its adherents, fince its firft inftitution, and that, both in the Heathen and Chriftian world. They have made it undeniably appear, that it was oppofed and condemned by the beft and wifeft men both Heathens and Chriftians in every age *. Its very defenders do all

pretend

---

* Particularly at Athens, where it firft had its birth, both Tragedy and Comedy were foon abolifhed by public authority; and among the Romans, tho' this and other public fhews were permitted in a certain degree, yet fo cautious were that wife people of fuffering them to be frequent, that they did not permit any public Theatre, when occafionally erected, to continue above a certain number of days. Even that erected by M. Scaurus, which is faid to have coft fo immenfe a fum as a million Sterling, was fpeedily taken down. Pompey the Great was the firft who had power and credit enough to get a Theatre continued. The

pretend to blame the abuse of it. They do indeed alledge that this abuse is not effential to it, but may be feparated from it; however all of them, fo far as I have feen, reprefent this feparation as only poffible or future; they never attempt to affign any Æra in which it could be defended as it then was, or could be affirmed to be more profitable than hurtful. Some writers do mention a few particular plays of which they give their approbation. But thefe have never yet, in any age or place, amounted to fuch a number, as to keep one fociety of players in conftant employment, without a mixture of many more that are confeffedly pernicious. The only reafon of bringing this in view at prefent when it is not to be infifted on, is, that it ought to procure a fair and candid hearing to this attempt to prove, That the ftage, after the greateft improvement of which it is capable, is ftill inconfiftent with the purity of the Chriftian profeffion. It is a ftrong prefumptive evidence in favour of this affertion, that, after fo many years trial, fuch improvement has never actually taken place.

It is, perhaps, alfo proper here to obviate a pretence in which the advocates of the ftage greatly glory, that there is no exprefs prohibition of it to be found in fcripture. I think a country-

man

The opinion of Seneca may be feen in the following paffage, *Nihil eft tam damnofum bonis moribus, quam in aliquo fpectaculo defidere. Tunc enim per voluptatem facilius vitia furrepunt.*

As to the primitive Chriftians, fee *Conftit. Apoft. lib. 8. cap. 32.* where actors and ftage-players are enumerated among thofe who were not to be admitted to Baptifm. Many different councils appoint that they fhall renounce their arts before they be admitted, and if they return to them fhall be excommunicated. *Tertullian de Spectaculis, cap. 22.* obferves, That the Heathens themfelves marked them with infamy, and excluded them from all honours or dignity. To the fame purpofe fee *Aug. de Civ. Dei, lib. 2. cap. 14. Actores poeticarum fabularum removent a focietate civitatis---ab honoribus omnibus repellunt homines fcenicos.*

The opinion of Moderns is well known, few Chriftian writers of any eminence having failed to pronounce fentence againft the ftage.

than of our own † has given good reasons to believe, that the apostle Paul, in his epistle to the Ephesians, 5th chap. 4th ver. by *filthiness, foolish talking and jesting*, intended to prohibit the plays that were then in use. He also thinks it probable that the word Κωμος, used in more places than one, and translated *revelling*, points at the same thing. Whether his conjectures are just or not, it is very certain that these, and many other passages, forbid the abuses of the stage, and if these abuses be inseparable from it, as there is reason to believe, there needed no other prohibition of them to every Christian. Nay, if they never had been separated from it till that time it was sufficient, and it would be idle to expect that the scripture should determine this problematical point, Whether they would ever be so in any after age. To ask that there should be produced a prohibition of the stage, as a stage, universally, is to prescribe to the holy Ghost, and to require that the Scripture should not only forbid sin, but every form in which the restless and changeable dispositions of men shall think fit to be guilty of it, and every name by which they shall think proper to call it. I do not find in Scripture any express prohibition of masquerades, routs and drums, and yet I have not the least doubt, that the assemblies called by these names are contrary to the will of God, and as bad, if not worse than the common and ordinary entertainments of the stage.

In order to make this enquiry as exact and accurate as possible, and that the strength or weakness of the arguments on either side may be clearly perceived, it will be proper to state distinctly, what we understand by the stage or stage-plays, when it is affirmed, that in their most improved and best regulated state they are unlawful to Christians. This is the more necessary, that there is a great indistinctness and ambiguity in the language used by those who, in writing, or conversation, undertake to defend it. They analize and divide it into parts, and take sometimes one part, sometimes another, as will best suit their purpose. They ask, What there can be unlawful in

the

B

† The late Mr. Anderson.

the stage abstractly confidered? Comedy is expofing the folly of vice, and pointing out the ridiculous part of every character. And is not this commendable? Is not ridicule a noble mean of difcountenancing vice? And is not the ufe of it warranted by the fatire and irony that is to be found in the holy fcriptures? Tragedy they fay is promoting the fame end in a way more grave and folemn. It is a moral lecture, or a moral picture, in which virtue appears to great advantage. What is hiftory itfelf but reprefenting the characters of men as they actually were, and plays reprefent them as they may be. In their perfection, plays are as like hiftory and nature, as the poet's art and actor's fkill can make them. Is it then the circumftance of their being written in dialogue that renders them criminal? Who will pretend that? Is it that they are publicly repeated or acted over? Will any one pretend, that it is a crime to perfonate a character in any cafe, even where no deceit is intended? Then farewell parables, figures of fpeech, and the whole oratorial art. Is it a fin to look upon the reprefentation? Then it muft be a fin to look upon the world which is the original, of which plays are the copy.

This is the way which thofe who appear in defence of the ftage ordinarily take, and it is little better than if one fhould fay, What is a ftage-play? It is nothing elfe abftractly confidered but a company of men and women talking together; Where is the harm in that? What hinders them from talking pioufly and profitably, as well as wickedly or hurtfully? But, rejecting this method of reafoning as unjuft and inconclufive, let it be obferved, that thofe who plead for the lawfulnefs of the ftage, in any country, however well regulated, plead for what implies, not by accident, but effentially and of neceffity the following things. (1.) Such a number of plays as will furnifh a habitual courfe of reprefentations, with fuch changes as the love of variety in human nature neceffarily requires. (2.) Thefe plays of fuch a kind, as to procure an audience of voluntary fpectators, who are able and willing to pay for being fo en-

entertained. (3.) A company of hired players, who have this as their only bufinefs and occupation, that they may give them-felves wholly to it, and be expert in the performance. (4.) The reprefentation muft be fo frequent as the profits may defray the expence of the apparatus, and maintain thofe who follow this bufinefs. They muft alfo be maintained in that meafure of luxury, or elegance, if you pleafe, which their way of life, and the thoughts to which they are accuftomed muft make them defire and require. It is a thing impracticable to maintain a player at the fame expence as you may maintain a peafant.

Now all thefe things do, and muft enter into the idea of a well regulated ftage, and, if any defend it without fuppofing this, he hath no adverfary that I know of. Without thefe there may be poets, or there may be plays, but there cannot be a play-houfe. It is in vain then to go about to fhow, that there have been an inftance or two, or may be, of treatifes wrote in the form of plays that are unexceptionable. It were eafy to fhew very great faults in fome of thefe moft univerfally applauded, but this is unneceffary. I believe it is very poffible to write a treatife in the form of a Dialogue, in which the general rules of the Drama are obferved, which fhall be as holy and ferious, as any fermon that ever was preached or printed. Neither is there any apparent impoffibility in getting different perfons to affume the different characters, and rehearfe it in fociety. But it may be fafely affirmed, that if all plays were of that kind, and human nature continue in its prefent ftate, the doors of the play-houfe would fhut of their own accord, becaufe no body would demand accefs *; unlefs there were an act of parliament to force atten-

B 2   dance,

* This furnifhes an eafy anfwer to what is remarked by fome in favour of plays, that feveral eminent Chriftians have endeavoured to fupplant bad plays by writing good ones ; as Gregory Nazianzen a father of the Church, and a perfon of great piety, and our countryman Buchanan. But did ever thefe plays come to repute ? Were they formerly, or are they now acted upon the ftage ? The fate of their works proves that thefe good men judged wrong in attempting to reform the ftage, and that the great majority of Chriftians acted more wifely who were for laying it wholly afide.

dance, and even in that cafe, as much pains would probably be taken to evade the law obliging to attend, as are now taken to evade thofe that command us to abftain. The fair and plain ftate of this queftion then is, Whether it is poffible or practicable, in the prefent ftate of human nature, to have the above fyftem of things under fo good a regulation, as to make the erecting, and countenancing the ftage agrecable to the will of God, and confiftent with the purity of the Chriftan profeffion.

And here let us confider a little, what is the primary, and immediate intention of the ftage, Whether it be for amufement and recreation, or for inftruction, to make men wife and good. Perhaps, indeed, the greateft part will choofe to compound thefe two purpofes together, and fay it is for both: For amufement immediately, and for improvement ultimately, that it inftructs by pleafing, and reforms by ftealth. The patrons of a well regulated ftage have it no doubt in their power to profefs any of thefe ends in it they pleafe, if it is equally capable of them all; and therefore, in one part or other of this difcourfe, it muft be confidered in every one of thefe lights. But as it is of moment, becaufe of fome of the arguments to be afterwards adduced, let the reader be pleafed to confider, how far recreation and amufement enter into the nature of the ftage, and are, not only immediately and primarily, but chiefly and ultimately intended by it.

If the general nature of it, or the end propofed from it when well regulated, can be any way determined from its firft inftitution, and the fubfequent practice, it feems plainly to point at amufement. The earlieft productions of that kind that are now extant are evidently incapable of any other ufe, and hardly even of that to a perfon of any tafte or judgment *. They ufually

ac-

---

* This is confeffed by a defender of the ftage who fays, ' Such of the co-
' medies before his (that is Menander's) time, as have been preferved to
' us, are generally very poor pieces, not fo much ludicrous as ridiculous, e-
' ven a mountebank's Merry Andrew would be hiffed, now a days, for fuch
' Puerilities as we fee abounding in Ariftophanes.' *Rem. on Anderfon's Pofiti-*
ons concerning the unlawfulnefs of ftage-plays, page 8th.

accompanied the feasts of the ancients in the houses of the rich and opulent *, and were particularly used in times of publick rejoicing. They have, indeed, generally been considered, in all ages, as intended for entertainment. A modern author of high rank and reputation †, who would not willingly hurt the cause, considers them in this light, and this alone, and represents their improvement, not as lying in their having a greater moral tendency, but in the perfection of the poet's art, and the refinement of the taste of the audience. It is only of late that men have begun to dignify them with a higher title. Formerly they were ever considered as an indulgence of pleasure, and an article of luxury, but now they are exalted into schools of virtue, and represented as bulwarks against vice. It is probable, most readers will be apt to smile when they hear them so called, and to say to their defenders, This is but overdoing, preserve them to us as innocent amusements, and we shall not much contend for their usefulness. It is, indeed, but an evidence of the distress of the cause, for their advocates only take up this plea when they are unable to answer the arguments against them upon any other footing. It may also appear that they are designed for amusement, if we consider who have been the persons in all ages who have attended them, *viz.* The rich, the young, and the gay, those who live in pleasure, and the very business of whose lives is amusement.

But not to insist upon these circumstances, I think it is plain from the nature of the thing, that the immediate intention of plays is to please, whatever effects may be pretended to flow afterwards, or by accident, from this pleasure. They consist in an exact imitation of nature, and the conformity of the personated

to

---

* *Plut. de Glor. Athen. & Sympof.* lib. 7. quest. 8. ' As for the new comedy, it is so neceffary an ingredient of all publick entertainments, that so ' to speak, one may as well make a feast without wine, as without Menander.'

† Shaftsbury.

to real characters. This is the great aim, and the great perfection, both of the poet and actors. Now this imitation, of itself,
gives great pleasure to the spectator, whether the actions represented are good or bad. And, in itself considered, it gives only
pleasure; for the beauty of the imitation, as such, hath no moral
influence, nor any connection with morality, but what it may
derive in a distant way from the nature of the actions which the
poet or actors choose to represent, or the spectators are willing
to see. Every person who thinks impartially, may be from this
convinced, that to please, or attempt to do so, is essential to
the stage, and its first, or rather its main design; how far it pol-
lutes or purifies is accidental, and must depend upon the skill
and honesty of its regulators and managers.

Having thus prepared the way, the following arguments are
humbly offered to the consideration of every serious person, to
shew, that a public theatre is inconsistent with the purity of the
Christian profession: which if they do not, to all, appear to
be each of them singly conclusive, will, I hope, when taken together, sufficiently evince the truth of the proposition.

In the first place, If it be considered as an amusement, it is
improper, and not such as any Christian may lawfully use. Here
we must begin by laying it down as a fundamental principle, that
all men are bound supremely to love, and habitually to serve
God; that is to say, to take his law as the rule, and his glory
as the end, not of one, but of all their actions. No man, at any
time or place is, or can be, absolved from this obligation. Every
real Christian lives under a habitual sense of it. I know this
expression, aiming at the glory of God, is called a cant phrase
and is despised and derided by worldly men. It were easy, however, to vindicate it from reason; but it will suffice, to all those
for whose use that discourse is intended, to say, It is a truth
taught and repeated in the sacred oracles, that all things were
made for, that all things shall finally tend to, and therefore, that
all

all intelligent creatures should supremely and uniformly aim at the glory of God.

Now we glorify God by cultivating holy dispositions, and doing pious and useful actions. Recreation is an intermission of duty, and is only necessary because of our weakness ; it must be some action indifferent in its nature, which becomes lawful and usefull from its tendency to refresh the mind, and invigorate it for duties of more importance. The use of recreation is precisely the same as the use of sleep ; though they differ in this, that there is but one way in which sleep becomes sinful, *viz.* by excefs, whereas there are ten thousand ways in which recreations become sinful. It is needless to adduce passages of Scripture to verify the above assertion concerning our obligation to glorify God. It is the language of the whole, and is particularly applied to indifferent actions by the apostle Paul, *Whether therefore ye eat or drink, or whatsoever ye do, do all to the glory of God* *.

If there were upon the minds of men, in general, a just sense of this their obligation, stage-plays, nay, and a thousand other amusements now in use, would never have been heard of. The truth is, the need of amusement is much less than people commonly apprehend, and, where it is not necessary, it must be sinful. Those who stand in need of recreation may be divided into two sorts, such as are employed in bodily labour, and such as have their spirits often exhausted by study and application of mind. As to the first of these, a mere cessation from labour is sufficient for refreshment, and indeed of itself gives great pleasure, unless when the appetites are inflamed and irritated by frequent sensual gratifications : and then they are importunately craved, and become necessary to fill the intervals of work. Of this sort very few are able to afford so expensive a recreation as the stage. And even as to the other, *viz.* those whose spirits are exhausted by application of mind, only a very small number of them will chuse the diversion of the stage, for this very good reason, that social converse, and bodily exercise

will

* 1 Cor. 10. 31.

will anfwer the purpofe much better. Indeed, if we confider the juft and legitimate end of recreations, and compare it with the perfons who moft frequently engage in them, we fhall find, that, ninety nine of every hundred, are fuch as do not need recreation at all. Perhaps their time lies heavy upon their hands, and they feel an uneafinefs and impatience under their prefent ftate; but this is not from work, but from idlenefs, and from the emptinefs and unfatisfying nature of the enjoyments, which they chafe with fo much eagernefs, one after another, vainly feeking from them that good which they do not contain, and that fatisfaction which they cannot impart.

From this I think it undeniably appears, that, if no body were to attend the ftage, but fuch as really needed recreation or amufement upon Chriftian principles, and of thefe fuch only as were able to pay for it, and of thefe only fuch as did themfelves choofe it, there is not a place this day, in the world, fo large as to afford a daily audience. It will be immediately objected, This argument, make as much of it as you pleafe, is not compleat, for it hinders not but that fome, however few, may attend in a proper manner, and with warrantable views. But let it be remembered, that I attack not a play fingly as a play, nor one perfon for being witnefs to a thing of that nature, but the ftage as a fyftem containing all the branches I have enumerated above. This cannot fubfift without a full audience, and frequent attendance, and therefore is, by its conftitution, a conftant and powerful invitation to fin, and cannot be maintained but by the commiffion of it. Perhaps, fome will ftill object, that the argument is too finely fpun, that it feems to demand perfection, and to find fault with every practice, in which there is a probability that fin will be committed. That, if this holds, we fhould no more contribute to the eftablifhment of churches than play-houfes, becaufe we have a moral certainty, that no congregation ever will meet together on earth, but much fin will be committed, both by minifter and people.

people. But there is a great difference between a commanded duty which is attended with sin by defect, and what is no where commanded, which necessarily invites to sin by its nature, and is in substance sinful to the great majority of those who attend it.

But further, the stage is an improper, that is to say, an unlawful recreation to all without exception, because it consumes too much time. This is a circumstance which, however little impression it may make upon those who find their time often a burden, will appear of the greatest moment to every serious Christian. In proportion as any man improves in holiness of heart, he increases in usefulness of life, and acquires a deeper and stronger sense of the worth and value of time. To spend an hour unprofitably appears to such a person a greater crime, than to many the commission of grofs sin. And, indeed, it ought to appear very heinous in the eyes of those who believe the representation given by our Lord Jesus Christ of his own procedure at the day of judgment, *Cast ye the* UNPROFITABLE *servant into utter darkness, where there shall be weeping and wailing, and gnashing of teeth* *. Mark this, ye lovers of pleasures, ye sons of gaiety and mirth, who imagine you are sent into the world for no higher end than your own entertainment, and who, if you are free from, or able any how to palliate your grosser sins, never once reflect on the heavy account against you of wasted time.

Though there were no other objection against the stage as a recreation but this one, it is surely faulty. If recreations are only lawful because necessary, they must cease to be lawful when they are no longer necessary. The length and duration of regular comedy and tragedy is already fixed and settled by rules of long standing; and, I suppose, whatever other circumstance may be confessed to need reformation, all men of taste will agree, that these shall continue as they are. Now I leave to all who know how much time the preparation for such a public appearance,

C

* Matth. xxv. 30.

85

pearance, and the neceſſary attendance, muſt take up, to judge, whether it is not too much to be given to meer recreation.

This holds particularly in the caſe of recreation of mind, between which and bodily exerciſe there is a very great difference. For bodily exerciſe, in ſome caſes, for example, when the health requires it, may be continued for a long time, only for this reaſon, that it may have effects laſting in proportion to the time ſpent in it. But giving the mind to pleaſure by way of recreation muſt be ſhort, or it is certainly hurtful; it gives men a habit of idleneſs and trifling, and makes them averſe from returning to any thing that requires ſerious application. So true is this, and ſo applicable to the preſent caſe, that I could almoſt reſt the whole argument upon it, that no man, who has made the trial, can deliberately and with a good conſcience affirm, that attending plays has added ſtrength to his mind, and warmth to his affections, in the duties of devotion; that it has made him more able and willing to exert his intellectual powers in the graver and more important offices of the Chriſtian life; nay, or even made him more diligent and active in the buſineſs of civil life. On the contrary, it is commonly to ſuch length as to produce a ſatiety and wearineſs of itſelf, and to require reſt and refreſhment to recruit the exhauſted ſpirits, a thing quite abſurd and ſelf-contradictory in what is called a recreation.

But the ſtage is not meerly an unprofitable conſumption of time, it is further improper as a recreation, becauſe it agitates the paſſions too violently, and intereſts too deeply, ſo as, in ſome caſes, to bring people into a real, while they behold an imaginary diſtreſs. Keeping in view the end of recreations, will enable us to judge rightly of this. It is to refreſh and invigorate the mind. Therefore when, inſtead of reſt, which is properly called relaxation of mind, recreations are uſed, their excellence conſiſts in their being, not only a pleaſant, but an eaſy exerciſe of the intellectual powers. Whatever is difficult, and either requires or cauſes a ſtrong application of mind, is

con-

contrary to their intention. Now it is plain, that dramatick reprefentations fix the attention fo very deeply, and intereft the affections fo very ftrongly, that, in a little time, they fatigue the mind themfelves, and however eagerly they are defired and followed, there are many ferious and ufeful occupations, in which men will continue longer, without exhaufting the fpirits, than in attending the theatre.

Indeed, in this refpect, they are wholly contrary to what fhould be the view of every Chriftian. He ought to fet bounds to, and endeavour to moderate his paffions, as much as poffible, inftead of voluntarily and unneceffarily exciting them. The human paffions, fince the fall, are all of them but too ftrong; and are not finful on account of their weaknefs, but their excefs and mifapplication. This is fo generally true, that it hardly admits of an exception; unlefs it might be counted an exception, that fome vitious paffions, when they gain an afcendancy, extinguifh others which oppofe their gratification. For, though religion is confiftent throughout, there are many vices, which are mutually repugnant to, and deftructive of each other. But this exception has little or no effect upon the prefent argument.

Now, the great care of every Chriftian is to keep his paffions and affections within due bounds, and to direct them to their proper objects. With refpect to the firft of thefe, the chief influence of theatrical reprefentations upon the fpectator, is to ftrengthen the paffions by indulgence, for there they are all exhibited in a lively manner, and fuch as is moft fit to communicate the impreffion. As to directing them to their proper objects, it will be afterwards fhown, that the ftage has rather the contrary effect, in the mean time, it is fufficient to obferve, that it may be done much more effectually, and much more fafely, another way.

This tendency of plays to intereft the affections, fhows their impropriety as a recreation on another account. It fhows that

C 2   they

they muſt be exceeding liable to abuſe by exceſs, even ſuppoſing
them in a certain degree, to be innocent.   It is certain there is
no life more unworthy of a man, hardly any more criminal in a
Chriſtian, than a life of perpetual amuſement, a life where no valuable purpoſe is purſued, but the intellectual faculties wholly employed in purchaſing and indulging ſenſual gratifications.   It is
alſo certain, that all of us are by nature, too much inclined thus
to live to ourſelves, and not to God.   Therefore, where recreations are neceſſary, a watchful Chriſtian will particularly beware
of thoſe that are enſnaring, and, by being too grateful and delicious, ready to lead to exceſs.   This diſcriminating care and
caution, is juſt as much the duty of a Chriſtian, as any that
can be named.   Tho' it is immediately converſant only about
the temptations and incitements to ſin, and not the actual commiſſion of it, it becomes a duty directly binding, both from the
command of God, and the neceſſity of the thing itſelf.   *Watch
and pray, that ye enter not into temptation* *, ſays our Saviour
to his diſciples; and elſewhere, *What I ſay unto you, I ſay unto
all, Watch* †.   And the apoſtle Paul to the ſame purpoſe, *See
then that ye walk circumſpectly, not as fools, but as wiſe, re-
deeming the time becauſe the days are evil* ‡.

And if we conſider the light in which the ſcripture ſets our
preſent ſituation, and the account there given of the weakneſs
of human reſolution, the ſame thing will evidently appear to be
our duty.   It is impoſſible that we can reſiſt the ſlighteſt temptation, but by the aſiſtance of divine grace.   Now, how can this
be expected if we put our conſtancy to unneceſſary trials, not
only contrary to reaſon, and a prudent regard to our own ſafe-
ty, but in the face of an expreſs command of God to be watch-
full.   *Lord, lead us not into temptation*, is a petition, which we
are taught to offer up, by him who knew what was in man.   But
how much do thoſe act in oppoſition to this, and even in contempt of it, who make temptations to themſelves.   And are
                                                                        not

* Matth. xxvi. 41.   † Mark xiii. 37.   ‡ Eph. v. 15.

not stage-plays temptations of the strongest kind, in which the mind is softened with pleasure, and the affections powerfully excited ? How little reason is there to hope that men in the use of them will keep within the bounds of moderation ? If any expect, in such circumstances, to be preserved by divine power, they are guilty of the sin, which is in scripture called *tempting God*.

It is this very circumstance, a liableness to abuse by excess, that renders many other amusements also ordinarily unlawful to Christians, tho' perhaps, in their general nature, they cannot be shown to be criminal. Thus, it is not easy to refute the reasonings, by which ingenious men endeavour to show that games of hazard are not in themselves sinful; but by their enticing, ensnaring nature, and the excess which almost inseparably accompanies them, there can be no difficulty in pronouncing them highly dangerous, lawful to very few persons, and in very few cases. And, if they were as publick in their nature as plays, if they required the concurrence of as many operators, and as great a number of persons to join in them, I could have little scruple in affirming, that, in every possible case, they would be sinful.

The preceeding considerations are greatly confirmed by the following, That when plays are chosen as a recreation, for which they are so exceedingly improper, it is always in opposition to other methods of recreation, which are perfectly fit for the purpose, and not liable to any of these objections. Where recreations are necessary, if there were only one sort to be had, some inconveniences could not be so strong an argument against the use of them. But where there are different kinds, to prefer those which are less, to those which are more fit, must needs be sinful. Such a tenderness and circumspection is, indeed, in this age, so rare and unusual, that, I am affraid, it will be almost impossible to fix a sense of its importance upon the mind of the reader; or, if it be done in any measure for a time, the example of a corrupt world, who are alto-

gether

gether void of it, will immediately efface the impreffion. But, however few may *have ears to hear it,* the thing is certain, that, as the progrefs of his fanctification is the fupreme defire and care of every Chriftian, fo he is continually liable to be feduced by temptation, and infected by example; and, therefore, from a diftruft of his own refolution, will not voluntarily and unnecef-farily prefer a dangerous to a fafe amufement. To prefer a very difficult and doubtful mean of attaining any worldly end, to one fure and eafy; to prefer a clumfy improper inftrument, to one perfectly fit for any piece of work, would be reckoned no fmall evidence of folly in the affairs of civil life. If one in ficknefs fhould choofe a medicine of a very queftionable nature, of ve-ry dangerous and uncertain operation, when he had equal ac-cefs to one entirely fafe, of approved reputation, and fuperior efficacy, it would be efteemed next to madnefs. Is there not then a real conformity between the cafes? Is not a like care to be taken of our fouls as of our bodies? Nay, is not the obliga-tion fo much the ftronger, by how much the one is of greater value than the other? The different conduct of men and their different fate, in this refpect, is well defcribed by the wife man, *Happy is the man that feareth alway, but he that hardeneth his heart fhall fall into mifchief* *.

It ought not to be omitted in fhewing the impropriety of the ftage as a recreation and amufement for Chriftians, that it is coftly and expenfive, and that this coft is altogether unneceffa-ry, fince the end might be obtained, not only as well, but much better, at a far cheaper rate, perhaps, in moft cafes, at no ex-pence at all. I know this argument will be treated with great con-tempt by thofe who live in affluence, and know no other ufe of riches but to feed their appetites, and make all the reft of mankind fubfervient to the gratification of their violent and ungovernable defires. But tho' none in this world have any title to hinder them from difpofing of their wealth as they pleafe, they muft be

called

* Prov. xxviii. 14.

called to confider, that they have a mafter in heaven. To him they muft render an account at the laft day, and, in this account, the ufe that they make of their riches is not to be excepted. The great have, no doubt, the diftinguifhed honour, if they pleafe to embrace it, of contributing to the happinefs of multitudes under them, and difpenfing, under God, a great variety of the comforts of this life. But it would abate the envy and impatience of the lower part of the world, and moderate their appetite after riches, if they would confider, that the more that is committed to them, the more they have to account for. The greateft and richeft man on earth hath not any licence, in the word of God, for an unnecefary wafte of his fubftance, or confuming it in unprofitable and hurtful pleafures; and, under the one or both of thefe characters, that muft fall, that is laid out upon the ftage.

Let not any reader, who cannot find a fatisfying anfwer to thefe objections againft the ftage as an unchriftian amufement, from the word of God, take the practice of the world as a refuge or fanctuary, and fay, This is carrying matters to an extreme, if thefe maxims are rigidly adhered to, you will exclude from the number of Chriftians, not only the far greateft part of mankind, but many otherwife of excellent and amiable characters. Tho' this is the weakeft of all arguments, it is, perhaps, that which hath of all others the ftrongeft effect, and moft powerfully contributes to fet peoples mind at eafe in a doubtful or dangerous practice. How hard is it to make men fenfible of the evil of fuch fins, as cuftom authorizes and fafhion juftifies? There is no making them afhamed of them, becaufe they are common and reputable, and there is no making them affraid of what they fee done without fufpicion by numbers on every hand. But is there any reafon to believe, that the example of others will prove a juft and valid excufe for any practice at the judgment-feat of Chrift? Will the greatnefs or the number of offenders fcreen them from his power? Or can that man expect a

gra-

gracious acceptance with him, who has suffered his commands to be qualified by prevailing opinion, and would not follow him farther than the bulk of mankind would bear him company.

I shall close the reflections upon this part of the subject by observing, that there are two general characters of the disciples of Christ, which will appear, if we consult the scriptures, to be essential to them, and which seem altogether inconsistent with theatrical amusements. The first is self-denial and mortification. Tho' we should not insist upon the particular objections against the stage, there is something of pomp and gaiety in it, upon the best possible supposition, that is inconsistent with the character of a Christian. The gospel is the religion of sinners, who are saved from wrath by the rich mercy and free grace of God. The life of such, then, must be a life of penitence, humility, and mortification. The followers of a crucified Saviour must bear the cross, and tread in the same path of suffering and self-denial, in which he hath gone before them. In their baptismal covenant they renounce the world, by which is not meant such gross crimes as are a violation of natural light, as well as a transgression of the law of God, but that excessive attachment to present indulgence, which is more properly expressed by the pomp and vanity of the world *. It is true there are many precepts in

Scripture

* It is not improper here to consider the ancient form of baptism, and what was supposed by the fathers to be implied in it, *Apost. Constitut.* lib. 7. cap. 41. αποτασσομαι τω σατανα, &c. ' I renounce Satan and his works, and his " pomps, and his service, and his angels, and his inventions, and all things ' that belong to him, or are subject to him.' *Ambros. de Initiatis. Ingressus es regenerationis sacrarium,* &c. ' Thou hast entered into the holy place of " regeneration ; repeat what you were there asked, and recollect what you ' answered ? You renounced the devil, and his works, and his world, and " his luxury and pleasures. *Hieron. Com. in Matth.* xv. 26. *Renuntio tibi diabole,* &c. ' I renounce thee Satan, and thy pomp, and thy vices, and ' thy world, which lieth in wickedness.' And that we may know what they had particularly in view by the pomps of the world which they renounced, they are sometimes expresly said to be the public shews. Thus Salvian. *de*

provi-

Scripture which require us to maintain a habitual gratitude and thankful frame of spirit, nay, to rejoice in the Lord alway. But there is a great difference between this joy, and that of worldly men; as they do not rise from the same source, so they cannot possibly express themselves in the same way.

Another branch of the Christian temper, between which, and theatrical amusements, there appears a very great opposition, is spirituality and heavenliness of mind. All real Christians are, and account themselves pilgrims and strangers on the earth, set their affections on things above, and have their conversation in heaven. Whatever tends to weaken these dispositions they will carefully avoid as contrary to their duty and their interest. Is not this the case with theatrical amusements? Are they not very delicious to a sensual and carnal mind. Do they not excite, gratify and strengthen these affections, which it is most the business of a Christian to restrain? Are not the indulgence of worldly pleasure, and heavenliness of mind, mutually destructive of each other? This is so plain, that anciently those who gave themselves up to a life of eminent holiness and piety, used to retire wholly from the commerce of the world and the society of men. Tho' this was wrong in itself, and soon found to be very liable to superstitious abuse, it plainly shows how much they err upon the opposite side, who being called to wean their affections from

the

provident. lib. 6. page 297. *Quæ est enim in baptismo, &c.* ' For what is the ' first profession of a Christian in baptism? What, but that they profess to ' renounce the devil, and his pomps, his shows, and his works. Therefore ' shows and pomps, by our own confession, are the works of the devil. How, ' O Christian, wilt thou follow the public shows after baptism, which thou ' confessest to be the works of the devil?'

There are some that pretend, that Christians were only kept from the shows, because they were mixed with idolatrous rites: But it is to be noted, that in the time of Salvian idolatry was abolished, and the shows were no longer exhibited in honour of idol Gods. Cyril of Jerusalem also, after idolatry was destroyed, continues the charge against the shows.

D

'the world, do yet voluntarily and unnecessarily indulge them-selves in the most delicious and intoxicating pleasures.

What is offered above, I hope, will suffice to show that the stage, considered simply as an entertainment, cannot be lawful-ly used by a Christian. But we must now proceed in the second place, To consider the modern pretence, that it is useful and in-structive, or to speak in the language of one of its defenders, ' A warm incentive to virtue, and powerful preservative against ' vice *.' The same author gives us this account of tragedy, ' True tragedy is a serious lecture upon our duty, shorter than ' an epick poem, and longer than a fable, otherwise differing ' from both only in the method, which is dialogue instead of ' narration; its province is to bring us in love with the more ' exalted virtues, and to create a detestation of the blacker and ' (humanly speaking) more enormous crimes,' On comedy he says, 'an insinuating mirth laughs us out of our frailties by mak-' ing us ashamed of them. Thus, when they are well intended, ' tragedy and comedy work to one purpose, the one manages ' us as children, the other convinces us as men.' In order to treat this part of the subject with precision, 1 must beg the rea-der to recal to mind the account formerly given of what is im-plied in the stage, even under the best possible regulation ; be-cause unless this be allowed me, I confess the argument to be defective. It is not denied, that there may be, and are to be found, in some dramatick performances, noble and excellent sentiments. These, indeed, are much fewer than is commonly supposed, as might be shown by an examination of some of the most celebrated plays. There is a great difference between the shining thoughts that are applauded in the world by men of taste, and the solid and profitable truths of religion. However it is allowed, that there are some things to be found in plays, against which no just objection can be made ; and it is easy to form an
idea

* Remarks on Anderson's Positions concerning the unlawfulness of stage-plays.

idea of them still more pure than any that do yet exist; but the question is, Whether it is possible now to find, or reasonable to hope to find, such a number of pieces, in their prevailing tendency, agreeable to the holiness and purity of the Christian character, as are necessary to support a publick theatre. Till this is accomplished, all that is done to support the theatre in the mean time, is done to support the interest of vice and wickedness; whatever it may be in itself and singly considered. And if such an entire reformation be impossible, a partial reformation, or mixing a few good things with it, is not only ineffectual but hurtful. It makes a bad cause a little more plausible, and therefore the temptation so much the more formidable.

There is a discourse of a foreigner of some note, in which he exerts all his eloquence in commendation of plays, when used in the public schools, for the improvement of youth in action and elocution, under the direction of their masters. As this gentleman was a clergyman, his authority is often used on this subject. But it ought to be observed, that as he was a young man when he employed his eloquence in this cause, so, what he says, strongly supports the propriety of the distinction I have laid down. He expresly confines the argument to such plays as were represented by youth in the schools, and rejects with great abhorrence the public stage, and such as were acted by mercenary players. Of the last sort he hath the following strong words. *At hic vereor A. ne qui sint inter vos qui ex me quaerant : Quid agis adolescens ? Tunc comoedos, Histriones, mimos, ex eloquentiae studiosis facere paras ? Egone ? Histriones ? Quos ? An viles illos qui in scenam prodeunt mercede conducti ? Qui quaestus causa quamlibet personam induant ? qui passim per urbes vagantes artem suam venalem habent ? Qui, merito, Romano jure, infamia notantur ? —— Absit a me absit, ut in hac impietatis schola teneros adolescentium animos eloquentia imbui velim. Quanticunque eam facio, tanti tamen non est. Satius esset balbutire, imo satius mutum esse, quam non sine summo animi peri-*

culo

culo eloquentiam difcere *. Which paſſage may be tranſlated
thus, ' But here I am affraid ſome of you will be ready to chal-
' lenge me, and to ſay, what is this you aim at young man ? Do
' you intend to make all who ſtudy eloquence comedians, play-
' ers, buffoons? Do I indeed ? What ſort of players? Thoſe
' contemptible wretches, who are hired to come upon the ſtage,
' and who for gain will perſonate any character whatever ? Who
' go about through different cities making merchandiſe of their
' art ? Who are juſtly marked with infamy in the Roman law ?
' —— Far, far be it from me to propoſe, that the tender minds
' of youth ſhould be taught eloquence in this ſchool of impiety.
' However much I value it, I value it not at this rate. Better it
' were they ſhould ſtammer in ſpeech, nay, better that they were
' dumb and incapable of ſpeech, than that they ſhould learn the
' art of eloquence, by putting their ſouls in the moſt imminent
' danger.' Now, whether this author's ſcheme was right or not,
I have no occaſion at preſent to debate with him as an adverſary,
for he rejects with abhorrence the imputation of favouring the
cauſe againſt which I plead.

When a public theatre is defended as a mean of inſtruction, I
cannot help thinking it is of importance to obſerve, that it is a
method altogether uncommanded and unauthorized in the word
of God.   This will probably appear a very weak argument to
many, but it will not appear ſo to thoſe who have a firm belief
of, and a juſt eſteem for that book of life. Such will not expect,
that any method will prove effectual to make men *wife unto
falvation* without the bleſſing of God, and they will hardly be
induced to look for his bleſſing upon the ſtage. And let it be
remembred, that it is now pled for in a higher light, and on a
more important account than merely as an amuſement, *viz.* as
proper to ſupport the intereſt of religion ; it ſhould therefore
have a poſitive warrant before it be employed in this cauſe, left
it ſhould meet with the ſame reception that all other human
devices

---

⁹ Werenfels Oratio de Comœdiis.

devices will meet with, *Who hath required these things at your hands?*

And that none may use a delusory sort of reasoning, and shift from one pretence to another, saying, it becomes a lawful amusement by its tendency to instruct, and an effectual instruction by its power to please at the same time; it must be observed, that a sinful amusement is not to be indulged on any pretence whatsoever, for we must not *do evil that good may come*. Nay, call it only a dangerous amusement, even in that case, no pretence of possible or probable instruction, (tho' such a thing were not contrary to the supposition) is sufficient to warrant it. Nothing less than its being necessary could authorise the practice, and that I hope none will be so hardy as to affirm.

It can never be affirmed to be necessary, without a blasphemous impeachment of the divine wisdom. If the holy scriptures, and the methods there authorised and appointed, are full and sufficient for our spiritual improvement, all others must be wholly unnecessary. And if they are the most powerful and the most effectual means, no others must be suffered to come into rivalship and competition with them; on the contrary, they must be condemned as wrong, or laid aside as comparatively weak. The truth is, the stage can never be defended on a more untenable footing, than when it is represented as having a moral or virtuous, that is to say, a pious or religious tendency. What Christian can hear such a plea with patience? Is the *law of the Lord perfect, converting the soul? Is it able to make the man of God perfect, throughly furnished to every good work?* What then are its defects which must be supplied by the theatre? Have the saints of God, for so many ages, been carried safely through all the dark and difficult steps of their earthly pilgrimage, with his law as a *light to their feet, and a lamp to their path*, and yet is it now necessary, that they should have additional illumination from a well-regulated stage? Have there

there been for fo long a time paftors employed bearing a divine
commiffion? ordinances adminiftred according to divine inftitution? Have thefe been hitherto effectual for *perfecting the
faints, for the work of the miniftry, and for edifying the body of
Chrift?* And fhall we not count them among the fcoffers that
were to come in the laft days, who pretend to open up a new
commiffion for the players to affift. If any fhall fay there needs
no divine inftitution, all men are called to inftruct one another,
the lips of the righteous fhould feed many, and this way of the
drama is but a mode of the inftruction we all owe to one another. I anfwer, it is as a mode I attack it. This very mode
has been fhown to be dangerous, nay finful, as an amufement;
who then can fhew its neceffity, in the fame mode, for inftruction
or improvement.

If the ftage be a proper method of promoting the interefts of
religion, then is Satan's kingdom divided againft itfelf, which
he is more cunning than to fuffer it to be. For, whatever debate there be, whether good men *may* attend the theatre, there
can be no queftion at all, that no openly vicious man is an
enemy to it, and that the far greateft part of them do paffionately love it. I fay no *openly* vitious man, for, doubtlefs,
there may be fome hypocrites wearing the habit of the Chriftian
pilgrim, who are the very worft of men, and yet may fhew a-
bundance of zeal againft the ftage. But nothing is more certain, than that, taking the world according to its appearance,
it is the worft part of it that fhews moft paffion for this entertainment, and the beft that avoids and fears it, than which there
can hardly be a worfe fign of it, as a mean of doing good.
Whoever believes the following words of our bleffed Redeemer,
will never be perfuaded that poets and actors for the ftage have
received any commiffion to fpeak in his name. *My fheep hear
my voice, and I know them, and they follow me* *.—*A ftranger
will*

* John x. 27.

will they not follow, but will flee from him, for they know not the voice of strangers †. ‡

This leads us to obferve, that the ftage is not only an improper method of inftruction, but that all, or the far greateft number of pieces there reprefented, muft have, upon the whole, a pernicious tendency. This is evident, becaufe they muft be to the tafte and relifh of the bulk of thofe who attend it. The difficulty of getting good authors for the theatre, I fhall not infift upon, but whatever the authors are able or willing to do, it is certain, that their productions in fact, can rife no higher in point of purity, than the audience fhall be willing to receive. Their attendance is not conftrained, but voluntary ; nay, they pay dearly for their entertainment ; and therefore they muft, and will have it to their tafte. This is a part of the fubject that merits the particular attention of all who are inclined to judge impartially, and it proves, in the ftrongeft manner, the abfurdity of forming chimerical fuppofitions of a ftage fo regulated, as, inftead of being hurtful, to promote the interefts of piety and virtue.

Here

† John x. 5.

‡ It is to be obferved here, to prevent miftakes, that the argument fa founded on the general and prevailing inclination of the greateft part of each character, and not upon particular inftances, in many of which, it is confeffed, it will not hold. For, as it is difficult to know the real character of fome perfons, in whom there are fome marks and figns of true religion, and at the fame time, fome fymptoms of unfoundnefs, fo, it is ftill more difficult to determine the quality of fingle actions. Therefore, it is little or no argument that any practice is fafe or good, becaufe one good man, or one fuppofed to be good, has been known to do it ; or on the contrary, ill, becaufe one bad man has been known to do it. But as, when we retire further from the limit that divides them, the characters are more clearly and fenfibly diftinguifhed, fo, whatever practice is paffionately defired by wicked men in general, and fhunned by the good, certainly is of bad tendency. If it were otherwife, as faid above, Satan's kingdom would be *divided againft itfelf,* and the God *who keepeth covenant and truth for ever,* would fail in his promife, of *giving* his people *counfel,* and *teaching them the way in which they ought to walk.*

Here let fome truths be called to mind which are frequently mentioned in the holy fcriptures, but feldom recollected, and their confequences very little attended to. There is a diftinction often ftated, both in the Old and New Teftament, between the children of God and the men of the world. Thefe are mixed together in the prefent ftate, and cannot, in many cafes, be certainly diftinguifhed by their outward appearance; yet is there at bottom, not only a real diftinction of character, but a perfect oppofition between them, as to the commanding principle of all their actions. And as there is an oppofition of character between them, fo there muft be an oppofition of interefts and views. Our bleffed Redeemer when he came into the world, was *defpifed and rejected of men*; and he every where tells his difciples, that they muft expect no better treatment. *Bleffed are ye when men fhall revile you, and perfecute you, and fhall fay all manner of evil againft you falfely, for my fake. Rejoice and be exceeding glad: for great is your reward in heaven: for fo perfecuted they the prophets that were before you* *. And on the other hand, *Wo unto you when all men fhall fpeak well of you, for fo did their fathers to the falfe prophets* †. Again, *If ye were of the world, the world would love his own; but becaufe ye are not of the world, but I have chofen you out of the world, therefore the world hateth you* ‡. His apoftles fpeak always the fame language: Thus the apoftle Paul, *And be not conformed to this world* §. Nay, he lays it down as an univerfal pofition, *Yea, and all that will live godly in Chrift Jefus fhall fuffer perfecution* ‖. Now I afk, Whether thofe who have a ftrong and rooted averfion at true holinefs, which is the character of the fincere Chriftian, will voluntarily croud to the theatre, to hear and fee fuch performances as breathe nothing but what is agreeable to the pure uncorrupted word of God? Will thofe who revile, injure, and perfecute the faints themfelves,

---

* Mat. v. 11, 12.   † Luke vi. 26.   ‡ John xv. 19.   § Rom. xii.
‖ 2 Tim. 3. 12.

felves, delight in the ftage, if honour is there put upon true religion, and be pleafed with that character in the reprefentation which they hate in the original ? This would be to expect impoffibilities. And therefore, while the great majority of thofe who attend the ftage are unholy, it is certain, that the plays which they behold with pleafure cannot, upon the whole, but have a criminal tendency.

If any allege, that the poets art may be a mean to make religion amiable to them, I anfwer, that he cannot make it amiable, but by adulteration, by mixing it with fomething agreeable to their own tafte, and then it is not religion that they admire, but the erroneous, debafed and falfe refemblance of it. Or even fuppofing, that, in a fingle inftance or two, nothing in fubftance fhould be fet before them but true religion, and this dreffed to the very higheft advantage by the poet's genius and actor's fkill, there would be little gained ; becaufe thefe human arts only, would be the object of their admiration, and they would always prefer, and fpeedily procure, a difplay of the fame arts, upon a fubject more agreeable to their corrupt minds. This, indeed, we are not left to gather by way of inference and deduction from other truths, but are exprefly taught it in the word of God. For *the natural man receiveth not the things of the fpirit of God : for they are foolifhnefs unto him, neither can he know them, becaufe they are fpiritually difcerned* *. Experience is a ftrong proof of this ; for if any man will take the pains of making up a fyftem of the morality of the ftage, I do not mean the horrid prophanity and fcandalous obfcenity that is to be found in the worft, but of that which is called virtue in the beft of the pieces wrote for the theatre, he will find it exceeding different from Chriftian morals ; and, that an adherence to it would be, in moft inftances, a wilful departure from the rules of a holy life.

However plainly this is founded upon the word of God and

E   found

* 1 Cor. ii. 14.

found reafon, there are fome very unwilling to think, that even
their duty as Chriftians fhould conftrain them to be at odds with
the delicacies of life, or the polite and fafhionable pleafures of
the age. And, as the mind of man is very ingenious in the defence of that pollution which it loves, they fometimes bring in
criticifm to their aid. They alledge that by the *world* is underftood, generally thro' the New Teftament, thofe who were
Heathens by profeffion; and that the fame oppofition to true
religion, in judgment and heart, is not to be afcribed to thofe
who are members of the vifible church. It is anfwered, the
word did indeed fignify as they fay, for this plain reafon, that
in the early days of Chriftianity, when it was under perfecution,
few or none would make profeffion of it unlefs they did really
believe it. But is not the meaning ftill the fame? Can we fuppofe that the hatred of the then world was at the name of religion only, and not at the fubftance? Was the devil *the prince
of this world*, then? And has he not now equal dominion over,
and is he not equally ferved by thofe who are profane in their
lives, though they were once baptifed? Was he the fpirit that
then worked, and is he not the fpirit that *now works* in the children of difobedience? The truth therefore remains ftill the
fame, thofe who are in a natural and unregenerate ftate, who
hate true religion in their hearts, muft have fomething very different before they can be pleafed with feeing it on the ftage*.

That

---

* There is an excellent paffage to this purpofe in an effay againft plays,
to be found in one of the volumes publifhed about a hundred years ago by
the gentlemen of the Portroyal in France, a fociety of Janfenifts, of great
parts and eminent piety. This effay in particular, is by fome faid to have
been written by the prince of Conti. Section 15th of that effay, he fays,
' It is fo true that plays are almoft always a reprefentation of vicious paffi-
' ons, that the moft part of Chriftian virtues are incapable of appearing upon
' the ftage. Silence, patience, moderation, wifdom, poverty, repentance,
' are no virtues the reprefentation of which can divert the fpectators; and
' above all, we never hear humility fpoken of, and the bearing of injuries
' It

That this argument may have its proper force, we ought to confider, how great a proportion of perfons under the dominion of vice and wickednefs there muft always be among thofe who attend the theatre. The far greateft number of the world in general are ungodly. This is a fact which could hardly be denied, even tho' the following paffage had not ftood in the oracles of truth. *Enter ye in at the ftrait gate; for wide is the gate, and broad is the way that leadeth to deftruction, and many there be which go in thereat: Becaufe ftrait is the gate, and narrow is the way that leadeth unto life, and few there be that find it* †. And as none can attend the ftage, but thofe in higher life, and more affluent circumftances than the bulk of mankind, there is ftill a greater proportion of them who are enemies to pure and undefiled religion. Thus, fays our Saviour to his difciples, *Verily I fay unto you, that a rich man fhall hardly enter into the kingdom of heaven. And again I fay unto you, it is eafier for a camel to go through the eye of a needle, than for a rich man to enter into the kingdom of God* ‡. To the fame purpofe the apoftle Paul fays, *Ye fee your calling, brethren, how that not many wife men after the flefh, not many mighty, not many noble are called* ||. This does not at all fuppofe, that thofe in high life are originally more corrupt in their nature than others, but it arifes from their being expofed to much greater and ftronger temptations. Now if, from the fmall number of real Chriftians in the upper ranks of life, we again fubftract fuch as

count

‘ It would be ftrange to fee a modeft and filent religious perfon reprefented.
‘ There muft be fomething of great and renowned according to men, or
‘ at leaft fomething lively and animated, which is not met withal in Chri-
‘ ftian gravity and wifdom, and therefore, thofe who have been defirous to
‘ introduce holy men and women upon the ftage, have been forced to make
‘ them appear proud, and to make them utter difcourfes more proper for the
‘ ancient Roman heroes than for faints and martyrs. Their devotion upon
‘ the ftage ought alfo to be always a little extraordinary.

† Mat. vii. 13, 14. ‡ Mat. xix. 23, 24. || 1 Cor. i. 26.

count the stage unlawful or dangerous, or have no inclination to it, there will very few remain of those who are *the salt of the earth*, to season the unhallowed assembly. What sort of productions then must they be, which shall have the approbation of such judges? How much more proper to pollute than to reform, to poison than to cure? If such in fact the great bulk of plays have always hitherto been, from what has been said it ought not to be wondered at, because it cannot be otherwise.

It is very possible, that some may be all this while holding the argument very cheap, and saying with lord Shaftsbury, ' The true genius is of a nobler nature than servilely to submit ' to the corrupt or vitiated taste of any age or place; —he works ' not for gain, but despises it ;—he knows, and will not swerve ' from the truth of art ;—he will produce what is noble and ' excellent in its kind ;—he will refine the public ear, and teach ' them to admire in the right place. These, tho' I do not cite any particular passage, are all of them sentiments, and most of them expressions, of that author so much admired among modern philosophers. But the objection is easily solved. The observation is allowed to be just, and to hold with respect to the poetic, oratorial, or any human art, because we know of no higher standard in any of these, than what human nature, in its present state, will most admire when it is exhibited to view. Accordingly the great poet and the great orator, tho', through the prevalence of a bad taste, they may find it difficult at first to procure attention, yet they will procure it at last : And when they are heard, they carry the prize from all inferior pretenders ; and indeed, their doing so is the very touchstone and trial of their art itself. In this case, there lies no appeal from the judgment of the public or the multitude, (as David Hume has said for once according to truth,) to the judgment of a wiser few.

But there cannot be any thing more absurd than to suppose,
that

that the same thing will hold in morals and religion. The dramatic poets in Athens, where the stage was first established, improved upon one another, and refined their own taste, and that of their audience, as to the elegance of their compositions. Nay, they soon brought tragedy, as a great critic * observes, to as great perfection as the nature of the thing seems to admit of. But whoever will from this infer, that they improved in their morals in the same proportion, or by that means, will fall into a very gross mistake. This, indeed, seems to be the great error of modern infidels, to suppose, that there is no more in morals than a certain taste and sense of beauty and elegance. Natural talents in the human mind are quite distinct from moral dispositions, and the excellence of the one is no evidence at all of the prevalence of the other. On the contrary, the first are many times found in the highest perfection, where there is a total absence of the last. And therefore, that true genius is the object of universal approbation, hinders not but that true goodness is the object of general aversion. The scripture assures us, that all men are by nature under the power of sin, *that every imagination of the thoughts of man is only evil from his youth, and that continually* †. *That the carnal mind is enmity against God, and,* till it be renewed by divine grace, *is not subject to the law of God, neither indeed can be* ‡.

Now it is utterly impossible and self-contradictory, that men should approve and delight in that which is contrary to the habitual prevailing temper of their hearts; and to bring about a change in them is not in the power of any human art, but with the concurrence of the spirit and grace of God. In this he has given no authority to the players to act under him, nay, he has expresly told us, that he will not ordinarily, in any way whatever, make use of the perfection of human art, but of the plainest and weakest outward means. Thus the apostle Paul tells us his Master sent him, *To preach the gospel, not with wisdom of words,*

lest

* Aristotle.   † Gen. vi. 5.   ‡ Rom. viii. 7.

left the cross of Christ should be made of none effect *.——And, *after that in the wisdom of God, the world by wisdom knew not God, it pleased God by the foolishness of preaching to save them that believe* †. He also professes that his practice had always been conformed to this rule, *And I, brethren, when I came to you, came not with excellency of speech or of wisdom, declaring unto you the testimony of God* ‡. *And my speech and my preaching was not with enticing words of man's wisdom, but in demonstration of the Spirit and of power. That your faith should not stand in the wisdom of men but in the power of God* ‖ §.

It may be necessary here, to obviate an objection, that in the holy scriptures themselves we find several passages which seem to signify, that true religion, though it is not the choice of all men, is yet the object of universal aprobation. Thus we are told, that *the righteous shall be in everlasting remembrance, but the memory of the wicked shall rot.* Nay, we are exhorted by the apostle Paul to the practice of our duty, in such terms as these, *Whatsoever things are true, whatsoever things are lovely,*

what-

---

* 1 Cor. i. 17.   † Ibid ver. 21.   ‡ 1 Cor. ii. 1.   ‖ Ibid ver. 4, 5.

§ Perhaps some will ask here, Is then human art, and are natural talents, which are the gifts of God, wholly excluded from his service? I answer, they are not. And yet the instances of their being eminently useful are exceeding rare. Such is the imperfection of the human mind, that it can hardly at the same time, give great attention and application to two distinct subjects; and therefore, when men give that intense application to human art, which is necessary to bring it to its perfection, they are apt to overlook the power and grace of God, without which all art is vain and ineffectual. Agreeably to this, when men of eminent talents have been of service in religion, it has been commonly by the exercise of self-denial, by making a very sparing and moderate use of them, and showing themselves so deeply penetrated with a sense of the important truths of the everlasting gospel, as to despise the beauties and embellishments of human skill, too great an attention to which is evidently inconsistent with the other. Well, say refined observers, this is the very perfection of art to use it with great reserve, and keep it out of view as much as possible. And it is, indeed, the perfection of art to have the appearance of this, but it is peculiar to a renewed heart to have it in reality.

whatsoever things are of good report, if there be any virtue, if there be any praise, think on these things. But these must surely be explained in such a manner, as to be confistent with the clear and strong passages mentioned above; which is not difficult to do. The matter of many good actions, particularly social virtues, the duties of the second table of the law, wicked men do often approve, nay, they may not only see some beauty, but feel some pleasure in them, from natural tho' unsanctified affections leading to them. But truly good actions, instances of holy obedience to God, in their manner, and in the principles from which they ought to flow, they neither can approve nor perform.

Nothing can be done agreeable to the will of God, but what hath the following properties. It must be done from a sense, not only of the unalterable obligation, but the perfect excellence of the law of God *; renouncing all pretence of merit in the actor †; depending for affistance entirely on divine strength ‡; and with a single eye to the divine glory ||. It is not the matter of an action that renders it truly holy, but the prevalence of these principles in the heart of the performer. And they are so far from being generally approved, that they are hated and despised, and the very profession of most of them at least, ridiculed by every worldly man. The truth is, it is not easy to discover these principles otherwise than by narration. They ly deep in the heart, they do not seek to discover themselves, and the shewing them on the stage would be a fort of contradiction to their nature. I believe it would exceed the art of most poets or actors, to exhibit by outward signs, true self-denial, without joining to it such oftentation as would destroy its effect. Or if it could be done, it would be so far from being delightful to those who *through the pride of their heart will not seek after God,* that it would fill them with difguft or difdain. So that all friends of the ftage ought to join with David Hume, who hath excluded self-denial,

* Rom. vii. 12.   † Gal. ii. 20. Phil. iii. 3.   ‡ John xv. 5.
|| 1 Cor. x. 31. 1 Pet. iv. 11.

denial, humility, and mortification from the number of the virtues, and ranked them among the vices.

From this it appears, that worldly men will bear a form of
godliness, but the spirit and power of it they cannot endure.
When therefore, the scriptures represent religion, or any part
of it, as amiable in the eyes of mankind in general, it is only
giving one view of its excellence in itself or in its matter : But
this can never be intended to make the judgment of bad men its
standard or measure. Or, when the approbation of men is proposed as an argument to duty, it cannot be considered in any o-
ther light, than as an assistant subordinate motive to preserve
us from its violation ; for the scriptures will never warrant us
to aim at the praise of men as the reward of our compliance.

If there be any more than what is said above in the testimony
which wicked men give in favour of religion, it is but the
voice of natural conscience, that is, the voice of God in them,
and not their own ; and as it is extorted from them against their
will, they do all in their power to destroy the force of the evidence. This we may be sensible of, if we will recollect, that it
is always general, and that many speak well of something which
they call religion, in general, when yet there is hardly any of
the servants of God, in whose character and conduct they will
not endeavour either to find or make a flaw. The truth is, tho'
some few heroes in profanity, vilify religion in itself directly,
and in all its parts, the plurality of scoffers only tell you, this
and the other thing is not religion, but superstition, preciseness,
fancy or whim, and so on. But at the same time, if you take
away all that by some or other is reflected on under these appel-
lations, you will leave little behind. Which plainly teaches us
this truth, that no man will cordially approve of such a scheme
of religion as he does not believe and embrace, or inwardly and
without dissimulation applaud a character that is better than his
own : at least, than his own either is, or he secretly hopes it to
be * .

be *. For this reafon, the apoſtle John gives it as a mark or e-
vidence of regeneration, *We know that we have paffed from death
to life; becaufe we love the brethren,* that is to fay, a fincere and
prevalent love to a faint as fuch, can dwell in no heart but that
which is fanctified.

It will be proper here to take notice, becaufe it has fome relation to this fubject, of what the advocates of the ſtage often
make their boaſt, that before a poliſhed audience things groſly
criminal are not fuffered to be acted ; and that it is one of the
rules of the drama, that, if ſuch things be ſuppoſed, they muſt
be kept behind the ſcenes. We are often put in mind of the
pure taſte of an Athenian audience, who, upon one of the actors

---

* For aſſertaining the fenſe, and confirming the truth of this paſſage, it is
proper to obſerve, That by the word [better] is not fo much to be underſtood
higher in degree, as different in kind. Tho' even in the firſt fenſe, it feems
to hold pretty generally, in comparifons between man and man. Men commonly extend their charity to thoſe who have leſs, and not to thoſe who
have more goodneſs than themſelves. There are very few, who, when they
fee others more ſtrict and regular in their conduct than they are willing to be,
do not aſcribe it either to weakneſs, or hypocriſy. Perhaps, indeed, the
reafon of this may be, that a gradual difference as to the actions done, is confidered as conſtituting a ſpecific difference in the moral character ; and men
condemn others not for being better than themſeves, upon their own notion
of goodneſs, but for placing religion in the extremes which they apprehend
ought to be avoided. This confirms the remark made above, that every
man's own character is the ſtandard of his approbation, and ſhows at the
fame time its confiſtency with that humility which is eſſential to every Chriſtian. Wherever there is a real approbation, and fincere confeſſion, of fuperior worth, there is alfo an unfeigned imitation of it. The Chriſtian, not
only knows himſelf to be infinitely diſtant from God, whom yet he fupreme-
ly loves, but thinks himſelf leſs than the leaſt of all faints ; but he could
neither love the one nor the other, if he had not a real, however diſtant like-
neſs ; if he had not the feeds of every good difpoſition implanted in him, the
growth of which is his fupreme defire, and the improvement of which is the
conſtant object of his care and diligence.

F

tors expreffing a profane thought, all rofe up and left the theatre. A famous French tragedian, Corneille, alfo takes notice of it as an evidence of the improvement of the ftage in his time, that one of his beft written pieces had not fucceeded, ' Becaufe ' it ftruck the fpectators with the horrid idea of a proftitution to ' which a holy woman had been condemned.' As to the cafe of the Athenians, it were eafy to fhow from the nature and circumftances of the fact, that this refentment at the profanity of the poet, tho' it was expreffed in the theatre, was by no means learned there. But it is needlefs to enter into any nice difquifition upon this fubject, for all that follows from any fuch inftances, is, that there are fome things fo very grofs and fhocking, that, as but a few of the moft abandoned will commit them, fo, the reft of the world can have no delight in beholding them. There is, no doubt, a great variety of characters differing one from another in the degree of their degeneracy, and yet all of them effentially diftinct from true piety.

To fet this matter in a juft light we muft remember, that, as has been confeffed above, the matter of many good actions, or a defective imperfect form of virtue is approved by the generality of the world; and, that they are very much fwayed in their actions by a view to public praife. Therefore, they are mutually checks to one another, and vice is not feen on a theatre in a grofs, but commonly in a more dangerous, becaufe an engaging and infinuating form. The prefence of fo many witneffes does reftrain and difguife fin, but cannot change its nature, or render it innocent. The purity of the theatre can never be carried farther by the tafte of the audience, than what is required in converfation with the polite and fafhionable world. There vice is in fome meafure reftrained; men may be wicked, but they muft not be rude. How much this amounts to, is but too well known; it is no more than that we muft not difguft thofe with whom we converfe, and varies with their character. This is fo far

from

from being agreeable to the rules of the gospel, that a serious Christian is often obliged, from a sense of duty, to be guilty of a breach of good manners, by administring unacceptable reproof.

Thus it appears, that, in the stage, the audience gives law to the poet, which is much the same thing as the scholar choosing his own lesson, and whether this be a safe or profitable method of instruction is easy to judge. Every one who knows human nature, especially who believes the representation given of it in Scripture, must conclude, that the young will be seduced into the commission, and the older confirmed and hardened in the practice of sin, because characters fundamentally wrong will be there painted out in an amiable light, and divested of what is most shameful and shocking. By this means conscience, instead of being alarmed and giving faithful testimony, is deceived and made a party in the cause. In short, vice in the theatre must wear the garb, assume the name, and claim the reward of virtue. How strong a confirmation of this have we from experience? Have not plays in fact commonly turned upon the characters most grateful, and the events most interesting to corrupt nature? Pride, under the name of greatness of mind, ambition and revenge, under those of valour and heroism, have been their constant subjects. But chiefly love: this, which is the strongest passion, and the most dangerous in the human frame, and from which the greatest number of crimes, and crimes the most atrocious, have sprung, was always encouraged upon the stage. There, women are swelled with vanity, by seeing their sex always deified and adored; there, men learn the language, as well as feel by sympathy, the transports of that passion; and there, the hearts of both are open and unguarded to receive the impression, because it is covered with a mask of honour. Hath this then been only the case at particular times of occasional corruption, or for want of a proper regulation of the stage? No, It is inseparable from its constitution. Such hath been the nature and tendency of plays in all former ages, and such, from the taste and disposition

F 2

of

of thofe who attend them, it is certain they will for ever con-
tinue to be *.										Ano-

* Perhaps, it will be alledged, that the whole force of this reafoning may
be evaded, by fuppofing a ftage directed by the magiftrate, and fupported at
the public charge. In this cafe the performers would be under no temptation, for gain, to gratify the tafte of the audience, and the managers would
have a quite different intention. It is confeffed, that this fuppofition feems
confiderably to weaken the arguments above ufed, though, perhaps, more in
theory than it would do in practice. But I would afk any who make fuch
a fuppofition, Why this inviolable attachment to the ftage? Why muft fo
many efforts be made to preferve it in fome fhape or other? What are its
mighty benefits, that it muft be forced as it were out of its own natural courfe
in order to make it lawful, rather than we will give it up as pernicious? ---
It is alfo to be obferved, that, however ufeful an ordinance of God magiftracy be for public order, there is very little fecurity in the direction of magiftrates, for found and wholefome inftruction in religion or morals. We can
never depend upon them for this, unlefs they are themfelves perfons of true
piety, and not always even when that is the cafe, becaufe they may be guilty of many errors in judgment. Now it is not reafonable to hope, that
magiftrates, in any country, will be always, or even generally, perfons of
true piety. Such, with the other qualifications neceffary to magiftrates, are
not always to be found. Neither is there any neceffity for it; becaufe, tho'
doubtlefs, thofe who fear God will be the moft faithful magiftrates, and the
moft dutiful fubjects, yet the greateft part of the duties of both may be performed without this, in a manner, in which the public will fee and feel
very little difference. Magiftracy has only the outward carriage, and not the
heart for its object, and it is the fenfible effect which the public looks for,
and not the principle from which any thing is done. Therefore, as on the
one hand, if a fubject obeys the laws, and outwardly fulfills the duties of his
ftation, the magiftrate hath nothing farther to demand, tho' it be only for
wrath, and not *for confcience fake*; fo on the other, if a magiftrate be diligent
in preferving order and promoting the general good, though the motive of his
actions be no better than vanity, ambition, or the fear of man well concealed, the public reaps the benefit, and has no ground of complaint, even whilft
his character is deteftable in the fight of God. But this magiftrate can never
be fafely trufted with the direction of what regards our moral or fpiritual improvement, and he would be going out of his own fphere fhould he attempt it.
------After all, it makes little difference whether the magiftrate or any body
elfe directs the ftage, while the attendance is voluntary; for in that cafe, it
muft either be fuited to the tafte of the audience, or it will be wholly deferted.

Another argument which shews the stage to be an improper method of instruction, or rather that it is pernicious and hurtful, may be drawn from its own nature. In its most improved state it is a picture of human life, and must represent characters as they really are. An author for the stage is not permitted to feign, but to paint and copy. Tho' he should introduce things or persons ever so excellent, if there were not discerned a resemblance between them and real life, they would be so far from being applauded, that they would not be suffered, but would be condemned as a transgression of the fundamental rules of the art. Now, are not the great majority of characters in real life bad? Must not the greatest part of those represented on the stage be bad? And therefore, must not the strong impression which they make upon the spectators be hurtful in the same proportion?

It is a known truth, established by the experience of all ages, that bad example has a powerful and unhappy influence upon human characters. Sin is of a contagious and spreading nature, and the human heart is but too susceptible of the infection. This may be ascribed to several causes, and to one in particular which is applicable to the present case, That the seeing of sin frequently committed, must gradually abate that horror which we ought to have of it upon our minds, and which serves to keep us from yielding to its sollicitations. Frequently seeing the most terrible objects renders them familiar to our view, and makes us behold them with less emotion. And, from seeing sin without reluctance, the transition is easy, to a compliance with its repeated importunity, especially, as there are latent remaining dispositions to sinning in every heart that is but imperfectly sanctified. It will be difficult to assign any other reason, why wickedness is always carried to a far greater height in large and populous cities, than in the country. Do not multitudes, in places of great resort, come to perpetrate calmly and sedately, without any remorse, such crimes, as would surprize a less knowing

ing

ing finner fo much as to hear of ? Can it then be fafe, to be prefent at the exhibition of fo many vitious characters as always muft appear upon the ftage ? Muft it not, like other examples, have a ftrong, tho' infenfible influence, and, indeed, the more ftrong becaufe unperceived.

Perhaps fome will fay, This argument draws very deep, it is a reproaching of providence, and finding fault with the order which God hath appointed, at leaft permitted, to take place in the world, where the very fame proportion of wicked characters is to be feen. But is there not a wide difference between the permiffion of any thing by a wife, holy, and juft God, or its making part of the plan of providence, and our prefuming to do the fame thing, without authority, and when we can neither reftrain it within proper bounds, nor direct it to its proper end. There are many things which are proper and competent to God, which it would be the moft atrocious wickednefs in man to imitate. Becaufe it is both good and juft in God to vifi. us with ficknefs, or to take us away by death when he fees it proper, would it therefore be lawful in us, to bring any of them upon ourfelves at our own pleafure ? I fhould rather be inclined to think, that thefe fportive reprefentations on the ftage, inftead of being warranted by their counterpart in the world, are a daring profanation, and, as it were, a mockery of divine providence, and fo to be confidered in a light yet more dreadful, than any in which they have been hitherto viewed. Befides, it ought to be remembred that, tho' evil actions, as permitted, make a part of the will of God, yet, hitherto, all who deferve the name of Chriftians have affirmed, that what is finful in any action is to be afcribed to the will of the creature as its adequate caufe ; and therefore, exhibiting human actions and characters upon the ftage, is, not only reprefenting the works of God, but repeating the fins of men.

The criminal and dangerous nature of fuch a conduct, will farther appear from this, that it is, by juft and neceffary confequence,

quence, forbidden in the word of God. There we find, that tho', in his fovereign providence, he permits the commiſſion of fin, fuffers his own people to continue mixed with finners in this ſtate, and makes their connexion with them in ſome mea- fure unavoidable, as a part of their trial, yet he hath expreſly prohibited them from having any more communication with fuch, than he himſelf hath made neceſſary. We are warned in ſcripture, that *evil communications corrupt good manners*, and therefore, that we muſt fly the ſociety of the ungodly. The Pfalmiſt tells us, *Bleſſed is the man that walketh not in the coun- fel of the ungodly, nor ſtandeth in the way of finners, nor fitteth in the feat of the ſcornful* *. Agreeably to this the characters of good men in ſcripture are always repreſented. Thus the Pfalmiſt David records his own refolution, *I will fet no wicked thing before mine eyes, I hate the work of them that turn afide, it ſhall not cleave to me. A froward heart ſhall depart from me, I will not know a wicked perfon* † The fame fays elſewhere, *I am a companion of all them that fear thee, and of them that keep thy precepts* ‡. *Depart from me ye evil doers, for I will keep the commandments of my God* ‖.

But there is no need of citing paſſages of ſcripture to this purpoſe ; it is well known, that good men, tho' they will be very cautious of raſhly determining characters that are doubtful, and will far leſs diſcover a proud and phariſaical contempt of any who may yet be veſſels of mercy, will however, carefully avoid all unneceſſary communication with finners. They will neither follow their perfons from inclination, nor view their conduct with pleaſure. On the contrary, when they cannot wholly fly from their ſociety, it becomes a heavy burden, and in ſome cafes intolerable, and ſo as to require the interpofition of the fame kind providence that *delivered juſt Lot, vexed with the filthy converfation of the wicked*. Is there any confiſtency be- tween fuch a character, and attending the ſtage with delight? Will

* Pfal i. 1. † Pfal. ci. 3, 4. ‡ Pfal. cxix. 63. ‖ Ib. ver. 115.

Will thofe who *behold tranfgreffors, and are grieved,* crowd with eagernefs to the theatre, where the fame perfons and acti-ons are brought under a review ? Will what affected them with forrow in the commiffion, be voluntarily chofen, and made fub-fervient to their pleafure in the repetition.

I cannot help here calling to mind the anxious concern, which wife and pious parents ufually fhew for their children, on ac-count of the fnares to which they are unavoidably expofed in an evil world. How carefully do they point out, and how folemn-ly do they charge them to fhun the paths in which deftroyers go. They ufe this caution with refpect to the world, even as under the government of God, and in fo doing they follow the example of their Saviour, who, in the profpect of leaving his dif-ciples, after many excellent advices, puts up for them this inter-ceffory prayer ; *And now I am no more in this world, but thefe are in the world, and I come to thee. Holy Father, keep thro' thine own name thofe whom thou haft given me, that they may be one, as we are.——I pray not that thou fhouldft take them out of the world, but that thou fhouldft keep them from the evil *. Can any expect that this prayer will be heard in their behalf, who are not content with feeing the world as it is ordered by a wife and holy God, but muft fee it over again, in a vile imitation, by a finful man.

It will probably be faid, that this ftrikes as much againft Hi-ftory, at leaft the writing and reading of human, commonly cal-led profane hiftory, as againft the writing and feeing of drama-tic reprefentations. But the cafes are by no means the fame ; the knowledge of hiftory is, in many refpects, neceffary for the great purpofes of religion. Were not this the cafe, there would be little difficulty in admitting the confequence. Perhaps, even as it is, it had been better for the world that feveral ancient facts and characters, which now ftand upon record, had been buried in

* John xvii. 11, 15.

in oblivion *. At any rate, it may be safely affirmed, that romances and fabulous narrations are a species of composition,
from which the world hath received as little benefit, and as
much hurt, as any that can be named, excepting plays themselves, to which they are so nearly allied. The first are only
exceeded by the last, as to their capacity of doing mischief, by
the circumstances of action, and the presence at once of so many
persons, among whom, by mutual sympathy, the spiritual poison
spreads faster and penetrates deeper.

Least it should be pretended, that such a turn is given to
things in the representation, as that, tho' the greatest part of
the actions represented are ill in themselves, yet vice is reproached;

---

* Perhaps, some will be surprized at what is here said on the subject of
History, who have not usually viewed it in this light. And, indeed, this
is the great difficulty in the whole of the present argument, to overcome
strong prepossessions, and to shew men the sin and danger of a practice, which
they know to be common, and have been long accustomed to look upon as
lawful and safe. For this reason, it is probable, that the best way of proving that the above assertion on the subject of History, is agreeable to scripture and reason, will be, by a case perfectly similar, but more frequently
handled. Do not all Christian writers, without exception, who treat of
the government of the tongue, lay down this as a rule, that we are not to
report the sins of others, tho' we know the truth of the facts, unless where
it is necessary to some good end? Now, why should there be any different
rule in writing than in conversation? What is done either way is the same
in substance, *viz* communicating information; and writing, which may be
called visible speech, is much more lasting in its nature and extensive in its
effects. If any ask, How, or why the knowledge of history is necessary to
the purposes of religion? I answer, It is necessary for proving the truths of
natural, and confirming those of revealed religion, for repelling the attacks
of adversaries, and giving us such a view of the plan of Providence, as may
excite us to the exercise of the duties of adoration, thankfulness, trust, and
submission to the supreme disposer of all events. Real facts only are proper
for this purpose, and not feigned stories, in the choice and dressing of which,
experience teaches us, the great end is, that man may be pleased, and not
that God may be glorified.

G

ed or ridiculed, virtue set upon a throne, rewarded and honoured; Let it be called to mind, that, as has been shewn above, the author is not left at liberty to do in this as he pleases. He must gratify the public taste, and the rules he is obliged to observe have rather the contrary effect. For he must divest his bad characters of what is most horrid and shocking, and present them less deformed than they really are. Besides, tho' he may conceal a part, he must not alter nature so far as he goes, but take it as he finds it. Accordingly, some of our modern critics tell us, that there ought to be no particular moral in a dramatic performance, because that is a departure from nature, and so not in taste.

It ought not to be forgotten, that attending dramatic representations is not only seeing a great plurality of bad characters without necessity, and seeing them with patience, but it is seeing them with pleasure. Whether or not entertainment be yielded to be the only or ultimate effect of plays, surely, it cannot be denied to be one effect sought and expected from them, and from every part of them. An actor is as much applauded, and gives as much pleasure to the spectators, when he represents a bad character to the life, as a good. Is there no danger then, that a heart softned by delight, should be more liable to infection from evil than at other times ? Is there no danger, that an association should be formed in the mind, between the sense of pleasure and the commission of sin ? Will any person affirm, that, in such circumstances, he feels that. holy indignation against sin, which every Christian ought to conceive upon seeing it committed ? Or, that he is able to preserve that awe and fear, which he ought to have of the just judgment of God, when he sees the crimes that merit it boldly re-acted, and finely mimicked in a personated character.

So far is this from being the case, that every person attending the representation of a play, enters in some measure himself, as well as the actors, into the spirit of each character, and the

more

more fo the better the action is performed. His attention is ftrongly fixed, his affections are feized and carried away, and a total forgetfulnefs of every thing takes place, except what is immediately before him. Can the various paffions be fo ftrongly excited as they are fometimes known to be, and no effect remain? Will not the paffion of love, for example, after it has been ftrongly felt by the fpectator in fympathy with the actor, be a little more ready to recur, efpecially as nature prompts, and various folliciting objects are daily prefented to his eyes? The author terminates his plot as he fees beft, and draws what conclufions he thinks proper from his characters, but he has no reafon to think, that he can controul the paffions which he raifes in the fpectators in the fame manner, and not fuffer them to exceed the bounds of his defcription. Will not the paffion of revenge, that right hand of a falfe greatnefs of mind, after it has been ftrongly excited in the theatre, be apt to rife again upon every real or fuppofed provocation? Some learned obfervers of nature tell us, that every paffion we feel caufes a new modification of the blood and fpirits; if there is any truth in this, then every paffion excited in the theatre takes poffeffion for a time of the very animal frame, makes a feat to itfelf, and prepares for a fpeedy return.

Having thus endeavoured to fhew, that the ftage, whether amufement or inftruction be aimed at in it, cannot be attended by any Chriftian without fin; there is a third general argument againft it, which merits confideration. It is, that no perfon can contribute to the encouragement of the ftage, without being partaker of the fins of others. This is proper to be attended to, as it is againft a public theatre that the arguments in this effay are chiefly levelled; fo that, if it be criminal at all, every perfon attending it, is not only faulty by his own proper conduct, but is farther chargeable with the guilt of feducing others. Befides without this, the argument, to fome, would not be altogether compleat, for after all that has been advanced, there

G 2 may

may be a few, who in a good meafure yield it to be true, and yet have another fubterfuge remaining. They acknowledge, perhaps, that it is a moft hazardous amufement, to which others ought ordinarily to be preferred ; That the bulk of plays will, much more probably, pollute than improve the far greateft part of thofe who attend them. Yet ftill, they are apt to figure to themfelves particular cafes as exceptions from the general rule, and to fuppofe, there are *fome* plays which may be attended, or at leaft, that there are *fome* perfons who have fo much clear-nefs of judgment, and fo much conftancy in virtue, as to fepa-rate the corn from the chaff. At a particular time, they fup-pofe, a perfon of this kind may, without receiving any hurt, be improved by the fine fentiments contained in plays ; and al-fo learn fomething, to be applied to other purpofes, of that force and juftnefs of action, that grace and beauty of behaviour, which is no where feen in fo great perfection as on the ftage.

Upon this fubject in general, it may be affirmed, that thofe who have this confidence in the ftrength of their own virtue, are far from being the perfons who may be moft fafely trufted in a place of danger. On the contrary, thofe will probably be moft truly ftedfaft, when expofed to temptation, who are moft diffi-dent of themfelves, and do not wantonly run into it. Yet, fince fome may take encouragement from fuch apprehenfions, it is proper to obferve, that, tho' there were truth in their pre-tence, yet would it not therefore be lawful for them to attend the theatre. They could not do fo without contributing to the fins of others, a thing exprefly prohibited in the holy fcrip-tures, and, indeed, diametrically oppofite to the two principal branches of true religion, concern for the glory of God, and compaffion to the fouls of men.

There are two ways in which the occafional attending of plays, by thofe who are of good character, even fuppofing it not hurtful to themfelves, contributes to the fins of others. (1.) By fupporting the players in that unchriftian occupation. (2.)

(2.) Encouraging, by their example, thofe to attend all plays indifcriminately, who are in moft danger of infection.

Firft, It contributes to fupport the players in an unchriftian occupation. After what has been faid above, and which I now take for granted, on the impropriety of plays as an amufement, and the impoffibility of furnifhing a ftage with nothing but found and wholefome productions, little doubt can remain, that the occupation of players is inconfiftent with the character of a Chriftian. Whatever occafional prefence may be to fome fpectators, continual performing can never be lawful to the actors. On the very beft fuppofition, it is a life of perpetual amufement, which is equally contrary to reafon and religion. It is a mean proftitution of the rational powers, to have no higher end in view, than contributing to the pleafure and entertainment of the idle part of mankind, and, inftead of taking amufement with the moderation of a Chriftian, to make it the very bufinefs and employment of life. How ftrange a character does it make for one to live, in a manner, perpetually in a mafk, to be much oftener in a perfonated than in a real character ? And yet this is the cafe with all players, if, to the time fpent in the reprefentation, you add that which is neceffary to prepare for their public appearances. What foul polluted minds muft thefe be, which are fuch a receptacle of foreign vanities, befides their own natural corruption, and where one fyftem or plan of folly is obliterated only to make way for another.

But the life of players is not only idle and vain, and therefore inconfiftent with the character of a Chriftian, but it is ftill more directly and grofly criminal. We have feen above, that, not only from the tafte of the audience, the prevailing tendency of all fuccefsful plays muft be bad, but that, in the very nature of the thing, the greateft part of the characters reprefented muft be vitious. What then is the life of a player? It is wholly fpent in endeavouring to exprefs the language, and exhibit a perfect picture of the paffions of vicious men. For this purpofe, they muft

ftrive

strive to enter into the spirit, and feel the sentiments proper to
such characters. Unless they do so, the performance will be
quite faint and weak, if not wholly faulty and unnatural. And
can they do this so frequently without retaining much of the
impression, and, at last, becoming in truth what they are so
often in appearance. Do not the characters of all men take a
tincture from their employment and way of life? How much
more must theirs be infected, who are conversant, not in outward occupations, but in characters themselves, the actions,
passions and affections of men? If their peformances touch the
audiencs so senfibly, and produce in them so lafting an effect,
how much more must the same effects take place in themfelves,
whose whole time is spent in this manner.

   This is so certain, and, at the same time so acknowledged a
truth, that even those who are fondest of theatrical amusements,
do yet, still, esteem the employment of players a mean and for-
did profeffion. Their character has been infamous in all ages,
juft a living copy of that vanity, obscenity, and impiety which,
is to be found in the pieces which they reprefent. As the world
has been polluted by the stage, so they have always been more
eminently so, as it is natural to suppofe, being the very cisterns
in which this pollution is collected, and from which it is distributed to others. It makes no difference in the argument, that
we must here suppofe the stage to be regulated and improved,
for, as it has been shown, that it can never be so regulated as
to be fafe for the spectators, it must be always worfe for the actors, between whom and the audience the same proportion will
still remain. Can it then be lawful in any to contribute, in the
leaft degree, to support men in this unhallowed employment? Is
not the theatre, truly and effentially, what it has been often
called rhetorically, the fchool of impiety, where it is their very
bufinefs to learn wickednefs? And will a Chriftian, upon any
pretended advantage to himfelf, join in this confederacy against
                                                      God,

God, and affift in endowing and upholding the dreadful feminary?

Secondly, Men of good character going occafionally to the
theatre contributes to the fins of others, by emboldening thofe
to attend all plays indifcriminately, who are in moft danger of
infection. If there be any at all, efpecially if there be a great
number, to whom the ftage is noxious and finful, every one
without exception is bound to abftain. The apoftle Paul exprefly commands the Corinthians to abftain from lawful things,
when their ufing them would make their brother to offend, that
is to fay, would lead him into fin. *But take heed, left by any
means, this liberty of yours become a ftumbling-block to them that
are weak. For if any man fee thee which haft knowledge fit at
meat in the idols temple, fhall not the confcience of him that is
weak, be emboldened to eat thofe things which are offered to idols?
And thro' thy knowledge fhall the weak brother perifh, for whom
Chrift died. But when ye fin fo againft the brethren, and wound
their weak confcience, ye fin againft Chrift. Wherefore, if meat
make my brother to offend, I will eat no flefh while the world
ftandeth, left I make my brother to offend* *.

There are many who feem to have entirely forgot that this
precept is to be found in the word of God, and difcover not the
leaft fenfe of their obligation to comply with it. If, by any
plaufible pretences, they imagine they can vindicate their conduct with regard to themfelves, or palliate it with excufes, they
are quite unmindful of the injury which they do to others. I
fpeak not here of offending, in the fenfe in which that word is
commonly, tho' unjuftly taken, as difpleafing others. Such as
are difpleafed with the conduct of thofe who attend the theatre,
becaufe they efteem it to be finful, are not thereby offended in
the Scripture fenfe of that word, except in fo far, as fome few
of them are provoked to unchriftian refentment, or induced to
draw rafh and general conclufions, from the indifcretion of particular

* 1 Cor. viii. 9.---13.

123

ticular perfons, to the prejudice of whole orders of men. But vaft multitudes are truly offended or made to offend, as they are led into a practice, which, whatever it be to thofe who fet the example, is undoubtedly pernicious to them. Is it poffible to deny, that, under the beft regulation of the theatre that can reafonably be hoped for, to great numbers it muft be hurtful, efpecially as it is enticing to all? And, if that be but allowed, perfons of character and reputation cannot attend without con-tributing to the mifchief that is done.

Perhaps it will be objected to this application of the paffage of fcripture cited above, that the particular danger there pointed out by the apoftle, is inducing men to venture upon a practice with a doubting confcience. I think it highly probable, that this very precife cafe happens with many, who go to the theatre following the example of others. They are not entirely fatis-fied of its lawfulnefs, they ftill have fome inward reluctance of mind, but adventure to gratify a carnal inclination, being em-boldened by the example of thofe who are efteemed men of un-derftanding and worth. But, even where their implicit truft is fo ftrong as fully to fatisfy them, and fet their minds at eafe, the apoftle's argument holds with equal force, if, thereby, they are unavoidably led into fin.

This will probably be looked upon as a very hard law, and it will be afked, Is a man, then, never to do any thing that he has reafon to believe will be mifinterpreted, or abufed by others to their own hurt? The hardnefs of the law will wholly evanifh, if we remember, that it is confined to things indifferent in their nature. In duties binding of their own nature, we are under no obligation to pay any regard to the opinions of others, or the confequences of our conduct upon them. But in things originally indifferent, which become duties, or not, precifely on account of their confequences, there, we are to beware of mak-ing our brother to offend. The fcripture rule is this, We muft not commit the leaft fin under pretence of the moft important end.

end, tho' it were to fave multitudes from fins incomparably more heinous. But in matters of indifference, we are not to value the moft beloved enjoyment fo highly, as to endanger the falvation of one human foul by enfnaring it into fin. And can a real believer have the fmalleft objection, the leaft rifing thought, againft this equitable law ? Shall we value any prefent gratification equally, nay, fhall we once put it in the ballance with the fpiritual intereft of an immortal foul ? Now, who will be fo fhamelefs as to affert, that attending a public ftage is to him a neceffary duty ? Or what defender of the ftage will be fo fanguine as to affirm, that it is, or that he hopes to fee it regulated fo as to be fafe or profitable to every mind ? And yet till this is the cafe, it evidently ftands condemned by the apoftolic rule.

Since writing the above, I have met with a pamphlet juft publifhed, entituled, *The Morality of Stage-plays ferioufly confidered.* This author convinces me, that I have, without fufficient ground, fuppofed, that no body would affirm attending plays to be a neceffary duty ; for he has either done it, or gone fo very near it, that probably, the next author upon the fame fide will do it in plain terms, and affert, that all above the ftation of tradefmen who do not go to the play-houfe, are living in the habitual negleft of their duty, and finning grievoufly againft God. If this looks ridiculous, it is none of my fault, for I fpeak it ferioufly ; and it is a much more natural confequence from his reafoning, than any he has drawn from it himfelf.

He confiders the paffage of the apoftle Paul, and fays, (which is true) that it holds only in the cafe of indifferent actions, but that we are to ' do good in the face of prejudice.' The way in which he fhews it to be doing good, is pretty fingular, but I pafs it by for a little, and obferve, that probably, he is not much accuftomed to commenting on fuch paffages of fcripture, for, even granting his unreafonable fuppofition, doing good indefinitely is not oppofed to indifferent actions in this, or any fimilar cafe. An action that is good in itfelf is indifferent when it may be exchanged for another ; when one as good, or

H   better,

better, may be put in its place. Nothing is oppofed to indifferent actions here, but what is indifpenfibly neceffary, and abfolutely binding, both in itfelf, and in its circumftances. And
indeed, tho' he is afraid at firft to fay fo, he feems to carry the
matter that length at laft, making his conclufion a little broader
than the premifes, and faying in the clofe of the paragraph up-
that fubject, ' What they do to this purpofe, either in oppof-
' ing the bad, or promoting the good, is MATTER OF DUTY,
' and their conduct in it is not to be regulated by the opinion
' of any perfon who is pleafed to take offence*.'

But how fhall we refute this new and wonderful doctrine of its
being neceffary that good men fhould attend the theatre. I cannot
think of a better way of doing it, than tearing off fome of the dra-
pery of words, with which it is adorned and difguifed, and fet-
ting his own affertions together in the form of a fyllogifm, ' The
' manager of every theatre muft fuit his entertainments to the
' company, and, if he is not fupported by the grave and fober,
' he muft fuit himfelf to the licentious and prophane.'——' We
' know that in every nation there muft be amufements and pub-
' lic entertainments, and the ftage has always made one in every
' civilized and polifhed nation. We cannot hope to abolifh it.'
——*Ergo,* According to this author, it is the duty of good
men to attend the ftage. But I leave the reader to judge, Whether, from the firft of his propofitions, which is a certain truth,
it is not more juft to infer, that, till the majority of thofe who
attend the ftage are good, its entertainment cannot be fit for a
Chriftian ear; and, becaufe that will never be, no Chriftian
ought to go there.

And what a fhameful begging of the queftion is his fecond
propofition, ' That we cannot hope to abolifh it.' It is hard
to tell what we may hope for in this age, but we infift that it
ought to be abolifhed. Nay, we do hope to abolifh it juft as
much as other vices; we cannot hope to fee the time when there
fhall be no gaming, cheating or lying, but we muft ftill preach
againft

againft all fuch vices, and will never exhort good men to go to gaming tables, to perfuade them to play fair, and leffen the wickednefs of the practice. In fhort, it is a full refutation of the extravagant affertion of good men being obliged, as matter of duty, to go to the theatre, that no fuch thing is commanded in the word of God, and therefore it is not, and cannot be neceffary to any †. And, fince it is evidently pernicious to great numbers, it can be lawful to none.

It would give Chriftians a much more juft, as well as more extenfive view of their duty, than they commonly have, if they would confider their relation to, and neceffary influence on one another. All their vifible actions have an effect upon others as well as themfelves. Every thing we fee or hear makes fome impreffion on us, though for the moft part unperceived, and we contribute, every moment, to form each others character. What a melancholy view, then, does it give us of the ftate of religion among us at prefent, that, when piety towards God has been excluded from many moral fyftems, and the whole of virtue confined to the duties of focial life, the better half of thefe alfo fhould be cut of, and all regard to the fouls of others forgotten or derided. Nothing, indeed, is left but a few expreffions of compliment, a few infignificant offices of prefent conveniency : For that which fome modern refiners have dignified with the name of virtue, is nothing elfe but polifhed luxury, a flattering of each other in their vices, a provocation of each other to fenfual indulgence, and that *friendfhip of the world*, which *is enmity with God*.

I would now afk the reader, after perufing the preceeding arguments againft the ftage, Whether he is convinced that it is inconfiftent with the character of a Chriftian, or not ? If he fhall

---

† It is proper here to remark, how natural it was to fuppofe, that the argument would be carried this length, when the ftage came to be pled for as ufeful in promoting the interefts of virtue. And therefore I have, above, taken notice, that thefe prophets run unfent, the propriety of which remark will now clearly appear.

shall anfwer in the negative, if he has ftill fome remaining argument in its defence, or fome method, which has not occurred
to me, to take off the force of the reafoning, I would next afk,
Whether it does not at leaft render it a doubtful point? Whether, joined with the concurrent teftimony of the beft and wifeft
men in all ages againft it, as it appeared among them, and the
impurity and corruption that ftill attends it, there is not at leaft
fome ground of hefitation? And, if fo much be but allowed, it
becomes on this very account unlawful to every Chriftian, who
takes the word of God for the rule of his conduct. There,
clear evidence, and full perfuafion is required before an action
can be lawful, and where doubt arifes we are commanded to
abftain. *Happy is he that condemneth not himfelf in that thing
which he alloweth : and he that doubteth is damned, if he eat :
becaufe he eateth not of faith, for whatfoever is not of faith is
fin* *.

Hitherto we have reafoned againft what is called a *well-regulated ftage*. That is to fay, inftead of attacking the corruptions
which now adhere to it, we have endeavoured to fhow, that
from the purpofe intended by it, from the prefent ftate and general tafte of mankind, and the nature of the thing itfelf, a public theatre is not capable of fuch a regulation, as to make it
confiftent with the purity of the Chriftian profeffion to attend
or fupport it. If any complain, that part of the above reafoning is too abftracted, and not quite level to the apprehenfion of
every reader, let it be remembered, that it is directed againft an
idea fo abftracted, that it never yet did, and, from what we have
feen, there is reafon to believe it never can exift. It is indeed
altogether imaginary, and is dreft up by every author who de-
fends it, in the manner and form that beft pleafes himfelf; fo
that it is infinitely lefs difficult to refute or fhew the unlawfulnefs of a well-regulated ftage, than to know what it is.

If the authors on this fubject would enter into particulars,
and give us a lift of the ufeful and inftructive plays with which

our

* Rom. xiv 22-23

our stage is to be served; lay down a plan of strict discipline, for introducing and preserving piety and purity among the actors; and shew us by whom the managers are to be chosen, and their fidelity tried, with some general rules for their conduct; it might soon be determined by plain and simple arguments, Whether such an entertainment could be safely permitted to a Christian, or not. But, when they give us no farther account of it, than by calling it a stage properly regulated, they involve themselves, at once, in obscurity, as to the very subject of their discourse. It is no wonder then, that they can make a parade with a few glittering, unmeaning phrases, as, picture of nature, moral lecture, amiable character, compassion for virtue in distress, decency of the drama, and several others. We are put to a stand what to say to such things, for if we speak of the impure sentiments of authors, or the wanton gesticulations of actors, all these are immediately given up, and yet the fort remains as entire as ever. Therefore, the method taken in this treatise, with all the disadvantages that attend it, was looked upon to be the best and the clearest that could be chosen; to shew, that those from whom a reformation of the stage must come, are neither able nor willing to make it; that the very materials of which this fine system is to consist are naught, and therefore, so must the product be always found upon trial.

It may indeed be matter of wonder, that among the many schemes and projects daily offered to the consideration of the public, there has never been any attempt to point out a plausible way, how the stage may be brought into, and kept in such a state of regulation, as to be consistent with the Christian character. There have been attempts to shew how money may be in a manner created, and the national debt paid, or the annual supplies raised, without burdening the subject. Some, who have nothing of their own, have endeavoured to persuade the rest of mankind, that it is the easiest thing imaginable to grow rich in a few years, with little labour, by the improvement of moor, moss, or bees. But none, so far as I have heard or seen, have
been

been so bold as to lay down a diftinct plan for the improvement
of the ftage. When this is added to the confiderations already
mentioned, it will confirm every impartial perfon in the belief,
that fuch improvement is not to be expected.

I hope therefore, there may now be fome profpect of fuccefs,
in warning every one who wifhes to be efteemed a difciple of
Chrift againft the ftage, as it hitherto has been, and now is. Experience is of all others the fureft teft of the tendency of any
practice. It is ftill more to be depended on than the moft plaufible and apparently conclufive reafoning, upon what hath never
yet been tried. Let us then confider, what hath been the fpirit
and tendency of almoft the whole plays which have been reprefented, from time to time, upon the ftage. Have not love and
intrigue been their perpetual theme, and that not in a common
and an orderly way, but with refiftance and impediments, fuch
as, rivalfhip and jealoufy, the oppofition of parents, and other
things of a fimilar nature, that the paffions may be ftrongly excited, and that the force of love, and its triumph over every ob-
ftacle, may be fet before the audience as a leffon? Is not the polite well-bred man the hero of fuch plays, a character formed
pon the maxims of the world, and chiefly fuch of them as are
moft contrary to the gofpel? Are not unchriftian refentment and
falfe honour the characterifticks of every fuch perfon?

What is the character of a clergyman when it is taken from
the ftage? If the perfon introduced is fuppofed to poffefs any
degree of ability, hypocrify is the leading part of the character.
But for the moft part, aukwardnefs, ignorance, dullnefs and
pedantry are reprefented as infeparable from men of that function. This is not done to correct thefe faults when appearing in
fome of that profeffion, by comparing them with others free
from fuch reproachful defects, but it is the character of the clergyman in general, who is commonly introduced fingle, and compared with the men acquainted with the world, very little to
his advantage. The truth is, it feems to be a maxim with dramatic authors, to ftrip men of every profeffion of their feveral
· ex-

excellencies, that the rake may be adorned with the spoils: even learning is commonly ascribed to him; how consistently with truth or nature, and consequently with taste itself, I leave the reader to determine.

And where can the plays be found, at least comedies, that are free from impurity, either directly, or by allusion and double meaning? It is amazing to think, that women who pretend to decency and reputation, whose brightest ornament ought to be modesty, should continue to abet, by their presence, so much unchastity, as is to be found in the theatre. How few plays are acted which a modest woman can see, consistently with decency in every part? and even when the plays are more reserved themselves, they are sure to be seasoned with something of this kind, in the prologue, or epilogue, the music between the acts, or in some scandalous farce with which the diversion is concluded. The power of custom and fashion is very great, in making people blind to the most manifest qualities and tendencies of things. There are ladies who frequently attend the stage, who if they were but once entertained with the same images in a private family, with which they are often presented there, would rise with indignation, and reckon their reputation ruined if ever they should return. I pretend to no knowledge of these things, but from printed accounts, and the public bills of what plays are to be acted, sometimes by the particular desire of ladies of quality, and yet may safely affirm, that no woman of reputation (as it is called in the world) much less of piety, who has been ten times in a play-house, durst repeat in company all that she has heard there. With what consistency they gravely return to the same schools of lewdness, they themselves best know.

It ought to be considered, particularly with regard to the younger of both sexes, that, in the theatre, their minds must insensibly acquire an inclination to romance and extravagance, and be unfitted for the sober and serious affairs of common life. Common or little things give no entertainment upon the stage, except when they are ridiculed. There must always be something grand

grand, furprizing and ftriking. In comedies, when all obftacles are removed, and the marriage is agreed on, the play is done. This gives the mind fuch a turn that it is apt to defpife ordinary bufinefs as mean or deride it as ridiculous. Aſk a merchant whether he chooſes, that his apprentices fhould go to learn exactnefs and frugality from the ftage. Or, whether he expects the moft punctual payments from thofe whofe generofity is ftrengthened there, by weeping over virtue in diftrefs. Suppofe a matron coming home from the theatre filled with the ideas that are there impreffed upon the imagination, how low and contemptible do all the affairs of her family appear, and how much muft fhe be difpofed, (befides the time already confumed), to forget or mifguide them ?

The actors themfelves are a fignal proof of this. How feldom does it happen, if ever, that any of them live fober and regular lives, pay their debts with honefty, or manage their affairs with difcretion ? They are originally men of the fame compofition with others, but their employment wholly incapacitates them for prudence or regularity, gives them a diffipation of mind and unftaidnefs of fpirit, fo that they cannot attend to the affairs of life. Nay, if I am rightly informed, that variety of characters which they put on in the theatre deprives them of common fenfe, and leaves them in a manner no character at all of their own. It is confidently faid, by thofe who have thought it worth while to make the trial, that nothing can be more infipid than the converfation of a player on any other fubject than that of his profeffion. I cannot indeed anfwer for this remark, having it only by report, and never having exchanged a word with one of that employment in my life. However, if it holds, a degree of the fame effect muft neceffarily be wrought upon thofe who attend the ftage.

But folly or bad management is not all that is to be laid to the charge of players : They are almoft univerfally vitious, and of fuch abandoned characters, as might juftly make thofe who defend the age afhamed to fpeak of learning virtue under ſuch masters. Can men learn piety from the profane, mortification from the sensual, or modesty from harlots? And will any deny that hired stage-players have always, and that deservedly, born these characters? Nay, tho' it could be supposed, that the spectators received no hurt to themselves, how is it possible that the performances of such persons can be attended, or their trade encouraged without sin?

This shews also, that attending a good play, even supposing there were a few unexceptionable, cannot be vindicated upon Christian principles. It is pled for the new tragedy lately introduced into our theatre, that it is an attempt to reform the stage, and make it more innocent, or more useful. What this piece is in itself, no body can say with certainty till it be published, tho' the account given of it by report is not exceeding favourable. But, let it be ever so excellent in itself, the bringing of one good play upon the stage is altogether insufficient; nay, is a method quite improper for reforming it. An author of a truly good piece would rather bury it in oblivion, than lend his own credit, and that of his work, for the support of those that are bad. A Christian can never attend the stage, consistently with his character, till the scheme in general be made innocent or useful. He must not sin himself, nor contribute to the sins of others, in a certain degree, because, unless he do so, they will sin without him in a higher degree. In short, such an attempt can be considered in no other light, than as encouraging a pernicious practice, and supporting a criminal association. The better the play is, or the better the characters of those who attend it are, the greater the mischief, because the stronger the temptation to others who observe it.

There is one inducement to attendance on the stage which hath more influence than all the arguments with which its advocates endeavour to colour over the practice: That it is become a part of fashionable education. Without it young persons of rank think they cannot have that knowledge of the

I   world

world which is neceſſary to their accompliſhment ; that they will be kept in ruſticity of carriage, or narrowneſs of mind, than which nothing is more contemptible in the eyes of the reſt of mankind ; that they will acquire the character of ſtiff and preciſe, and be incapable of joining in polite converſation, being ignorant of the topics upon which it chiefly turns. No better than theſe, it is to be feared, are the reaſons that many parents ſuffer their children to attend this and other faſhionable diverſions. How then ſhall we remove this difficulty ? Why truly, by ſaying with the apoſtle John, to ſuch as will receive it, *All that is in the world, the luſt of the fleſh, and the luſt of the eyes, and the pride of life, is not of the Father, but is of the world*. It is certainly the greateſt madneſs to ſeek the knowledge of the world by partaking with the wicked in their ſins. Whatever knowledge cannot otherwiſe be acquired, is ſhameful, and not honourable. How cruel then are theſe parents, who, inſtead of endeavouring to inſpire their children with a holy and manly reſolution, of daring to appear ſingular in an adherence to their duty, ſuffer them to be plunged in ſin, that they may not be defective in politeneſs. Why ſhould the world, or any thing elſe, be known, but in order to our ſpiritual improvement † ? There-

fore

---

* 1 John ii. 16.

† This is not meant to condemn all human accompliſhments, which have not an immediate reference to our religious improvement, but to affirm, that they ought to be kept in a juſt ſubordination and ſubſerviency, to the great and chief end of man. There are, no doubt, a great number of arts, both uſeful and ornamental, which have other immediate effects, than to make men holy ; and, becauſe they are, by the greateſt part of the world, abuſed to the worſt of purpoſes, they are conſidered as having no connexion with religion at all. But this is a miſtake ; for a good man will be directed in the choice and application of all ſuch arts, by the general and leading purpoſe of his life. And, as he who eats for no other or higher end than pleaſing his palate, is juſtly condemned as a mean and grovelling ſenſualiſt, ſo, whoever has no farther view in his education and accompliſhment, than to ſhine and make a figure in the faſhionable world, does not in that act the part of a **Chriſtian.** In ſhort, theſe arts are among the

number

fore, all that is truly valuable, muſt, by the very ſuppoſition, be innocently learned, and to bear with a noble diſdain the ſcoffs of more experienced ſinners is the greateſt glory.

Like to the above is another argument in favour of the ſtage, that men muſt have amuſements, and, that the ſtage is much better than many others, which would probably be put in its place. It is ſaid, that of all the time ſpent by the faſhionable part of the world, at preſent, in diverſions, that which they allot to the ſtage is moſt innocently, or leaſt hurtfully employed. Is there any more in this, than a declaration of the ſhameful luxury and degeneracy of the preſent age, an alarming token of approaching judgment? Do not ſuch perſons know, that all ſerious Chriſtians condemn every one of theſe criminal pleaſures, and will never allow it as any advantage to exchange one of them for another. But it is leſs ſurprizing to hear ſuch palliative arguments uſed in converſation: an author above referred to has been bold enough in print, to reaſon in the ſame way. He ſays, ' That no abuſe was ever ' admitted on any ſtage, but might paſs for perfect decency, ' when compared to what may have been often heard of, at a ' goſſipping, a merry-making, or a meeting of young fellows †.' Again, after telling us, that we cannot hope to aboliſh the ſtage, he ſays, ' And if we could, we ſhould only make way ' for the return of drunkenneſs, gaming, and rude cabals, which ' the more decent converſation and manners of civilized times ' have in a great meaſure aboliſhed.' I lay hold of this gentleman's reaſoning, who pleads for civilizing the world, and not ſanctifying it, as a confeſſion of the weakneſs of his cauſe, and a confirmation of all the arguments adduced in this treatiſe againſt the ſtage. For, if he meant to ſhow, that ſtage-plays

were

number of indifferent things, which ſhould be ſupremely and ultimately directed to the glory of God. When they are not capable of this, either immediately, or remotely, much more when they are contrary to it, they muſt be condemned.

† Morality of Stage plays ſeriouſly conſidered, p. 19.

were agreeable to the purity of the gospel, that drunkenness is worse (if indeed it be so) could be no evidence of it at all. He must therefore, if he speaks to any purpose, plead for the toleration of sinful diversions, because they are comparatively less sinful than others; and if that is the case, I detest his principles, and so will every Christian.

Having mentioned this author, perhaps it may be expected, that I should take some notice of the other arguments brought by him in defence of the stage. It is not easy either to enumerate, or comprehend them, they are thrown together in such confusion, and expressed in such vague and general terms. He says, (page 3d) ' The people of this island are not inferior to ' those of any other age or country whatever. This will be a ' presumption, that if plays are a poison, it is at least but slow in ' its operation.' And (p. 17.) ' We may venture to ask, Whether ' knowledge, whether industry and commerce have declined in this ' city (Edinburgh) since the play-house was first opened here. ' It will be owned, that they have rather increased.' I would venture to ask, What sort of an argument this is, and what follows from it, tho' both his assertions were allowed to be true, which yet may easily be in many respects controverted. If the stage, as he would insinuate, be the cause of our improvement, then is his argument self-contradictory, for we ought to be greatly inferior in purity to the people of other countries, who have enjoyed the reforming stage much longer, which is contrary to his supposition. The truth is, the stage is not the cause, but the consequence of wealth; and it is neither the cause nor consequence of goodness or knowledge, except in so far as it certainly implies more knowledge than uncultivated savages possess, and is only to be found in what this author calls civilized nations. How easy were it for me to name several vices unknown to Barbarians, which prevail in places of taste and polished manners. Should I at the same time insinuate, that these vices have contributed to improve us in knowledge and

taste,

taste, it would be just such an argument as is here used in favour of the stage, and the plain meaning of both is, the abuse of knowledge is the cause of it.

It were worth while to consider a little our improvements in knowledge in this age, which are often the boast of not the most knowing writers. Perhaps it may be allowed, that there is now in the world a good deal of knowledge of different kinds, but it is plain we owe it to the labours of our predecessors, and not our own. And therefore, it is to be feared, we may improve it no better than many young men do, who come to the easy possession of wealth of their father's getting. They neither know the worth nor the use of it, but squander it idly away, in the most unprofitable or hurtful pursuits. It is, doubtless, an easy thing at present, to acquire a superficial knowledge, from Magazines, Reviews, Dictionaries, and other helps to the slothful student. He is now able, at a very small expence, to join the beau and the scholar, and triumphs in the taste of this enlightened age, of which he hath the comfort to reflect, that he himself makes a part. But, for our mortification, let us recollect, that, as several writers have observed, human things never continue long at a stand. There is commonly a revolution of knowledge and learning, as of riches and power. For as states grow up from poverty to industry, wealth, and power, so, from these they proceed to luxury, and vice, and by them are brought back to poverty and subjection. In the same manner, with respect to learning, men rise from ignorance to application, from application to knowledge, this ripens into taste and judgment, then, from a desire of distinguishing themselves, they supperadd affected ornaments, become more fanciful than solid, their taste corrupts with their manners, and they fall back into the gulph of ignorance. The several steps of these gradations commonly correspond ; and if we desire to know in what period of each, we of this nation are at present, it is probable, we are in the age of luxury as to the first, and, in the eve at least, of a false and frothy taste as to

learn-

learning, and may therefore fear, that as a late very elegant writer expresses it, We shall relapse fast into Barbarism.

Another argument adduced by this author, is, that the apostle Paul, in preaching at Athens, quotes a sentence from one of the Greek poets, and, in writing to the Corinthians, has inserted into the sacred text a line from a Greek play which now subsists.—— ' This, (he says), is sufficient to connect the defence of plays ' with the honour of scripture itself.' The fact is not denied, though he has given but a poor specimen of the knowledge of this age, by mistaking, in the first of these remarks, the expression quoted by the apostle : for, this sentence, *In him we live, and move, and have our being*, which, he says, is a very sublime expression, and beautifully applied by the apostle, was not cited from the poet, but the following, *For we are also his offspring*. But supposing he had, (as he easily might) have hit upon the true citation, What follows from it ? Did ever any body affirm, that no poet could write, or no player could speak any thing that was true ? And what is to hinder an inspired writer from judging them out of their own mouths ? What concern has this with the stage ? If it implies any defence of the stage in general, it must imply a stronger defence of the particular play and poem, from which the citations are taken. Now, I dare say, neither this author, nor any other will affert, that these are in all respects agreeable to the Christian character. These citations do no other way connect the defence of the stage with the honour of scripture, than a minister's citing, in writing or discourse, a passage from Horace or Juvenal, would connect the defence of all the obscenity that is to be found in the rest of their works, with the honour of preaching.

The only thing further in this essay not obviated in the preceeding discourse, is what he says on the subject of the poor. ' That the expence laid out on the stage does not hinder the ' charitable supply of the poor, and that they suffer no loss by ' it, for it comes at last into the hands of the poor, and is paid

' as

' as the price of their labour.—Every player muft be maintain-
' ed, clothed and lodged.' It does not fuit with any prefent purpofe to enter into controverfial altercation, or to treat this author with that feverity he deferves ; and therefore I fhall only
fay, that his reafoning upon this fubject is the very fame from
which doctor Mandeville draws this abfurd and hated confequence, ' Private vices are public benefits.'

The truth is, a ferious perfon can fcarce have a ftronger evidence of the immorality of the ftage, than the perufal of thefe
little pieces of fatyr, which have been publifhed, in fo great a
variety, againft the prefbytery of Edinburgh, within thefe few
weeks, becaufe of their public admonition againft it. They offer no other defence, but deriding the preaching of the gofpel,
blafphemoufly comparing the pulpit with the ftage, and recri-
mination upon fome who are fuppofed to live inconfiftently with
their character. It is not worth while to fpend three words in determining, whether drunkennefs, deceit and hypocrify are worfe
than the ftage or not, but if that is the ftrongeft argument that
can be offered in its fupport, wo to all thofe who attend it. The
new reformed tragedy, has, indeed, been very unlucky in its advocates. There is an old faying, that a man is known by his
company. If this be true alfo of a play, which one would think
it fhould, as it muft be chiefly to the tafte of congenial minds,
by thofe who have appeared in defence of Douglafs, it is a work
of very little merit.

It may be expected, that, having brought this performance
on the field, I fhould add fome further reflections, upon the
aggravated fin of *minifters* writing plays, or attending the ftage.
But, though it is a very plain point, and indeed becaufe it is fo,
it would draw out this treatife to an immoderate length. If any
man makes a queftion of this, he muft be wholly ignorant of the
nature, and importance of the minifterial character and office.
Thefe therefore it would be neceffary to open up diftinctly, and
to confider the folemn charge given to minifters in fcripture, to
                                                    watch

watch over the souls of their people, as those *who must give an account unto God*; to give themselves wholly to their duty, since some of those committed to them are, from day to day, entering on an unchangeable state, whose blood, when they die unconverted, shall be required at the hand of the unfaithful pastor. None can entertain the least doubt upon this subject, who believe the testimony of Moses and the prophets, of Christ and his apostles, and, if they believe not their writings, neither will they believe my words.

Instead therefore of endeavouring to prove, I will make bold to affirm, that writing plays is an employment wholly foreign to the office, and attending theatrical representations an entertainment unbecoming the character of a minister of Christ? And must not both, or either of them be a sacrilegious abstraction of that time and pains, which ought to have been laid out for the benefit of his people? Is it not also flying in the face of a clear and late act of parliament, agreeably to which the lords of council and session not long ago found the stage contrary to law, in this country? And tho' the law is eluded, and the penalty evaded, by advertising a concert after which will be performed *gratis*, a tragedy, *&c.* Yet, surely, the world in judging of characters, or a church court in judging of the conduct of its members, will pay no regard to the poor and shameful evasion. Can we then think of this audacious attempt at the present juncture, without applying to ourselves the words of Isaiah, *And in that day did the Lord God of hosts call to weeping, and to mourning, and to baldness, and to girding with sackcloth, and behold joy and gladness, slaying oxen and killing sheep, eating flesh and drinking wine: let us eat and drink for to morrow we die. And it was revealed in mine ears by the Lord of hosts, surely, this iniquity shall not be purged from you till ye die, saith the Lord of hosts*, Isa. xxii. 12, 13, 14.

F I N I S.

5 An address to the Synod of Lothian and Tweedale Concerning Mr Home's Tragedy and Mr Hume's Essays

Written in 1757 after David Hume's dedication had been printed in his *Four Dissertations*, the anonymous writer attacks both him and John Home as heretical authors. The main thrust of the argument is that Home as a Scottish clergyman has brought the Church into disrepute by writing plays which condone unchristian acts such as suicide. Furthermore, he has compounded this error by neglecting his parishioners in order to indulge in this blasphemy. The 'theatrical clergy' are also attacked because of scandal they have brought, not just to Edinburgh, but to Britain as a whole. John Witherspoon is cited as having provided incontestable arguments confirming the sinfulness of the stage. Also of note is his reference to George Anderson, who provided arguments against the stage long before the *Douglas* controversy in his *The Use and Abuse of Diversions: A Sermon on Luke XIX 13* (1733), and was instrumental in closing down the theatre which Allan Ramsay had established.

An *Address* to the *Synod of* Lothian *and* Tweedale, *concerning Mr* Home's *Tragedy and* Hume's *Moral Essays.*

Reverend Fathers and Gentlemen,

AS you are now met in a synodical way, to cognosce the conduct of your several presbyteries, and to hear complaints, and to approve or disapprove their conduct and management concerning what hath been before them since last synod; you are appointed both by God and man to be watchmen over your different flocks, and in a synodical way to watch over and inspect the conduct of one another. You are guardians of your own and your people's spiritual rights and privileges, and bound to do all in your power to keep them from being invaded; and also guardians of the precepts, laws, and statutes of Christ the head, and of his church you represent.

Seeing you are met to look into the conduct of your several presbyteries, and members whereof they are made up, and to hear what complaints are made concerning them; and how far they have acted agreeably to the rules of Christ in his word, and the rules agreeable thereto given them by the orders and acts of this church, and to approve or censure as you find cause; you know the eyes of God and the world are upon you at this time in a special manner, as there have been sinful and disorderly deeds done by some of your members, such as, considering all aggravating circumstances, surely the like was never done before by any clergyman Protestant or Popish, which hath given great offence and scandal to all that have the glory of God, the interest of religion, and credit of this church, at heart.

That tragedy of Douglas, composed and sold, in order to be acted by Mr John Home, hath put such an affront on the church of Scotland, as your greatest indignation and highest censure will not be sufficient fully to countervail. Surely such a nonsensical, profane, blasphemous, atheistical piece, worse was never wrote by any Pagan. How contemptible must the church of

Scotland now be in the eyes of other proteſtant churches!
She once their glory, now their reproach. No doubt
you have heard what noiſe and work was at London, what wonder and curioſity it raiſed to ſee the monſtrous thing, a play wrote by a Scotch clergyman, ſold
by him to be acted in a public theatre; a monſtrous
thing indeed, ſuch as was never heard of in the world
before.

How do the numerous infidels and profane glory o-
ver you, and in you, now when they have got the
Scotch clergy on their ſide? Thoſe that were wont to
be ſo ſtrict in their doctrine and diſcipline, now many
of them ſcarce differ from them in any thing; as we ſee
an openly profeſſed infidel dedicating his eſſays (ſome
of which were prohibite printing by the influence of the
Engliſh clergy, on account of their wickedneſs) to the
now famous Mr John Home, as his dearly beloved
friend; telling the world, he differs from him only in
a few ſpeculative points, which is a thing few, if any,
doubt of; neither can the world have any better opinion
of ſuch as appear for his vindication and protection.
It is well known what intimacy that infidel gentleman
hath with many of our clergy, and how much they
have befriended him, ſo as perſons cannot help thinking they are no enemies to his principles.

It is owned, ſome of reputation among the Engliſh
clergy have wrote tragedies, yet a very rare thing, and
what gave offence. But were they ſo abominably wicked as the tragedy of Douglas? or did they ſeveral times
leave their charge for many months, travelling from
one nation to another, to ſell them at a high price,
bringing them to ſtateſmen and play-actors to get them
acted? No; they wrote them for amuſement, not to be
acted, yet were they very ill employed, as their doing it
countenanced, and is pled in behalf of others, which is
no juſt reaſoning, ſeeing the beſt of men have done bad
things. It is no better employment than David's when
writing to Joab concerning Uriah, and giving him his
own dead-warrant to carry; even ſo do ſuch writers
betray ſimple fools to their deſtruction. Was it ever
heard of that a clergyman, after having wrote a play
and ſold it, went openly to ſee it acted, complimented
tickets to his pariſhioners, and carried his elders with

him? Oh such shameful impudence, daring God and the church! What reproach to Christianity and this church doth it bring? who can hear of it, but must be filled with indignation and abhorrence? The highest church-censure is by far too little; he deserves not only to be cast out of the church, but out of Christendom. The immorality and sinfulness of the stage hath been fully laid open by many judicious divines; none who deserve a religious character will ever vindicate it. Mr Law hath clearly proved attendance upon and encouraging of the stage to be absolutely inconsistent with real piety and the power of godliness. Mr Witherspoon hath sufficiently answered all the vain pretences and cavillings that are offered in behalf of the stage. None can be ignorant of the sinfulness of it, but such as are wilfully or judicially blind, and given up to the power of corrupt passions.

You see what manner of spirit they are of who write and appear in defence of the stage; how they ridicule and reproach the least evidence or concern for the interests of religion, what infidelity, profanity, and malignity their scurrilous papers are stuffed with. And as for those of the ministry that appear in vindication of the stage, or of the theatrical brethren, that is not the only exceptionable part of their character; the unsoundness of their doctrine, their immorality and offensive behaviour otherwise, makes it no surprise that they do so. And the many infidel gentry, with the profane rakes and lascivious debauchees, and the poor vain ladies, who spend their time, and live like butterflies, unprofitable to themselves or others, these are the stanch advocates for the play-house.

It is needless to say any thing concerning the immorality and sinfulness of the stage, seeing it hath ever been testified against, and looked on as diametrically opposite to the power of godliness. All that are taught of God are taught to deny and abhor it, seeing it is not a covered snare, but the broad way to destruction. We know there are many carnal nominal professors of different characters who attend and vindicate the stage, but such are not to be esteemed real Christians: and whatever high station or repute for worldly wisdom such may have, their sentiments concerning spiritual things, or even the morality of things, are not to be regarded, seeing their light is but darkness, and they are under the power of corrupt affections. It is certain the stage was first erected by Pagans, at the instigation of the devil whom they worshipped; and when public calamities befel them, their oracles ordered them to erect theatres, and frequent them more; which we must suppose to be the reason why our modern infidels or heathens are so mad upon plays now in the time of public calamity.

Play writers and actors pretending to teach morality, and reform the world by the stage, do but act such a part as the seven sons of Scheva the Jew, who pretended to cast out devils, which answered them, " Jesus I " know, and Paul I know, but who are ye?" and the man, in whom the devil was, overcame them, and wounded them. So shamefully will they be disappointed, if any expect to learn morality there. It is not Christianity, it is only morality play-actors pretend to teach. Surely none that go there ought to pretend to have more morality than their teachers; or why do they go to learn at them? It is well known how moral the lives of play-actors are. But a little morality is all the religion such as attend the play-house seek after as the whole of their religion, and scarce any of them come that length, but become like the Pharisees disciples seven-fold more the children of the devil than before. The play-house is as evidently the synagogue of Satan as your houses for public worship are the churches of Christ; and play-actors appear as much and more the ministers of Satan than many of you the ministers of Christ. And what can those ministers be esteemed to be, who will appear to vindicate it, or any that have countenanced it? Christian charity doth not teach to think well of them. How do they contradict and invalidate their profession? Dare any such say to their people, " Be ye followers of me, as I am of Christ?" Wo to the world because of offences, and wo to them by whom such offences come. What a scandalous thing is it to hear of judges and elders attending the rendezvous of infidels and profane debauchees, who wallow in lascivious wickedness, and attend the play-house to feed their adulterous eyes? and our gentry and burghers

sending their children to the devil's school to learn lasciviousness, prodigality, and vanity? what a dreadful account will such parents have to give?

I have seen a pamphlet wrote in a smooth sophistical
way, proving the morality of the stage, but it can take
with none but such as are wilfully blind. It is said to
be wrote by a preacher, successor to David Home Esq;
the infidel; indeed the author appears to be of the same
stamp; and he pretends to prove it from scripture;
but by his manner of arguing he will as soon prove the
sanctity of the devil by his confessions of the most important truth.

It is boasted by the theatrical clergy, that Mr Home
and his brethren in iniquity have transgressed no act of
assembly or church-law. It may be remembred by
the same gentlemen, how that when that argument was
justly pled on the behalf of the reverend and faithful
Mr Gillespie, they answered he had transgressed against
the spirit of all acts and church-laws, though his pleading the benefit of them was made a ground of his deposition. If the conduct of Mr Home and his brethren
be not diametrically opposite to the spirit of Christianity,
and the intention of all acts of assembly and church-laws
concerning the behaviour and conduct of the ministers
of this church, it is now before you to determine.
There are none of you but know what scandal and offence those ministers have given in Edinburgh, at London, and through all Britain; and no doubt is or will
soon be known through many places of the world. It
will be inquired what you have done concerning them;
the glory of God, the interest of religion, and honour
of this church, is at stake; you are under no difficulty,
if you eye the directions given in scripture and by this
church; but if you be conducted by modern and civil
policy, you will be perplexed. The eyes of the English
clergy are upon you in a special manner. Oh! let not
the enemies of religion, and those that watch for your
stumbling, be permitted to glory over you. Blessed be
God there are yet some among you that have the interest of religion, and honour of this church, at heart:
Oh that they, like Phinehas, may now appear zealous,
and be made instruments of turning away wrath.

The conduct of the presbytery of Haddington will

come before you. Notwithstanding the letters sent them by the presbytery of Edinburgh and others, their conduct looks like an approbation of their dear brother. But the truth is, little or no better could be expected of them. It is hoped you will take notice of them, and approve or censure as you find cause.

It is also hoped the conduct of the presbytery of Edinburgh will be laid before you by those faithful ministers who entered their dissent, or by some others who have the glory of God, the interest of religion, and honour of this church, at heart. The presbytery was brought under a kind of necessity to go forward with the process which the deceast worthy Mr Anderson had begun before them concerning Home's Moral essays, because the council for the delinquent not only permitted but desired them, as he knew Mr Home had so many friends among them; yet it surprised some, that they should judicially accept of a pamphlet, said to be wrote by the author of the essays, as an answer to the objections made against them by Mr Anderson and others, and yet never require who the author was.

It is presumed the essays and objections made against them by Mr Anderson and others, learned judicious gentlemen and ministers, with Mr Anderson's verification by many fair and candid quotations from the essays, with the author's answer to them, are known to most of you; as also, what the presbytery of Edinburgh have done in the process. There was indeed some of the presbytery, who before them did read some passages of the essays, and exposed the wicked and blasphemous principles they contained; but the friends of the essays, knowing they were better able to carry their point by votes than arguments, answered nothing. You all know what just ground of offence that book hath given to Christians. It is evident, both by the essays and answers to the objections against them, the author is careful of being suspected to be a Christian: though he sometimes speaks of revealed religion, but though he writes as a philosopher, and not as a theologue, yet by his reasonings he saps the foundation of our Christian faith.

Indeed he appears to be in the dark and bewildred, and knows not how to reconcile himself, yet the most candid interpretation will not allow one to think one of his station to be so weak, as to write in such a way with a good intention. You know, it is the ordinary way of erroneous and heritical preachers and writers, to give and take, to mix and confound truth and error, that so they may stagger, jumble and perplex their hearers or readers, leaving a way to escape to themselves if questioned, and when questioned, do pick out what truth may be found as a salvo for their herefy. He speaks of a feelling, I suppose peculiar to himself, which he calls deceitful, imposed by God, as if rational creatures could not so well be governed without it, and yet makes this deceitful feelling to be the only sure test by which we know the truth of things. Whatever the author's intention might be, evident it is, the scope of those essays in their native tendency would lead the reader to scepticism and infidelity, or as I see it exprest in the introduction of the letter to the presbytery of Haddingtoun, to teach the wicked how to take a short cut with a condemning conscience.

It may be justly expected, that the reverend Synod and assembly will take the consideration of these essays into their own hand, as they are so dangerous and liable to stagger the belief of such as are not well fixed in their principles, and of strengthning the hands of the many infidels, sceptics and profane among us.

It is known, that when the consideration of David Home Esquire's infidel and profane books was laid before, and urged by, some faithful ministers in the committee of overtures, in order to be laid before the last assembly, on the slight pretence that it was the way to make them more sought after, it was rejected; but how did infidels, and the profane, triumph in finding so many ministers befriend them.

However, it is yet hoped there will be found some faithful and zealous members of the ensuing assembly, that will yet get them brought in with the essays, in order that those books may be stigmatized, and the authors censured, especially as one of them is said to be done by an elder of this church.

With too much truth it is said, Popery greatly prevails among us, but we have good ground to think infidelity prevails much faster; all we have to boast of, is pure standards, and good acts of assembly, which is only a standing witness against us.

It is the obfervation of fome, that notwithftanding the corruption that prevails, yet ferious religion, and real godlinefs, is not fuch a rare thing in city or country as among our gentry and minifters, who mutually corrupt one another both in principle and practice. How many are there among them who like the fons of Eli, make the facrifices of the Lord to be abhorred ? If you the fathers of the church do not reftrain and frown on thofe who make themfelves vile (fome of whom break the public peace, and deferve to be profecute before civil courts) confider what was threatned againft Eli and his fons, and how foon it was inflicted.

How many tender Chriftians are racked in their confcience? They fee the evil of feparation, yet cannot countenance their parifh minifters, becaufe of the unfoundnefs of their doctrine and fcandal of their lives ; it is not peoples giddinefs, but their tendernefs, that makes fo many leave the eftablifhed church.

Thefe plain truths, in a coarfe drefs, are not laid before you to offend and fhame you before the world, but to awaken your attention : they are things manifeft, and deferve the moft ferious attention of a Synod or Affembly: as each of you have a particular charge, fo all of you have a general charge of the whole church. Things will probably come before you that will evidence what manner of fpirit you are of: as faid before, the eyes of God, and other churches, efpecially the Englifh clergy, are upon you; and your conduct in thefe things, fo important to the truth and the honour of the church and religion, will be enquired after.

Oh let it not be faid of this church as it is, Ifaiah li. " There is none to take her by the hand, of all the " fons fhe hath brought up ;" and Lam. i. 8, 10. " All " that honoured her defpife her, becaufe they have " feen her nakednefs; for they have feen the heathen " entered into the fanctuary, whom thou didft command " fhould not enter into the congregation."

Bleffed be God there is yet a goodly number thro' the different corners of the church, of faithful gofpel minifters ; Oh that they were fo filled with a fpirit of zeal for the glory of God and intereft of religion, that if our church judicatories do not exoner themfelves, and give public teftimony againft our growing evils, yet that they may do it jointly for their own exoneration.

6 A Letter to the Reverend the Moderator, and the Members of the Presbytery Of Haddingtoun

This anonymous tract prefaces its letter with an attack on the Moderates for defending David Hume's writings while praising the efforts of George Anderson who unsuccessfully attempted to bring heresy charges against him. The tract finds it reprehensible that Hume shows not the slightest shame for his 'infidelity'. The letter itself berates John Home for neglecting his parishioners while attempting to sell them tickets for his play, a play which contains 'intrigue, revenge, bloodshed and self-murder'. Hume's work on suicide is cited as the source for the doctrine of self-murder that the author finds so abhorrent. The punishment for the author of the tragedy should not merely be deposition, but excommunication.

A
LETTER

TO THE REVEREND

The MODERATOR,

AND

MEMBERS

OF THE

Presbytery of HADDINGTOUN.

Matth. xviii. 17.——*Tell it unto the church.*
Col. iv. 17. *And say unto Archippus, Take heed to the ministry which thou hast received in the Lord.*——
Isaiah lviii. 1. *Cry aloud and spare not, lift up thy voice like a trumpet, shew my people their transgressions.*——

EDINBURGH:
Printed in the Year M,DCC,LVII,

UNTO the faithful ministers of the church of Scotland, be it known, that the disorders in churchmen are now come to the greatest height. What by error in doctrine, what by error and neglect in discipline, and what by the light, vain, indecent, and disorderly practices and conversations of her ministers and managers, in delity and profanity grows and increases so fast, that it threatens to overrun all: it hath now audaciously gathered head, and openly brow-beats and bears down the very form of religion. Now when they find so great a party among the clergy countenance and protect the authors of the vilest infidel-books ever was printed, infidels apprehending they have so many of the clergy that favour their principles, and their number so increasing, are emboldned to proceed still in composing and printing books in favour of Infidelity.

Now the reverend Mr George Anderson is dead, who valiantly appeared for the cause of his God and his Saviour; yet he was suffered to stand alone, to the reproach of Edinburgh.

Indeed the presbytery of Edinburgh took the process he commenced against the author and publishers of Hume's moral essays into their own hands; but dismissed it at an after meeting, by only remarking it contained many unguarded expressions and exceptional passages, which might be dangerous to some good people. In the debate some there were who approved the book, yet some condemned it as heretical. Mess. W--st--r & L---say dissented, so it is open to the synod. It was generally said, the author appeared to have no bad intention; yet many think the intention appears to be, to teach the wicked how to take a short cut with a condemning conscience —— But David Home is not afraid nor ashamed to own his Infidelity; how far it is your duty, and the interest of this Christian church, to permit him, and other professed Infidels, to enjoy a right to the privileges of Christians, do you determine.

By the judicious, matters appear to be near some remarkable crisis. If you thus supinely sit still regardless, and do not rouse up to some effectual endeavours, many will suffer whose blood will be required at your hand. If you are afraid or ashamed to own the cause of God according to your profession, God will raise up instruments to do his pleasure. If you be not ashamed, you have nothing to fear; you have the laws of God and man on your side, which not only permit, but command you. Oh that those cool sedate easy men, who love to slumber, and care not to disturb their own repose, could be roused up to put to their hand when they see their enemies so active to undermine them; or take some moderate method of their own, agreeable to the polite world, that may be effectual to suppress vice, and bring about reformation, and not appear yet more void of zeal than passions.

Esther iv. 14. For if thou altogether holdest thy peace at this time, then shall there deliverance arise to the church from another place; but thou and thy father's house shall be destroyed. Isaiah lvi. 10. Ezek. xx. 30. Zeph. iii. 18. Amos 6. and Mic. iii. throughout.

A

LETTER, &c.

EDINBURGH for eight or ten days hath been filled with the clamour, that Mr John Home in Athelstane-ford, one of your number, has composed and sold the tragedy of Douglas, in order to be acted in the play-house of the Canongate at Edinburgh, and which play hath accordingly been acted there, to the offence and scandal of all who have any regard to religion. And so impious hath he been, that out of zeal to promote the interest of Satan, he sent out a considerable number of tickets to one or more of his own elders, to be distributed among his parishioners, in order to seduce them to come in and see the play, which they did accordingly. And he himself was witness several times to the acting of the play; as were also several other ministers, of whom some came from a considerable distance. But how consistent this is with the profession and character of a minister of Jesus Christ, and with the doctrine and spirit of Christianity, let all real Christians judge.

And as the acting of all plays exhibites scenes of vanity, lewdness and impiety, so this tragedy of his is, in a special manner, horridly wicked. It is wholly made up of intrigue, revenge, bloodshed and self-murder, intermixed with strange oaths,

A 2

oaths, and blafphemous fpeeches againft God, which filled many of the fpectators with horrour and abhorrence at the profanation of facred things; and the moft folemn act of religious worfhip towards God is profaned in an open ftage, before the crowd, by one of the moft abandoned of all characters, exhibited praying: and in the play he fets forth, not for caution, but rather for example, the curfed principles and doctrine of his intimate acquaintance and beloved friend, David Home the Infidel, concerning the warrantablenefs of felf-murder.

Have players been banifhed both by Pagans and Papifts; and fhall minifters of the church of Scotland be allowed to fupport and furnifh materials for them wherewith to ferve the devil in feducing fouls? are not thofe who furnifh them materials firft and moft criminally guilty? yea, are not they as Beelzebub to the inferior devils, who furnifh materials, and fet fuch vile creatures a-work to feduce and deftroy fouls?

He is a ftrange kind of bifhop who employs play-actors for his curates; however, the doctrines, curates and bifhop, appear to be all of a piece. We fee, by the growth of Infidelity, the fatal effects of thus permitting David and John Homes to go on after the manner they do without being cenfured. John Home's is fuch audacious and impudent wickednefs, that it is only parallelled by Zimri's, Numb. xxv. 10. and juft fo timed as his was, who, when the congregation were weeping before the Lord, under the immediate effects of the juft vengeance of God for that particular fin, brings out his whore in the fight of the congregation; even fo hath he done, and proftituted religion to finful diverfion

by

by such abandoned creatures.　Shall none of our priests be found like Phinehas, who was zealous for his God and for his people, and turned away the wrath of God, so as the plague was stayed?

It is now said to you, who is on the Lord's side? Exod. xxxii. 26. Confider what is said, Deut. xxxiii. 9. of the sons of Levi, how they gathered themselves to Moses, and regarded not parents or brethren in the caufe of God.——— It is now said to you, who will rise up for me againſt the workers of iniquity? Pfal. xciv. 16. who will ſtand up for me againſt the evil doers?

Do you not fee the pernicious effects of your complying with the way of the world, and of your ſupine careleſneſs and negligence? hath not God faid to the ſons of Eli, 1 Sam. ii. 30. " They that honour me, I will honour, but " they that deſpiſe me, ſhall be lightly efteem- " ed?" Is it not ſo at this day? Mal. ii. 9. " Therefore I have made you contemptible and " baſe before all people, according as ye have " not kept my ways, but have been partial in " the law." How have miniſters made them- ſelves contemptible by acting ſo much below and unſuitable to their character, in miniſtring to and attending the play-houſe? Edinburgh, for ſeveral days, was filled with deriding contem- ptuous ſpeeches and converſation in all companies concerning them: what wanton, ludicrous pa- pers have been fold and handed about, to their reproach? One would think, tho' there were no- thing of the Spirit of God to ſtir up, the ſpirit of men of honour would ſtir them up, and not ſuffer their reputation and profeſſion to be ſo reproached, ſtained and polluted.

Let it not be ſaid of the church of Scotland, that ſhe harbours and protects ſuch enemies to

the gospel, and allows the ministers of the play-
house, to fill her pulpits, and enjoy her bene-
fices. Do you think such can serve the interest
of Christ? is Satan's kingdom divided? will
Satan cast out Satan? or should one be allowed
to partake of the table of the Lord and the table
of devils, by harbouring such as they? do not
the profane say, You are all alike, and think
you approve his conduct? " Purge out there-
" fore the old leaven ;" and let it be seen the
whole lump is not yet leavened, 1 Cor. v. 7. I
hope you do not want number so much, had
you spirit and zeal. While you enjoy your be-
nefices, will you appear to be like Gallio, Acts xviii
17. caring for none of those things? Let it be seen
we have yet some ministers who dare to appear
zealously for the glory of God, the interests of
Christ, and credit of religion. You must either
depose and cast out John Home and his adherents, or be cast off yourselves. What
tender Christian can cordially join with them
who adhere to and join themselves with him as
a brother? surely none that would show due
regard to the glory of God, and the benefit of
their own souls, can do it.

Deposition is as much the ordinance of Christ
as ordination, excommunication as baptism.
Though there was no particular church act a-
gainst ministers composing or attending plays,
seeing it could hardly be supposed any would
be so openly profane, you have enough to lay
to John Home's charge, for which he deserves
not only to be deposed, but excommunicated.
Neither can you sufficiently exoner yourselves
without doing it. I have heard there was a
process commenced against Mr Home before
                                                his

his presbytery, with difficulty begun, and shame-
fuly deserted: and it is long since it was said,
that if he could find bread any other way, he
wanted to demit. Now that he hath joined
himself with another kind of society, let them
have him altogether, seeing it suits his genius
and disposition so well: but by no means ought
a dimission to be received from him; he ought
to be solemnly cast out.

Wherefore, out of obedience to Christ, and
love to the offender, put away from among yourselves that wicked person; deliver him over to Satan for the destruction of the flesh, that the spirit
may be saved in the day of the Lord, 1 Cor. v.5.

Ah the church of Scotland, once the glory
of the Protestant churches for the purity of her
doctrine and discipline, now become a reproach
to Christianity; while she permits the profane
and erroneous, yea Infidels, to bear office in
her, and casts out such as faithfully and sted-
fastly adhere to her doctrine and discipline! those
who in times past would have been excommunicate the congregation, are permitted to serve
in the sanctuary and at the altar!

According to the advertiser a solemn farce
should have concluded the play, called the Address, and the five principal characters in their
true colours. But it came out to be only five
lords of session and barons of exchequer exhibiting their regard to the act of parliament
prohibiting the play-house; and several of John
Home's fellow-presbyters, brethren in iniquity,
exhibiting themselves in their true colours.

But we may venture to assure the public, that
though the house of Baal was for six or seven
nights filled from end to end, scarce ever any of
the

the true worshippers of God could be found in it.

The church can be at no loss in wanting such ministers, however agreeable to those of their own kidney in their facetious way, allowing and taking all freedoms ; whose gifts are only to soothe the simple, and stir up the angry passions of the judicious ; whose cloke is so thin and ragged they seldom wear it, nor even carry it to the pulpit. I am, &c.

IT is certain that the stage is the device of Pagans, instigate by the devil whom they worshipped. Is it rational to suppose the devil intended the exposing of vice to ridicule, or virtue for imitation? or dare any say that the stage ever had that effect? or can it be denied but that it hath been the chief means of introducing all kind of impiety, lewdness, effeminacy and debauchery? hath not the ruin of empires and cities been attributed to the stage by many learned and judicious writers? is not the dismal state of Britain at this day chiefly to be attributed to the stage, which hath introduced such manner of living, that our statesmen and chief officers in army & navy are so effeminate and unmanned, counsel, conduct and courage withdrawn, and also the whole nation overrun with licentiousness both in church and state, so that we are become a reproach to Christianity and derision to our enemies?——How evident is it, that since the stage got footing in Edinburgh, infidelity, contempt of religion, and all manner of lasciviousness, profanity and debauchery, hath increased still more and more, to the ruin of many families and once hopeful youths? and its baneful influence is spread through the whole nation.———God hath long warned us by his word, now he cries by his providence. Britain appears near some remarkable crisis: sword and famine threaten us. Edinburgh sinks under the burden of guilt and expence incurred by the stage.——If judges and magistrates, in obedience to God and the king, will not now suppress, but rather countenance and protect, that fountain of our sin and misery, let them answer it to God and posterity.——But let ministers be faithful to those for whom they must be accountable, and not be afraid or ashamed in plain words to warn and exhort all against the stage, and publickly debar from the Lord's table all such as approve themselves in their partaking of the table of devils, which joining in the play-house doth evidently infer. Then shall ministers be so far kept from accession to the sins of others, and that just ground of offence be removed, 1 Cor. x. 20, 21.

HUME'S DEDICATION AND RESPONSE

7 David Hume's *Dedication*

Hume's ostentatious tribute to *Douglas* was signed, on the 3rd of January 1757, less than a month after the first Edinburgh performance of the play. The tone of the piece is deliberately overstated, for Hume hoped that his position as a critic of note would draw attention and debate to his friend's work. The storm that surrounded the dedication, and the blizzard of critical response, shocked even the mild-mannered philosopher, to the extent that he attempted to suppress it, fearing that his support of the play would become another stick with which the Church could beat the playwright. On the 20th January he instructed his publisher in London to pull the dedication from his *Four Dissertations*, one of which was the sceptical essay, 'The Natural History of Religion'. However, the dedication began to appear in editions published in February 1757, and it went on to appear in several weekly papers, and in the *Scots Magazine* the following June. Writing to Adam Smith, Hume felt that he ought to do all that he could to assist his fellow countryman whose path to fame had, according to him, come under some 'unaccountable obstructions'. The dedication is the basis for much of the literary response to the play, both in Scotland and England and was highly successful in attracting a keen focus on the work, even if a significant number of the responses to it were savagely critical.

TO

The Reverend Mr. Hume,

Author of DOUGLAS, a Tragedy.

MY DEAR SIR,

IT was the practice of the an-
tients to addrefs their compofitions
only to friends and equals, and to render their dedications monuments of
regard and affection, not of fervility
and flattery. In thofe days of ingenuous and candid liberty, a dedication
did honour to the perfon to whom it

a   was

was addreffed, without degrading the author. If any partiality appeared towards the patron, it was at leaft the partiality of friendfhip and affection.

ANOTHER inftance of true liberty, of which antient times can alone afford us an example, is the liberty of thought, which engaged men of letters, however different in their abftract opinions, to maintain a mutual friendfhip and regard; and never to quarrel about principles, while they agreed in inclinations and manners. Science was often the fubject of difputation, never of animofity. *Cicero*, an academic, addreffed his philofophical treatifes, fometimes to *Brutus*, a ftoic; fometimes to *Atticus*, an epicurean.

I   I HAVE

I HAVE been feized with a ftrong defire of renewing thefe laudable practices of antiquity, by addreffing the following differtations to you, my good friend: For fuch I will ever call and efteem you, notwithftanding the oppofition, which prevails between us, with regard to many of our fpeculative tenets.   Thefe differences of opinion I have only found to enliven our converfation; while our common paffion for fcience and letters ferved as a cement to our friendfhip.   I ftill admired your genius, even when I imagined, that you lay under the influence of prejudice; and you fometimes told me, that you excufed my errors, on account of the candor and fincerity, which, you thought, accompanied them.

a 2   BUT

But to tell truth, it is lefs my admiration of your fine genius, which has
engaged me to make this addrefs to
you, than my efteem of your character
and my affection to your perfon. That
generofity of mind which ever accompanies you; that cordiality of friendfhip, that fpirited honour and integrity,
have long interefted me ftrongly in
your 'behalf, and have made me defirous, that a monument of our mutual amity fhould be publicly erected,
and, if poffible, be preferved to pofterity.

I own too, that I have the ambition
to be the firft who fhall in public exprefs his admiration of your noble tragedy of Douglas; one of the moft
inter-

interefting and pathetic pieces, that
was ever exhibited on any theatre.
Should I give it the preference to the
Merope of *Maffei*, and to that of *Voltaire*, which it refembles in its fubject;
fhould I affirm, that it contained more
fire and fpirit than the former, more
tenderness and fimplicity than the latter;
I might be accufed of partiality: And
how could I entirely acquit myfelf,
after the profeffions of friendfhip,
which I have made you? But the unfeigned tears which flowed from every
eye, in the numerous reprefentations
which were made of it on this theatre;
the unparalleled command, which
you appeared to have over every affection of the human breaft: Thefe
are inconteftible proofs, that you poffefs the true theatric genius of *Shakefpear*
and

and *Otway*, refined from the unhappy
barbarifin of the one, and licentioufnefs
of the other.

My enemies, you know, and, I
own, even fometimes my friends,
have reproached me with the love of
paradoxes and fingular opinions; and
I expect to be expofed to the fame imputation, on account of the character,
which· I have here given of your
DOUGLAS. I fhall be told, no doubt,
that I had artfully chofen the only time,
when this high efteem of that piece
could be regarded as a paradox, to
wit, before its publication ; and that
not being able to contradict in this
particular the fentiments of the public,
I have, at leaft, refolved to go before them.   But I fhall be amply com-
penfated

penſated for all theſe pleaſantries, if
you accept this teſtimony of my regard,
and believe me to bè, with the greateſt
ſincerity,

DEAR SIR,

Your moſt affectionate Friend,

and humble Servant,

EDINBURGH, 3,
Jan. 1757.

DAVID HUME.

8 The Tragedy of Douglas Analysed

Published in London in April 1757, this anonymous pamphlet broadly agrees with Hume's celebration of the play arguing that it is the 'ingenuous critic's task to rise up in its defence, and put it in the most glaring point of light'. A brief recap of events is provided before the author gives lengthy quotations from the tragedy in order to convey the beauty of the language. A short review of the London performance also appears, as well as some consideration of the prologue, which had been given a richer British flavour in the version available in England.

THE

TRAGEDY

OF

DOUGLAS

ANALYSED.

Amicus *Plato*, amicus *Socrates*, sed magis amica *Veritas*.
ENGLISHED,
I honour Mr. *David Hume*; but *Truth* more!

L O N D O N,

Printed for J. DOUGHTY, in Pater-noster Row.

MDCC LVII.

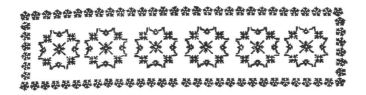

THE

TRAGEDY

OF

DOUGLAS ANALYSED.

WHILE fo many whifpers are propagated by the emiffaries of a certain dramatic perfonage againft the *real Tragedy of Douglas*, it is the ingenuous critic's tafk to rife up in its defence, and put it in the moft glaring point of light, that not a fpeck therein may efcape the eyes of the malevolent; wherefore it is thought not improper to indulge them with a tranfcript of the commendatory part of this tragedy, from the very ingenious and taftefully learned Mr. *David Hume*'s Dedication to his friend, the author Mr. *John Hume*; prefixed to his four laft publifhed Effays.

" I own too, that I have the ambition to be the
" firft who fhall in public exprefs his admiration of
" your noble Tragedy of *Douglas*, one of the moft
" interefting and pathetic pieces that was ever ex-
" hibited

" hibited on any theatre. Should I give it the
" preference to the *Merope* of *Maffei*, and to that
" of *Voltaire*, which it refembles in its fubject;
" fhould I affirm that it contained more fire and
" fpirit than the former, more tendernefs and fim-
" plicity than the latter, I might be accufed of
" partiality : and how could I entirely acquit my-
" felf, after the profeffions of friendfhip which I
" have made you ? But the unfeigned tears which
" flowed from every eye, in the numerous repre-
" fentations of it on this theatre ; the unparalleled
" command which you appeared to have over every
" affection of the human breaft : Thefe are incon-
" teftible proofs, that you poffefs the true theatric
" genius of *Shakefpear* and *Otway*, refined from the
" unhappy barbarifm of the one, and licentioufnefs
" of the other."

This virtuous glow of friendfhip, by whofe in-
tenfity each fquinting *Zoilus* affects to be offended,
and turn afide from, fhall be made appear not to
have ftretched beyond the bounds of truth ; nay,
receive additional luftre from a candid examination ;
in writing which, there is an unfpeakable pleafure
to herald undoubted merit, and at the fame time,
filence all malignant diffenters from the refpectable
authority of Mr. *David Hume* ; whofe fanction
(had any modefty been left among our ftage fmat-
terers) ought to have awe-ftruck unlettered jab-
berers,

berers, and injudicious criticlings, who are ever guiltlefs of the praife-worthy foible,

" T'admire fuperior fenfe, and doubt their own."

But wordy declarations are vague and inconclu-five ; can be as eafily denied, as advanced, with as much juftice and vehemence : therefore let us pro-ceed to proofs ; and, that methodically.

The PLOT or FABLE,

Is as nobly fimple as any antiquity hath tranf-mitted to us, and founded on the hiftorical tale of an old ballad ; from which flender bafis to have raifed fo noble a fabric, evinces the creative energy of the author's invention. All in this tragedy is uncopied, unborrowed ; all written from himfelf. Although the fubject be fomewhat like that of *Merope*, yet fcarce a thought or expreffion is refem-bling: a new proof of our author's merit, which widely diftinguifhes him from his cotemporary-patchwork, pilfering limpers after *Melpomene*.

An ancient and hereditary feud raging between the houfes of DOUGLAS and SIR MALCOLM, *Ba-larmo's* lord; the fon of the latter faved that of the former in battle. From which generous act, a virtuous and inviolable friendfhip fprang. Sir
                                                            Malcolm's

Malcolm's daughter is feen by young *Douglas* (difguifed at her father's houfe) beloved, and courted.
With her brother's confent, by his tutor, a prieft,
they are married.

A few weeks after, the two friendly heroes were
fummoned to their refpective ftations in the field,
where they both were flain, as was alfo young Sir
Malcolm's tutor. The diftreffed young lady, wi-
dowed of a hufband fhe adored, robbed of a brother fhe affectionately loved, and deprived of the
only witnefs of her marriage, determined not to
exafperate her father with the knowlege of a fecret,
which would fill him with horrour at the apprehenfion of his daughter, and now only child's giving
him an heir from the hated blood of *Douglas*.

She entrufted her own nurfe with the care of her
new-born infant, and fome valuable jewels for his
fupport, to be reared in private, agreeable to her
declaration in the play.

On filence and concealment I refolv'd,
Till time fhould make my father's fortune mine.

I appeal to all tender-hearted readers, if, from the
many circumftances, ever beauty in affliction has
been fo interestingly fituated ? or more juftly fo to
modern and chriftian bofoms an object of *terrour*
and *compaffion*, as this young lady, whofe diftreffes
must

muſt certainly affect us more than thoſe of a *Hecu-
ba, Andromache,* or *Merope*; which is an obvious
proof of the author's taſte in making choice of a
ſubject in every body's hands, and in appropriating
it to himſelf. With ſuch a genius, *Horace*'s maxim
will always prove true,

> *Publica materies privati juris crit.*

Glenalvon, lord *Randolph*'s heir, had attempted to
commit a rape on her, which ſhe was reſcued from
by the latter, ignorant of the former's being the
intentional raviſher. To ſhelter her beauty from
any ſuch attack, ſhe married lord *Randolph. Glenalvon* ſtill nurſes his paſſion, hoping one day or
other to ſatisfy it. Although foremoſt in favour
with his kinſman lord *Randolph,* he ſchemes to
make him the dupe of his villainy : and ſo far de-
ceives himſelf, as to think that the lady knows not
that it was he had attempted the rape ; and that
all rebukes to him in his interview with her, glance
only at his baſely daring to declare a paſſion for the
wife of his friend.

Lady *Randolph,* on the anniverſary of her huſband and brother's deaths, mourns in remembrance
of them, mentioning only the latter to her huſband ; and this is the reaſon of her wearing ſable,
the dreſs of ſorrow, which ſome ſuperficial critics

B   have

have objected to. The eighteenth anniverſary our author has judiciouſly choſen for the time of action; and on this very day, the ungrateful *Glenalvon* has formed an aſſaſſination-plot againſt the life of his benefactor lord *Randolph*, who in a winding dale is aſſailed by four hired ruffians, whom he judged to be rovers from the enemy's camp; and who would have inevitably murdered him, if not defeated by the lucky interpoſition of a young ſtranger, whom in gratitude he receives to his boſom and friendſhip. Lady *Randolph* is actuated by an inſtinctive fondneſs for him.

Glenalvon is irritated by the miſcarriage of his conſpiracy, and the additional diſgrace of its having introduced a new favourite into the family.

A priſoner is brought in, ſuppoſed to have been one of the intentional aſſaſſins. By the ſifting of, and jewels found about him, lady *Randolph* comes to a natural and unſtrained knowledge, that the young ſtranger, who had ſaved lord *Randolph*, is her ſon by *Douglas*, whom ſhe had ſo long mourned for as loſt.

Glenalvon, unacquainted with the motive of lady *Randolph*'s fondneſs for the young ſtranger, which is carefully kept a ſecret from him, reſolves to poiſon lord *Randolph*'s breaſt with jealouſy againſt the youth, and practiſes on *Douglas*'s venal follower,

lower, who treacheroufly gives to him *(Glenalvon)* a letter fent from the mother, lady *Randolph*, to her fon *Douglas*, appointing a place where they fhould meet and fettle matters ; which honeft intent *Glenalvon* perverts to an adulterous affignation, that appears to him the more flagrant from her having freed the prifoner.

Having communicated the letter and his thoughts thereon to lord *Randolph*, he gives it to the mifcreant fervant, in order (as if nothing had intervened) to be delivered to his mafter ; whom, in the mean time, he purpofely accofts; and, by fparing, ftrives to wreft the fuppofed fecret from him, but is difappointed. He brings lord *Randolph* to the rendezvous between his lady and her fon. As foon as they are parted, he fets lord *Randolph* on *Douglas* ; himfelf determined on the double murder of them both, and fo to remove all obftacles between him and lady *Randolph*.

Douglas difarms lord *Randolph*, kills *Glenalvon* ; who, as is after difcovered, had wounded him in the back, of which wound he dies. The ftrongeft imagination cannot picture to itfelf any thing beyond lady *Randolph*'s affliction, which fhe confummates by throwing herfelf off a rock. Lord *Randolph*, in expiation of his rafh and fatal error,

B 2 feeks

feeks the embattled enemy, there to meet and provoke the death he wifhes for.

The old faithful fhepherd, *Norval*, remains by
the corps of his adopted fon, and newly-difcovered
mafter.

THE CHARACTERS.

Lady RANDOLPH is affliction's ftandard.

Lord RANDOLPH, a gallant, open, undefigning
man.

GLENALVON, a fubtle, dark villain.

DOUGLAS, a fhining inftance that nobility of
birth cannot be depreffed by a lowly education;
and, on the firft intimation of that it is, breaks forth
with a luftre proportioned to the time of its having
lain concealed.

NORVAL, an ingenuous, trufty fhepherd.

ANNA, a confident to lady *Randolph*.

The *Manners, Sentiments,* and *Diction.*

The firft are manifefted by the two laft. Some
pieces are rich in fentiment, but poor in diction;
others are ftrong in diction, but weak in fentiment.

Douglas is happy in both, and its moft remarkable beauties are not fuch as can be detached from
the place where they are, and equally fit in any
other, as *Horace* judicioufly paints fuch writing,

Purpureus

Purpureus late qui fplendeat unus et alter
Affuitur Pannus.

From the few following quotations fome idea
may be formed of the ftyle of the whole. The
beauties whereof being obvious, I fhall not take up
the reader's time in unneceffarily pointing them out.

Lady RANDOLPH.

Sincerity,
Thou firft of virtues, let no mortal leave
Thy onward path! altho' the earth fhould gape,
And, from the gulph of hell, deftruction cry
To take diffimulation's winding way.

And when that fon came, like a ray from heav'n,
Which fhines, and difappears ———

Lord RANDOLPH.

Free is his heart who for his country fights:
He, in the eve of battle, may refign
Himfelf to focial pleafure: fweeteft then,
When danger to a foldier's foul endears
The human joy that never may return.

Lady RANDOLPH.

At every happy parent I repine!
How bleft the mother of yon gallant *Norval!*
She, for a living hufband, bore her pains,
And heard him blefs her, when a man was born;
She nurs'd her fmiling infant to her breaft;

Tended

Tended the child, and rear'd the pleafing boy :
She, with affection's triumph, faw the youth
In grace and comelinefs furpafs his peers :
Whilft I to a dead husband bore a fon,
And to the roaring waters gave my child.

PRISONER.

Heav'n blefs that countenance, fo fweet and mild !
A judge like thee, makes innocence more bold.
O fave me lady ! ——

                         As I hope
For mercy at the judgment feat of God,
The tender lamb that never nipt the grafs,
Is not more innocent than I of murder.

Alas ! I'm fore befet ! let never man,
For fake of lucre, fin againft his foul !
Eternal juftice is in this moft juft !
I, guiltlefs now, muft former guilt reveal.

The needy man, who has known better days,
One whom diftrefs has fpited at the world,
Is he whom tempting fiends would pitch upon
To do fuch deeds, as make the profperous men
Lift up their hands and wonder who could do them.
And fuch a man was I ; a man declin'd,
Who faw no end of black adverfity :
Yet, for the wealth of kingdoms, I would not
Have touch'd that infant, with a hand of harm.

                                      Lady

[15]

Lady RANDOLPH.

Reaching from heaven to earth, *Jehovah*'s arm
Snatch'd from the waves, and brings to me my son!
Judge of the widow, and the orphan's father!

But now I long to fee his face again,
Examine every feature, and find out
The lineaments of *Douglas*, or my own.
But moſt of all, I long to let him know
Who his true parents are, to claſp his neck,
And tell him all the ſtory of his father.

ANNA.

If a cherub, in the ſhape of woman,
Should walk this world, yet defamation would,
Like a vile cur, bark at the angel's train. ———

Lady RANDOLPH.

As he does now, ſo look'd his noble father,
Array'd in nature's eaſe: his mien, his ſpeech,
Were ſweetly ſimple, and full oft deceiv'd
Thoſe trivial mortals, who ſeem always wiſe.
But, when the matter match'd his mighty mind,
Uproſe the hero: on his piercing eye
Sat obſervation; on each glance of thought
Deciſion follow'd, as the thunderbolt
Purſues the flaſh.

How many mothers ſhall bewail their ſons!
How many widows weep their husbands ſlain!

Ye

Ye dames of *Denmark!* ev'n for you I feel,
Who, sadly sitting on the sea-beat shore,
Long look for lords that never shall return.

GLENALVON.

When beauty pleads for virtue, vice abash'd
Flies its own colours, and goes o'er to virtue.

Lady RANDOLPH.

The truly generous is the truly wise;
And he who loves not others, lives unblest.

GLENALVON.

He seldom errs
Who thinks the worst he can of womankind.

This impiety against the fair sex is uttered by a
profest villain; and the author makes him expiate
it, and his other crimes with death. This is infinitely more excuseable than the licentious invective against the ladies, with which *Castalio* ends
the third act of the *Orphan.* The description of
the *Hermit*, and his cell, is beautiful.

NORVAL.

Pleas'd with my admiration, and the fire
His speech struck from me, the old man wou'd shake
His years away, and act his young encounters:
Then, having shew'd his wounds, he'd sit him down,
And all the live-long day discourse of war.
To

184

To help my fancy, in the smooth green turf
He cut the figures of the marshall'd hosts ;
Describ'd the motions, and explain'd the use
Of the deep column, and the lengthen'd line,
The square, the crescent, and the phalanx firm.

They exchang'd forgiveness :
And happy, in my mind, was he that died ;
For many deaths has the survivor suffer'd.
In the wild desart on a rock he sits,
Or on some namelefs stream's untrodden banks,
And ruminates all day his dreadful fate.
At times, alas ! not in his perfect mind !
Holds dialogues with his lov'd brother's ghost ;
And oft each night forsakes his sullen couch,
To make sad orisons for him he slew.

The setting sun,
With yellow radiance lighten'd all the vale,
And as the warriours mov'd, each polish'd helm,
Corslet, or spear, glanc'd back his gilded beams.
The hill they climb'd, and halting at it's top,
Of more than mortal size, tow'ring, they seem'd,
An host angelic, clad in burning arms.

This is a fine description, and an improvement
on *Virgil*'s
————*Campique armis sublimibus ardent.*

The following is a fine night piece.

C   Douglas.

185

DOUGLAS.

This is the place the centre of the grove.
Here ftands the oak, the monarch of the wood.
How fweet and folemn is this mid-night fcene !
The filver moon, unclouded, holds her way
Thro' fkies where I could count each little ftar.
The fanning weft wind fcarcely ftirs the leaves ;
The river, rufhing o'er its pebbled bed,
Impofes filence with a ftilly found.
In fuch a place as this at fuch an hour,
If anceftry can be in ought believ'd,
Defcending fpirits have convers'd with man,
And told the fecrets of the world unknown.

When I inhabit yonder lofty towers.
I, who was once a fwain, will ever prove
The poor man's friend ; and, when my vaffals bow,
NORVAL fhall fmooth the crefted pride of DOUGLAS.

If in this ftrife I fall, blame not your fon,
Who if he lives not honour'd, muft not live.

Lord RANDOLPH.

The nobleft vengeance is the moft compleat.

DOUGLAS.

But who fhall comfort thee ?

Lady RANDOLPH.
Defpair ! defpair !

Her

Her lamentation for her murdered son is heart-rending.

My fon ! my fon !
My beautiful ! my brave ! how proud was I
Of thee, and of thy valour ! My fond heart
O'erflow'd this day with tranfport, when I thought
Of growing old amidft a race of thine,
Who might make up to me their father's childhood,
And bear my brother's and my hufband's name :
Now all my hopes are dead ! A little while
Was I a wife·! a mother not fo long !
What am I now ?---I know.---But I fhall be
That only whilft I pleafe ; for fuch a fon
And fuch a hufband make a woman bold.

[*Runs out.*

ANNA.

She ran, fhe flew like ligh'tning up the hill,
Nor halted till the precipice fhe gain'd,
Beneath whofe low'ring top the river falls
Ingulph'd in rifted rocks : thither fhe came,
As fearlefs as the eagle lights upon it,
And headlong down————

O had you feen her laft defpairing look !
Upon the brink fhe ftood, and caft her eyes
Down on the deep : then lifting up her head
And her white hands to heaven, feeming to fay,
Why am I forc'd to this ? She plung'd herfelf
Into the empty air.

C 2   The

The opening of this tragedy is artful, as it marks the time and place. Lady *Randolph*'s coming on the stage to pour out her lamentations is truly tragic. Her story and character unfolded to *Anna*, the discovery of, and recognition with her son, bears some affinity to the affecting scenes between *Electra*, *Chryfothemis*, and *Oreftes*, in the tragedy of *Sophocles*. The progressive action grows naturally from what has preceded. The first act shews lady *Randolph*'s affliction, and the cause of it. The second introduces *Douglas*, who has defeated the attempt against lord *Randolph*'s life. The third exhibits *Norval* a prisoner, by whom we come to a knowledge of *Douglas*. The fourth intricates the fable by the villainy of *Glenalvon*. The fifth, by the death of *Douglas* and lady *Randolph*, terminates the action. To the objecting critics against the death of innocence, lord *Randolph* answers.

There is a deftiny in this strange world,
Which oft decrees an undeferved doom :
Let schoolmen tell us why.

In the performance Mr. *Barry* figured, and acted well the affectionate noble-minded *Douglas*. Mrs. *Woffington*'s deportment was fine throughout ; but particularly where she questions the shepherd, recognizes her son, and weeps over his body ; the fentimental part she delivered with intelligence, dignity, and spirit. Mr. *Sparks* was so excellent

in

in his part, that he henceforward deferves to be called the good fhepherd *Norval*. To point out where this piece fuffered in the reprefentation is an invidious tafk I chufe not to enter on.

The *Prologue* is a fine picture of the heroic hof-pitality practifed between the chieftains of the contending realms of *England* and *Scotland*, in days of yore.

The *Epilogue* is an ingenious and laudable attempt to banifh all immoral and obfcene ones off the ftage ; which chafte example, it is hoped, will be followed.

The rules of the *Drama* obferved, as appears by this tragedy, are not enemies, but rather auxiliaries, to genius. There is not a beauty in *Shakefpear* but what is reducible under them ; all his faults they difclaim.

This gentleman hath been glorioufly anathema-tifed by an otherwife refpectable body of gentlemen, from a pious partiality to themfelves, and not having fufficiently confidered, that the heart and paffions militating in the fervice of virtue, advance her intereft infinitely more than the cold, dry, and un-affecting precepts from the pulpit.

If the virtuous part of fociety is obliged to **Mr.** *Hume* for having furnifhed them with fo moral and
fublime

fublime an entertainment, what ought to be the
thanks of the fons of genius to that great man,
who, from amidft the weightier concerns of the
ftate, turns a *Mecænas* eye on (under his *Saturnian*
predeceffor) the too long neglected mufes, truly
fenfible that the contempt of art is fymptomatic of
the decay of empire. Until revived by his be-
nign afpect, the author's lines in the mouth of lady
Randolph, might have been applied to himfelf.

Have you not fometimes feen an early flower
Open it's bud, and fpread it's filken leaves,
To catch fweet airs, and odours to beftow ;
Then, by the keen blaft nipt, pull in it's leaves,
And, tho' ftill living, die to fcent and beauty ?

In anfwer to the mechanical objection of there
not being *ftage-bufinefs* enough in *Douglas*, that is,
buftle, and trick for the eye, let the underftanding
provide for itfelf, we refer them for fuch ftuff to
the two late horrours, to wit, *Barbaroffa* and *Athel-
ftan* ; but by preference to the latter, promifed to
us above a year before its exhibition, as a very
wonder. In the latter of thefe tragical farces, replete with all machinal jugglings of the fcene
(which may our candid author always live in ignorance of) the hero is made wantonly and unnecef-
farily the affaffin of his only child : but, to reconcile himfelf to the audience for fo horrid a deed,
                                                    and

and make his peace with heaven, he dies on the stage of *cold sweats*, and the *hiccup*.

The dull fosterer, and presumptuous obtruder of such absurdities on the town, (which he boasts, and not without some foundation, that he can whistle to, and make implicitly swallow whatever nonsense he pleases) arrogantly rejected *Douglas* as undramatical; undramatical indeed, according to his *Antisophoclean* ideas; and which to vilify, his menial junto, are now hard at work, under the inspection of their preface-read, would-be *Aristarchus*. But such an attempt will be productive of new infamy to them, as it must certainly expose his and their impotent malice, and unlimited ignorance. Against which, and all other attacks,

The blood of Douglas *will* defend *itself*.

F I N I S.

9 A Letter to Mr David Hume

Another anonymous publication in London in April 1757, this pamphlet concludes that Hume has sacrificed critical accuracy for national promotion, and as a result has reduced those critical stocks 'almost to bankruptcy'. The author is receptive to Hume as a critic, and admits to turning his attention to the play because of the warm recommendation that he bestowed upon it. In an attempt to demonstrate that he is not attacking Hume on nationalistic grounds, he cites Dr Arbuthnot as an arbiter of good taste and sound poetical judgement, who cautions that one ought only to promote what is actually found in poetry, and not what one would wish there to be. Specific mention is made of *The Tragedy of Douglas Analysed*, which the author believes to be little more than the conclusion to Hume's unconsidered praise of the play. To address this, he proceeds to embark on a short critical analysis of the language and diction of the play, before finally offering support to Garrick for his rejection of the play in the first instance.

A

LETTER

TO

Mr. DAVID HUME,

ON THE

TRAGEDY

OF

DOUGLAS,

It's ANALYSIS.

AND THE

CHARGE againſt Mr. GARRICK.

By an ENGLISH CRITIC.

——— — *Sic ais, aſt ego contra.*
So thou ſayeſt ; but I am of a contrary Opinion.

LONDON,
Printed for J. SCOTT, in Pater-noſter Row.
MDCCLVII.

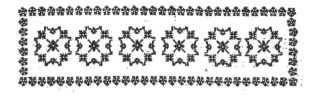

A

L E T T E R

T O

Mr. DAVID HUME.

SIR,

HAVING for a long time conceived the higheſt eſteem for the variety of your literary merit, a recommendation from you was almoſt a ſanction to pre-engage my implicit approbation. How high were my expectations raiſed by your dedicatory commendation of *the tragedy of Douglas*; but, alas! how fallen, from ſeeing its repreſentation : nor has a peruſal ſince won me over as an admirer of it.

Had

Had the tragedy of *Douglas* been uſhered into the world as the promiſe of a dramatic genius; as ſuch it ought to have been received with applauſe; but its having been forced upon us authoritatively, in competition with all antiquity and the moderns, two obvious effects were produced in the minds of men; to wit, curioſity was excited in ſome, jealouſy provoked in others. I am ſorry to inform you, Sir, that in conſequence, your *national* judgment has been greatly run upon here, and your critical ſtocks reduced almoſt to bankruptcy.

For my part, when I firſt read your panegyrical paragraph, I for ſome time heſitated as to the ſincerity of it, and could not help reflecting on the paſſage in *The Art of Sinking in Poetry*, written by your truly ingenious countryman Dr. *Arbuthnot*.

" Take all the beſt qualities you can find in the
" moſt celebrated heroes; if they will not be re-
" duced to a conſiſtency, lay them *all in a heap*
" upon him. But be ſure they are qualities which
" your *patron* would be *thought to have*; and to
" prevent any miſtake which the world may be
" ſubject to, ſelect from the alphabet thoſe capital
" letters that compoſe his name, and ſet them at
" the head of a dedication."

But, on a ſecond reading of it, I changed opinion, and have moreover been aſſured, that
what

what is written you meant, to which, in amaze, I used the famous reply of " *Eft il poffible*," is it poffible ?

The four great and revered names, *Maffei*, *Vol-taire*, *Otway*, *Shapefpear*, which you have employed as supporters of *Douglas*, put me in mind of the ftatue of Lewis XIV. in *Paris*, where the four nations *Germany*, *Spain*, *Holland*, and *England*, are chained round him as vanquifhed, aud lavifhly accompanied with all the tokens of fubjection. However this may pleafe the national vanity of the *French*, all foreigners with reafon laugh at the folly of the defign, and unpardonable foppery of the execution.

I refpect you too much, Sir, to make any unmannered or indelicate applicaton; fuch as " All fools admire, but men of fenfe approve;" and fhall impeach you by an evidence whom I dare fay will not be objected to, yourfelf---and from the ftandard of tafte.

" Strong fenfe united to delicate fentiment, im-
" proved by practice, perfected by comparifon, and
" cleared of all prejudice, can alone entitle critics
" to this valuable character; and the joint verdict
" of fuch, whenever they are to be found, is *the*
" *true ftandard of tafte and beauty.*

" Juft

" Juft expreffions of paffion and nature are fure,
" after a little time, to gain public vogue, which
" they maintain for ever."

According to this juft and admirable doctrine,
what is likely to be the fate of *the tragedy of Douglas ?* Neglect and oblivion : however illumined for
the prefent by the flambeau, you (forgive the expreffion,) too partially, or in the mildeft terms, too
fanguinely, hold before it.

Not fatisfied to have preluded to the affured
triumph of this tragedy in your dedication, an un-
provoked and congenial enforcer of the extravagance of its merit, has been artfully diffufed thro'
the public under the title of *The Tragedy of Douglas
Analyfed*, a feeming attack, which the difappointed
reader finds to be the fecond part of the fame tune
you had begun in your dedication, and which is
there quoted, in order to be illuftrated true in every
article ; therefore, to join iffue the fooner, we fhall
follow the method therein obferved.

From page feven to twelve is a tedious hiftorical
account of the fable, quite too long for the propofed limits of this letter, to be quoted, and therefore I refer to it.

The next heads proceeded to, are the characters,
manners, and diction. Having nothing to object
againft

againſt what the analyſer ſays relative to the two former, the following citations will ſufficiently ſhew that our diſapprobation ariſes not from caprice, but very juſtifiable motives.

Lady RANDOLPH.

For in your ſhades I deem ſome ſpirit dwells,
Who from the *chiding* ſtream, or *groaning* oak,
Still *hears*, and *anſwers* to MATILDA's moan.

Wherefore *chiding*, *groaning*, *hears*, *anſwers?* This may be founded on ſome tradition, or popular errour of *Scotland*; but to *Engliſh* underſtandings, if not altogether nonſenſical, is at leaſt chimerical.

Thou do'ſt not think ſo: *woeful* as I am.——
Woeful indeed!

But whither goeſt thou now?
Is a queſtion in the low familiar.

The miſplaced and *Hors d'Oeuvre* compliment to the union ——

A river here, there an ideal line, &c.
is tedious and inſipid; the line it cloſes with flat,

The youthful warriour, is a *clod* of *clay*.

Clod and *clay* are not only mean words, but alſo cacophonous to the ear.

B · ANNA.

ANNA.

> To dry
> Thefe piteous tears, I'd *throw* my life *away*.

For but a confident, there is a quality-eafe in
this offer to oblige a friend.   But fhe foon relapfes
into a diction more appofite to her condition ;

> I-will-fpeak-fo-no-more,

and prefents us at the fame time with a nafty image.

> But filent mix
> My tears with hers.

Lady RANDOLPH.

> Can thy feeble pity
> *Roll* back the *flood* of never *ebbing* time.

Is this ftrictly correct, *ebb* and *flood* being oppo-
fites ?   *Roll* is indequate here.

> And with him,
> In fpite of all my tears did MALCOLM go.

That tears fhould have been fhed rather to detain
her but three weeks married hufband *Douglas*, than
an unfubftitutive brother, will be affented to by all
young married ladies who are fo unfafhionable as to
love their hufbands.

> Fault'ring I took
> An oath·equivocal, that I ne'er would
> Wed one of *Douglas'* name.

> This

This is a pretty jefuitical device, fhe having been married to one already.

ANNA.

Never did I hear
A tale fo fad as this.
Nor any body elfe.

Lady RANDOLPH.

The good prieft
Who join'd our hands, my brother's antient tutor,
With his lov'd *Malcolm* in the battle fell,
They *two, alone,* were privy to the marriage.

The poet is hard run here, in order to diftrefs his *heroine.* Why kill the prieft in battle? Perhaps this action happened in the days of the *Church militant!*

Acrofs the *Carron* lay
The *deftin'd* road.

This name of a river in *Scotland,* from its likenefs in found to our *Englifh* word *carrion,* is grating to the ears of a *London* audience. Why *deftin'd* road?

ANNA.

The hand that fpins th'uneven thread of life,
May fmooth the length that's yet to come of yours.

This may appear a pretty figure to thofe acquainted with the art of fpinning, tho' it does not

B 2   to

to me. The laſt line is monoſyllabically harſh, a
fault our author is often guilty of.---To *Anna* replies

Lady RANDOLPH.

Not in this world.
I ſhould be glad to know in what other.

Never were vice and virtue pois'd ſo ill
As in GLENALVON's unrelenting mind.

On the contrary, I think never better, if he
played his varied parts with that ſubtlety and *pro-
tean* art ſhe aſcribes to him.

Lord RANDOLPH.

Bluſh not, *flower* of *modeſty*,

Is an odd expreſſion from one man to another,
and would be better addreſſed to one of the gentle
ſex.
Lady RANDOLPH.

I will be ſworn thou wilt not.

This is inelegant, and not ſuited to the rank of
the ſpeaker.

Lord RANDOLPH.

Go with me, NORVAL, and thine eyes ſhall ſee
The choſen warriours of thy native land,
Who languiſh for the fight, and beat the air
With brandiſh'd ſwords.

I diflike this picture of *Scotch* warriours *beating the air*; the renowned Don *Quixote* indeed encountered windmills.

GLENALVON.

And *waves* the *flag* of her difpleafure o'er me.

This would not be improper from a fea-officer.

Perfiftive wifdom is the *fate* of man.

I do not underftand this line; and confefs my ignorance of what *perfiftive* means.

We found him lurking in the hollow *glynn*.

Glynn is a word ufed in *Scotland* and *Ireland*, but not in the meridional parts of *England*.

NORVAL.

Red came the river down, and loud and oft
The angry fpirit of the water fhriek'd.

The meaning of *red* here, and the *angry fpirit of the water fhrieking*, are unknown to us *South Britons*.

By the moon's light I faw, whirl'd round and round,
A bafket: foon I drew it to the bank,
And neftled curious there an infant lay.

Quite

Quite the contrary, and all drenched in water, is moft likely, unlefs the bafket had been purpofely caulked, from a fore-knowledge of the event.

Sir MALCOLM of our barons was the *flower*

Our author feems fond of the word *flower*, to mark male-eminence ; wherefore, purfuant to the baptifmal vows you have made for him as his fponfor, (not at all alluding to the fong) let him be called the *flower* of *Edinburgh*'s tragic writers ; for, on this fide of the *Tweed*, nothing more will, or ought to be allowed him.

The panegyrical analyfer, who has quoted many indifferent, has, in my fenfe, omitted feveral of the moft beautiful paffages, which, as they occur, I fhall infert in this letter ; for inftance.

Lady RANDOLPH.

What does my ANNA think
Of the young eaglet of a valiant neft ?
How foon he gaz'd on bright and burning arms,
Spurn'd the low dunghill where his fate had thrown
                                                [him
And tower'd up to the region of his fire !

ANNA.

Myfterious nature, with the unfeen cord
Of powerful inftinct, drew you to your own.

                                             A

A *cord* is a vifible fubftance; befides, this is too grofs and material an image of the power of in-ftinct.

GLENALVON.

The field
Muft man to man, and foot to foot, be fought.

This rather excites an idea of two armies wreftling, than fighting with offenfive weapons.

Here follow other unpardonable omiffions by the analyfer.

Lord RANDOLPH.

An army knit like ours would pierce it thro':
Brothers, that fhrink not from each other's fide,
And fond companions, fill our warlike files:
For his dear offspring, and the wife he loves,
The hufband, and the fearlefs father arm.
In vulgar breafts heroic ardour burns,
And the poor peafant mates his darling lord.

The Crofs of Chrift. Chriftian Crofs would found lefs harfh to the ear; what follows is a fine picture of decayed beauty, and fome judicious fentiments.

Lady RANDOLPH.

Arife, my fon! in me thou doft behold
The poor remains of beauty once admir'd:
The autumn of my days is come already;

For

For forrow made my fummer hafte away.
Yet in my prime I equall'd not thy father ;
His eyes were like the eagle's, yet fometimes
Liker the dove's ; and, as he pleas'd, he won
All hearts with foftnefs, or with fpirit aw'd.

Thou doft not know what perils and injuftice
Await the poor man's valour.   O ! my fon !
The nobleft blood in all the land's abafh'd,
Having no lacquey but pale poverty.

There burft the fmother'd flame !

How do bad women find
Unchanging afpects to conceal their guilt ?
When I by reafon, and by inftinct urg'd
Full hardly can diffemble with thefe men
In nature's pious caufe.

The following remark deferves the attention of all
men ambitious of the matrimonial ftate.

Lord RANDOLPH.

Let no man after me, a woman wed
Whofe heart he knows he has not ; tho' fhe brings
A mine of gold, a kingdom for her dowry.

GLENAL-

GLENALVON.

> She too that seem'd
> *Pure* as the *winter ſtream* when *ice emboſſ'd*
> *Whitens* its courſe.

This is ſtrained, quaint, and affected; and what follows ſheer bombaſt.

> He's in a proper mood
> To chide the thunder if *it at him roar'd.*

Glenalvon is anſwered with a ſenſible, and manly ingenuity by *Douglas*.

> Sir, I have been accuſtomed all my days
> To hear and ſpeak the plain and ſimple truth:
> And tho' I have been told that there are men
> Who borrow friendſhip's tongue to ſpeak their ſcorn,
> Yet, in ſuch language I am little ſkill'd.
> Therefore I thank *Glenalvon* for his counſel,
> Tho' it ſounded harſhly.

GLENALVON.

> What will become of you?

is an unheroic interrogation.

> Thy truth! thou'rt all a lye.

This brutality does not meet with an inſtantaneous and proper retort from one of young *Douglas's* ſuppoſed feeling, which, by the following ſentiments, is farther manifeſted.

C   DOUGLAS.

DOUGLAS.

To the liege lord of my dear native land
I owe a fubject's homage: but, ev'n him,
And his high arbitration I'd reject.
Within my bofom reigns another lord;
Honour, fole judge and umpire of itfelf.
If my free fpeech offend you, noble *Randolph*,
Revoke your favour, and let *Norval* go
Hence as he came, alone, but not difhonour'd.

Impofes filence with a *ftilly* found.

What means *ftilly* here? is it tantamount to *ftilling?* I know the word is in *Shakefpear*, but do not underftand it, in the place he ufes it.

NORVAL.

And *ever* and *anon* they vow'd revenge.

Ever and *anon*, are no doubt, fuppofed defenfible, becaufe in a fhepherd's mouth, and in imitation of *Homer*'s practice, are in p. 60, faithfully repeated by *Douglas* to his mother.

DOUGLAS.

May heav'n infpire fome fierce gigantic *Dane*
To give a bold defiance to our hoft!
Before he fpeaks it out, I will accept!

How accept it before he fpeaks it out? Does

Sad *fear* and *melancholy* ftill divide
The empire of my breaft with *hope* and *joy*.

This, Sir, is an abridgement of your Diſſertation on the Paſſions.

Lady Randolph.

Too well I ſee
Which way the current of thy temper *ſets*;
Drives would perhaps be more explicit.

The ſentiments of dying *Douglas* are not amiſs; nor is the mother's affliction ill drawn; nay, ſome-what affecting. But why ſhe ſhould plunge from a precipice head-foremoſt into the ſea, I cannot ſee any reaſon, nor for her, or her ſon's deaths. He might have killed *Glenalvon*, tho' previouſly woun-ded by him in the back, but, not mortally; and lord *Randolph*, in expiation of his groundleſs jealouſy and raſh attempt reſign to victorious *Douglas* his rightful inheritance.

The prologue, a learned alluſion to the old ſong of *Chevy-Chace*, is of the true *poetical profound*.

In *ancient times* when *Britain*'s *trade* was arms,

Why not *pride* inſtead of *trade*; but the *Scotch* have always ſneered at the *Engliſh* as a trading nation.

And the lov'd muſic of her youth alarms.

C 2

The

The fenfe of this line, not intelligible to us, alludes rather to tne mufical alarms of *Highland* bagpipes.

It would be too much to take in the whole *prologue* here ; to read it is enough ; where it emerges from confufion and obfcurity, it gently fubfides in kindred lines to this,

They knock'd alternate at each other's gate !

It concludes with an humble petition in behalf of *Scotland.*

The epilogue is a priggifh affectation ; and I hope will never be relifhed by a genuine *Britifh* audience. The far-fetched comparifon of the *Nile* is ftolen. I object to the epithet of *celeftial* joined to *melancholy* in the laft line. Heaven, by all information I have ever had of it, is the kingdom of joy, it is therefore a *diffenting* opinion to make it the abode of *melancholy.*

Why has the panegyrift taken notice but of three performers, and natives of *Ireland?* fhameful partiality ! This appears a flagrant combination of the *Scotch* and *Irifh* againft the true fons of old *Englifh* roaft-beef, as if, forfooth, the former are only qualified to write tragedy, and the latter to perform. But, to thy teeth, partial Analyft, I will do my country-folks the juftice they deferve.

He

He who figured in the character of *Glenalvon*, manifested a projectile spiritedness of person, and strictly adherent to *Horace*'s rule, *Semper sibi constans*, without any variation throughout: now, this is what may be called, supporting a character.

The actor of lord *Randolph* was self-collected, having the curb of his passions in hand. He exhibited a commanding calmness of deportment, and a level, stomach-fetched, dignity of voice.

The liquid toned actress of *Anna* irradiated sorrow with her smiles; how sweetly did she speak?

Thy vassals grief great nature's order break
And change the noon-tide to the midnight hour.

I should not have been surprised if the superior beings descended from heaven to her pretty manner of uttering this invitation.

                        Ye ministers
Of gracious heav'n who love the human race,
Angels and seraphs who delight in goodness!
Forsake your skies, and to her couch descend!
There from her fancy chase those dismal forms
That haunt her waking; her sad spirit charm
With images celestial, such as please
The bless'd above upon their *golden beds.*

I owed this to my country; so now my mind is at ease. *Golden beds* savours of *Epicurism.*

                                 The

The ground-work of the play is an abfolute abfurdity, for either the lady *Randolph* muft have been very artful, who had a chopping boy eighteen years before, to pafs on her hufband for a maid; or he, lord *Randolph* muft have been very unacquainted with the affairs of women. I fear the latter cafe; and from ineffectual nights fprung the daily caufe of her tears; and certainly a very material one. *Penelope*, it is true, mourned twenty years for *Ulyffes*; but then fhe did not admit an *apathic* lover to tantalize her in bed.

The fhepherd, the jewels, and recognition of this doleful piece, are worn-out devices of the ftage, and expletive pegs of the human invention.

The protracted monotony of lady *Randolph*'s grief is irkfome. One character often exhibited in the fame piece, muft be agitated by variety of paffions, otherwife we grow tired of the famenefs.

After the difcovery of *Douglas* he is not thrown into any interefting fituation, nor is there any dramatic anxiety throughout, arifing from the intricacy of the plot; for from the beginning to the end, it is an uninterrupted downhill greenfword courfe, entirely againft the revolutionary fpirit of the fcenic laws, which perhaps, (nay, by your mifcalled Differtation, or rather Differtatiuncle on tragedy, it appears)

pears) you are not acquainted with. We had, however, a right to expect at leaft, unexceptionable correctnefs of ftile, in a work by you fo immoderately praifed, not to fay, profanely.

I now take leave of *Douglas*, this *Aurora borealis* of tragedy, that had fo long corufcated over us from the North, to execute the laft part of my tafk, to wit, to defend Mr. *Garrick*, by difculpating him from a heavy charge, diffeminated every where from the Drawing-room in *St. James's* to the Nightcellars; which is, that he had the impudence to refufe *The Tragedy of Douglas*, the beft play ever acted, not only on the *Englifh* ftage, but on any other antient, or modern.

The author not only abfolves, but apologifes for Mr. *Garrick* by his motto.

Non ego fum vates, fed prifci confcius ævi.
" I am not a poet ; but well read in old ballads. "

Mr. *Garrick* acquiefced to the former part of his confeffion ; and told him that but poor materials for the ftage could be derived from the latter. This is the upfhot of his crime. Has he then deferved all the foul-mouthed abufe that has been lavifhed on him ? I think not, who am not partial
im.

The

The pulpit and clergy of *Scotland* are irreverently treated in the *Analysis*, which ends with a bullying line, that might waggishly be retorted, to wit,

The blood of *Douglas* will *defend* itself.
That is, people will keep aloof from it, because,

Nemo impune lacessit.
No body rubs to it with impunity.

The drift of the whole being now seen through; with a dislike to your partiality, but, esteem and veneration for your *genius* and erudition,

I am, SIR,

Your, &c.

F I N I S.

10 Remarks upon the Play of Douglas in a letter by a Gentleman to his friend in the Country

This anonymous critic is of the opinion that there is significant merit in the play, and that the tragedy is far from immoral, although it is also far from perfect. He believes that the play lacks both an overall moral, and a hero, as Norval has done nothing during the performance that can allow him to be identified as such. Finally he asserts that Lady Randolph is a character 'neither *natural* nor *commendable*', primarily because he cannot accept that she would allow a figure as benevolent as Lord Randolph to marry her without returning to him any of the affection which he has bestowed upon her.

REMARKS

PLAY of DOUGLAS,

IN A

LETTER by a GENTLEMAN to his Friend in the Country.

S I R,

I Send you, according to your Defire, a Copy of the PLAY, *DOUGLAS*, with fome general Remarks upon it.

I am far from having an ill Opinion of the Stage, or Stage-plays in general: I think, good Plays, well acted, afford not only an innocent Amufement, but may be of great Ufe in improving the Mind, Language, Behaviour and Morals of the Hearers, and efpecially of our young People.

As for this Play, it is far from being an immoral one; on the contrary, there lie, difperfed in it, many fine Sentiments and moral Reflections well expreft.

But confidering it, as a Critick, it is far from being a compleat Piece. It has not what can be properly called, A MORAL; neither is there in it A HERO; and as to the HEROINE, her Character is neither *natural* nor *commendable.*

The Sum of the Story reprefented feems to amount to this, a Lady marries, clandeftinely, a Gentleman of a great Family, enjoyed him three little Weeks; he was foon thereafter killed in Battle, along with her Brother; fhe happened to be with Child: But being obliged to conceal that from her Father, fhe fent it off with its Nurfe, and believed it was drowned in a River, on occafion of a Storm: She lamented the Lofs many Years; but at laft was induced by her Father, contrary to her own Inclination, to marry *Randolph*, a worthy and deferving Nobleman; but ftill the Lady goes on lamenting her Loffes for feven Years more, when it was at laft difcovered that her Boy had been miraculoufly preferved; and fcarce has fhe had the Comfort of feeing him, and letting him know who he really was, when he is cruelly killed by a Villain, who is alfo difpatched in the Scuffle; upon which the poor Lady turns mad, and drowns herfelf.

Now, what is the Moral of this whole Story? What good Meaning has it? I own I can fee no obvious Inftruction that arifes from it; and yet I cannot but commend the Author's Ingenuity, in dreffing up fuch a fimple Story in fuch a Manner, as, in different Places of the Play, to move the Compaffion of the Audience, tho' from the *whole*, taking it as *one Piece*, there arifes no Moral.

Another Fault I find in this Performance, is, That *Douglas*, who is defigned for the HERO, has done nothing that can make him be confidered as a Hero.

While he was a Shepherd, he was fprightly, killed the Captain of a Band of Robbers, took a Liking to warlike Atchievements, and
when

when he is feeking after an Opportunity for thefe, he happens to refcue a Nobleman, who was attacked by four Ruffians. Thefe are all the heroick Deeds that he did, before he was acquainted of his Birth; after which he is foon cut off.

The Hero of a Play ought always to do fome very grand and heroick Actions, fuch as may raife a high Efteem and Affection for him: 'Tis from this that a juft Sorrow and Compaffion rifes in the Minds of an Audience, when they fee the Hero brought into Diftrefs, or fuffer unjuftly; but in this Play, the Hero does nothing of fuch Moment, as can raife any great Degree of Efteem for him, before he is untimely cut off.

If the Author had not been in fuch Hafte to difpatch his Hero, but had carried him to the Wars, made him deftroy the *Danes*, and relieve his Country, then he would have done fomething worthy of a Hero.

The Author feems to have been fenfible of this, when he makes *Douglas* die, lamenting that he had not fallen, as his brave Forefathers fell, turning with great Effort the Tide of Battle: But had it not been a more compleat Piece to have made *Douglas* rather *act*, than only *fpeak as a Hero*.

As to the HEROINE; the Lady no Doubt met with two great Loffes, her beloved Husband, and her fine Boy, (this laft as fhe thought;) but thefe Afflictions are not fo uncommon as to merit a perpetual Grief and Lamentation; and when fhe was prevailed upon, tho' contrary to her own Inclination, to marry a worthy Man, how unaccountable was it in her to perfevere in her fullen Grief for no lefs than feven Years, without giving her deferving Husband decent Affection, or complacent Kindnefs! When I read thofe Words of *Randolph*,

———————— *Seven long Years*
Are paft fince we were joined by facred Ties;
Clouds all the while have hung upon thy Brow,
Nor broke, nor parted by one Gleam of Joy.

I cannot but pity the poor Nobleman, and at the fame time have a juft Indignation againft the Lady's unreafonable Obftinacy.

This inceffant Grief of hers for her firft Husband, may, by fome romantick Readers, be thought a Piece of high Virtue; but I can never juftify the indulging any Paffion that is contrary to Reafon, and can never anfwer any good Purpofe.

A Woman may have fuch a Regard for a firft Husband, as to refolve never to marry another; but if fhe is induced, tho' contrary to her Inclination, to marry another Man, 'tis contrary to all Reafon, that fhe fhould not indulge him with fome Gleam at leaft of Joy, efpecially if he proves a deferving and affectionate Husband; and therefore, I cannot admire the Character that our Author has drawn of his HEROINE.

As to her ruinous End, it being a natural enough Confequence of her new Surprife and exceffive Grief, I make no Reflections upon it.
I am, Sir,

Your moft humble Servant.

218

FERGUSON'S MORALITY OF THE STAGE AND CRITICAL RESPONSE

11 The Morality of Stage Plays Seriously Considered

This account of the stage and Home's tragedy by Adam Ferguson (1723-1816) is the most effective defence of the pro-*Douglas* pamphleteers. Although he would go on to achieve great acclaim as a moral philosopher in his own right, at the time of the controversy Ferguson was a little-known unemployed former minister. Nevertheless, he marshalled a wide variety of examples to demonstrate that the theatre was not the immoral den of iniquity that its Popular opponents had labelled it, and instead sought to prove that there were in fact multiple examples of stage craft and stage production generously scattered throughout the Christian tradition. Ferguson states that the function of the play is to teach and instruct its audience. This method is comparable to the parables of Christ, because they both employ stories to provide moral instruction. Ferguson reminds his readers that, far from blasphemy, plays were never banned in scripture so there is no religious justification for objecting to a morally sound work. Like Witherspoon, he concedes that corrupt plays are evident, but firmly asserts that *Douglas* is not in this category. Indeed it is far less licentious than Restoration comedy according to Ferguson, and this progression of moral refinement would in turn lead to the removal of inappropriate stage plays. Contemplation of morals via the outlet of theatrical representation would consequently result in an increase in the moral good. Alongside the moral significance of the play Ferguson was also concerned to address economic issues, seeking to dispel accusations that the theatre was a luxurious plaything of the rich devouring funds that could be more profitably distributed to the poor. A theatre would necessarily create industry around it, providing jobs for set-builders, wig makers, and costume makers, as well as the actors themselves. Conscious of cultural and national perspectives, Ferguson also believed that the ascendancy and success of *Douglas* would bring about the end of English dominance of the stage. In this respect the play was a powerful literary motor that would provide Scotland with a solid identity and a potent means of expressing it.

THE

MORALITY

OF

STAGE-PLAYS

SERIOUSLY

CONSIDERED.

EDINBURGH:
Printed in the year M,DCC,LVII.
(Price Sixpence.)

THE

MORALITY

OF

STAGE-PLAYS

SERIOUSLY CONSIDERED.

NOTHING can be more alarming, to every well-wisher to true religion, than to find disputes arising among its Professors, which may end in divisions and animosities hurtful to the spirit of religion itself. People who begin such disputes have much to answer for, unless they have sufficient reason for what they do. It is well known, that the people of this country are well disposed, sober and religious; that they are ready to take every public offence much to heart, and, as far as their disapprobation will operate, that they strenuously contribute to remove it. We should therefore beware of trifling with their honest zeal, or of making them waste, against objects of a harmless or indifferent nature, that opposition,

A   which

which fhould be all employed againft real vices and corruptions. Miftakes in this article are attended with many ill confequences ; they miflead our apprehenfions of duty ; they create ill-will, and become a fource of groundlefs antipathy between perfons, who fhould entertain fentiments of kindnefs and charity towards one another. I am forry that there fhould be any appearances of this kind amongft us at prefent, and would think myfelf very happy in contributing to remove them. We are alarmed with an imputation of irreligion, which is caft upon the entertainments of the Theatre ; and it may be apprehended, that perfons who liften to this charge will think very unfavourably, if not with fome degree of antipathy, of their neighbours, who continue to take any part in fuch entertainments. I hope that no perfon would chufe to bear the imputation of hating his brother without a caufe, and that every well-difpofed perfon will be glad to hear any obfervations which may help us to form a right judgment of one another.

The Stage has fubfifted in *Britain* about two hundred years ; it has been during this period the entertainment of people of diftinction, and of others too, who were enabled to partake of it. Whether it has corrupted our people in any degree, is a queftion not eafily determined. I am inclined to believe, that, confidering the mixture of good and
bad

bad men which are to be found in every age, the people of this island are not inferior to those of any other age or country whatever. This will be a presumption, that, if Plays are a poison, it is at least but flow in its operations. Another observation which I will make by the way, is, that however the Stage may have corrupted our people, the manners of the people have so far prevailed, as, in some respects, to have reformed the Stage. On this head we may come to a sure conclusion, because we may compare Plays that were admitted during some part of this period, with those which are now chiefly in repute. In making this comparison it will appear, that a certain degree of indecency and licentiousness once permitted, is now rejected, and that Plays more pure, and of a better moral tendency are either chosen from our antient stock, or that these qualities at least are expected from every Writer of the present age. We cannot be too anxious in forwarding this reformation, when it is in any degree incompleat. But I am sensible that it is in vain to speak in this manner, whilst an opinion remains, that the very name and form of a Play is offensive and pernicious. I confess that I am at a loss fully to account to myself for the prevalence of such an opinion. It is not derived from Scripture; for I cannot recollect any thing like a warning against the Stage, either in the Old or New Testament.

Our

Our Saviour, who appeared at a time when Plays were in high repute in different parts of the *Roman* Empire, says nothing to warn us of their immorality. The Apoſtle *Paul*, in writing his Epiſtle to the *Romans*, amidſt various inſtructions and cautions which he gives, is ſilent on the ſubject of Plays, which were then in high repute amongſt the people he was writing to. In preaching at *Athens*, the ſame Apoſtle expreſsly quotes a ſentence from one of the *Greek* Poets, Acts xvii. 28.; *For in him we live, and move, and have our being; as certain of your own Poets have ſaid.* This is a very ſublime expreſſion, and beautifully applied by the Apoſtle, as will appear on conſulting the context. It ſhows that he was ſenſible of the inſtructions and good impreſſions which we may receive from poetry, and was directed, by that Spirit which ſupported him in his Miniſtry, to apply it ſo properly to thoſe purpoſes. Nor is this the only proof he has given of an eſteem for good performances of this nature. He has, in the firſt Epiſtle to the *Corinthians*, xv. 33. inſerted into the ſacred text a line from a *Greek* Play, which now ſubſiſts : *Be not deceived, evil communications corrupt good manners.* Who does not ſee that ſuch ſentiments, and ſuch inſtructions muſt be improving to mankind, wherever they are found, whether in proſe diſcourſe, or in a Play ? And, if the whole ſtrain of a Play is framed to this purpoſe, pofe, it furely deferves efteem and encouragement from every well difpofed perfon, who has the means of filling up his vacant hours with fuch entertainments. I am forry that any perfon fhould have overlooked this confideration, or given reins to a headlong zeal againft the Stage, fo unlike the wifdom and difcernment of the holy Apoftle, whom we have quoted. The Stage indeed may be abufed, and fo may the wifeft inftitutions of mankind: Religion itfelf can hardly be preferved from corruption: The Papifts, and other Sectaries, daily mifapply the doctrines of Scripture, to ferve their own unlawful purpofes. The pulpit, in the poffeffion of every party, into which Chriftians are unhappily divided, has often rung with other founds than thofe of the Gofpel of peace; and put us in mind, that when the beft things fall into the hands of corrupt men, then the wifeft and moft facred inftitutions may fuffer fome abufe: But this will furnifh no argument againft any fubject which is fo abufed. I fhould be forry to offer any apology for abufes which may have appeared on the Stage: I hope that every audience, in our times, will have judgment and feverity enough to reject examples of this nature: But I cannot admit any fuch abufe, as a valid argument againft the Stage in general. We do not prohibit the ufe of food and drink, becaufe fome men abufe them to excefs; nor do we forbid all

relaxation

relaxation from bufinefs, becaufe fome unhappy perfons do mifchief in their fports: Neither fhould we condemn every poetical compofition, intended for the Stage, becaufe fome Writings of this kind have been found faulty and licentious. People, who are acquainted with performances of this nature, are fenfible that a number of grave, moral and edifying pieces, would, by fuch an undiftinguifhing ruin, be loft to mankind. The Authors of fuch works have been efteemed worthy of great praife, and have been thought to bear a confiderable part in promoting the intereft of virtue. We cannot doubt of this, when we find any degree of regard paid to them in Holy Writ; and what we have obferved to this purpofe above, is fufficient to conne&t their defence with the honour of Scripture itfelf. This is more than apology fufficient for endeavouring to fhow, that fuch performances may not only be innocent, but be of great benefit to mankind. I am fenfible that perfons who need much information on this head, may likewife need to be told what is the nature of a Play; and I will now give fome notion of it, that every perfon, if poffible, may be enabled to judge for himfelf.

Plays are of two kinds, called *Tragedy* and *Comedy*; the one reprefents the a&tions of common life, and compofitions of this nature have been the moft liable to abufe; becaufe

caufe wit and ridicule are fometimes found to be petulant, and the familiarity of this ftyle is more eafily mixed with indecencies : But the perfection of Comedy confifts in expofing to juft ridicule the follies and abfurd vices of ordinary men ; where it fails in this purpofe, the abufe is manifeft, and will be condemned by every judicious audience. Tragedy, on the other hand, is ferious, grave and majeftic; it reprefents the actions of great men, and their conduct chiefly on great and interefting occafions, their ftruggles in difficult and diftreffing fituations, where the fentiments they exprefs raife admiration or pity, and where the very faults they commit become fo many warnings to the fpectator. Every Tragedy therefore contains a ftory, and may convey inftruction in the fame manner with a parable or fable; it differs only in the form, and not in the effect. In a Parable, the ftory is related ; in Tragedy, the fubject is expreffed by fome action and converfation which is reprefented, and we are left to collect the ftory from the fpeeches of the perfons concerned in it. In a Parable, we wait for the moral till the ftory is concluded, when the whole appears to have been an illuftration of fome moral precept; in a good Tragedy, we have a continued moral from beginning to end ; the characters, the fentiments, and the obfervations, which come from the perfons who fpeak, are calculated to move and inftruct us; and

and we are deeply engaged by such reprefentations, becaufe we take part with amiable
characters, and become anxious about the e-
vent. It muft appear ftrange, to fay, that
every ftory, parable or fable, either in the
form of narration, or in that of a Tragedy,
muft be a wrong thing in itfelf. One ftory,
indeed, however told, may be dull, tirefome,
and leave bad impreffions ; but another ftory,
we all know, may be agreeable, entertaining,
and leave the beft impreffions on the hearts
of the hearers. We cannot therefore condemn the ftory reprefented in any Tragedy,
till we know of what kind it is, till we know
whether it tends to leave good impreffions or
bad ones, in the minds of the hearers. If it
is found to leave good impreffions, it fhould
certainly be commended, and highly deferves
the countenance which the Apoftle *Paul* hath
given to fuch works, altho' written even by
Heathens. In order to fhow in what manner
a tender and affecting ftory improves the
heart, and ftrengthens every good difpofition,
I fhall confider the hiftory of *Jofeph* and his
cruel brothers in that view. We find the elder brothers moved with envy and malice a-
gainft an innocent child, becaufe he had his
father's affection, and was diftinguifhed by
forebodings of Divine favour. They refolved to fhed his blood, when he came to them
alone, in the defart ; but being diverted from
this cruel purpofe, they fold him as a flave
to

to ftrangers who were paffing thro' the wil-
dernefs. Every humane perfon, who reads
this piece of hiftory, will be moved at the
diftrefs of the innocent fufferer, and will feel
a horror at the cruelty of the brothers. Here
then we may obferve, that compaffion for the
diftreffed, and indignation at the wicked, are
the beft difpofitions which men can entertain ;
and that every ftory which leaves fuch impreffions muft be very edifying and inftructive
to good men. The remaining part of this
hiftory is very beautiful, and we cannot help
confidering it. *Jofeph* was preferved, and,
by the Divine favour, came to a ftation of
honour and great power. Famine obliged
his brothers to feek relief in that country
where he was become a ruler. When they
appeared before him, he difguifed the firft
emotion of his foul, under an afpect of feverity. He queftioned them about his father's
condition ; and, when mention was made of
his younger brother, who had no fhare in
the cruel offence committed againft him, he
difcovered an earneft defire to fee him. When,
at laft, he declared himfelf to be their brother
Jofeph, they were ftruck with remorfe and
terror : But he repaid their former cruelties
with a generous forgivenefs ; he relieved their
diftrefs ; he faw again his aged father, and
paid the duty of a grateful child. Whilft
we are attending to a ftory of this kind, it
nourifhes every good difpofition of the heart,

B   and

and we are the better prepared by it to act a noble, generous and compaffionate part towards our fellow-creatures. If we can imitate fuch circumftances in the ftory of a Tragedy, we may prefume that the effect will be fimilar ; and it muft appear ftrange, to find any Tragedy cenfured, before we pretend to fhow that it fails in this point. The fubject we are now upon has been brought in queftion, on occafion of the Tragedy of DOUGLAS ; and no perfon fure can judge of that performance, who is not acquainted with the conduct of the ftory on which it is built. But, if any perfon has proceeded fo far, from a general difapprobation of the Stage, I am perfuaded, that a few reflexions upon the reprefentations of this performance, would be fufficient to reconcile him to it. It was well received by every audience, and feemed to make a deep impreffion. , The fentiments it excites are thofe of admiration of virtue, compaffion to the diftreffed, and indignation againft the wicked caufe of their fufferings. In every ftory of diftrefs, which is not merely accidental, wicked characters muft appear, as well as good ones ; for we cannot impute injury and cruelty to any other but the wicked : Their appearance however improves the mind, by foftering our averfion to wickednefs, in the fame degree as the view of amiable characters heightens our love of virtue, by engaging our hearts in its behalf. Hence

the

the generofity of *Jofeph*, and the wickednefs
of his brothers, are equal matter of improvement and edification to our minds.

When the Tragedy of *Douglas* becomes yet
more public, it will appear to have a tendency
fimilar to this. The defigns of one perfon are
painted in fuch colours of hateful depravity,
as to become a neceffary object of deteftation.
The miftakes of another awaken our caution,
and become a leffon of prudence. The generous and elevated mind of a third, warm
and exalt our fentiments ; and that perfon, on
whom the chief diftrefs of this ftory falls,
moves to compaffion, and proves at laft a
warning againft rafh and fatal defpair. Agreeable to this fhort reprefentation, the performance has found a favourable reception with
the public, and given proof how far grave
and ferious compofitions may engage the
minds of men, and convey inftruction under
the fhew of amufement. It has likewife had
the ordinary teftimony of diftinguifhed merit; it has ftruck out fome fparks of envy and
fpite. This kind of fire, we may believe, is
feldom extinct, but it only flames upon extraordinary occafions, when any remarkable
merit, or a rifing fame is to be confumed.
People who carried it in their breaft, have
paid their duty regularly to every good Writer in every age ; in fo much that their attendance is now required to compleat his honours : Their filence therefore would have
been

been the fevereft blow they could have ftruck
at the Author of *Douglas*. I think very diffe-
rently indeed of thofe who are fincerely anxious for the intereft of religion, and who
cenfure every Writer of a Play, becaufe they
apprehend fomewhat immoral and offenfive in
the very nature of the Stage. I refpect the
intentions of fuch, however I may think them
miftaken in this particular, and flatter myfelf,
that, whilft we agree in condemning any particular abufes which may have place on the
Stage, we fhall likewife be of one mind in
applauding whatever will contribute to render
the amufements of that place inoffenfive and
inftructive. This is the only point I have la-
boured in this Paper, and only plead againft
an opinion which would place all Theatrical
performances upon the fame level. With
the people who are likely to oppofe me, the
very name of a Play implies fomewhat criminal and immoral. A near view of the fubject fhould be fufficient to correct this apprehenfion ; but, whilft any refpectable authority continues in favour of it, we can fcarcely
expect to remove it entirely. The authority
of the Chriftian Church is fuppofed by fome
to be clearly on that fide of the queftion :
But will any body fay, that the Chriftian
Church has invariably difcouraged good Plays.
In the times of our Saviour and his Apoftles,
the pureft times of the Chriftian Church, no
fuch marks of difapprobation appear. The
Fathers

Fathers of the Church, whofe authority is probably referred to on this occafion, ought furely to have very little credit with us on their own account : A great part of the fuperftition of the Church of *Rome* is derived from their inventions; and we have already totally rejected the authority of them and their Oral Traditions, when we reformed the corruptions of the Popifh Church. We may however, in charity, allow, that they might have had fome reafon for their oppofition to Stage-Plays. Chriftianity, in their times, was ftruggling for a full eftablifhment; and they thought that Stage-Plays, being of Heathen compofition, and having frequent reference to Pagan Divinity, might recal the minds of men to their former fuperftition. We have reafon to believe, that, if Plays of a Chriftian ftrain had appeared, they would have met with no oppofition from the friends of Chriftianity: For *Gregory Nazianzen*, a Father of the Church, and a perfon of great piety, endeavoured to fupplant Heathen Plays, by introducing one which he wrote himfelf, on the moft interefting fubject of our religion. And we muft fo far confefs that he acted a wife part: For, when corrupt performances are admitted on the Stage, the beft thing we can do is to reject them, and fupply their place with compofitions more favourable to the important concerns of religion and morality. If the Plays on our Stage have not. hitherto

hitherto been altogether pure, we have certainly been unlucky in the long silence we have kept on that subject; and doubly unlucky in breaking out with our censure, at a time when one very successful attempt was made to supply the Stage with a Play, which might contribute to its reformation. The Popish Clergy, we know, exclaimed against the Stage, when it took part with the Reformers, and helped to overturn their own power: For it is well known, that Plays were acted at the Reformation, which very much helped on that work, by exposing the vices and absurdities of the Popish Clergy : It is no wonder therefore that they were enemies to the Stage; but we cannot surely have any resentment to the Stage in our days, because it formerly offended the Popish Clergy in promoting the Reformation.

When we come to consider the law and doctrine of our Church with respect to Stage-Plays, it will appear that the censure which performances of this nature now meet with, doth not arise from any law, statute or established doctrine in this Church. We may even venture to affirm, that the prejudice to Plays in general is of late origin. The only act of this Church relating to Stage-Plays, which I have ever heard quoted, is an act of the Assembly which met in the year 1574. An act in the following terms. * " That no
" Comedies

* Vid. Petrie's Church History.

" Comedies or Tragedies or such Plays should
" be made on any subject of canonical Scrip-
" tures, nor on the *Sabbath Day*. If any Mi-
" nister be the Writer of such a Play, he
" shall be deprived of his Ministry: As for
" Plays of another subject, they also should
" be examined before they be propounded
" publickly." This act of Assembly, we see,
supposes that Plays are allowable, and that
Ministers may write Plays on the subject of
any history, which is not taken from canonical Scripture. So far the practice is agreeable
to the laws of this established Church, and it
is not pretended that there is any other ecclesiastical law now in being with respect to
Stage-Plays. We hear indeed of certain Proceedings of the Presbytery of *Edinburgh* about
thirty years ago, when they published an admonition to discourage the Stage. We would
willingly believe, for the honour of the dead,
that they took this step in opposition to some
faulty and immoral Plays which were then
acted, and that they would have been loth to
discourage performances of a better tendency,
which might promise a reformation of such
abuses. Their example, at any rate, is no
law; and to follow them without examination would imply a concession of infallibility,
which they never laid claim to. It is needless
to mention the names of Clergymen of un-
questioned reputation in the Christian Church,
who have written Plays for the Stage; or to
                                            mention

mention how frequent it is to confider a right tafte and judgment in fuch performances, as an accomplifhment neceffary to every man of letters, whether Clergyman or layman. Such authorities can be but of little avail after we have had the fubject itfelf before us, and an opportunity of judging for ourfelves. I fhall therefore go on to take another view of the Stage, and confider fome inconveniencies which are fuppofed to attend it. Few things of human concern are free from inconveniencies; we need not therefore be furprized, that fome are apprehended to belong to the Stage. We may fufpect that Theatrical Entertainments engage the minds at leaft of our youth too much, and carry them away from other fubjects of attention, which make a part either of their bufinefs or their education. This fufpicion is equally well grounded with refpect to every other amufement: For people who are difpofed to be idle, will eafily find avocations from bufinefs; and the Stage has one peculiar advantage, its being the amufement only of a ftated time, and not always at hand to tempt people who are idly difpofed. This objection goes upon a fuppofition that perfons of all tempers run with equal eagernefs to the amufements of the Stage; they differ however greatly from one another in this particular, and they who are the moft captivated with them, acquire a degree of coolnefs and indifference from time and familiarity. We may

venture

venture to afk whether knowledge, whether induftry and commerce have declined in this City fince the Play-houfe was firft opened here. It will be owned that they have rather increafed. We may appeal to perfons who have the care of the education of youth in other places, whether they would not gladly fee their pupils come to the Theatre, and mix with grave and decent company, if by that means they could break up more dangerous meetings for low gaming and riot, where youth have no good example to lead them, and no reftraint from a fenfe of decency or fhame. The Stage, I think, may well bear a comparifon with other amufements which youth will devife for themfelves, if they are debarred from this. When we confider the ftrain of thofe Plays which have met with the moft favourable reception from the public, obfervations will occur to the honour of human nature; for they are Plays which excel in moving compaffion, which intereft an audience in behalf of amiable characters, which give the proper applaufe to virtue, and treat vice with ignominy and reproach. A tragedy, which fails in exciting thefe emotions, or which would fhock our favourable apprehenfions of virtue, would foon be rejected with difguft. We may confult on this point an author, whom we hold in fuch efteem, that we make our children read his works, almoft as early as their catechifm. He has obferved, that

C   a

a Play, tho' defective in ornament, and without any affectation to pleafe by pompous and
founding expreffion ; if it is furnifhed with
a juft moral and true reprefentation of nature,
will carry the preference with every audience
from more fplendid and fhowy performances.
When we fee an audience therefore in tears
for an object of compaffion, when we find
them affected with the generous fentiments
which come from a virtuous character, deeply
engaged in wifhes for the fuccefs of the good,
and for the difappointment of the wicked ; it
would fcarcely occur that fuch an audience
could be better employed in an hour of lei-
fure. Whatever our peculiar occupations are,
virtue is the bufinefs of all, and we fhould not
be excluded from any place where it may be
learned. We know how few amufements
there are for which this plea can be offered:
It is well, we think, if they are innocent re-
laxations from bufinefs, we feldom expect to
find them fchools of morality. But were this
plea laid afide, we ought to make fure that o-
ther amufements, lefs favourable to the habits
of bufinefs, may not come in the way of our
youth ; and that our pretended feverity may
not prove the occafion of greater licentioufnefs. It will be faid that our youth may go
too often to the Play-houfe. They may go
too often to any amufement ; but we are affured here that they can go no oftener than
plays are acted, which is by no means fo frequent

quent, as other avocations from bufinefs may
occur to them. As there is a danger that
youth may exceed in every amufement they
are given to, thofe amufements fhould be
moft difcouraged, in which the excefs is moft
dangerous. I will venture to fay that no place
of public refort, under the influence of decency, and in the prefence of refpectable perfons,
can be fo dangerous, as cabals which are formed in fecret, and apart from fuch influence.
If any abufes yet remain on our Stage, we
fhould not delay to reform them. But I have
mentioned thefe abufes fo often, that fome of
my readers will begin to have a very terrible
notion of them : However, I will venture to
inform them, that no abufe was ever admitted
on any Stage, but might pafs for perfect decency, when compared to what they may have
often heard at a goffiping, a merry-making,
or a meeting of young fellows. The Play-
houfe is frequented by people of both fexes,
whofe rank, whofe age and manners, are fufficient to command refpect, and to bring decency along with them into any place. It is
an uncommon compliment we pay them, in
fuppofing that our youth are corrupted in
their company ; I fhould rather think, that,
confidering the nature of the entertainment,
and the refpect due to the company, we fhould
fee, with fatisfaction, fuch fpectacles become a
part in the amufements of our youth, and
hope that their idle hours would find there,
not

not only agreeable relaxation, but improvement too.

It has, I underftand, given offence of late, that perfons of grave and refpeÃ§lable chara- Ã§ter, were prefent at the reprefentation of a new tragedy, which they thought a good one. Great part of this offence fhould be removed, when we recolleÃ§t that this, and many fuch performances, have a tendency very favourable to fobriety and morality ; for they muft be very dignified charaÃ§ters indeed who muft keep at a diftance, when the advancement of virtue is in any degree concerned. Their part of the cenfure, however, is put in a new light. It is faid, that altho' a praÃ§tice may be innocent in itfelf, yet perfons of grave charaÃ§ter ought to avoid it, becaufe it gives offence to other people; and being thought immoral, their neighbour may by fuch an ex- ample, be fhaken and unfettled in what he thinks his own duty. We are inftruÃ§ted to this purpofe in the eighth chapter of *Paul's* epiftle to the *Corinthians*, where he confiders the praÃ§tice of eating meat, which had been offered to idols. The reader will be pleafed to obferve, that this inftruÃ§tion relates to aÃ§ti- ons, in their own nature indifferent, and cannot be applied to any other. The Apoftle ex- plains it in the eighth verfe in thefe words : " Meat commendeth us not to God : for nei- " ther if we eat are we the better, neither if " we eat not are we the worfe." He ends
the

242

the chapter with this conclusion ; " Where-
" fore, if meat make my brother offend,
" I will eat no flesh while the world stand-
" eth, left I make my brother offend." If
the eating of such meat had been criminal in
itself, he would have avoided, and forbid the
practice on that account. If on the contrary it had been right, and a commendable
practice, he would have embraced it, and
studied to correct the prejudice which any
person might have entertained against it. For
his whole life was a continued course of opposition to both *Jews* and *Gentiles*, where their
prejudices stood in need of correction. Let
us therefore apply the Apostle's instruction and
example to the present question. Is it perfectly indifferent to a man whether he goes to
a play or no ? I shall suppose that it is. Is it
likewise indifferent to the public what sort of
people compose the ordinary audience at our
Theatre ? I believe it is not. The Manager
of every theatre must suit his entertainments
to the company, and if he is not supported by
the grave and the sober, he must suit himself to the licentious and profane. We know
that the language of the theatre, or any other
language whatever, may be employed either
to recommend virtue, or to insinuate folly and
licentiousness. If licentious people alone frequent this entertainment, they will perhaps
encourage what they like to hear. But persons of sobriety, and regard to virtue, would
make

make that entertainment form itſelf to a very different ſtrain, and give the whole a very different influence on the manners of mankind. They would rejeet and condemn what was exceptionable, they would promote and encourage what was agreeable to ſound reaſon, and favourable to virtue. Happily for us, this is no new thing; for the Play-houſe has been long the reſort of perſons of both ſexes, who are the moſt ſcrupulous on the point of reputation and decency; and their preſence has, no doubt, contributed to reform ſome abuſes, which may have, at ſome times, crept into the ſtage. Their preſence therefore has done a great ſervice to mankind; and if any perſon is prejudiced enough to think otherwiſe, 'tis high time he was undeceived. The Apoſtle inſtruets us to refrain from an indifferent action, if it offend our brother; but he has often commanded, and has ſhown the example, to do good in the face of prejudice, and every ſuch prejudice in time will be correeted. We know that in every nation there muſt be amuſements and public entertainments, and the Stage has always made one in every civilized and poliſhed nation. We cannot hope to aboliſh it; and if we could, we ſhould only make way for the return of drunkenneſs, gaming, and rude cabals, which the more decent converſation and manners of civilized times, have in a great meaſure aboliſhed. We ſhould not even propoſe

pofe to abolifh an entertainment, which is
founded on the beft principles of human nature, the love of virtue, and compaffion to
the diftreffed : For who would ever go to a tragedy, if he had not a heart formed to pity,
and a mind fufceptible of the admiration due
to worthy characters. It is the duty of grave
and refpectable men to watch over an entertainment of this kind, that it may not de-
viate from the good purpofes which it is calculated to ferve. What they do to this purpofe, either in oppofing the bad or promoting
the good, is matter of duty, and their conduct in it is not to be regulated by the opinion of any perfon who is pleafed to take offence.

The ftate of the poor has been mentioned, as a confideration which muft render this
entertainment at prefent pernicious and criminal. We cannot be too attentive to every circumftance which can affect the ftate of the
poor, in the difficulties which they are now
threatened with ; and we have reafon to believe, that the Gentlemen of this country are
well difpofed to take any meafures which may
be thought proper for their relief. How the
Theatre comes to be thought any hindrance
to fuch meafures, we cannot eafily apprehend.
The poor may be divided into two claffes;
thofe who are indigent, but ftill in a condition to earn their bread by fome fort of labour
or induftry ; and thofe, on the other hand,
who

who, by reafon of age or ficknefs, are unable
to earn any fubfiftence. It is remarkable, that
of late years more care has been taken than
formerly to provide for the poor, who are unfit
for any kind of labour. Poor-houfes have been
built in many parifhes, under the management of the Gentlemen and people of fubftance, who have taxed themfelves for that
purpofe. It were cruel therefore to load the
body of our Gentlemen with an imputation of
neglect in this article, at a time when their
conduct deferves commendation. And it were
imprudent by fuch an imputation to encourage any perfon able to work in the expectation that he may be idle, and yet receive gratui-
tous charities. If any perfon were rich enough
for the undertaking, he could not poffibly do
a more fignal mifchief to his country, than
that of maintaining the whole poor of *Great
Britain* in idlenefs. It has pleafed Providence,
for wife purpofes, to place men in different
ftations, and to beftow upon them different
degrees of wealth. Without this circumftance
there could be no fubordination, no government, no order, no induftry. Every perfon
does good, and promotes the happinefs of fociety, by living agreeable to the rank in which
Providence has placed him. Whilft his gra-
tuitous charities relieve the poor who are unable to work, his other expence becomes a
fund for the fubfiftence of the induftrious;
nor is it proper that they fhould expect fubfiftence

fiftence upon any other terms than thofe of induftry and fobriety. The money which the rich expends is paid for the labour of the poor. Different trades live upon the profits of fur-nifhing his cloathing, his table, and his equi-page. It is evident how many poor induftri-ous people would ftarve, if he did not buy the works which they furnifh him. The ve-ry money he lays out for amufement comes at laft into the hands of the poor, and is paid as the price of their labour. A part of it we fhall fuppofe is laid out for the amufements of the Theatre, and the people who receive it there, are fo many hands who diftribute that money among the induftrious poor. Every Player muft be cloathed, maintained and lod-ged: The money which he receives therefor is paid at laft to the fpinftrefs, the weaver, the clothier, and other tradefmen who live by fur-nifhing the ordinary neceffaries of life. Whilft from humanity we indulge the poor in their ftation, we ought from juftice to indulge the wealthy in theirs, and to expect that they are to go on agreeable to the habits of living which belong to their ftation, and which in effect are neceffary to the order and good of fociety, and to the maintenance of the poor. If we fhut up our places of entertainment, and deprive people of diftinction of that fo-ciety and thofe amufements which they have a relifh for, they muft tire of living among us; and the few who yet remain will chufe

D   to

247

to remove to another place, where they will not meet with popular antipathy, on account of their moſt commendable amuſements. Then indeed the money they expend would be loſt to the poor of their native country. This and every other city would feel, in ſuch a caſe, that the reſidence of perſons of fortune is neceſſary to give any number of tradeſmen, and induſtrious poor, the means of ſubſiſtence. How hard muſt it appear then, to give any encouragement to the poor to murmur againſt a circumſtance from which their induſtry may derive ſuch advantage ? We may aſk, who are the moſt forward in this country to form charitable deſigns for the relief of the poor ? The Gentlemen of this neighbourhood, I think, have ſet the example; and they too who were the readieſt to ſhed tears, for the diſtreſſes repreſented in the Tragedy of *Douglas*, have been the moſt forward in compaſſion to the poor, and in liberal deſigns for their relief.

After all I muſt confeſs that one conſideration remains, which muſt renew my diffidence on this point. A body of men reſpectable for their learning and gravity, who conſtitute a judicature in this city, have, without any exception, declared their diſapprobation of the Theatre in general ; and, to ſhow that no exception could be admitted, have taken the alarm, juſt when the Tragedy, which I have had occaſion to mention, was introduced. I

cannot

cannot pretend to speak of their reasons for so doing, until they are pleased to publish them; but must entertain great expectations of their force, since they are sufficient to overpower what has appeared on the opposite side. Men of gravity are above trifling with the mistakes and misapprehensions of a people, and certainly cannot long ly under any such imputation. Men of learning need not be told, that part of every liberal education consists, in learning to distinguish between Theatrical performances which are faulty, and those which have a moral dignity and a good tendency; they know that a good Tragedy has been in all ages esteemed amongst the chief productions of human ability; that the authors of such works become more renowned with posterity than the princes and monarchs of the earth. The names of *Buchanan* and *Milton* are more respected than those of *Henry* and *James*; and the names of *Cyrus* and *Xerxes* are less celebrated than those of *Sophocles* and *Euripides*. I am, from these considerations, the more inclined to believe, that reasons have occured against the Stage, which will appear very urgent when they are produced; and cannot imagine, that objections which ly against bad Plays only are now all the objections they have to plead against a good one, which may be considered as an attempt to make the Stage truly useful and instructive.

This

This refpectable body of men have paffed a fevere fentence againft one of their number, for being prefent at this reprefentation we are fpeaking of. This likewife feems to proceed from fome powerful motive not fufficiently known : For they were not led to this act of feverity, in execution of any law or ftatute of this Church. It muft have been one of thofe extraordinary cafes where a difcretionary power is neceffary. Such a power indeed is not affumed by any court of judicature in Europe, except one, which I will not name on this occafion. It is happy for us, that the law of our Church has exprefsly forbid the exercife of any fuch arbitrary and dangerous power. See *Form of Procefs*, cap. 1. and 84. where it is exprefsly enacted, " That nothing " be admitted by any Church-judicature as the " ground of a procefs for cenfure but what " has been declared cenfurable by the Word " of God, or by fome act or univerfal cuftom " of this National Church."——They were perhaps led to a proceeding, in appearance fo little agreeable to the fundamental laws of their own fociety, by a zeal to fupport the laws of the State. People indeed are often more fond of work which they devife for themfelves, than they are of any bufinefs affigned them by others. It does not however appear, that they have done much honour to the legiflature by their interpofition on this occafion. They have caft an imputation of impiety

piety upon an amufement which the law for-
mally authorifes in the Metropolis, which
Our GRACIOUS SOVEREIGN honours with
his prefence, and which the moft refpectable
perfons in the legiflature of *Great Britain*
fupport by their countenance.

F I N I S.

12 The Players Scourge *and*
13 The second part of the Players Scourge

The *Players Scourge* is a response to Adam Ferguson's *Morality of Stage Plays*, and is thought to have been written by John Haldane. Haldane was an upholsterer by profession, living in Edinburgh, but was also a zealous Cameronian and took a hard line on the theatre. It is one of the most aggressive anti-theatre pamphlets to have been published, replete with fire and brimstone warnings over the punishments in store for those daring to put on plays. Haldane alludes to lines that have been removed from the printed version of the play to make it more acceptable to a Christian audience, but Home's actions still make him worse than 'idolatrous Papists and Pagans' in his eyes. He accuses Alexander Carlyle of Arminianism and Ferguson of being a deist. To those who have opposed the play he offers a modicum of praise, but goads them to more exacting, more overt, and more violent forms of retribution for the supporters of *Douglas*. The second part, mostly likely published in 1758, although dated 1768, uses largely the same arguments and sometimes even the same language as its predecessor. This time women are included in the list of degenerates who attend the theatre.

THE

PLAYERS SCOURGE:

OR A

DETECTION

OF

The ranting prophanity and regnant impiety of ſtage plays, and their wicked
encouragers and frequenters; and eſpe-
cially againſt the nine prophane Pagan
Prieſts, falſely called miniſters of the
goſpel, who countenanced the thrice cur-
ſed tragedy called *Douglas*.

A MONGST the many great and grievous ſins
and ſnares which prevail in this day, the wicked
and deviliſh deverſions of the ſtage are greatly
increaſing, and more encouraged than ever in this place,
to the great diſgrace of Chriſtianity and of all that is
ſacred.

Were the perſons who pretend to be miniſters and
magiſtrates acting up to their character, it would be their
endeavour, as it is their bound duty, to extirpate all wickednefs out of their juriſdictions, and to be a terror to
theſe imps of Satan, and actors of his devices the players.
Many famous councils, ſtates and republics, as well Popiſh as Proteſtant, have accounted the ſtage Satan's ſchool,
the ſeminary of the devil, and a nurſery for hell, which
Beelzebub

Beelzebub hath ever claimed as his own chief residence and rendezvous in the world, over which he superintends, and in which the actions practised are by his special command and suggestion. In like manner it is agreed on by sober Pagans themselves, that play-actors are the most profligate wretches, and the vilest vermine, that hell ever vomited out; that they are the filth and garbage of the earth, the scum and stain of human nature, the excrements and refuse of all mankind, the pests and plagues of human society, the debauchers of mens minds and morals, unclean beasts, idolatrous Papists or atheists, and the most horrid and abandoned villains that ever the sun shone upon; and therefore have banished, extruded and exterminated them out of their cities and communities; yea the laws of our own land, defective as they are at present, have declared these land-louping villains impudent sturdy-beggars, and idle vagabond rascals: so that, would these called rulers act up either to their own laws, or the example of the very heathens, they would order the playhouse in the Canongate, which hath not even the pretence of human authority, to be forthwith demolished, and razed to the foundation, and the very place where it is built to be salted with brimstone, in abhorrence of the abominations that have been committted there: and as these vile miscreants, Diggs, Heyman, Younger, Lewis, Love, Ryder, Holland, and the rest of Satan's artificers, who now act jugler plays there, have often blasphemed God with their mouths, and debauched their own and others bodies, it were a great mercy to themselves, and a favour to the society among whom they are, to cut the tongues out of their heads, and the ——— from between their feet, that they may not henceforth have it in their power to blaspheme their Maker, nor pollute their fellow creatures; and that they may for ever be distinguished from honest men, their faces should be marked with a burning iron, and they sent back to their native lands of England and Ireland, whence the most of our wickedness proceeds.

Moreover, the prime supporters of these devilish, hellish stage-plays, and of all other wickedness in the place,

place, be'ng the idle, loofe, ufelefs catives falfely called nobility and gentry, and efpecially thofe called judges and lawyers, to the great difgrace of their birth, education, offices and employments, it were highly neceffary and very honourable in thofe who gave them their honours, offices and employments, to diveft them of thefe till they abandon Satan's camp, and give evidence of their fincere repentance: and (if as indeed confidering the times,this cannot be expected) may we not hope, that all who have any fear of God will forbear employing thofe who attend the ftage, and fo do what is in their power to incapacitate them from making fuch a finful ufe of money? confidering further, that the ordinary haunters and frequenters of the playhoufe are, of men, the idle, prophane, godlefs, gracelefs and brutifh rakes, reprobates and panders for hell; and of women none but idle vagueing jilts, light cocquettes, ftrumpets, whores, bauds, and vile meretrixes, who have thus in effect renounced their baptifm, their creed, their Chriftianity, their bible and their God, and lifted themfelves under Satan's banner, giving up even with their fobriety, humanity, chaftity, honour and honefty. It were pity if any who are called minifters of the gofpel, who know the impoffibility of partaking of the cup of the Lord and the cup of devils, fhall hereafter admit thefe foul-murdering, inconfiftent wretches to fealing ordinances, or other church privileges, until they fhall give evidence of their unfeigned humiliation and forrow for their apoftafy.

But, alas! the far worft is yet to come. Was it ever heard of in Scotland, a land which hath often renounced the devil and all his pomps, that the minifters of the gofpel wrote jugler plays, and attended the ftage, until thefe falfe brethren, viz. J—n H——e at A—— d, A——r C——e at M——h, J——n W——e at L——n, M——w D——t at E——s, W——m H——e at P———t, F—— s S——t at W——r, G——— c G———s at S —— n, J——n S——i at S———r, and A——m T——— n Chaplain to I—d J——n M ———'s regiment, lately chofen by thofe black-birds the faculty of advocates to be the keeper of

their

their library, did it? Now concerning this unhallowed number, it might be observed in general, that they
were intruded upon their charges by the force of Popish
patronages; all of them ride upon the top of the kirk,
and lead on in all their black measures; all of them shew
by their light behaviour and supine negligence in the
discharge of their office, that their profession of the ministry is, in gross, hypocrisy, and for a piece of bread;
and all these have by resorting to, and haunting Satan's
accursed jugler plays and routs, contemned their sacred
callings, grieved all in whom any spark of piety remains,
and hardned a prophane, mad and distracted generation.
But because they deserve a more glaring stigma, we observe more particularly,

That the chief ring-leader in all this black work is
J—k H——e, remarkable for his lightness, madness,
impudence, prophanity, impiety, swearing, sabbath-
breaking, contempt of his superiors, neglecting, and
oft deserting, his poor people, and infecting them with
the husks of error and prophanity, which has made most
of them as wicked as himself, oppressing and calumnia-
ting of ministers and others who retain any measure of
integrity; wenching, dancing, gaming, drinking, wa-
stery: and that, like his master Satan, he may involve
others in the same misery with himself, he hath wrote,
and caused to be acted and published, his cursed play
called D o u g l a s, which, for its prayers to and for the
dead, swearing by the most blessed cross, by the heavens,
yea, as is lately proven, (though the printed copy con-
ceals it) by him who died on the accursed tree to save
mankind, &c. its imprecations, appeals, self-murdering
principles; his doctrine of a necessity of sinning, and
so making God the author of sin, and other blasphemies,
exceeds the wickedness of idolatrous Papists and Pagans.
To excuse his wickedness, we have been told that this
apostate play-hunter makes his boast that the prince of
W——s, the dukes of C———d and A———e, and
Mr P—t, &c. take him by the hand: but though this
were true, while others deny it, he may rest assured that
though all the rakes great and small in the three kingdoms were to take him by the hand; and let him likewise

wife take in the affiftance of the tyrant of France, the tyger of Savoy, the witch of Endor, with her daughters the bloody witches of Hungary and Lapland, yet they will never be able to fcreen him from the leaft drop of the Mediator's vengeance, whofe authority he hath contemned; but that woe pronounced againft the man by whom offence cometh will purfue him until his name be made a curfe and an execration upon the face of the earth, for a beacon to all pofterity, unlefs he fpeedily fly to God for mercy.

C ———— e deferves the next place, being an ignorant, empty, frothy, foolifh, light mountebank, who fcarce acknowledges God out of the pulpit, either in his family or elfewhere, entertains his people with reading a ballad of other mens compofing, which is the more intolerable that he culls out fuch fermons as are moft ftuffed with Arminianifm, and therewith intermixes paffages from plays. He fcarce hath the form of vifiting and catechifing his parifh; or if at any time he does it, he makes ufe of a catechifm. He is quite remifs in difcipline, admits all to the facraments who will but claim that privilege, connives at adultery in his own parifh, and keeps company with the perfons reputed guilty, and lets baudy language pafs without a check; fpends the whole fabbath, except the fhort time he is in the kirk, with vifiting the gentry, or gallanting the ladies; is a great frequenter of routs and other public entertainments, at which he drinks exceffively, dances unweariedly, and calls for prophane fongs, as De'il ftick the minifter, and the like; plays at cards both for money and pleafure; is an open reforter to rehearfals and plays, a conforter with that vile meretrix Sarah Ward, and the other comedians, and a great daubler with, and encourager of, thofe who write and fet forth curfed ftage-plays; on all which accounts he is the darling of the whole malignants in the place, many of whom appear openly in his defence, while yet they abhor thofe with whom he holds communion, being themfelves of the Epifcopal, or none.

W———te, alias Black, doth anxioufly tread the fame path: he not only connives at all the wickednefs committed in the parifh, but is fhrewdly fufpected of being the

the father of the baftard brats begotten in his own houfe, and poifons his people with heterodoxy; but being an ig-norant blockhead, a dumb idle drone, and fo lazy that he hath compared the pleafant, the honourable work of the miniftry to carrying the ftone-barrow, he is not ca-pable of fo much mifchief as either of the two above named ramblers are.

The pitiful body D ——— t deferves the next place in this cabal, being more taken up with fidling, fling-ing, dancing and training up his children in thofe wick-ed amufements, than with preaching; adventures to the pulpit without a bible, and yet dare fcarce lift his head off his ballad; an ignorant, hen-picked, cowardly, beaft-ly animal; a contented c———d; carried his whole fa-mily to the playhoufe; and one who allows himfelf to be dragged where-ever his imperious wife and m ous daughters will have him.

H——e in P——— t, an airy, proud, fwaggering blade, C———les, that prophane, brauling, fighting, light mountebank, and S——l, a frothy fool, fitter indeed for a ftage than a pulpit, muft be kept all on one ftring, be-caufe, if the current report of the country be true, they are efpecially fond of drinking, dancing and whoring together; and to them all conjunctly H———'s maid is faid to have brought forth two bumpkin gytlings at one birth; and fince fhe affirms they all had ado with her, it is but juft they fhould all pay her largely, equally and punctually: accordingly the whore calls on all the kittle three to be exact in their payment, certifying them that the perfon who fails fhall be publicly expofed, and the brats laid down at his door, which makes the guilty brotherhood as prompt in their payment to her as they are to the vagabond juglers.

S l in S——— r, though of a grave countenance, is noted for a pedantic, foolifh, flory; a conftant com-panion of the prophane and gracelefs; a great drunkard, and therefore was eafily prevailed on to attend the play-houfe; and pretended to be fo foolifh as to expect he could be affifted by the doctrine of devils taught there how to inftruct his people; though at other times he a-vows, that they being only coalliers are not worth any man's pains or ftudy. F——n

F —— n is left to bring up the rear, though he rather deferves the van, being a more avowed deift, play-
hunter, and companion to the wicked, than any of the
former ; a bold defender of, and champion for the ftage,
and a vile blafphemer and maligner of our Lord and his
apoftles in his pafquil called The morality of the ftage,
as hath been clearly proved againft him in feveral pamphlets lately publifhed.

When thefe abandoned wretches had thus exerted
themfelves for the fupport of Satan's kingdom, to the
everlafting contempt and difgrace of all religion, morality and decency, to the utter ruin and perdition of themfelves and others, it might have been expected that if
any fpark of God's fear had remained with the pref-
byteries whereof they are members, they would immediately have conveened, and deprived them of any
further opportunity of difgracing their facred character,
and polluting the pulpit ; but no fteps have been taken
with the moft, and any little thing that hath been done
by the reft hath been no better than Eli's velvet-mouth'd
reproof to his fons. The presbyteries of E———h
and D———h began tolerably ; the one in advertifing
the other presbyteries of the offence given by their brethren, and calling W——e to account ; and the other
for putting a libel into C——e's hand : but what hin-
dered them that they did no more ? why did thefe two
presbyteries confine their inquiry to the ftage-play ? why
did E———h presbytery overlook F—— n, and their
own brethren W———ce, C——g, W———t and
H———n, who, 'tis faid, went to the plays in London ? why did they fufpend W——e only for a month,
and recommend to W——n, who intimated the fham
fentence, to ufe their dear brother W——te gently ? which
he did with a witnefs, behaving in fuch a way as if he
had come to recommend him to his people as more deferving of their favour : and why did the presbytery of
D———h, after finding C—— le's libel both relevant
and fully proven, diveft themfelves of the power of cen-
furing him given them by laws religious and civil, and
refer the matter to the fynod, who probably will only
fhave the head they fhould cut off ? and why did they
refufe

refufe to read informations given in to them by C——le's elders of his negligence and immoral practices? Thefe things may convince all men that the presbyteries now named are either unwilling or unable to do their duty, and poffibly they are both: and as for the presbyteries of H —— n, A——r and the M——fe, no better than a total overlooking of the matter was expected from them; the whole members in fome of them, and the generality in others, being remarkably loofe and diffolute, in fo much that they will not do any one good thing but what the love of their ftipend obliges them to perform.

To conclude this paper, would it be any wonder tho' many Pagan ftates and rulers, the apoftate Julian not excepted, fhould rife up in judgment againft the rulers in thefe days? for they extruded and banifhed players and play-poets out of their kingdoms and ftates; whereas the prefent rulers fuffer, yea entertain, fupport and cherifh them in their bofoms, until, as vipers, they fting, poifon and plague them: and will not the primitive churches alfo condemn the prefent Laodicean church? for the former excommunicated all, both minifters and hearers, who frequented ftage-plays, as giving up with Chriftianity, and renouncing their baptifm; whereas the latter connives at and fuffers not only the hearers, but deacons and elders, yea minifters, to perfift in countenancing thefe Pagan and hellifh diverfions without a check. " Let God arife, let his enemies be fcattered; " let them alfo that hate him fly before him: as fmoke " is driven away, fo drive them away; as wax melt- " eth before the fire, fo let the wicked perifh at the pre- " fence of God."

H. I.

THE

SECOND PART

OF THE

PLAYERS SCOURGE

Exhibited to the World.

Wherein is contained .

The true Character of Playhoufes, Play-actors,
and Play-haunters.

WITH

An humble Advice to the Occupant upon the
Throne.

By J—n H——ne.

PRINTED IN THE YEAR MDCCLXVIII.

TRUE CHARACTERS

OF THE

Players and Play-haunters.

THE fathers of the primitive church, and other divines, ftyled the playhoufes the devil's temples, his chapels, his fyna-gogues, chairs of peftilence, and the dens of lewdnefs and filthinefs, the fchools of bawdry and uncleannefs, the ftews of fhame and immodefty, the fhops of Satan, the plague and poifon of mens fouls, and a Babylonifh brothel-houfe, alias, a bawdyhoufe.

And fuch as erect or build them, (which no true Chriftian dare do), or contribute in the leaft to their fupport, affiftance, and maintenance, are liable to the heavy curfe and malediction of the ever-living God upon their fouls and bodies, the temporal and fpiritual interefts of themfelves, fa-milies, and pofterity, except they fincerely repent in time.

It is agreed by all Chriftians, and even by fober Pagans themfelves, that play-actors are the moft profligate wretches, and vileft vermin that ever hell vomited out; that they are the filth and garbage of the earth, the fcum and ftain of human nature, the excrements and refufe of all man-kind, the plague of all human focieties, the de-bauchers of mens minds and morals; and are all unclean beafts, idolatrous Papifts, or Atheifts.

A 2

Befides,

Befides, they are ordinarily common thieves, robbers, pilferers, and pick-pockets. In fhort, they
are the moft horrid abandoned villains that ever
the fun fhone upon. Therefore they have been
juftly banifhed, extruded, and exterminated out
of many cities, countries, and communities (both
Pagan and Chriftian as fuch). Yea, the laws of
the land, defective as they are in this point, have
juftly declared them land-louping villains, impudent fturdy beggars, vile ftrolling vagabonds,
rogues, and rafcals. And above all, thefe vile
wretches are notorious epicures, greedy gormands,
hellifh belly-gods, and voracious vultures, who
fpend more upon their ftinking bellies and vile
carcafes, than would maintain fifty honeft families, that are both ufeful and beneficial to the public; when thefe wretches are a burden and a
plague; which cannot fail to bring a dearth upon
vivres, where-ever thefe ufelefs mountebanks refide.

Moreover, thefe mifcreants are all tainted with
the difeafes and botch of Egypt, and efpecially
with that hafty, noifome, foul difeafe, anciently
called the glengore; which cannot but affect all
that come near them, with their poifonable ftink;
which, if their natural fenfes were not as vitiated
as their fpiritual fenfes are depraved, and tainted
with the faid malady, they would foon perceive,
and avoid fuch noxious company; for inftance
their chief juggler Rofs, who was tainted and
fmitten with the forefaid crimes and difeafes in
their perfection, as is to be feen in his vile perfon
at this day. And further, being a wretch of fuch
prodigious wickednefs, he was caft off by his
father and family, for his wicked life and his hellifh

lifh trade; and for any other to take him by the
hand, or to own and countenance fuch a monfter,
is a fhame and a fin in folio.

Now, if thofe called rulers acted up either to
their own laws, or the example of the very Heathen, they would order the timber of the play-
houfe to be taken down, and being fet up as a
gallows, would hang them all thereon, and the
play-houfe builders along with them, as a piece
of pure juftice to the nation.

The play-haunters, the prime fupporters of
thefe wicked, hellifh, curfed ftage-plays, and all
other wickednefs in the land and place, are the
profane, idle caitiffs, falfely called nobility and
gentry; efpecially thofe called judges and lawyers; to the great difgrace of their birth, education, offices, and employments; and fome of
them were fo wofully feduced by their light play-
haunting wives, who fpent fo much time and money
at thefe wicked plays, to the hurt and neglect of
their families, as did drive their hufbands to debt
and danger; and it were highly neceffary, and
very juft, to diveft fuch judges and lawyers of their
honour, offices, and employments, till they a-
bandon Satan's camp and company, and give evidences of their repentance.

And as to the other fort of play-haunters of a
lower degree, they are all the idle, the profane,
godlefs, gracelefs, brutifh rakes, reprobates, and
panders for hell, a plague to the earth and the
place they live in.

A third fort of play-haunters are women, who,
being left to bring up the rear, are none but idle
vagabond jilts, light coquets, ftrumpets, bawds,
and

and vile meretrixes, who have in effect renounced
their baptifm, (as all that frequent ftage-plays do),
their creed, their Chriftianity, their Bible, and
their God, and have lifted themfelves under Satan's banner; yea, have given up even with fobriety, humanity, chaftity, honour, and honefty,
for the wicked, finful, and filthy pleafure of curfed
ftage-plays; which bring no glory to God, nor
good to themfelves, but much hurt and damage.

And it is a matter of deep lamentation, that
the minifters of this prefent church fhould be fo
dumb and filent at thefe fo crying fins of thefe
wicked and devilifh plays. For if they have a
trumpet and a mouth, they fhould cry aloud, and
not fpare, and warn their people of the danger
of thefe land-deftroying and confcience-feducing
plays, which enfnare their fouls to perdition.
But it feems they rather encourage them, and
promote thefe horrid wickednefles. For when
nine of their unhallowed band attended thefe hellifh Pagan plays, all the cenfure that they put upon them, fcarce amounted to a Why do you fo ?
And their play-haunting people they admit to
fealing ordinances, without fo much as a rebuke,
or the leaft fign of repentance or reformation.
And fince they partake of their fin, they will fhare
of their plagues; and the blood of their fouls will
be required at thefe dumb watchmens hand, who
neglect to give faithful warning againft fuch ram-
pant fins.

And as to the magiftrates of this city and elfewhere, inftead of being a terror to evil-doers,
and encouragers of thofe that do well, they encourage and countenance all wickednefs, by allowing,

lowing, suffering, and countenancing these hellish Pagan plays, not only to reside within their bounds, but by giving them ground and liberty to build a temple to the devil, to worship him therein, to their everlasting reproach; which will not fail to bring down the judgments of God upon the places and persons, who suffer and encourage such tremendous wickedness and profanity; as these hellish plays are, and ever have been since Satan set them up, and supported his servants and votaries to haunt them; they being the spring and fountain whence all immorality, profanity, and all manner of idleness and filthiness proceeds; as all nations, cities, and countries, and true Christians, can bear witness.

And the primitive church did excommunicate all players and play-haunters, not only from the sacraments, but from the society of all Christians; and never received them in again, until they gave real evidences and signs of their repentance and reformation; for which they will rise in judgment against this secure and play-encouraging generation, &c.

But that which surpasseth all manner of impudence and audacity is, that these vermin of hell, the play-actors, have styled themselves his Majesty's servants. Now, what Majesty can these miscreants mean? Surely, it can be no Christian Majesty, if he deserve the name, or will ever take the servants of Satan to serve him; for they cannot serve two masters faithfully. Neither can they mean a Pagan Majesty; for all virtuous and sober Pagans banished plays and their actors out of their dominions. Except they mean Nero and
Caligula,

Caligula, and fuch as they, who fat at, and acted plays themfelves. Now, fuch mafters and fuch fervants will agree together; and their only ma-fter is Satan, who reigns and rules in thofe who are the children of difobedience.

But if they mean by Majefty, the Occupant upon the throne of Britain; if he look to his own honour, he fhould chaftife them foundly, for of-fering fuch an affront, difhonour, and difgrace to him, when they are the fworn flaves of Satan and their own lufts, and their whole trade is to de-bauch and pollute the minds, and corrupt the man-ners of the people, and lead them into fin and guilt, unto their everlafting perdition; which they will furely feel, if they do not make a fudden retreat from thefe foul-ruining, profane, and flagi-tious plays. So that all the beft fervice that the kingdom or country can do, fhould be to extirpate them out of the world, and from all human fo-ciety, as the greateft plague and peftilence that ever the nation faw.

But if it be true, as it is reported, O! Occupant, that you have given and granted liberty to erect and fet up Satan's kingdom in Scotland, by al-lowing them to build a temple for his fervants to act therein; if fo, you have done more than your commiffion is worth, or you will ever be able to anfwer for, at the great and laft day, when you will be called to a ftrict account for all your ac-tions, and efpecially for your arrogating a power to fet up profane ftage-plays, in oppofition to, and in contempt of Chriftianity.

For I know that there is one J E S U S, who was dead, and is now alive, and lives for ever more, and

is

is Lord of heaven and earth, that will not give his glory to another, nor his praise to any creature of clay, that dares to usurp his power, and dishonour or rob him of his royal prerogative.

But if it be by force of evil counsel that you have done this deed, more than your own inclination, then to be sure banish them from your court and presence, or else your throne will never be established in peace or truth. Remember what mischief bad counsellors have done in all ages. By hearkening to them, Rehoboam lost the greatest part of his kingdom; and the like wicked counsel made Jeroboam forsake the true God, and build two play-houses, the one at Dan, the other at Bethel, and place players in them of the lowest of the people, to act and serve the devils and calves which he had made.

Another crew of wicked counsellors persuaded Ahab to a journey, where he lost both soul and body, and his kingdom too, at Ramoth-Gilead.

Another wicked counsellor would persuade Ahasuerus to massacre the best people of his kingdom, although contrary counsel restrained him from it, and brought the wicked counsellor to his deserved end. And it were just, that all that act like him got the same desert; and that Jack and David Humes, the one an apostate, the other an Atheist, were among the first to satisfy justice for their high crimes, and bad service to the nation.

Moreover, there is another set of wicked counsellors, as noxious and bad as the other, viz. the Antichristian Knights of the Black Order, alias Bishops. And what pests and plagues they have

B   been

been to church and state since ever Satan and the Pope set them up, and what havock they have made of the best people in all places where-ever they had power, by seducing and hounding out kings and princes to murder and persecute all that would not bear up their train, bow to their mitre, and worship the false gods that they set up, and drink the deadly poison of error, and idle ceremonies, which in all ages have pestered and polluted the church of God, all true histories can witness. For Jesus Christ, the alone head of the church, never gave them a commission to lift themselves above their brethren, or to lord it over God's heritage, but to be ensamples to feed the flock. He never made them idle drones, or dumb dogs, and to lie about kings courts, and feed their idle bellies, and starve their flocks, or else to turn them over to a parcel of ignorant, scandalous, and naughty curates, to feed the poor people with the husks of error, Pagan and Popish ceremonies, and with a dead and lifeless carcase of formality, the mass-book in English, with the like trash of Pelagian and Arminian errors, and others forged out of their own brain. Now, it were just and equal to clip their wings, prick their pride, and reduce them to their primitive institution, viz. to single congregations, and cause them to preach the gospel truly; or else to banish them all to Rome, their mother, from whence they came.

To conclude: Now, O! Occupant, take my humble advice, I pray you; which will be happy for you and these kingdoms, will make your tranquillity lasting, and procure to you both the favour

vour of God and good men; and that is, to ba-
nith and expel out of all your dominions, Popery,
Prelacy, and all idolatry, Atheifm, and profanity,
with all their trumpery; I fay, to banifh them quite
out of thefe lands; to break down all play-houfes,
and banifh thefe idle dogs the actors to the mines,
to work hard under fevere difcipline. And likewife, O! Occupant, renounce that facrilegious
title of head of the church, which belongs neither
to man nor angel, but wholly and alone to JESUS
CHRIST, without any competitor either co-ordi-
nate or fubordinate. Let the fin, the fhame, and
the heavy curfe reft upon the hellifh Pope, who
ufurps the fame. And moreover, remove from
off the church's neck that heavy and finful yoke
of patronage, which came from Rome in the
feventh century, from curfed Pope Valentine.
And likewife you would do well to fupprefs that
horrid fin of fwearing, whereof a great part of
the land is guilty; and if they will not forbear,
execute King Donald of Scotland's law upon them.
Punifh fabbath-breakers and adulterers as the law
of God requires, and be a terror to all evil-doers,
and an encourager of all thofe that do well, and
fear God. Let thefe be the men of your counfel,
and fcatter the wicked from your throne, if you
expect it fhould be eftablifhed in righteoufnefs.
But if you do the quite contrary to this good advice, and go on in your former courfe of fupporting Satan's kingdom, be you affured your peace
fhall not be as a river, and it will be bitternefs in
the latter end. This addrefs is from a lover of
truth, and one who is a lover of the welfare of
the fouls of all men.

B 2   POST-

POSTSCRIPT.

Amongſt the many and regnant ſins of the day, that of flattering the powers that be, is not the leaſt. What ſhame, ſin, ſorrow, and ruin, it hath brought upon the flatterers and flattered, is evident enough to all through the world. For wicked Herod allowing his flatterers to deify him, was ſmitten of God, and eaten of worms, for allowing them ſuch wicked flattery. There were threeſcore and twelve Roman emperors between Julius Cæſar and Auguſtulus, and but three of them died in their beds in peace. All the others came to black and diſmal ends, for their cruelty, tyranny, and wicked life, encouraged by their flatterers, either by their own hands, or by their injured ſubjects, or by the hands of ſtrangers, for their horrid and tremendous wickedneſs. Now, to come to our own land, the wicked furious malignant party, by their cruelty and flattery, have brought many of their kings and people to ruin both in ſoul, body, and eſtate: for they perſuaded them to rule above all law of God and man; that they were accountable to none on earth for any of their actions; that the lives and goods of their ſubjects were all at their diſpoſal; and that they can do no wrong, although they ſhould bring in the Turkiſh Alcoran, and murder all the people of the land for refuſing it, as they did for refuſing a maſs-book of the like kind. Such helliſh and ſlaviſh principles ought to be abhorred by all rational creatures; and if they were not themſelves ſlaves to Satan and their own luſts, they would

renounce

renounce fuch madnefs with indignation for ever. The other fort of flatterers, of the malignant kind, are the black band of Bifhops. What perfecutions they have driven their kings to act, and what cruelty, trouble, and vexation, they brought upon the beft people of the land, all true hiftories bear witnefs. Yea, what wreck, trouble, and mifchief, they brought upon the king and country, and upon themfelves likewife, by their wicked counfels, and bafe flattery, is evident in the whole courfe of life, and hiftory of Becket, Beaton, and Laud.

It is to be bewailed, that this Eraftian church, and the felfifh and malicious Seceders, are guilty of the fame fin of flattering their princes in their iniquity. They are never fo faithful as to warn the Occupant upon the throne, of the deluge of blood and perjury that lies about the throne for a long time unpurged away, of the great fin of ufurping the fupremacy over the church, and of his bearing down the church with the heavy yoke of patronage, a bondage that came from hell and Rome. Neither do they warn him of the great fin of pardoning murderers, and other crimes, which the law of God condemns; and although many account it a grievance, yet they ufe no effectual endeavours to remove it. Neither do they warn him to abolifh and banifh all ftage-plays and interludes out of thefe lands, which will procure the curfe and vengeance of almighty God upon perfons or places where they are either tolerated or connived at. Now, if the Occupant were doing his duty, he would fharply rebuke both the flattering church and Seceders, for being fo cruelly

unfaithful

unfaithful to him, in not warning him of his sin, and the judgments which therefore are hanging over our heads; which will undoubtedly fall out upon them, without a speedy repentance.

Another dreadful effect of stage-plays is, that they cause an apparent breach of all God's commandments.

1. Of the first, in honouring, applauding, invocating, representing, and extolling Pagan idols, gods and goddesses, by the names of God; in reviving their infernal ceremonies, rites, and worship; and in propagating atheism and idolatry.

2. Of the second, in making the images and pictures, shapes and statues, representing the persons, vices, ceremonies, and customs of these hellish Pagan devil gods; and in relating their histories, pedigree, acts, and mad monuments.

3. Of the third, in profaning and blaspheming the name of the true God, by cursed oaths and horrid execrations, frequent in their interludes; by traducing and profaning the holy name and word of God; by deriding the sincere worship and service of God; and by taking all God's names, titles, attributes, and ordinances in vain.

4. Of the fourth, by profaning the Lord's day in a notorious manner; not only spending it in idleness, and neglect of all manner of worship, but even in getting and repeating their parts of these profane plays; and in drawing men to idleness

nefs on other days, by their either reading, hearing, or feeing thefe plays.

5. Of the fifth, by difhonouring, reproaching, traducing, and ridiculing minifters and magiftrates, lawful and religious, upon the ftage; who, in the regular and lawful exercife of their offices, are the fathers and mothers of church and ftate.

6. Of the fixth, in occafioning and recommending murders, quarrels, duels, tyranny, and cruelty; by murdering the good names of other men; by teaching plots to poifon, betray, and ruin others; above all, in murdering innumerable fouls of men and women, whom ftage-plays caufe to perifh.

7. Of the feventh, in fomenting and exciting unchafte affections in the actors and fpectators, drawing them on to fornication, adultery, and other detefable uncleanneffes, which Chriftians fhould abhor to name or think upon.

8. Of the eighth, in teaching men to cheat and cozen one another; in picking other mens purfes, by receiving money for exercifing of thefe unlawful wicked plays, which God never ordained as a mean to get gain by; the taking of which money for fuch a trade is plain theft.

9. Of the ninth, in flandering, by perfonating and traducing particular perfons and fafhions on the ftage; and cafting falfe afperfions, with terms

of

of ignominy and fcorn, upon the faints and ordinances of God.

10. Of the tenth, in caufing children and pro-
digals to wifh and defire the death of their parents,
that fo they may enjoy and prodigally wafte their
patrimony and portions on their lufts and vain plays;
and in caufing men to covet the pomp, the pof-
feffions, the wives, the fervants, and the goods of
other men ; as players, whores, and others who
refort to ftage-plays, learn to do, and daily practife.

To conclude in the words of famous Mr William Prinne, in his *Hiftrio-maftix*, p. 62. " If we
" furvey the ftyle or fubject-matter of all our po-
" pular interludes, we fhall difcover them to be
" either fcurrilous, amorous, and obfcene ; or
" barbarous, bloody, and tyrannical ; or hea-
" thenifh and profane ; or fabulous and fictitious ;
" or impious and blafphemous ; or fatirical and
" invective ; or at the beft but frothy, vain, and
" frivolous. If then the compofure and matter
" of our popular ftage-plays be but fuch as this,
" the plays themfelves muft needs be evil, unfeem-
" ly, and unlawful unto CHRISTIANS."

F I N I S.

14 Some Serious Remarks on a Late Pamphlet, entituled, The Morality of Stage-Plays Seriously Considered

This piece, often attributed to a certain Reverend Harper, was written in response to Ferguson's assertion that evidence in the Scriptures points to a Church history which is more open to the moral benefits of plays. This tract offers a more learned criticism than the hard line stage opponents, while still remaining true to the remit of the Popular opposition. Rather than dismiss Ferguson as an infidel, Harper chooses to engage him on his composition, language and biblical understanding. Demonstrating that he is also learned in both the Scriptures and the classics, Harper attempts to counter Ferguson's arguments for the morality of stage plays in the Church's history.

SOME

SERIOUS REMARKS

ON

A Late PAMPHLET,

ENTITULED,

The MORALITY of STAGE-PLAYS Serioufly confidered.

In a LETTER to a LADY.

Bleffed is the Man that walketh not in the Counfel of the Un- godly, nor ftandeth in the Way of Sinners, nor fitteth in the Seat of the fcornful.

PSAL. i. 1.

I have not fat with vain Perfons, *nor will I go in with* Dif- femblers.

PSAL. xxvi. 4.

EDINBURGH:

Printed in the Year M.DCC.LVII.

A
LETTER, &c.

MADAM,

I Have read the Pamphlet you sent me Yesterday, entituled, *The Morality of Stage Plays seriously considered*, &c. I am sorry to hear, that has been, of late, the Subject of much Controversy, (I ought rather to have said) the Subject of much Contention here, for really Truth and Argument are all on one Side of the Question.

Many Years are past since I had settled my Opinion of that Matter, and was so fully satisfied and determined, that I have not read the Papers which have come abroad on either Side, and perhaps never would, if your Ladyship had not desired I should read this one, and give you my Opinion of it.

I own I have no Talent at compounding Matters between Wisdom and Folly, Virtue and Vice, or Christ and Belial; nor would I attempt it, unless I were first made certain, that Men may get to Heaven upon their own Terms, and that it is not the Privilege of our Creator and Redeemer to prescribe to his own Creatures, or to settle the Conditions upon which their Forgiveness, and his Mercy, are to be obtained.

A   As

As I do not know the Author of this Performance, I may treat him with the lefs Ceremony: Whoever he is, he feems more Mafter of Language, than of Logick, and to have ftudied more the Smoothnefs of his Stile, than the Truth of his Narrative, or the Force of his Arguments.

I have confidered his Performance as *ferioufly*, and perhaps as fully as he has done; and that you may not think I am unjuft to him, I will lay before you a few Samples of his Reafoning, and leave you to judge how lucky he has been in his Choice of Topicks, how difcreet and fit his Premiffes, and how fair and confequential his Inferences are.———Not that I will pretend to equal him in his Flow of Words, or in his Arts of Soothing, and Infinuation: If I could imitate him in this, I would not, for Truth needs no painting to increafe its Beauty; it appears beft in its native Colours, and plain Drefs.

After a long artful Preface, (by which he would perfwade the Reader, that he had nothing in his View, but the Peace of Society, and the Good of Mankind) he brings forth his firft Argument in favour of the Stage; an Argument which I tremble to repeat, it borders fo nigh upon Blafphemy, fomething like that of the ancient *Pharifees*, who accufed our Saviour of cafting out Devils by *Belzebub*.

He fays, (Page 4th) " Our Savionr, who " appeared at a Time when Plays were in high
                                          " Repute

" Repute in different Parts of the *Roman* Em-
" pire, fays nothing to warn us of their Immo-
" rality."——Now, Madam, fuppofe this were
true, it would conclude nothing; it is at beft
but a negative Argument, of which every one
knows the little Force, and that it is againft all
the Rules of Reafoning, *from Silence to infer
Approbation.* I do not remember to have read
in the Gofpel that our Saviour has faid any
Thing directly to warn us of the *Immorality of
Suicide,* and yet I hope this Author will not
hence infer, that Self-murder is lawful.

But I wifh the Author had ferioufly confidered the Defign of our bleffed Lord's coming
into the World, the Manner of his Appearance
in it, with the Aim and Tendency of his
Doctrines, his Precepts and Example, to fee
whether any of thefe would yield the leaft
Shadow of Authority, or but Apology for the
Play-houfe.——The Defign of his Incarnation
was to fave Sinners.——And for that End, not
only to make an Atonement for them by his
Blood, but by his Word and Spirit to rectify
the Diforders which were got into our Nature,
which fet and kept us at Diftance and Enmity with God, to enable us to reftrain and fub-
due our finful Lufts and Paffions, to make us
new Creatures, transformed from earthly, fenfual, devilifh, into fpiritual, holy, and heavenly
minded.

The Manner of his Appearance, the Condition of Life he chofe, was that of Poverty and
Contempt, fubject to Hunger, Thirft, Weari-
nefs, and the common Feelings of Sympathy

and Compaffion.—He went about doing Good, doing the beft Things, and fuffering the worft: In fhort, he appeared in the Form of a Servant, which Form he affumed, not of Neceffity but Choice, as moft conducive to his gracious Defign, which was to inculcate thofe Virtues, which, I hope, even this Gentleman will not fay, are taught in the Play-houfe.——

His divine Doctrines and Precepts all point the fame Way with his holy Example.——He enjoins Purity and Peacefulnefs, Meeknefs and Mercy, Self-denial, taking up the Crofs, and Mortification of our fenfual Lufts and Appetites.——Are thefe Virtues taught and learned in the Play-houfe?——

We read in the Gofpel, that our bleffed Saviour was often in the Temple and Synagogues, but not once in the Theatre: That he fpent watchful Nights in Devotion, but none in Diverfions: That he withdrew from the Crowd for the Purpofes of Meditation and Prayer, but not that he reforted to it for Frolick or Amufement. —— My Charity obligeth me to think this Author had not ferioufly confidered all this, and that the Character of a Believer or Chriftian indeed, implies a careful Imitation of Chrift's Example, &c. If he had, he could not have had Audacity enough to mention this Argument for the Play, in a Country profeffing Chriftianity; at leaft while the Liberty we boaft of, is (I hope) not as yet fuppofed to imply a Liberty to blafpheme.

When our Lord Jefus Chrift enjoined his Followers to " fearch the Scriptures to find e-

" ternal Life," had he given a Hint in favour
of Comedies and Tragedies, and bid them read
or hear, and ftudy Plays, as a needful or proper Appendix and Supplement to his holy
Word.

When he eftablifhed his Church upon Earth
as a Society, diftinct from thefe of the World,
appointing and fending Men chofen by him,
on Purpofe to inftruct and govern that Society,
with Commiffion and Authority, to teach and
baptize, that is, to make Difciples, and initiate
them into the Belief and Practice of his Religion, and Privileges of his Kingdom, telling
them for their Encouragement in that difficult
Work, That " to defpife, or not to hear them,
was" in Effect to defpife him.——Had he then
put in a *Salvo* in favours of the Writers and
Actors of Plays, and fent his Difciples to the
Theatre, for fupplying the Deficiencies of their
authorized, ordinary Guides.

When he wrought miraculous Cures, and
bid the Perfons recovered " fhew themfelves to
" the Priefts, and make their Acknowledgments
" to God by the proper Oblation;" had he
told them they might be churched in the Play-
houfe.

When he warn'd his Difciples, That " the
" Way to Heaven is ftrait, and the Gate nar-
" row, and that there are but few who find it."
Had he fent them to the Theatre, to learn how
to widen the Entrance, or to foften and fmooth
the Difficulties occurring in the Paffage to it.
Had all this been true, this Gentleman might
have

have said something to Purpose for the Stage, but the direct contrary appears to be the Case.

I am really concerned and grieved, Madam, to find the Gospel of our Salvation thus burlesqued, and the blessed Author of it thus ridiculed and trifled with. Certainly this hardy Writer must have a poor Opinion of the Understanding and Virtue of his Readers, when by such a Mixture of Profaneness and Audacity, he questions or affronts all their Attainments in Christianity and common Sense.——— I will finish this Article with my earnest Prayers for him, that God would bring him to a better Mind, and not lay this Sin to his Charge.

His next Argument is in the same Page; there he tells us, That " the Apostle *Paul* in " writing his Epistle to the *Romans*, among " various Instructions and Cautions which he " gives us, is silent on the Subject of Plays, " which were then in high Repute amongst " the People he was writing to."

This Argument is so much of a Piece with the former, that the same Answer will suffice. It is plainly negative, and you have already seen what Weight it can have, and that from simple Silence or Omission, it is not safe to infer Consent or Approbation.

But had this Author seriously considered this excellent Epistle, or but the first and twelfth Chapters of it, 'tis possible he might have made a very different Conclusion.———Towards the End of the first Chapter, the Apostle gives a

most

moſt dreadful Deſcription of the Religion in Faſhion among the Heathen *Romans* at that Time. One can ſcarce read it without pitying their Ignorance, Stupidity and Debauchery, to which the Theatre had contributed not a little, as will appear by and by, from unexceptionable Evidence fetched out of their own Philoſophers and Poets.

He begins the 12th Chapter with exhorting them " to offer themſelves to God, a holy, " living and acceptable Sacrifice, *&c.* and " that they ſhould *not be conformed to this* " *World*, but be transformed by the renew- " ing of their Mind, that they might prove " what is the good and acceptable, and perfect " Will of God." And in the reſt of that Chapter, he gives many Inſtructions and Ex- hortations, not to duelling, fighting, or Suicide; not to cheating or robbing; not to intrigueing, procuring, or Amours, (which are often exhi- bited upon the Stage, and (I am ſorry to ſay it) more frequently and more barefacedly upon the preſent *Britiſh*, than it was of old upon the Pagan *Greek*, and *Roman* Theatres; but to other Du- ties and Purpoſes, to Diligence in our Buſineſs, Modeſty in our Behaviour, Fervour in our Devotions, Charity without Hypocriſy——Almſ- giving and Hoſpitality, and Abhorrence of that which is evil, *&c. &c.* And which of theſe laſt Leſſons are often and plainly taught on the Stage, I think I may venture to leave this Author to tell.

He

He next proceeds to (what he would have pafs for pofitive Proof from Scripture) telling us, that, " In his preaching at *Athens*, the " fame Apoftle (*Paul*) exprefly quotes a Sen- " tence from one of the *Greek* Poets, *Acts* " xvii. 28. *For in him we live, and move,* " *and have our Being*, as certain of their own " Poets have faid. This, fays he, is a very " fublime Expreffion, and beautifully applied " by the Apoftle, as will appear on confulting " the Context. It fhews that he was fenfible " of the Inftructions, and good Impreffions " we may receive from Poetry, and was direct- " ed by that Spirit which had fupported him " in his Miniftry, to apply it fo properly to " thofe Purpofes. Nor is this the only Proof " he has given of good Performances of this " Nature. He has in the firft Epiftle to the " *Corinthians*, xv. 33. inferted upon the facred " Text, a Line from a *Greek* Play, which " now fubfifts, *Be not deceived, evil Commu-* " *nications corrupt good Manners*.".

The laft of thefe Quotations is from *Menan-der* a *Greek* Poet, and very properly it is brought on that Occafion. The Apoftle had been re-futing the *Epicureans*, whofe chief Aim was *Pleafure*, or *indulging their Appetites*, as ap-pears from the preceeding Verfe, taken like-ways from one of them, " Let us eat and " drink, for To-morrow we die." In Oppo-fition to this brutal Dogma, he brings forth this Line of *Menander*, " Be not deceived, *&c.*

" *&c.* And is there any Impropriety in fighting an Adverſary with his own Weapons? or can we think the Apoſtle, by this Citation, meant to enrol the Works of *Menander* into the Canon of Scripture?

The former Quotation, *Acts* xvii. 28. is taken from *Aratus*, one of the *Greek* Poets. Here the Apoſtle, at *Athens*, was engaged againſt the Stoicks, who denied that God made the World, but ſuppoſed it to have ſtarted into Exiſtence, by Chance medley, or a fortuitous Concourſe of Atoms. — Againſt this fanciful unphiloſophical Dream, the Apoſtle brings the Conceſſion of one of their own Poets, " In " him we live and move, and have our Being." Only what *Aratus* had aſcribed to *Jupiter*, the Apoſtle transfers to the true God, whom (at that Time) the People of *Athens* knew not.

I could have helped our Author to a third Citation from a Heathen Poet, which, for certain Reaſons, he did not chuſe to mention, and I do not remember to have met with any more in the New Teſtament; 'tis in *Titus* i. 12. " The *Cretians* are always Liars; evil " Beaſts, ſlow Bellies." This is taken from *Epimenides*, another *Greek* Poet, and very properly brought furth in an Admonition to *Titus*, who was left in *Crete* to eſtabliſh a better Religion amongſt them. But what avail all theſe Citations to the Cauſe, this Gentleman has taken upon him to defend? Of theſe three Heathen Authors, cited in the New Teſtament,

B

-ftament, two were only Poets, and but the third (*Menander*) wrote Comedies, or furnifhed any Entertainment for the Stage. —— A Heathen Poet may ftumble upon an Expreffion wife and true; an infpired Writer (for a particular Purpofe) cites that wife Saying. What can be inferred from thence? I hope not that both Authors are of equal Authority. The Devil fpoke Truth, when he informed againft *Job*.—— " Does " *Job* ferve God for nought? —— But will any Man infer from thence, that we may fafely apply to the Devil for Information, or Advice? ——No, Madam, Truth is God's Truth, whereever it is found ; like a Mine of Gold, it ftill belongs to the King in whofoever's Ground it is difcovered.—— Enough is faid, to fhew how modeft and juft that Expreffion of this Author is, Page 6th ; where he tells us, " The Authors " of fuch Works (*i. e.* Plays) have been e- " fteemed worthy of great Praife, and have " been thought to bear a confiderable Part in " promoting the Intereft of Virtue: We can- " not doubt of this, (fays he) when we find " any Degree of Regard paid to them in holy " Writ; and what we have obferved to this " Purpofe above, is fufficient to connect their " Defence with the Honour of Scripture itfelf." Madam, The Word of God in holy Scripture, is the Privilege, and greateft Bleffing in the Cuftody of Chriftians : We ought often to read, hear, and meditate upon it, with Attention, Reverence, Humility, and a teachable Difpofition,

Difpofition, free from Prejudice or Prepoffeffion, a Difpofition to believe whatever God fays,
and to obey whatever he commands. —— Unhappy and unwife are they, who do not confult and ftudy, and liften to thefe facred Oracles, for the Improvement of their Minds, and
the Conduct of their Lives. —— But I am a-
fraid there are many who read the Holy Scriptures for other Purpofes, and with ill Defign.——
Some read thefe facred Books as they do a
News Paper or a Romance, only for Curiofity, or for the Sake of Hiftory or Amufement: Others read them with Prejudice and
Prepoffeffion.——They have got fome favourite Opinion into their Heads, and therefore
they ranfack the Bible, and ftudy thofe Parts
of it which feem to carry fome Correfponden-
cy to the Opinion they have adopted ; thefe,
they rack, and fcrew into a perfect Conformity
with their own fond Conceits, and improve e-
very little Probability into a Demonftration.——
I wifh this Author may not have read in this
Way.

There are fome, who read the Word of
God infidioufly, on Purpofe to find Matter of
Objection and Cavil againft it, only that they
may get free of its Reftraints, and the Yoke it
lays upon them : But there are others, who to
Malice add *Contempt*, who not only ftifle and
refift its divine Precepts, but alfo revile and ridicule them, arraign the Wifdom of God, and
pronounce his Laws to be weak and impertinent,

nent, lay their Scenes of ridiculous Mirth in the Bible, rally in the facred Dialect, and play the Buffoons with the moft ferious Thing in the World.

Whether this Defcription will take in the *Britifh* Stage, I will leave to others to judge.

Tho' neither my Circumftances nor Inclination lead me to attend the Stage, I am not fo unacquainted with what is exhibited (and fometimes applauded) there, but that I fear, the holy Name of God, his Word, his Ordinances, and his Minifters, &c. are often made the Subject of their profane Wit and Drollery: If my Books do not deceive me, I could point to the very Plays and Places where thefe Things occur.

And if we are come to this impious Licentioufnefs, I cannot forbear thinking it is one of the Wonders of God's long Suffering, that there are not as many eminent Inftances of the Vengeance, as there are of the Guilt.——Certainly this Abufe in Men, who ftill feem to own the Bible as the Word of God, is more monftrous than in thofe Deifts who deny it: Thefe look upon it as a common Thing, and ufe it as fuch; but for thofe who ftill confefs it facred, thus to proftitute and profane it, or to encourage them that do fo, is a flat Contradiction, as much againft the Rules of Decency and Civility, as of Religion.——'Tis to offer the fame Abufe to Jefus Chrift in his Word, which the rude Soldiers did to his Perfon, to bow the

Knee

Knee before it, and yet expofe it as an Object of Scorn and Laughter.——Men may flatter themfelves that thefe lighter Frolicks will pafs for nothing, fo long as they do not *ferioufly* and malicioufly oppofe God's Word: But tho' they be in Jeft, they may find God in earneft; and that he who has *magnified his Word above all Things*, will not brook that we fhould make it vile and cheap, by playing and dallying with it for our Sport and Paftime; nor will be pleafed to have his own Words echoed back to him in profane Drollery.

That this Author I am now *ferioufly confidering*, has read the holy Scriptures with fome of the bad Intentions I have mentioned, there is (befide what is already faid) a ftrong Prefumption in his 8th to 13th Page; there he brings a profane, faucy, impertinent Parallel between the Hiftory of *Jofeph* and the late Tragedy of *Douglas*.

I have not feen this late Tragedy, which has made fo much Noife, and is like to be hurtful in its Confequences, but have been told (by them I can truft) what the Author's Plan is, and how he has wrought it up. And really, Madam (without infifting upon the great Odds between true and falfe, Hiftory and Fable, or facred and profane,) I can difcover no fuch Proportion or Refemblance between the two Cafes, as can juftify a Comparifon.

By this Gentleman's own Account of Tragedy (Page 7th and 8th) " it ought to be feri-
" ous,

" ous, grave and majeftic; to reprefent the A-
" ctions of great Men, and their Conduct chief-
" ly on great and interefting Occafions, &c."
—— " We can't therefore (fays he) condemn
" the Story reprefented in any Tragedy till we
" know of what Kind it is, till we know whe-
" ther it tends to leave good Impreffions or
" bad ones in the Minds of the Hearers."——
Now let us apply thefe two Cafes to his own
Rule. The firft fhews us a pious, modeft, innocent young Man, engaged in a Variety of Trials
and Dangers, Snares and Diftreffes.—He ftill
preferves his Integrity, refifts Temptations, and
adheres to God and Duty; and after his Virtue had been fufficiently tried, and held out in
the Trial, at laft it conquers all Oppofition,
and is rewarded even in this World.

In the other is reprefented an unfortunate
Lady, ftruggling againft many Counter-blafts
of Fortune, and Storms of adverfe Fate: For
fome time fhe ftands the Shock, and has Re-
courfe to Tears and Prayers, and Expoftula-
tions with God. But at laft her Patience is
worn out, fhe finds no Benefit in drawing nigh
to the moft High, Why fhould fhe wait upon
God any longer: fo fhe falls into Defpair, runs
mad, and kills herfelf.

The firft fets before us a noble Example of
Fortitude, Conftancy, and Perfeverance in Virtue and Holinefs, the other exhibits an Inftance
of Defpair and Self-murder. I would ask this
Apologift, which of the two is moft imitable,
and

and leaves the beſt Impreſſions on the Minds of the Hearers?

After this Author had inſinuated (P. 12th) " That the Chriſtian Church has not invaria- " bly diſcouraged good Plays." He tells us, (Page 13th) " That the Fathers of the Church, " whoſe Authority is probably referred to on " this Occaſion, *ought ſurely to have very lit- " tle Credit with us on their own Account.* " That a great Part of the Superſtition of the " Church of *Rome* is derived from their Inven- " tions, and that we have already totally re- " jeſted the Authority of them, and their oral " Traditions, when we reformed the Corrup- " tion of the Popiſh Church."

This Gentleman ſeems to be unacquainted with the Popiſh Controverſy, and the Hiſtory of the Reformation from the Errors of that Church; had he *ſeriouſly conſidered* theſe, he would have found, that the Popiſh Errors were confuted, not by Texts of Scripture only, but by concurring Teſtimonies from the Fathers of the early Ages, who lived and wrote, and were in high Eſteem, long before what we call Popery had prevailed in the World, however little Va- lue he may now ſet on them.—Had he known this, I hope he would not have made the Church of *Rome,* ſo valuable a Preſent as that of the Fathers; this is really throwing too much Weight into their Side of the Balance. Howe- ver, as Plays ſtill ſubſiſt in Popiſh Countries, that is one of the Corruptions of the *Roman* Church,

Church, not yet reformed, which this Author seems very unwilling to part with.

In the same Page he says, " *Gregory Nan-* " *zianzen,* a Father of the Church, and a Per- " son of great Piety, endeavoured to supplant " Heathen Plays, by introducing one which " he wrote himself, on the most interesting " Subject of our Religion.——

I know that *Gregory Nanzianzen* lived in the 4th Century, was a good Scholar, and (what is more) a good Man, that he wrote *Greek* in as great Purity as any one of his Time; insomuch that they substituted his Writings in place of the ancient *Greek* Authors, as the Standard of that Language.——But what then, may not one be a good Scholar without writing Plays?——My Books tell me that he wrote 55 Discourses or Sermons, and yet a greater Number of divine Poems: But must every Poet be a Comedian?

I know too that there was a spurious Piece, a Tragedy, entituled, *The Sufferings of Christ,* once ascribed to him ; but I hope this Author does not mean to palm that upon us at this Time of Day, as the Work of *Nanzianzen,* after the best Judges, and most learned Critics (such as Doctor *Cave* and *Dupin*) have declared it unworthy of him, and delivered his Character from that Imputation.

But what if, to oblige our Author, I should give up *Gregory Nanzianzen* as a Friend to the Stage, it would profit him very little, when all his

his Contemporaries, and the Fathers both before and after him, (whether single or united
in Councils) have bore Teſtimony on the o-
ther Side.

It would not be difficult for me to lay before your Ladyſhip the Sentiments of the early
Fathers on this Subjeſt.—— Of *Theophilus* of
Antioch, and *Tertullian* in the 2d Century,
(this laſt is deciſive, and has exhauſted the Argument;) of *Clemens* of *Alexandria*, *Mi-
nutius Felix* and *Cyprian* in the third; and
after them of *Laċtantius*, *Chryſoſtom*, *Hierom*,
and *Auguſtine*.——I might alſo ſet before you
the Decrees or Canons of Councils, both in
Europe and *Africa*, againſt the Stage, down to
the 5th Century, and I would come no lower
than to thoſe good Times of Truth, Piety and
Purity, before Popery (properly ſo called) had
got Footing in the World.

But I foreſee this would be tedious, and
ſwell this Letter beyond the Bulk I intended;
beſides, I am afraid our Author would have no
Regard for the Sentiments of thoſe old holy
Men, (ſome of them Martyrs too;) tho', if the
Grace of God ſhould touch his Heart ſo far,
as *ſeriouſly* to conſider their Reaſonings on this
Subjeſt, I dare ſay he would alter his Opinion
of the modern as well as the ancient Stage, and
not think ſo contemptibly of them that oppoſe
it, as at preſent he ſeems to do.

There is one Thing I would beg Leave to in-
ſert here, though it is out of its proper Place.

C   Upon

Upon a Review of *Tertullian*, I find a Paſſage which I ought to have remembered, when I was animadverting upon the Author's firſt Claſs of Arguments for the Stage, *i. e.* thoſe from Scripture. As it eſcaped me there, I will give it Room here, though it might have done better in another Place.——It ſeems the Sentiments and Faſhions of ſome, have been the ſame in all Ages.——*Tertullian* ſays, That in his Time, " ſome People's Faith was either too full of " Scruples, or too barren of Senſe, and that " nothing would ſerve to ſettle them but a Text " of Scripture: That they hovered in Uncer- " tainty, becauſe it is not as expreſly ſaid, Thou " ſhalt not go to the Play-houſe, as it is, Thou " ſhalt not kill.——But this looks more like " Fencing than Argument: For we have the " Meaning of the Prohibition, though not the " Sound, in the firſt Pſalm, *Bleſſed is the* " *Man that walks not in the Counſel of the* " *Ungodly, nor ſtands in the Way of Sinners,* " *nor ſits in the Seat of the Scornful.*

But it is poſſible, and not very unlikely, that this ſly Author is one of thoſe fine Gentlemen, (diſtinguiſhed by the good Name of Free-think- ers,) who ſtrut and vapour upon the Privileges and Extent of their Reaſon and natural Pow- ers.——And if he is, I would refer him to other Authorities againſt the Stage, to which he will probably pay more Reſpect; I mean thoſe of the ancient Heathen Sages, both *Greek* and *Roman* Philoſophers, Orators and Hiſtorians.

I am

I am convinced, that Nature was the fame, in the Days of *Socrates*, *Pythagoras*, *Plato* and *Ariftotle*, that it is now, (except that it is dignified by Jefus Chrift's affuming it) and that they enjoyed no lefs Clearnefs and Strength of natural Reafon, than a *Shaftsbary*, *Tindal*, *Toland*, *Collins*, *Woolfton*, *Bolingbroke*, or any other of the later Deifts do; notwithftanding all the Helps they have derived from Holy Scripture, for which they are very unthankful, and of which they have made a very bad Ufe.

Now, Madam, If it fhould appear that the beft and wifeft, and moft efteemed of the Heathen Fathers, did (for human and political Reafons) difapprove of the Stage, and that even in that Time of Darknefs and Infidelity, few or none did contend for, or furnifh Entertainment for the Stage, but poor, half-bred Scholars, whofe Wit was predominant for their Judgment, or who wrote either for Vanity, or Neceffity for Subfiftence, or an Affectation of Singularity. This might be worthy of our Author's *ferious* Confideration.

Plato banifheth Plays from his Commonwealth, becaufe (fays he,) they raife the Paffions, and pervert the Ufe of them, and therefore are dangerous to Morality. —— *Ariftotle* lays it down for a Rule, that the Law ought to forbid young People the feeing of Comedies, for very good Reafons which he there affigns.--- And *Xenophon* commends the *Perfians*, that they would not fuffer their Youth to fee any Thing amorous, becaufe it was dangerous to add Weight to the Bias of Nature.

Such

Such were the Sentiments of the wiſer *Greeks*: And accordingly *Plutarch* tells, that the *Lacedemonians*, (who were remarkable for the Wiſdom of their Laws, the Sobriety of their Manners, and their breeding of brave Men,) would not in their Government endure the Stage in any Form, nor under any Regulation.——And even the *Athenians*, who admitted the Play-houſe in their State, yet thought *Comedy* ſo unreputable a Performance, that they made a Law, ' That no Judge of the *Areopa-* " *gus* ſhould make one."

If we come down to the *Romans*, we ſhall find the ſame Impreſſions in the wiſeſt and beſt: *Cicero* cries out upon " licentious Plays and " Poems, as the Bane of Sobriety and an Hin- " derance to wiſe Thinking."——He ſays ex- preſly, " That Comedy ſubſiſts in Lewdneſs, " and that Pleaſure is the Root of all Evil." *Titus Livius* tells us the Origin of Plays a- mong the *Romans*, That they were brought in upon the Score of Religion, to pacify the Gods, and remove a Mortality: But then he adds, That the Motives are ſometimes good, when the Means are bad; that the Remedy in this Caſe was worſe than the Diſeaſe, and the Atonement more infectious than the Plague.

His Contemporary *Valerius Maximus* gives much the ſame Account of the Riſe of Thea- tres at *Rome:* But then he ſays, they occaſi- oned civil Diſtractions; that the State firſt bluſh- ed, and then bled for the Entertainment: And

ſo

fo he concludes the Confequences of Plays intolerable.

Seneca complains of the Extravagance and Debauchery of the Age, and how forward People were to improve in that which was nought; that fcarce any Body would apply themfelves to the Study of Nature and Morality, unlefs when *the Play-houfe was fhut,* or the Weather foul. —— That there is nothing more deftructive to good Manners than to run idling to fee *Sights; for there Vice makes an infenfible Approach, and fteals in upon us* in the Difguife of Pleafure.

Tacitus complains of *Nero,* that he hired decayed Gentlemen for the Stage: He fays, it was the Part of a Prince to relieve their Neceffity, but not to tempt it, and that his Bounty fhould rather have fet them above an ill Practice, than driven them upon it.——And in another Place, he tells us, the *German Women* were guarded againft Danger, and kept their Honour out of Harm's Way, by having no *Play-houfes* amongft them.

Nay, even *Ovid* himfelf, whofe Poems, (fome of them,) had contributed not a little Affiftance to Amours and Immorality, yet when he came to himfelf, he endeavours to make fome Amends for his Faults, and gives *Auguftus* a fort of Plan for a publick Reformation; and among other Things he advifes " the *fuppreffing of Plays* by *his Authority,* be-
" caufe

" cauſe they were the Promoters of Lewdneſs,
" and Diſſolution of Manners."

In the *Theodoſian Code*, *Players* are called
by a Name, which according to the ſofteſt
Tranſlation can mean no leſs than Perſons of
bad Character.——And upon this Text *Gotho-fred* ſays, " The Function of Players was (by
" the civil Law) counted *ſcandalous;* and that
" they who came upon the Stage to divert
" the People, had a Mark of Infamy ſet upon
" them."

But as *Theodoſius* was a Chriſtian, I ought
not to have mentioned him in this Place, tho'
he lived in the fourth Century, and long before
the Riſe of Popery.——Nor was it neceſſary, as
we may go back to the Times of Heathen
Rome to find the Government obſerving and
curbing the Stage. The *Roman Cenſors*, whoſe
Buſineſs it was to take Care of Regularity and
Manners, looked on theſe *Play-houſes* as no o-
ther than Batteries raiſed againſt Virtue and Sobriety, and for this Reaſon often pulled them
down before they were well built. —— So that
here we can argue upon the Precedents of Nature, and plead the wiſer Heathens againſt the
fooliſh. —— If Magiſtrates now ſhewed the
ſame Zeal, they could not eſcape our Author's
very ſevere Cenſure.——Upon this View *Pom-pey the Great*, when he built his dramatick
Bawdy-houſe, put a Chapel on the Top of it:
He would not let it go under the Name of a
Play-houſe, but conveened the People to a ſo-
lemn

lemn Dedication, and called it the Temple of
Venus; giving them to underſtand, that there
were Benches under it for Diverſion.——For he
was afraid, if he had not gone this cunning Way
to Work, the *Cenſors* might afterwards have
razed the Monument, and branded his Memory.——Thus a ſcandalous Pile of Building was
protected, the Temple covered the Play-houſe,
and the Care and Diſcipline of the Magiſtrate
were baffled by a Pretence of Religion.

This, Madam, was the Opinion of theſe *celebrated Authors* with reſpect to *Theatres*; they
charge them with the Corruption of Principles
and Manners, and lay in Cautions and Cave-
ats (very wiſe and judicious) againſt them; and
yet theſe Men had ſeldom any Thing but this
World in their Scheme, and formed their Judgments only upon natural Light, and common
Experience: All they aimed at was the Preſer-
vation of Virtue, Decency and good Order,
with the Peace and Safety of the States and
Countries they lived in: For they had little or
no Notion of a future Life, and were very uncertain about what ſhould become of them when
they died.

Now, one would think, that the Argument
ſhould riſe in its Force, and conclude much
ſtronger with us, who have Life and Immortality brought to Light by the Goſpel, are ſure
that there is a future Reckoning, where we
muſt account for the Manner in which we have
ſpent our Time here, and be finally doomed to
everlaſting

everlasting Misery or Happiness, according to our Behaviour.

It could never be the Design of God's Providence (wise and good) to send us into this World merely to frisk and sport, and play ourselves a while, (like young Beasts in a fine fruitful Meadow) and then tumble out of it with as little Care, or Thought (as they have) of what is to become of us hereafter.

It is a common Complaint, That Life is short, and the Term of it uncertain. Is it not then very surprising, that they who make this Complaint, spend so great a Part of this short Time, either to no Purpose, or to that which is worse than none, by running about from one idle Amusement to another, all of them unprofitable, and some of them dangerous?

Not that I intend by this to recommend Dulness and Solitude, and a total Abstraction from Company and the World, while we live in it, but only in so far as we have renounced it in our Baptism.——It is none of my Meaning to make People Monks or Hermits, nor to forbid proper Diversions and Recreations; only I would have them well timed, well chosen, such as may conduce to Health, Vigour, Activity, and the Improvement of our Minds and Manners; and I'm afraid the Entertainments of the Play-house conduce to neither.

I do not say the Action, or Oratory in the Pulpit, is equal to these on the Stage; but I think I may venture to affirm, there is more of

Truth,

Truth, Morality and good Senfe, in one well compofed Difcourfe, than has appeared in all the Plays exhibited on the *Britifh* Theatre ever fince we had one, *Cato* itfelf not excepted.

This brings to my Remembrance fome delicate Strokes of our Author, which I had almoft forgot to take Notice of.——He tells (Page 2d and 3d) '' That the Stage has fubfifted in
" *Britain* about Two hundred Years.—— That
" if Plays are a Poifon, it is, at leaft, but flow
" in its Operations.—— And that however the
" Stage may have corrupted our People, the
" Manners of the People have fo far prevailed,
" as in fome Refpects to have reformed the
" Stage. That on this Head we may come to
" a fure Conclufion, becaufe we may compare
" Plays that were admitted during fome Part
" of this Period, with thofe which are now
" chiefly in repute. In making this Compari-
" fon, it will appear, that a certain Degree of
" Indecency and Licentioufnefs once permitted,
" is now rejected, and that Plays more pure
" and of a better moral Tendency, are either
" chofen from our ancient Stock, or that thefe
" Qualities at leaft are expected from every
" Writer of the prefent Age." —— I remember to have read many Years ago a Book on that Subject, (written by a mafterly Hand) wherein a Parallel is carried on between the *Britifh* and the ancient Heathen (*Greek* and *Roman*) Stage.——He brings the Plays of *Æfchylus* and *Sophocles*, of *Plautus* and *Terence*, &c. or Paf-

D fages

sages from them, and collates with them the Compositions exhibited on the *British* Theatre, (such as the *Mock Astrologer*, the *Orphan*, the *Old Batchelor*, and *Double Dealer*; *Love Triumphant*, *Love for Love*, the *Provok'd Wife*, the *Relapse*, &c.) and shews evidently that, in Point of Immodesty and Profaneness, of Cursing and Swearing, of the Abuse of Religion and the Holy Scriptures, and the Abuse of the Clergy ——the Christian Stage (if it is not a Blunder, an Absurdity to call it so) is much less pure, and more faulty than the Heathen was. As I am afraid that excellent Book is now almost out of Print, if I was equal to the Charge, I would give it a new Impression; (it is but about 400 Pages in 8*vo*.) I would indeed forebear to mention the Author's Name, for Fear of lessening his Influence, at least with the Gentleman I now deal with, who seems to have a very poor Opinion of Men of that Complexion and Character. . But there is no such Danger in telling your Ladyship, that he was a Clergyman of the Church of *England*, and one of great Learning and Piety, who preferred Poverty, and the Peace of his Mind, to a good Benefice, and the Countenance of Men in Power.

'Tis true, this Apologist for the Stage has told us, that the Plays of our ancient Stock, *i. e.* those in Use long ago, are now reformed, and purged of every Thing offensive.——It may be so; but I have been told, that a Comedy lately

lately exhibited, (after all its Mutilations and Refinements) gave the Ladies some Use for their Fans, to cool and cover their Faces.——I dare say many, (and I hope all of them) would have taken it much amiss, to be addressed in the same Manner and Language at home, they were on the Theatre; and I cannot think, Indecency and Smutt are the less guilty, or ought to be the less offensive for being publick.

From the 16th Page and forward, this Author brings a Number of foreign Auxiliaries to support his Possession of the Play-house.——He asks, Page 27th, " Whether Knowledge, In- " dustry and Commerce are declined in this " City, since the Play-house was opened here. " That the Manager must suit his Entertain- " ments to the Company; and if he is not " supported by the Grave and the Sober, he " must suit himself to the Licentious and Pro- " fane. Page 21. That if we could abolish " the Stage, we should only make Room for " the Return of Drunkenness, Gaming, and " rude Cabals; and that the State of the Poor, " (whether indigent and reduced, or of the in- " dustrious and laborious) is much mended by " the Play-house.——That the first Class is re- " lieved by Poor-houses erected of late, and " that the other is employed, and thereby main- " tained, by furnishing the Tables, Cloathing " and Equipage of the Rich, &c. Page 23. &c.

Madam, It is none of my Business to follow him through all this wild Goose-chace he has
devised

devifed for himfelf. Had he thought his firft Principle (the *Morality* of the *Stage*) on which he fet out, fully eftablifhed on Scripture and Reafon, he had no Occafion for thefe mercenary Troops to maintain his Caufe. I am perfuaded, that an invariable Regard to Truth and Honefty, is the beft Policy, and the beft Logick too. But though my Intention carried me no further, than to wipe off the vile Afperfions he has thrown upon holy Scriptures, and the beft Authorities, I think it might not be from the Purpofe to afk him the following Queftions, naturally arifing from the Principles and Facts he has advanced in the Pages above referred to.

Whether fubftantial, ufeful Knowledge and Literature, are in a more flourifhing Condition now, than they were many Years ago?——— Whether the greateft Men now, in the Profeffions of Law, Phyfick or Theology, think themfelves, far fuperior in their feveral Profeffions, to a *Craig* of *Rickarton*, a *Forbes* of *Corfe*, a *Pitcairn?* and whether thefe great Men derived their moft extenfive Erudition from the Play-houfe? ——— Whether, if the Stage conduceth fo much to the Increafe of Literature, it was not a Blunder to forbid it in the Vicinity of the great Seminaries of Learning, *Oxford*, *Cambridge*, &c.?———Whether, if Induftry and Commerce have not declined in this City, fince the Play-houfe was opened here, being a Queftion of Facts, it may not be fit to afk it of the Merchants and Artificers? and if they fay thefe

are

are rather increaſed, it may nòt be fit to ask, whether that Increaſe is more owing to the Play-houſe, than to other Incidents?

"Whether, if the Manager of a Stage muſt "ſuit his *Entertainments to the Company*, and "if he be not ſupported by the *Grave* and "the *Sober*, he muſt ſuit himſelf to the *Licen-*"*tious* and *Profane*," be not to affirm, (in other Words) That if a Man cannot ſupport his Luxury by lawful Means, and honeſt Labour, he may have Recourſe to the High-way, not to beg, but to rob and murder?——Whether, if Clubs and Goſſipings concerted in the Play-houſe, have (after the Farce was over) been kept in the Tavern, where they have ſupped, drank, gamed, *&c.* to very late, or rather early Hours? And if this is true, whether there was Truth or Propriety in that Witticiſm of our Author, That if we could aboliſh the Play-houſe, we ſhould only make Room for the Return of Drunkenneſs, Gaming and rude Cabals? Whether, "If they who were the "readieſt to ſhed Tears, for the Diſtreſſes re-"preſented in the Tragedy of *Douglas*," were the moſt numerous, or moſt forward for erecting of poor Houſes? and if they were, whether they got their Impreſſions of Humanity and Pity from the Stage, where other Leſſons (thoſe of Gallantry and Revenge) are more frequently taught?

Whether the Rich and Great might not live according to that Rank in which Providence has placed them, and have *Cloaths, Table* and *Equipage*

Equipage fuited to their Station, tho' there were no Play-houfe to go to?——And if they may, Whether the *Spinfter*, the *Weaver*, the *Clothier*, and *other Tradefmen*, might not be as much employed, and as punctually paid for their Labour, if fo much Money was not fquandered for the Play-houfe?——Whether there is not as much Virtue in Charity, and as great Reward annexed to it, when Men give it only for the Love of God, and Obedience to his Law, as when (to the true and proper Motive) they add the Expectation of diverting themfelves? And whether it was not paying but a coarfe Compliment to *People of Figure and Fortune*, to infinuate, that if they had not the Play-houfe here, they would no longer live in *Edinburgh*, but muft go where they could find it?——Upon the whole, Whether this Author is true and juft in his Pleading for the Stage, or only fpecious and mifleading?

This Gentleman (Page 26, *&c.*) concludes his good Work, by infinuating his great Regard and Concern for a very *refpectable* Body, a Judicature in this City; tho' all the Compliment he pays to their Learning is taken away by a fly Imputation of Rafhnefs and Tyranny in their Proceedings. If he means the Prefbytery of *Edinburgh*, (as indeed he feems to do,) they are able enough to anfwer for themfelves, and vindicate the Conduct complained of.——Tho' I am no Member of that Society, I have had the Pleafure of being acquainted with feverals of them, whom I thought

Men

Men of Learning and Character. —— I have read their Admonition in last *January*, and in my poor Opinion, it is a wise, well expressed, and very seasonable Warning to their Hearers, who certainly owe them Thanks for it.

'Tis true, they have not entered deep into the Merits of the Cause, nor indeed could they, in so short a Paper; but they have very judiciously mentioned the Impropriety of running after these idle, expensive Entertainments in this Time of Dearth and Distress.

The present is a Time of Danger, or actual Calamity in most Parts of the known World. ——War rages on the Continent of *Europe*, in *Asia* and *America*, and did but very lately in *Africa*.——There is in many Places, Famine, in some, Pestilence, in others, Earthquakes, Inundations, Hurricanes, and Devastations by Fire.——God has not left himself without Witness, nor us without Remedy; he has not been wanting in the Means of our Amendment, but we have been wanting in the Use and Application.————He has sent abroad his Judgments to alarm our Fears, and awaken the World to Thought and Seriousness; but if Men will not listen to his Calls, he has provided no Cure for Obstinacy. He made us free Agents, and will not alter his Scheme, by forcing us to be wise, and good, and happy, whether we will or not.

After so many Differences in Opinion with our Author, there is one Thing wherein I must agree with him: He says (Page 1st) that " Dis-
" putes arising among the Professors of true
Religion.

" Religion, may end in *Divisions* and *Animo-*
" *sities*, hurtful to the Spirit of Religion it-
" self.——And that People who begin such Dis-
" putes, have much to answer for, unless they
" have sufficient Reason for what they do."——
I am of the same Sentiments, and believe, that
as Offences must come, there is a Wo de-
nounced against them by whom they come.——
But whether this Offence, and these Disputes,
came by the Play-house or the Presbytery, I
will leave the intelligent Reader to judge.

I love Peace, and do most sincerely wish it
prevailed in all the World.——At the same time
it might be too dearly paid for, if it is at the
Expence of Truth. If we cannot be in Friendship with Thieves and Robbers, but by ab-
rogating the Laws, and overturning the Government which restrains them, and preserves
Property. If we cannot be in Peace with the
Devil, and his Agents, without renouncing our
Creed, abjuring our Baptism, and giving up
our Bible; I think that Peace is purchased at
too high a Price, after all that this Gentleman
has said to bring us to a Meeting, and soften
the Terms of Accommodation.

My present Distress hinders me to write your
Ladyship with my own Hand: I am forced to
employ that of a Friend, who knows not to
whom I write. You will (I hope) not only
pardon this Freedom, but consider it as a Testimony of my Readiness to obey your Commands, and Zeal to approve myself in the best
Manner I can.

Your Ladyship's faithful Servant.

15 The Usefulness of the Edinburgh Theatre Seriously Considered with a Proposal for Rendering it more Beneficial

This is an ironical response to Ferguson's *The Morality of the Stage Seriously Considered*. Picking up on the moral philosopher's assertion that the theatre had an economic role to play, the author of the proposal argues that the theatre ought to be the principal measurement of a city's wealth. Such wealth is demonstrated by keeping idle a proportion of people for the luxury of others. The plan for Edinburgh is that it should furnish its cast of players not from visiting English actors, but from the people that make up Edinburgh society

THE
USEFULNESS
OF THE
EDINBURGH THEATRE
SERIOUSLY CONSIDERED.

WITH

A PROPOSAL for rendering it
more beneficial.

We may venture to afk whether KNOWLEDGE, whether INDUSTRY and COMMERCE have declined in this city fince the playhoufe was firft opened here.

Morality of the ftage ferioufly confidered, p. 17.

————duas tantum res anxius optat,
PANEM & CIRCENSES. *Juv. fat.* 10. ỳ 80.

EDINBURGH: Printed in the Year MDCCLVII.

[Price Two Pence.]

THE
USEFULNESS
OF THE
EDINBURGH THEATRE
SERIOUSLY CONSIDERED.

OF the many improvements our country has of late received, none ought to ſtrike the breaſt of a *North-Britiſh* patriot with ſo ſenſible a pleaſure, as the amazing progreſs we have made in cultivating a taſte for amuſements and diverſions.

Some years ago the puppet-ſhow, exhibiting a lively repreſentation of *Doctor Fauſtus and the Devil*, the *Babes of the wood* and *Robin Redtreaſt*, were the faſhionable entertainments of our fine ladies and gentlemen. In that happy period, the jokes of facetious *Punch*, who had long been obliged to retail his wit to the noiſy rabble of a country-fair, were liſtened to, with the higheſt ſatisfaction, by the moſt polite audience. To him ſucceeded the ſeven wonders of the world, from the wooden plates of *Henry Overton*; the dancing bear; the wonderful rhinoceros, and arithmetical dog; who were all in their turn honoured with crouded houſes of the *beau monde*. And now, to complete our happineſs, the *tuba* of the ancients (in plain *Engliſh* a trumpet), which proclaimed the arrival of theſe entertaining creatures, flouriſhes the en-

A   try

317

try of a mighty monarch, or founds the charge to a bloody battle on the ftage.

That fuch public fpectacles, and particularly ftage-plays, are of the utmoft confequence to the welfare of every nation, has been allowed by moft writers, who have duly confidered the fubject, either in a moral or political light. After their example, I fhall endeavour to fhow, with brevity, and yet I hope with perfpicuity enough to convince the candid and ingenious reader, that the encouragement given to theatrical entertainments amongft us, is the fource of numberlefs bleffings to this once defpifed, but now flourifhing city.

That from the theatre the WEALTH of every opulent city is principally derived, the flighteft reflection may convince every unprejudiced perfon. To pafs over the more remote examples of *Greece* and *Rome*, what reafon can be fo juftly affigned for the riches and fplendor of *London*, that great metropolis, but that when moft of the other cities and towns of *Great Britain* have no theatre, and fome few but one, fhe enjoys the fuperior privilege of two royal ones? Some little-minded people have, I know, falfely infinuated, that her wealth flows from the genius, the activity, and induftry of the inhabitants; without adverting, that where bufinefs brings one to town, idlenefs in poffeffion of money, and the pleafures of the theatre, bring twenty. To come nearer home, who are the beft cuftomers to the doctors, the kirk-treafurer, and to our taverns, but the feveral parties made at the concert-hall? Thefe, beyond queftion, confume the great quantities of wine, fpirits, and beer, from the confumption of which articles the good town's revenue is fo prodigioufly increafed.

Not to mention the quantity of paint, &c. furnifhed

ed by our fhopkeepers to lacker over the wan com-
plexions of half-ftarved heroes, and tawny necks of
hackney heroines; what a number of mercers, man-
tua-makers, milliners, hair-dreffers, peruke-makers,
woollen-drapers, and their retainers, does the theatre,
in a great meafure, fupport? Are not hundreds of
brawny chairmen (who otherwife would be obliged
to apply themfelves to fome mechanic or handicraft)
enabled, by the fame means, to eat the bread of idlenefs? That it is an advantage to a nation, to have a
number of its hands beft qualified for labour, kept
quite idle, or what with refpect to the public is the
fame, only miniftring to the luxury of others, a celebrated effay-writer has of late fufficiently proved.

The conftant attendance the young gentlemen of
the law, thofe hopes of their country, and true refto-
rers of ancient eloquence, give to the entertainments
of the theatre, fufficiently fhows from whence they
have catched that fire of elocution, that juftnefs of
action, and every other oratorial grace, fo confpicuous
in their daily pleadings.

The univerfity too (whatever fome of its pragmatical profeffors, who have imbibed narrow principles,
may think) finds the encouragement given to the
theatre turn greatly to its account. How rapid a progrefs do the young gentlemen-ftudents make through
the literary courfe, when, inftead of poring their eyes
out with midnight-lucubrations, the old-fafhioned way
of coming by knowledge, they repair to the playhoufe,
that feminary of wit, criticifm, and knowledge,
whence they receive a frefh recruit of fpirits, to be
expended on to-morrow's hard ftudy?

May we not alfo flatter ourfelves with the hopes,
that our promifing young clergy, freed at length from
the tramels of Prefbyterian ftiffnefs, which have fo

A 2   long

long and so miserably cramped every sublimer genius of our church, will now set about the improvement of pulpit-eloquence, by transfusing the flowery-buskined rhetoric of the stage into the solemn harangues of the pulpit? This reformation, I confess, is yet in its early dawn; but a constant attendance on dramatic entertainments, which, I hope, our sprightly reformers are fully resolved upon, will soon bring it to its meridian glory. *Thy modest merit*, O DOUGLAS author! as the *Caledonian Mercury* of *December* 4. has most emphatically phrased it, and the free and undaunted spirit of thy friends and brethren C—l—le and F—g—r, deserve a large tribute of gratitude from your obliged country: while B—n—ne and R—l——n shrunk back behind the scenes, you bravely fought your way to the forbidden box. Such honoured names shall swell the trump of fame, when those of your bigotted opposers shall be buried in oblivion.

We have now seen learning greatly promoted, the spirit of ancient eloquence revived, our industry quickened, our wealth increased, and the national taste much refined, by the noble entertainments of the stage: but as these are only the well-known advantages of the theatre in general, it seems proper to add some of the many advantages peculiar to our own proper theatre.

It was erected originally on a very charitable plan, to maintain actors who could gain their bread no where else; and, in pursuance of the same plan, is now become the asylum of plays banished from other theatres. With us even DOUGLAS, despised and friendless as he is, finds hearts and purses open to receive him.

As such a stage affords the best opportunity of shewing our Christian compassion to the poor and afflicted,

it

it demonſtrates what is ſtill more agreeable, our Chriſtian fortitude, in oppoſing the law of the land. While the followers of *Garrick* can enjoy at beſt only the inſipid pleaſure of a licenſed theatre, we reliſh all the pleaſures of forbidden fruit.

Here too, as a late author juſtly obſerves, " the " happy mixture of ſenatorial robes, and ſacerdotal " veſtments, with the gay cloathing of the fair aſſem- " bly, adds ſeverity to ſprightlineſs, and corrects the " levity of faſhion." In one box, we ſee the Divine unbending his pious mind, worn out with meditation and prayer; and in another, the J—ge, oppreſſed with the cares of the be—h, regaining his loſt ſpirits. Let *Drury-lane* and *Covent-garden* boaſt of ſuch illuſtrious characters exhibited in real life, and then vie with *Edinburgh* theatre.

Another advantage peculiar to the *North-Britiſh* ſtage is not ſo well known, but no leſs true. To this we owe the cure of that dark and deſperate wound given through *David*'s ſides to the liberty of the preſs. The public need not now lament the ſuppreſſion of his celebrated eſſay on the *lawfulneſs of ſuicide* : This is more beautifully repreſented in the character of *Lady Barnet*, who throws herſelf over a rock with more than *Roman* courage. Nor need we mourn the loſs of his incomparable treatiſe on the *mortality of the ſoul*, while viewing *Glenalven* nobly *riſking eternal fire*. It is hoped the next production of our Reverend author will ſolace us too for the want of the 'Squire's third and laſt eſſay, on the *advantages of adultery*, that we may have a complete triumph over the impotent malice of the late Ch——r and the B—-p of L——n, who murdered theſe eſſays in cold blood.

To this I might add, what is alſo of ſome conſequence : Our players are no mercenary hirelings; they

act

act from the moft difintereſted regard to the good of
mankind, without fee or reward. The richer part of
the audience pay, 'tis true, the fidlers; but the poor-
er fort, ſtudents and apprentices, &c. have the benefit of free tickets, when their own and their maſters
money is exhauſted.

There is another advantage that may be reaped from
our ſtage, of greater importance to the good town than
any of the foregoing; which is in ſhort this, to ſave
the whole revenue of her clergy. When the inhabitants have an opportunity, three times a-week at leaſt,
to hear, and *gratis* too, the pure goſpel of *Shakeſpear*,
of *Sopho*, and *St David*, is it not ridiculous, and
contrary to every rule of good policy, to ſquander a-
way ſome thouſand pounds, in maintaining above a
ſcore of pragmatical fellows, merely to retail the antiquated goſpel of *St Matthew* or *St John*, to ſpeak
evil of dignities, and bring a railing accuſation againſt
their worthy reforming brethren?

It cannot be pretended that public worſhip is neceſſary of a *Sunday*, to paſs away a few hours in ſeeing
and being ſeen, which might otherwiſe lie heavy upon the hands of our fine ladies and gentlemen; for
they have already agreed to divide the whole day between Mrs *J—p*'s at *P—ſt—n-p—ns*, the gaming-
table, the tavern, and the drawing-room; and as to
the manufacturers and day-labourers, &c. they are
to be allowed, you know, the uſe of fire-arms, at the
deſire of the c—mm—n of the k—k, for the due
fanctification of the Sabbath.

The good Dean's argument for ſupporting the clergy, in order to preſerve our breed ſound and entire,
does not apply to the preſent caſe; becauſe it is not
intended to ſet aſide that order of men in general:
my propoſal comprehends only the parſons of this
city

city and fuburbs, whofe parifhioners can without in-
conveniency attend the playhoufe: and if any defi-
ciency fhould happen as to the *numbers of mankind,*
from the want of thefe able-bodied divines, the R—d
Mr *W—ce* may be appointed to move in the Edinburgh or felect fociety, that a certain fum fhould be
annually given, by way of premium, to the clergyman,
married or *unma·ried,* (it being always underftood
of a found and wholefome conftitution), who fhall, on
the firft day of *January,* produce to the fociety, of his
own proper begetting during the currency of the pre-
ceding year, the greateft number of males, and another premium to the clergyman who fhall produce the
greateft number of females, under the conditions and
provifions above mentioned.

To this propofal I cannot figure any objection, but
the difficulty that thefe brethren might find in maintaining their numerous iffue; which will foon be happily
obviated by the foundling-hofpital to be erected here.

I have hitherto faid little or nothing concerning the
morality of our ftage. This is done to great advantage by a more mafterly hand, who, with the affiftance
of *Douglas,* has proved it to be the only fchool of
virtue. In this matchlefs play, where the *mighty matter matches the mighty mind,* young ladies are taught
to draw the vail of matrimony over the misfortunes of
their unguarded hours; young enfigns and lawyers to
fwear in a manly Chriftian ftyle, (*By the blood of the
crofs, and the wounds of him who died for us on the
accurfed tree,* founds glorioufly); and what feems more
praife-worthy, old bawds are taught to pray with divine
eloquence. He knew nothing of the exalted devotion of this enlightened age, who thought, that *from
the fame mouth bleffing and curfing fhould not proceed.*
From this fpecimen of the new doctrine of our ftage,
it

it appears unqueftionably good ; and the practical part is ftill better. Players are no dry, fpeculative mo-ralifts ; they bring all home in a warm application and fhow by example, the belt teacher, how every man and every woman ought to be fruitful in good works.

This will account in fome meafure for the late op-pofition of the p—b—ies of E—h and G—w to the entertainments of the ftage. They talk like H—n of the innate beauty of moral virtue, but don't love the applicatory part, which is Mrs W—a's chief accom-plifhment. But however they may differ with the fe-male preacher in this trifling punctilio, it is hoped they will have fome compaffion on the M—n—g—rs, who have exhaufted their fmall ftock in fupporting a needy brother. They would not willingly, I dare fay, fend thefe brave adventurers to the devil ; why then would they drive them to the abbey, which they dread a great deal more ? The difinterefted will allow, that it is far more becoming gentlemen of their humanity and cloth, to join in the fcheme I am now to propofe for ren-dering our theatre ftill more beneficial.

It has grieved me, and muft be a matter of ferious deep concern to every well-wifher of his country, that our theatre, the fource of fo many advantages, fhould be wholly fupplied with actors from *England.* We have *Scotfmen* who now actually brew porter, an *Englifh* drink ; others there are who can fatten hogs, and make bacon, though originally of *Englifh* invention ; and if thefe inftances fhould not be thought fo appli-cable, we have effay and play writers : Why then fhould we not furnifh our ftage with actors from our own country ?

It was certainly an omiffion in the fociety inftituted at *Edinburgh,* for the encouragement of arts, manufac-tures,

tures, and agriculture, not to aſſign a premium to the young DIVINE, PHYSICIAN, LAWYER, or MER-CHANT, who ſhould have ſpirit to renounce the drud-gery of his profeſſion, to embrace the more ſprightly, uſeful and honourable profeſſion of ſtage-playing. The ſociety will doubtleſs take the hint here given, and correct the omiſſion in their next publication of premiums.

That our country abounds with original actors, to whom the principal characters in our beſt plays would naturally fall to be aſſigned, I appeal to the Honour-able the G—tl—m—n M—n—g—rs, and to their Lord High Treaſurer, *though laſt, not leaſt in our e-ſteem*; whoſe patronage I here humbly implore, and in whoſe unblemiſhed intentions to ſerve the public, I truſt that my propoſal will, after due conſideration, be approved of, and executed as they in their wiſdom ſhall judge proper.

Objections may be raiſed as to the difficulty of exe-cuting my ſcheme: And to what ſcheme, however uſeful, may not plauſible objections be raiſed?

Some will be afraid, that if Mr *Digges*, with his mimic-train, ſhould be diſmiſſed, we may run a hazard of being deprived altogether of theatrical entertain-ments. Had I the leaſt apprehenſion of this propoſal being productive of ſo dreadful a conſequence, I ſhould be the firſt man to oppoſe it. For if that ſhould happen, (which Heaven avert), the final ca-taſtrophe of this nation would be faſt approaching. Then, and not ſooner, ſhould the good citizens of *Edinburgh* aſſemble themſelves, and humbly addreſs their ſovereign, That out of pity to his loyal ſubjects, he would graciouſly pleaſe to order a detachment of his merry ſervants, from either of the theatres royal, forthwith to repair to this his ancient city, and there,

B   by

by force of mufic, mimicry, and farce, to difpel all
gloomy apprehenfions from the minds of his harmlefs
and well-meaning fubjeĉts. But no fuch chimerical
fear torments me. I fee many worthy candidates for
the principal charaĉters of every play.

For inftance, can ever a *Ranger* be wanted, when
every young fellow, of a genteel perfon, and diffolute
morals, may have an opportunity, by appearing in that
favourite charaĉter, of making himfelf the darling of
the women, and envy of the men? Do you want a *Sir
John Brute?* feveral fine women could, and I dare
fay with juftice, recommend their hufbands as perfeĉt
mafters of that charaĉter. The family of *Wrongheads* are not wholly confined to *England*; we have
our *Wrongheads* as well as they, and doubtlefs fome
of ours have made their *journies to London* too.

I never had the pleafure of being entertained with
that refpeĉtful family on our ftage, but I could fee
that *Squire Richard* had feveral gaping brothers-ger-
man among the audience. Whether we could furnifh
out a *Mifs Jenny* of our own, the high regard I have
for the prefent race of accomplifhed beauties, forbids
me pofitively to affirm. Say, courteous reader, when
did thy eye furvey the ftreets or coffechoufes of this
populous city, and not prefent thee with a portly figure, in fhape, fize, and weight, a proper reprefenta-
tive of the humorous Sir *John Falftaff?*

As to fops, prudes, and coquettes, we need give ourfelves no trouble; thefe are the natives of moft countries, they play over their parts in moft drawing-rooms.
In fhort, were it not that I hate being perfonal, even
in praife, I could point out a number of diverting ori-
ginals, who, could they be perfuaded, for the good of
their country, only to fhow themfelves on the ftage,
their very figures and features would give more entertainment,

tertainment, and to more crouded audiences too, than ever *Stamper* gave in *Scrub*, or *Love* in *Falstaff*.

One thing, however, I am aware of, which the G—tl—m—n M—n—g—rs, should they approve of my scheme, will study to remedy. And it is this: As there may be several candidates for playing the same character, it may happen that their critical judgment may be puzzled to bestow it on the most deserving. Suppose, and the supposition is far from being unnatural, that the college of physicians should take it into their heads, at a meeting of that learned body *pro re nata* convened, to dispute, which of their members should be honoured with playing the *Mock Doctor*: In this case, the claims of the different contending parties might be so equally balanced, that it would be difficult to determine the preference, otherwise than by the decision of chance, or giving the character to every member of the college by rotation, in the same manner as they take the infirmary at present.

Competitions for theatrical fame, that may arise amongst the members of the other learned and R——d communities of this city, must be determined in similar cases by the same rule.

Thus I have touched at a few principal characters of the drama, to show that my scheme is practicable: to give more instances, would only tire the ingenious reader's patience; who, I dare say, will find it no difficult matter to supply our stage from the circle of his acquaintance, with more *original* entertaining actors, than have hitherto trode it in sock or buskin.

I profess, with more sincerity than most of my brethren proposal-writers, that I have no personal interest in endeavouring to promote the reformation of our stage. A nobler motive influences my heart, and directs my pen; the love of virtue, and of my country.

To

To increase her wealth, to quicken the industry of her inhabitants, to feed the *poor*, to divert the rich, to infuse a spirit for the mimic-art into her promising sons, were the sole motives of my writing. The inward satisfaction arising from a consciousness of meaning the public welfare, is all the reward I expect, and is indeed the highest I could receive.

F I N I S.

Pro-Douglas Pamphlets and Ballads

16 An Argument to Prove that The Tragedy of Douglas ought to be Publickly Burnt by the hands of the Hangman

Published as a direct response to the *Admonition and Exhortation* recently distributed by the Presbytery of Edinburgh, Alexander Carlyle intended this work to be a Swiftian defence of the play accumulating absurd arguments against it. However, in several instances it was misread as a robust attack on the performance and was held up by some in the Popular party as a solid example of anti-*Douglas* rhetoric. Carlyle remarked that both his sister and his aunt, ignorant of the author, believed the pamphlet to be serious, and thought it would be a blow to the tragedy. Despite these misinterpretations of the work, Carlyle felt that it elated friends of the play, while exasperating its enemies.

A N

ARGUMENT

To prove that the

Tragedy of Douglas

Ought to be

Publickly burnt by the hands of the Hangman.

A fect, whofe chief devotion lies
In odd perverfe antipathies ;
Who falling out with that, or this,
And finding fomewhat ftill amifs, ⸻
Compound for fins they are inclin'd to,
By damning thofe they have no mind to.

HUD.

E D I N B U R G H:
Printed in the Year M,DCC,LVII. [Price Threepence.]

A N

ARGUMENT, &c.

JOSEPH ADDISON, Esq; was certainly drunk, when he laid it down
as a maxim, in one of his spectators, "that
" a perfect tragedy is the noblest produ-
" ction of human nature." His opinion,
I know, but too universally prevails; and
I am aware of the dangers that attend
writing against received maxims. The
voice of the people, is justly held to be
the voice of God; and the author escapes
well, who suffers no greater loss than his
reputation, for having openly contradict-
ed the notions of the venerable multitude.
Yet, from I don't know what motive, whether it be the love of truth, or a regard to
the welfare of my fellow citizens, I feel an
irresistible inclination to write against the
favourite tragedy of *Douglas*, and endeavour to prove, by reasons that seem un-
answerable to me, that the author of that
much extoll'd piece deserves to be stigmatized,

tized, and his performance to be publickly burnt by the hands of the hangman.

And perhaps it may be found, after I have executed my charitable defign, that the majority are not on the fide the world imagines. The greateft part of the rich and gay, indeed, will always have a pride in fupporting what they believe to be the moft rational, elegant, and refined of all entertainments. But in this country of freedom, where every man has a right to chufe his opinion in all matters, facred and prophane; and where the bulk of people are filent, rather becaufe they do not know what to fay, than thro' any defect in the paffions; I am next to certain, that I fhall be able to open fuch an univerfal cry againft this minion of perfons of rank and tafte, as fhall forever condemn him and all his works, paft, prefent and future, not to oblivion, but to perpetual infamy and difgrace.

And having the trumpet to found, as it were, to fo great a body as the vulgar of my native country, I muft be allowed the liberty of ufing a confiderable variety of *notes*, that, if it be poffible, I may hit the *tone* of every puppy in the pack; that is to fay, (to defcend from the poetical ftile, ſtile, which I abhor) I will muſter up ſuch a number of arguments, as cannot fail, one or other of them, to reach conviction to every true presbyterian in Scotland: Nor ſhall I trouble myſelf much about their conſiſtency with each other; for I expect that every candid reader will be contented with that argument that hits his own fancy, and leave the reſt to his neighbours; always remembering, that my work is ſanctified by the ſincere deſign of opening the eyes of my deluded countrymen, and warning them to ſhun the paths that lead to perdition.

And here I ſhall omit all general declamations againſt the ſtage, for I aim only at particulars. I do indeed believe it to be an invention of the devil, and I cannot deny that it has always been ſupported by his agents: I know it is pernicious to the morals of men, and altogether inconſiſtent with true religion. But as I likewiſe believe, that puppet-ſhews, ballads in dialogue, romances, fictions of poets, not to mention muſick, and painting, and whatever elſe imitates the paſſions and manners of men, abſolutely unlawful, and tend to make us in love with lying vanities; and yet am not fully inſtructed in the ſeveral

ral *tastes* of my fellow-citizens; I do not chuse to cut down all the courts of Europe in a box, and Sir *William Wallace Wight*, and the *Pilgrim's progress*, and *Jack the giant-killer*, together with the *whole works of Henry Overton*, at a single blow; lest I should disoblige many good and worthy friends, and provoke them to a dislike of the whole of my following arguments. Besides, I am justified in this prudent measure by some great and reverend examples; for as the learned and pious clergy of this city, of whatever party or faction, (for fear of giving offence I suppose) have winked for many years at the diversions of the theatre, and permitted the most virtuous matrons, and tender virgins, to repair to that shop of iniquity unreprov'd, reserving the fire of their zeal till it should be blown up by motives purely ecclesiastical: In like manner, it is wise in me, their humble disciple and imitator, to wave the general argument, and apply my whole force in one direction against the celebrated tragedy of Douglas.

In the first place, there is hardly a single word of this admir'd piece true, from the beginning to the end of it; for tho' there was a paper printed under the title of *the full*

full and true hiftory, I can eafily prove that it is all an invention, and perfectly inconfiftent with the thread of Scottifh hiftory. As for inftance, he makes the landing of the Danes to have been in Eaft-Lothian; whereas, in reality, it was in the fhire of Air, and at the very town call'd by that name. Our author, I prefume, has falfified this important fact, to flatter the gentlemen and farmers of that rich county to fupport his play. In chronology too he has made a palpable error, when he reprefents his hermit as alive at the time of this invafion of the Danes; and yet fays, that in his youth he was a foldier under that warlike prince Godfrey of Boulogne. One would have imagined that after the juft and fevere cenfures that have been paft on the Latin poet Virgil, for fuch an error in chronology, our author might have taken warning. But the prefumption and folly of poets is infinite.—Thus it appears, that our boafted poet, is either entirely ignorant of the hiftory of his own country, or has wilfully falfified many important facts, fo that he muft be confider'd as a difgrace to his profeffion, and country, either by his ignorance, or want of veracity.

I have only touch'd upon the points

that

that are material, and can easiest be dif-
proved; for every other circumstance of
the story is the fiction of his own idle
brain, and contriv'd on purpose to deceive.
And what a gross immorality is implied
in such an action, I need not explain to
any person who is acquainted with the
first principles of religion. Nor is it any
excuse for, but a high aggravation of his
crime, that the whole story is wrought up
in such artful language, and made to have
so much similitude to truth, that many
persons of judgment and solidity, and o-
therwise of respectable characters, have
been seen to weep bitterly at the representation of it! wasting those precious tears,
that ought not to be shed but on the serious contemplation of human vanity, or
occasions of real distress. And indeed I
think it can be imputed to nothing but di-
abolical art, and the influence of that spirit,
who lies in wait to subvert human reason,
that men of sound minds can be brought
to weep at events that never happened,
and bewail the misfortunes of persons who
never existed.

Another reason is, that the tragedy of
Douglas is reported to be what they call a
good tragedy. Now, (not to dwell on
the

the contradiction in terms, for one may as well fay, a *good hypocrite*, or a *good atheift*, as a *good tragedy*) fuppofing the tragedy of Douglas to contain nothing but good fentiments to reprefent good characters, to have a good moral tendency, to paint virtue as amiable, and vice as odious; in fhort to have a good effect upon the minds of the whole audience, which is granting as much as ever was ask'd; yet, for the fake of thefe excellencies, if there was no other reafon, ought this piece to be publickly burnt by the hands of the hangman.

And here I muft be allowed to ufe a figure, not uncommon with authors of eminent fame; the affuming of that to be true, which I formerly declin'd to prove, from reafons of prudence: for it is neceffary for me now, to have it taken for granted, that ftage plays, and all dramatic entertainments are abfolutely unlawful, and directly contrary to the word of God: or at leaft, it muft be admitted me, that they do infinitely more evil than good; for altho' matters of this kind are faid to depend on very nice calculations, yet I fee clearly, that the bad confequences of conftant attendance at the theatre, are many and

B various;

various ; whereas I perceive not one single advantage to be gain'd by frequenting that temple of vanity. Now since it would be for the benefit of mankind that the stage was abolished, he who attempts to reform it, by writing within the rules of decency and virtue, is to be consider'd as a public enemy, who takes pains to gild a poisonous pill, in order to allure you to your ruin; and deserves equal praise with those conquerors of the earth, who by mild and equitable laws, have reconciled the conquer'd to the loss of their liberty. Whereas it is to be wish'd, that no piece were ever perform'd in the theatre, but what is shocking to humanity, and altogether abominable and detestable, that the people at last might be provok'd to drive it and all its cursed contents to hell, from whence it came. And for this reason I suppose it was, that the church of Scotland in ancient times made a law, prohibiting any of its members to form the plot of a play upon any part of scripture history, lest the people should have been insensibly led to favour the plays themselves, for the sake of that good book from which they were taken.

My next reason, which is level to the capacity

capacity of infinite numbers, and which I am certain will do great execution, is, that the fuppos'd author of Douglas is a clergyman: and what muft be carefully obferv'd, is faid to have fome peculiar qualities, fuch as learning, eloquence and wit, infomuch, that his company has been very much fought after by perfons of fuperior ftation; and what is worft of all, he is young. Now, as it is a thing perfectly new in this country, for a clergyman to write a tragedy, I do not fee what title this rafh young man had to go out of the common road. In our neighbouring country, a Dr. Young, or a Dr. Brown, may pafs uncenfur'd, after having written tragedies of fome little reputation; for they are dignified clergymen, and have a good right to fhew talents fuperior to moft other ecclefiafticks; but in this church, which is founded on presbyterian parity, he is a bold man indeed, who ventures to diftinguifh himfelf above his brethren.

Befides in the exercife of his poetical gifts, he muft have gone through a courfe of ftudy altogether foreign to his duty as a clergyman; he muft have wafted a great deal of precious time, in making himfelf mafter of the Greek and Roman poets, and

and other heathen authors of pernicious tendency; and indeed if he be a true poet, muſt have been guilty of the heinous ſin of idolatry, in paying little leſs than divine honours to his muſe.   And if our author poſſeſſes the ſuperior talents aſcrib'd to him, ſo much the more deſerving of puniſhment has he made himſelf, by proſtituting his genius to prophane uſes, and employing the parts beſtowed on him for important purpoſes, in the ſervice of *Melpomene* a goddeſs of heathen extraction.

Had this youth of genius followed the true theological track, and devoted himſelf to ſmoaking tobacco, to drinking of ale, and the ſtudy of controverſy, which has been ſo beneficial to the Chriſtian church, he might have made his name immortal, by ſome valuable treatiſe, like the late account of *the preſent ſtate of* Judas Iſcariot; or, *the candid and impartial eſtimate of the profit and loſs of religion.*   Had he employed himſelf in the ſtudy of city politics, and human nature, he would certainly have become a maſter in experimental preaching, and one day might have produc'd ſome ſuch ſearching piece of eloquence, as, *the riſe and fall of* Haman; or, the other characteriſtical diſcourſe of an eminent

nent author. Had he followed the useful occupation of farming, or sent the savings of his stipend as a venture to sea, or dealt in the gentlemany trade of horsecouping, he might have been tolerated; for such things are not without precedent among the brethren. Much more would he have been accounted blameless, or praise-worthy, had he spent his time in managing a burgh, or in sauntering about booksellers shops, or in diverting himself with his children by the fire-side, or in inclosing his glebe with his own hands, or in attending all the burial and christning feasts, or in digging his own garden, or any other inoffensive and profitable method of making the lazy hours pass lightly away, practis'd in city or country.

Besides, this gentleman, as I am informed, within the compass of nine or ten years, has made no less than two trips to London, for two or three months at a time, and thereby deserted his charge, and exposed himself to the high censure due for non-residence. It is very true, that many other ministers in Scotland, have been frequently absent from their charges for a longer space; and it is particularly the custom in this city, (where no man

can

can fay that minifterial duty is not carefully performed in all its parts) for the minifters annually to make a journey to the
country, efpecially during the harveft va-
cation, infomuch, that were it not for the
uncommon ftrength and benevolence of
one b——r, the inhabitants behoved to
call in the neighbouring minifters, to join
them together in wedlock, and chriften
their children. But then it muft be no-
ticed, that as the town is totally deferted
by people of condition at that feafon of the
year, any body is thought good enough
to preach to the vulgar citizens; fo likewife
there is a very wide difference betwixt the
employments of our young author, and
thofe of the pious and diligent paftors of
Edinburgh: for they, good men, are either travelling for their healths, or paying
court to their patrons, or relaxing their
minds, worn out with fpiritual cares, at
mineral waters, or fhewing the world to
their gentle fpoufes, and their gentle fpoufes
to the world, or ftrengthening their parties
in diftant presbyteries, or feeking ecclefiaftical preferment; whilft this extravagant
author, againft all order, regularity and
cuftom, is endeavouring to obtain for
himfelf a place in the annals of tafte and literature;

terature, by this detested tragedy of Douglas, which is the cause of all my perplexity and trouble. Thanks to the watchful guardian of this church, and the power worshipped by the uncontroulable ruler of the English stage! he has not yet been able to gratify the better half of his wishes; and in them I trust with joy, for the full disappointment of all his future endeavours.

There is one circumstance I cannot reflect upon, without the utmost surprize, grief and indignation. It is, that, according to the best information I can receive, this same audacious theatrical divine is extremely popular in his own parish; and not only popular, (for I have known pious ministers much admired for their preaching, and yet, thro' the malice of Satan, brought into contempt in other respects) but entirely esteemed and beloved by every single person there. Now, this circumstance concerning our young author, I the rather believe to be true, because it consists with my own observation, that many young brethren, much of the same stamp with himself, in spite of all the secret artifices, or open attacks of the g—ly, have some how or other preserved the e-
steem

fteem and affections of their parifhioners.
There is nothing that relates to the prefent
ftate of the church that hath given me
me more real affliction, or occafioned more
perplexing thoughts in my hours of defer-
tion. The wiles of Satan are as endlefs
as his malignity is great; and moft fuc-
cefsfully of all, he attacks religion in the
fhape of human virtue : by enduing
thofe fine modern minifters with candor,
openefs, humanity, and an affectionate
concern for the welfare of their parifhioners, he blinds the carnal minds of the
people, fo that they cannot perceive how
deficient they are in true grace : whereas,
by infufing cunning, envy, covetoufnefs
and fpiritual pride, into the hearts of many godly and orthodox brethren, he
weakens their hands, and deftroys the effects of all their zeal and labour.

My fourth reafon is, that the tragedy of
Douglas is faid by fome fanguine friends
of the author, to be an honour to our
country. It is true, that fome great men
of antiquity have thought it very honourable to be able to compofe a tragedy ; and
having acquired all other kinds of fame,
have repined when that could not be added to compleat their glory. But thefe
men

men have been generally heathens, and can in no respect become examples to us. Neither do I think it is very likely, that in this cold, barren, and remote country, in which there is so little encouragement for the industrious manufacturer, and adventrous merchant, much less for such useless members of society, as the composers of idle poems; or that out of the bosom of the poorest and most despised, tho' the best church in the world, there can possibly have arisen a tragic poet to rival Sophocles and Euripides, Corneille and Racine, Shakespear and Otway. For my part, I will not believe that he resembles any of these great prophane men but one, and that only in one single circumstance, *viz.* his having mistaken his employment. For Euripides was at first bred to be a wrestler; but he was soon found unfit for that manly and laborious profession, and therefore, like our author, obliged to turn a maker of tragedies.

But if it were really true that the tragedy of Douglas conduc'd so much to the honour of our country, it ought to be kept as dead a secret as the flourishing state of any of our manufactures; and no person who has the least regard for his native land, will be ever brought to own a truth so dangerous to our prosperity.

C

Have

Have we not the greatest reason in the world to fear that the English ministry, with whom we do not stand in a very favourable light since the rebellion, will take it very much amiss, that any body here should have the presumption to think he can write the English language as well as they can do in London? Is it not highly probable, that if such an insult should ever reach their ears, they will load us with some new tax, to keep down our ambitious spirit? I have often heard it affirmed, that the French duty would not have been demanded for claret, but things allow'd to go on as they have done since the union, had it not been for that superb and magnificent building call'd the *New-Exchange*, which no doubt will surpass all the exchanges in the world, when once it is finished.

As it is therefore of the utmost importance to the welfare of our country, to prevent any jealousy from rising in the minds of the English, let us industriously suppress every appearance of genius and spirit; and I am persuaded no good Scotsman, however prejudic'd he may be, will grudge to sacrifice our single tragedy of Douglas to the interest and prosperity of his country. What would David Garrick Esq; say, were it possible for him to hear,

that

that a tragedy he rejected, as cold and unaffecting, made the whole city of E-dinburgh almost mad for a fortnight, and drew endless tears and lamentations from every spectator? Let us, by one bold stroke, deliver ourselves from all future apprehentions. I am persuaded that a seasonable example of this kind, will deter other enterprizing young men, from turning their talents to the service of the stage; for, tho' it be true, that one precedent like Douglas, is enough to bring us an hundred tragedies in a year; yet I am very hopeful, that after this necessary severity shewn to that piece, there will be but very few hardy enough, to trouble us for a long time with compositions of that nature: Next Wednesday then, let it be publickly burnt by the hands of the hangman, and I shall exceedingly rejoice, that I have been instrumental (tho' unworthy) to save my country from ruin, and prevent the downfall of true religion.

My fifth reason is, that the tragedy of Douglas has certainly given great offence to the nobility and gentry of Scotland. For since it is accounted, however falsely, a proof of learning and genius to have written a successful tragedy, were not the laity intitled to lead in a matter of so much importance? and is it not the height of

of folly and prefumption, for this rafh
young man to ftep in before his betters,
and take upon him, forfooth, to raife the
reputation of his country higher than ever
it was before, for fine writing, which is
the firft and moft excellent of the fine arts?
Have not the gentry in Scotland been always jealous of the increafing power, and
abilities of the clergy? What elfe could
have induc'd them, againft their own intereft, to favour prefentations, of which
more than two thirds are in the hands of
the crown? Befides, from the fuccefs of
Douglas, and the boafted merit of that
performance, the laity have good ground
to fear, that the next application to parliament for an augmentation of ftipends,
will be more fuccefsful than the former; for
the Englifh lords and commons will no
doubt think it great pity, that men of fo
much learning and ability fhould be confin'd all their days to offices not fo lucra-
tive, tho' a little more honourable, than
thofe they eafily procure for a favourite
footman.

And here it is but juft to own, that religion has gain'd one confiderable advantage by the tragedy of Douglas. For feveral perfons, not remarkable heretofore
for their zeal and piety, have been lately obferv'd to exprefs themfelves with a
proper

proper degree of warmth, in behalf of religion, and the fanctity of the ministerial character. Thus it was likewise during the dependance of the augmentation scheme ; for there was then a manifest increase of zealous profeffors. I hope our new converts will perfevere, and bring forth fruit, longer than they did.

I have many other reafons to add, but underftand I am happily prevented by the zeal and vigilance of the presbytery of Edinburgh, who by their wife conduct have already rais'd fuch a cry, as the general affembly itfelf will hardly be able to filence. They have long been the leading presbytery in the church, and after this mafter-ftroke of ingenious zeal, I foon hope to fee them dictate to every other presbytery in Scotland. For obferve their admirable conduct ; they fcorn'd to attack the ftage on its weak fide of comedy, or even on that of exceptionable tragedies ; but have waited many years with the utmoft coolnefs and patience, till a tragedy appear'd with which every mortal was highly delighted, and which the beft judges pronounced to be one of the moft moral poems that ever was compos'd ; and that ftrongeft part of the ftage, to fhew their undaunted courage and zeal, they have manfully attack'd with all their forces.

ces. But further, to shew the world th goodness of their cause, they have broke through all the barriers of the sacred character, and overturn'd the independent jurisdiction of presbyteries by a single letter.

In this wonderful letter, they have taken an effectual course with those brethren, who had the assurance to go and see the tragedy of Douglas, in the presence of many of the judges of the land, the greatest part of the ruling elders in the church, and the best and worthiest persons of every parish in town; and who have been frequently heard to say, that they did not think tragedy unlawful, that it might often do good, and was by no means contrary to scripture, or the laws of the church. But these priests of Baal shall soon be made sensible how undecent it is for them to partake of the favourite amusment of persons of rank, and how dangerous to taste of pleasures, otherwise innocent, that their brethren do not care for.

I am informed too, that the reverend presbytery have prepared a warning and admonition, and are soon to volley the thunders of the church, against the supporters of the tragedy of Douglas. The storm no doubt will be very great, for it has been long in gathering. And as they

permit

permit you to fin on for two weeks longer, (for the paper is not to be read till the
laft Sunday of the month) you may firmly
believe, my fellow citizens, they will make
you fmart the more feverely for all. You
are well acquainted with the clear and regular, and impartial conduct of the prefbytery as a court, as well as with the decency, fobriety, and purity of a great many of the leading members in this affair.
Be not therefore fo head-ftrong, as to
judge for yourfelves in time to come ; but
be fo wife as to ufe the advantages you
poffefs, and furrender yourfelves implicitly to the direction of your paftors. What
tho' you have ground to believe, they do
not act in this matter precifely according
to their fentiments, remember that religion
is at ftake, and you muft forgive them.
Have but patience for a little while, and
they will foon flacken their difcipline. Wo
is me, that the nature of man cannot be
altered ! When this perfonal attack is once
over, what reafon have I to hope, that
they will take any more notice of plays,
than they did heretofore ! Some of thefe
devout father-confeflors have articled with
their fair young penitents for two plays
a week the reft of the winter, if they
would but abftain from the tragedy of
Douglas. What a key this private anec-
dote

dote is to a great part of their conduct!

I cannot conclude this work without congratulating the reverend presbytery upon their zeal and courage, and the success of their laudable endeavours; and admiring that wonderful concurrence of circumstances, that has produc'd such an *unusual* harmony of sentiments among them. If it should long continue, blest be the day that brought to light the tragedy of Douglas! for union and peace among brethren, are to be purchas'd at any expence.

But let not the chosen and faithful few be too confident in this temporary union, occasion'd perhaps by passions the simple reader is little aware of. Proceed ye, you sacred band! with vigour and resolution, before the children of this world recover their wisdom again; if you do not strike the blow now, never more hope to find them at your mercy; and as the first step to a full victory over this vile tragedy, move the presbytery to come in a body next Wednesday, to the place where the cross once stood, precisely at one o'clock, and you shall behold that abomination of abominations devour'd by flames hotter than your hottest zeal.

F I N I S.

17 A Song: Or, a Sermon. A New Ballad

The song is dated the 29th January 1757, a day before the *Admonition and Exhortation* of the Edinburgh Presbytery was released. Dr Alexander Webster as the figurehead of the Popular party and Patrick Cuming are the targets of the author's wit. Webster's weakness for drink is mentioned and the writer is eager to demonstrate the hypocrisy of his position: why should Webster be left to drink as he pleased while those who wished to go to the theatre were not allowed to attend?

A SONG:

OR, A

SERMON.

A

NEW BALLAD.

SINCE the Presbyt'ry sage,
  Attacking the Stage,
In the Churches 'gainst Tragedy rail;
  Before you repair
  To be catechis'd there,
Shall a Song or a Sermon prevail?

'TIS

'Tis *W———r* and *C———g*
That fet me a-humming,
By them more than Phœbus infpir'd;
Affift me, Divines,
And breath in my Lines,
The Zeal that your Bofoms hath fir'd.

SAY, was it Religion
Your Zeal fet an Edge on,
And mov'd you 'gainft Poets to rant?
Were you never afraid,
It by them fhould be faid,
That Poetry's better than Cant?

LESS

[3]

LESS furely's the Crime
In coupling a Rhime,
Than either to drink or to lie;
Yet wifely you chofe
To be filent on thofe,
And we all know a good Reafon why.

THE Doctor fo civil,
Would bow to the Devil,
Were the Devil a great Man in Pow'r;
And the Parfon fo able,
If Old Nick kept a Table,
Would dine, and call five Bottles more.

THERE's *W--k-r*, your Brother,
How durft he make a Pother?
If Acting's a damnable Sin,
He had need to pray ftout,
To fetch himfelf out;
We know that he fairly was in.

WHAT

WHAT Cause could incense,
 Or stir up Offence
In Divines so holy as these?
 Let 'em drink, lie and flatter,
 And each other bespatter,
We go to the Play when we please.

THEN good People all,
 Attend to my Call,
This Night to the Play-house repair;
 For To-morrow the Clergy
 Are gravely to charge ye,
There's no Sin, if you cease to go there.

18 Advertisement

This anonymous piece depicts the Presbytery of Edinburgh as puppet masters putting on a show of disapproval over the play that has newly emerged. The author refers to the *Admonition and Exhortation* when he states that no one 'can think himself at liberty to countenance the impious proceedings at the Theatre in the Canongate, after the 30th January current'. Webster is again the target for the pro-*Douglas* faction. All those under him are depicted as unthinking mouthpieces of the Presbytery, flocking around in support of the *Admonition*. The figure of 'Great Powell', described as the god of all puppets, is an allusion to Martin Powell, the famous puppeteer who travelled with his show in Europe during the early part of the eighteenth-century.

ADVERTISEMENT.

THAT there is lately come to town, A new set of curious PUPPETS, commissioned by the R———d P———y of *Edinburgh*, in order to afford a proper innocent entertainment for the remaining part of the winter-season; as no Person of any religious principle whatever, can think himself at liberty to countenance the impious proceedings at the Theatre in the *Canongate*, after the 30th of *January* current.

A neat stage is fitted up in *Allan's* close, near the New Exchange; and on *Monday* next, the 31st current, will be performed, by particular desire of the M——d——r, a new farce, called, *The Deposition*.———The following PROLOGUE, wrote upon the occasion by the P——y-cl——k, to be spoke by a puppet dressed in black.

IN a dark dismal corner long had stood
    Poor *Punchinello* in a pensive mood,
Sadly bemoaning his disastrous fate,
Who for sev'n years had not been heard to prate.

Unhappy

Unhappy *Punch*, unhappy friends, he cries,
Shall we no more attempt the long'd-for prize?
Shall *Caledonia*'s nymphs for ever be
Barr'd from that pleasure they receiv'd from me?
Shall they no more my witless squeaks approve?
Shall I no more their thoughtless laughter move?

Thus spoke the hero, ending with a groan,
While meaner puppets echo'd to his moan,
When, lo! an airy messenger appear'd,
And crav'd an audience quickly to be heard.

I come, he says, with wings of haste to chear
Your drooping hearts, and hence to banish fear.
Great *Powell* sent me, whom you all revere,
The god of puppets, now he dwells in air;
And thus thro' me he speaks, attention give,
And learn henceforth more patiently to live.
Soon shall fair *Scotia*'s capital again
Receive great *Punch*, and all his puppet train;
Soon shall her belles thy witless squeaks approve;
Soon shall thy barren jests their laughter move;
No more shall you by *Douglas* rival'd be,
W——r's your friend, and the whole P——y.

They

They long have mourn'd in filence your difgrace,
P——ts themfelves when in their proper place),
And griev'd to find that fuch refpect was fhown,
To wit and tafte fo different from their own ;
Fretted to fee the town fo much admire
The tragic mufe, and the poetic fire
Of *Athelftaneford*'s bard, their rage increas'd ;
And thus great *W*——*r* the k——k-c——t addrefs'd.
  " The pulpit and the puppets only can
Proper inftruction give to finful man.
The ftage is impious, 'caufe there vice is fhown
Horrid from reafon, not from fear alone :
And fhould it gain the pow'r men to perfuade,
Virtue to court by patterns, then our trade
Ufelefs may prove ; for we muft all allow,
Our precepts more than our examples fhow
The paths of virtue : therefore let us join
Our heads, and with united force combine
In this grand fcheme, to perfecute the ftage,
And all its followers, with the keeneft rage
Of c——h-rebuke, and make the croud believe,
Whom by ftrain'd fc—p—re-texts we oft deceive),
That nought but vice from ftage-plays can be learn'd,
And fure damnation by their lovers earn'd."

                                               Thus

Thus fpoke the p——n with becoming grace,
While cheartul affent fhone in ev'ry face.
Charm'd with the grateful plan they all agreed,
A folemn warning 'gainft the ftage to read,
In ev'ry c———h, that ev'ry flock might fee,
How good, how meek, how wife the P———try.

So fpoke the herald to the puppet crew,
And quick as lightning back to *Powell* flew.
But left he fhould be deem'd an impofition,
He left a copy of the *A—n—tion.*
Punch read with joy, and bade us all make hafte,
Hither to come, and fhew the cl—gy's tafte.
We ftraight obey'd; and here to night is fhown
A fcene entirely new, but which you'll own,
Points c—chm—s actions in their proper view,
And fhows what zealous c—gy—n will do.
If the plot pleafe you, I content fhall be;
If not, d—n all your pr—ts, but d—n not me.

F I N I S.

19 Votes of the Presbytery of Edinburgh *and*
20 By Particular Desire of the Reverend Members of the G----l As---m---y

This short broadside, dated the 29th December 1756, mocks the Presbytery of Edinburgh and its objections to the play. Although not mentioned by name, Alexander Webster and his profuse drinking habits are alluded to. The writer chooses to call him Dr *Bonum Magnum,* a nickname frequently used by his opponents. The second piece is in the style of a theatre announcement for a farcical opera featuring the protagonists in the controversy: Webster, Carlyle, Patrick Cuming, and possibly John Haldane (J—n H—e).

VOTES

OF THE

P——y of E————h.

Die Mercurii, die 29no Dec. 1756.

RESOLVED, That Learning, Genius, and Merit are the Bane of Society, and ought to be difcouraged.

Refolved, That Ignorance, Dulnefs, and Demerit are the Glory of this *covenanted* Church, and ought, therefore, to be encouraged.

Refolved, That every Propofition, which filly People alone maintain, is true.

Ordered, That the Crowd of wife Heads, who fill the Areas of the *T——th* K——k, be henceforth fovereign Arbiters of Tafte, Compofition, and Merit.

Refolved, That none but ignorant, fuperftitious, barbarous Nations have admired thofe Reprefentations of human Life, which are exhibited upon the Stage.

Ordered,

Ordered, That they be forthwith abolifhed, and that *Tam Thumb*, *Blind Hary*, *Totum*, *Punch*, and *Difhy Loof* be immediately fubftituted in their Place.

Refolved, That Improvements of all Sorts are hurtful to Society.

Ordered, That no Alteration be ever attempted to be made of the Principles, the Cuftoms, and the Manners of Men.

Ordered, That the Method of improving Land by inclofing and fallowing be immediately laid afide, becaufe ———— it is offenfive to the People.

Refolved, That the Poets are publick Nufances, and ought, like noxious Weeds, to be extirpated.

Refolved, That *Homer*, *Virgil*, *Milton*, *Shakefpear*, *Corneille*, and *Addifon* were Dunces, and that their Memories ought to be ftigmatifed.

Refolved, That the Author of the *Revenge*, of *Bufiris*, and of the *Brothers* is an impious Fellow, becaufe he wrote *Night Thoughts* and the *Centaur*.

Refolved, That the Author of *Athelftane* and of *Barbaroffa* is an Infidel, becaufe he made an Anfwer to the *Characterifticks* of the Earl of *Shaftesbury*.

Refolved, That Drunkennefs, Deceit, and Hypocrify are not *Chriftian* Vices.

Refolved,

Refolved, That notorious Drunkards, Idiots, and Villains *be* the moft zealous Chriftians.

Refolved, That a Man, who makes it the Bufinefs of his Life to hunt after Feafts and a good Bit, who guzzles more Liquor than fome Parifhes, and delights not only in drinking himfelf, but in encouraging others to get themfelves drunk; lead a fober exemplary Life, and has a mortal Averfion at Claret, becaufe ———— he thunders once a-Week againft *good Works.*

Ordered, That none of thofe *ætherial Spirits,* who fipple about the Cellars at *A———n,* apply the foregoing *Refolution* to Dr. *Bonum Magnum.*

Refolved, That one, who is come from acting on the Stage to pafs the greateft Part of his Time in the Company of his Harpficord, and———of Mrs. S———, is, therefore, grown a perfect Saint.

Refolved, That Mr. *C———g* and Mr. *J—ne,* Men, who it is notorious, have, on *all* Occafions, acted *without* felfifh Views, are actuated by Zeal *alone.*

Refolved, That the Favourites of Beauty, Wit and Spirit, are dangerous Rivals, and ought therefore to have no Friends.

Refolved, That *effectual* Means be ufed to remove them out of the Way of the Preferment of————

Ordered,

Ordered, That L —— d *M*——— take Care immediately after the Death of Mr. *G*—*e*, and Mr. *G*———*t*, to promote Mr. *C*——*g* and Mr. *J*———*ne*, for their remarkable Zeal in his Service.

Ordered, That they be furthwith *restored* to his Favour.

Ordered, That on the third *Sunday* of *March* next, a Table and a Half be not taken from the usual Compliment of the *T*———*h* K——k.

Die Mercurii, 12*mo Jan.* 1757.

Ordered, That no Pr———y presume to insult the Pr———y of *E*———*h*.

Resolved, That the present Time is the same with that of the *Covenant*.

Ordered, That the People of *Scotland* remain for ever in Barbarity.

Printed by Order of Dr. Bonum Magnum, *for* W——t——r P——t——r, W———m G———y, *and* J———s B——n.

FINIS.

BY PARTICULAR DESIRE of the Reverend Members of the G-------L As--M--Y.

ON SUNDAY NEXT,

Being the 5th of J U N E,

Will be performed A *CONCERT* of MUSIC,

Confisting of feveral Favourite OVERTURES.

After which will be prefented (*gratis*)

A *TRAGEDY*, called, THE

SUFFERINGS OF JOB.

[By W-------M W------E A------te.]

The Characters of Lord *JOB*, Lady *JOB*, and Friends, as will be exprefed in the next Bills.

To which will be added, a FARCICAL OPERA, revived from the GREEK, called,

THE REVELATIONS.

By the fame A U T H O R.

Four and Twenty Elders,——The Elders of the Pr--sb--ry of E------h.

Four B E A S T S full of Eyes before and behind.

1ft Beaft, Mr. W---b----r ;

2d Beaft, Mr. W--lk--r ;

3d Beaft, Mr. P---m---fe ;

4th Beaft, Mr. Pl---d----th.

Author of the Book fealed with feven Seals, Mr. J—n H—e ;

Angel offering Incenfe at the Golden Altar, Mr. C—m—g ;

And the Part of the Angel of Sardis, that was reproved, by Mr C--l—le,

[From the Canongate Theatre.]

N. B. As the Golden Candlefticks, Trumpets, Jewels, and other Decorations and Machinery, have coft the Undertakers a great deal of Money, and as this is the firft laudable Attempt towards a Reformation of the Theatre, fo much to be wifhed for, and fo earneftly recommended, we hope the R——d C——y will countenance, and the Nobility and Gentry will attend this Reprefentation. If you approve,

——————— " Back to the Mufe he flies,

" And bids your Scriptures in Succeffion rife.

21 Advice to the Writers in Defence of Douglas

This pro-*Douglas* poem encourages the advocates of the play to surmount the superstitious complaints of the Church of Scotland who would ban stage performances. According to the author, those that have penned tracts against the play have shown little in the way of taste or skill, and instead have succeeded only in publishing 'scandalising Anecdotes'.

A D V I C E

TO THE

W R I T E R S

In DEFENCE of

D O U G L A S

———— *Servum pecus! at mihi sæpe*
Bilem, sæpe jocum vestri movere tumultus.

HOR.

I Who's weak Numbers struggled to display
The hidden Beauties of our *Scottish* Play,
Zealous a rising Genius to commend,
And praise the Poet of my native Land
In Verse more lofty, now attempt to plan
The Vindication of the holy Man,
Instruct his Champions how to deal their Blows,
And overcome his superstitious Foes.

LET

LET not harſh Epithets affright the Nine,
Nor let a —— disfigure ev'ry Line,
Leſt puzzled Readers curſe the cautious Sot,
Who for each Name he writes muſt make a Blot.

FROM ſcandaliſing Anecdotes refrain,
And ſcorn to combat with a poiſon'd Pen;
If to provoke contending Parties loth
A *Janus bifrons* countenances both,
Let him ſecure his double Viſage ſhew,
Nor box and buffet that which ſmiles on you.
Or ſhould a Prophet all his Sorrows drown
In mighty Flaſks of Claret not his own,
Shall ye like HAM, 'gainſt whom God's Vengeance
    roſe,
A fuddled Father's Nakedneſs expoſe?
In all your meagre Writings ſtands confeſt,
Great Want of Liquor, and great Want of Taſte.
                    Good

Good Poets owe their Fury to the Vine,
But thin Potations weaken ev'ry Line.*

OR if each Prieſt to expiate his Crimes,
Muſt hitch and hobble in your trotting Rhimes?
His Character's peculiar Out-lines ſketch,
Nor by a Nickname ſingle out the Wretch,
As bungling Limners, who diſtruſt their Paint,
Write in plain *Engliſh* what their Pencil meant.

SUBDUED the Prize of Wit and Humour yield
Nor try the Sword of Ridicule to wield ;
Aukward you totter with that Sword oppreſt,
Like J E S S E's Boy in manly Armour dreſt.

YOUR Strength conſiſts, (Heav'n knows I don't de
In Compoſitions ſtay'd, ſedate and grave. [ceive
Ho\

* Nulla placere diu nec vivere carmina poſſunt,
Quæ ſcribuntur aquæ potoribus.———— HOR.

[4]

ow many lolling read in eafy Chair,
our foporifick, *ferious* Pamphleteer,
Whofe labour'd Periods uniformly dull
To fofteft Slumbers his Admirers lull.

NOR boafting venture falfly to affert,
That ev'ry Genius battles on your Part,
When Men impartial in the Balance weigh,
What Works deride, and what extoll the Play:
Then fhall poor DOUGLAS fee his Foes prevail,
And ftart at TEKEL written on his Scale.

F I N I S.

ANTI-DOUGLAS PAMPHLETS AND BALLADS

22 The Moderator Number II

The Moderator is a conscious emulation of John Witherspoon's *Ecclesiastical Characteristics*, selecting the same targets for its cultural attack, such as Lord Shaftesbury, but without achieving the damage or the accuracy that Witherspoon's arrows inflict. George Buchanan is provided as a model upon whom David Hume might base his own writings, particularly in the field of history. The cultural model of the Moderates comes under a sustained barrage from the author who professes that the ministers of the church should no longer preach sermons on religious matters, but ought instead to spread the word by writing about secular topics such as the science of morals and agriculture, with the Select Society paying for the best of these efforts. Home's abilities are distorted beyond all recognition, mocking the adulation of the Moderates, while David Hume's association serves only to bring the minister into further disrepute.

THE
MODERATOR.
NUMBER II.

THE public has, doubtless, suffered very much from my long silence, since the publication of the first number of this paper. To relieve them from their anxiety, I come now forth, assuring them that I am still alive, and that, during this long interval, I have not ceased, though in a different capacity, to promote the good end I proposed on my first setting out. Left any reader should not be able to call to mind the subject-matter of my first number, I am, as the title itself may partly inform him, a champion for the flourishing and prosperous cause of moderation in the church.

Such, it must be owned, is the thriving and vigorous state of that great interest at present, that it doth not appear to stand in much need of the assistance or support of a periodical writer, or indeed any writer at all. This, perhaps, was the reason why our friends showed so little sense of gratitude to my brother the author of the *Ecclesiastical Characteristics*, who thought fit to draw his pen in their defence. I am however rather inclined to think, that the gentleman failed in the execution of his design. He is plainly of a cold systematic turn, laying down a regular and uniform plan; which way of writing is at present quite disrelished, both in the world and in the church. His miscarriage therefore is little or no discouragement to me, who intend to use the shorter and more palatable method of essay-writing and miscellany. This the Noble Earl of *Shaftesbury* justly celebrates, under the

A   character

character of *learned ragout and medley*. He was the first who brought such treatises into reputation among men of taste; and shewed how the order, strength, and elegance of the ancients, might be concealed under the ease, irregularity, and apparent confusion of the modern form. He hath been my delight and pattern from my youth, not without some tolerable profit. And in entering upon the present attempt, that my periods may run with the same slipshod nimbleness of style, for which his Lordship was so eminent, I hope the reader will believe I have used every form of invocation.

Another reason may be given for the miscarriage of the author above named, *viz.* a wrong choice of his subject. There are but three distinct ends which a writer in support of any party can be supposed to have in view. The first is, to answer the objections, and refute the calumnies, of enemies; the second, to point out the paths of further improvement; and the third, to celebrate the characters of those eminent persons who are chiefly employed in leading and conducting it. The first of these the author of the *Characteristics* seems chiefly to have had in his eye; and therein he discovered the weakness of his judgment. Nothing can be more foolish in a party-writer, than to busy himself in answering objections. It is always a confession, and to many an information, that such objections are or may be made: and as the world hath a far greater tendency to believe ill than well of others, so it requires both longer time, and a stronger comprehension, to understand the answer to an objection, than to perceive the force of the objection itself. A deep wound may be given in a moment; but it takes a long time, as well as the application of remedies, effectually to cure it; and sometimes it is impossible fible wholly to remove the fcar. The fame thing ufes alfo often to bring to my mind the throwing of dirt upon a well-dreffed lady, which, after you have wiped off with ever fo great care, is ftill apt to leave fome ftain.

For thefe reafons, I defpife the work of anfwering objections. And there is the lefs occafion for it in our cafe, becaufe we are not now ftriving for power, but ufing it. We are poffeffed of abfolute and fupreme command; and if at any time a remaining enemy do prefume to throw out a reflection againft us, fecure of dominion, we glory in our ftrength, and mock the ineffectual dart. As fimilitudes feem to flow upon me at prefent in great plenty, I muft give them vent; affuring the reader, that, as all comparifons ought to do, they prefent themfelves arifing naturally out of the fubject, and are not induftriously hunted for by me, and forced into the fervice. Once more then, we refemble a traveller, who may be fometimes annoyed with the yelping of a cur at his horfe's heels upon the road. It would be both below his dignity, and would but more provoke the animal, to fpeak to him, or command him away; and therefore he ought wholly to defpife the impotent and feeble fury, unlefs the creature be fo incautious as to come within his reach, and then he may take fignal and heroic vengeance, and give him a mortal blow in return for his barking.

Leaving then this vindicating and objection-anfwering method, as unprofitable or hurtful, it is upon the fecond and third views of a party-writer that my prefent and following papers are to turn, viz. pointing out the meafures proper to be followed, and celebrating the characters of thofe who lead the way. With this defign, my firft number endeavoured to direct the

citizens

citizens of the capital of this church and nation in the choice of three paftors to fupply fo many vacant charges. In that inftance the victory was not complete; yet my attempt was not wholly ineffectual, if the world and my friends have not flattered me. I intended alfo to have given directions in the laft election, and was moved by feveral perfons fo to do; but came too late by the precipitate conduct of the managers of that affair. However, there are a few things for the public emolument, which I fhall now humbly propofe. Some of them, indeed, a penetrating eye may eafily, from the prefent tendency and courfe of things, difcern to be future. Such may lightly efteem my propofals, as being little elfe than what will naturally happen in a fhort time: but, befides that I fhall add fome things not quite fo obvious, even thefe future bleffings are of fuch value, that I fhall reckon my pains well beftowed, if I contribute in any meafure to accelerate their approach.

1/t, Let it be obferved, that there is a great penury of m——s at prefent in this c——h fit for the M——r's chair. This is evident from the two laft elections. In the firft of them, a *public teacher* * was chofen, a creature equivocally generated between a c——n and layman, like a mule, who is neither horfe nor afs. In the other, a well-known perfon was chofen for the fecond or third time, who is now in the decline of life and character, and, being a great lover of pre-eminence, is put to very hard fhifts to preferve it. Having long ferved the great with the moft affiduous and flavifh fubjection, he is at laft reduced to the ftill more ignoble fervitude, of flattering and cajoling beardlefs boys, that he may be fuffered to go before them.

* This is the phrafe which that gentleman always ufes inftead of *Minifter of the Gofpel.*

It

It is therefore propofed, that the ancient cuftom which prevailed in Mr *George Buchanan*'s time, be revived, cf chufing a layman. The benefits that may arife from this alteration, will occur to every reader; and therefore I wholly pafs them, and humbly recommend to the choice of the enfuing a——y, *Sopho*, whofe learning, piety, and other qualifications, are evident from his writings, and his ftation. This honour would ferve to wipe off fome unjuft afperfions which have been thrown upon him in former affemblies. For my part, I heartily approve of him, both as a man and as a writer; and find no fault in his effays, except a ftarting and convulfive motion in the ftyle, which was probably owing to fome diforder in his nervous fyftem.

D—— H——, Efq; might alfo be on the leet, becaufe, like *Buchanan*, he has been a governor to young gentlemen, and is a great admirer of K. *James*, who was *Buchanan*'s pupil. Like him too, he is an hiftorian; at leaft it is faid he has written, and is writing a hiftory. However, I wifh *Sopho* may carry the chair, becaufe Mr *H——* feems to have fomething of a party-man about him; whereas *Sopho*'s catholic principles about the delufory nature of confcience, in which he is really of no body's, and, by confequence, in the centre of every body's opinion, muft incline him to hear all fides with the utmoft impartiality.

2*dly*, It is propofed, that the *Edinburgh* bookfellers concerned in Mr *H——*'s hiftory fhould prefent a petition to the committee of bills, bearing, " That " whereas Mr *D—— H——* hath, with incredible " pains, and patience, written a hiftory, wherein great " honour is done to the church of *Scotland*, by fhew- " ing, that fhe excels all other churches in the purity

A 3 " of

" of her worſhip and diſcipline ; and this repreſenta-
" tion being evidently given by the author, not from
" any prejudice in favour of the church of *Scotland*,
" but from an inadvertent regard, for once, to truth,
" it muſt therefore make a deeper impreſſion upon the
" minds of Mr *H——*'s admirers in and about *Edin-*
" *burgh*, and diſpoſe them, as ſoon as they ſhall be-
" come ſerious, and ſettled in any principles at all, to
" join in communion with the church of *Scotland* :
" yet ſo it is, that the book does not ſell, except a-
" mong theſe ſame admirers of his at *Edinburgh* ; and
" your petitioners, through the corrupt taſte of the
" age, are like to loſe *L.* 400 *Sterling* ;" therefore
praying " to be indemnified to that extent out of his
" Majeſty's bounty of *L.* 1000, or that the whole
" impreſſion be bought up by the ſociety for propa-
" gating Chriſtian knowledge, to be diſperſed in the
" highlands and iſlands, where it may be very uſeful
" in preventing the growth of Popery, and, by the
" fine ſtyle in which it is written, ſerve to introduce
" the *Engliſh* language."

3*dly*, That, as the world has been long plagued and
tired with endleſs repetitions in ſermons upon religious
ſubjects, which have alſo a woful tendency to keep a-
live enthuſiaſm and ſuperſtition ; therefore every
m——r in *Scotland*, for a year to come, ſhall preach
on the different branches of trade and manufacture,
(in towns), and of agriculture, (in landward pariſhes).
This would relieve men from the gloom of devotion
mentioned by Mr *H——* in his hiſtory, and would agree
better with the *Scotch* taſte than pictures or proceſſions.
It would certainly make the congregations of ſome de-
ſerted paſtors thronger than before, and prevent people from ſleeping when they do attend ; as the young
gentlemen might poſſibly underſtand ſomething of
theſe

these subjects, and might also probably speak with a little more force and energy than they usually do. It would likewise draw the country-gentlemen to church, who have so long utterly deserted it ; and would be a mean of good correspondence between the m——r and his heritors, whom he must consult upon the applicatory part of every sermon, lest he mislead their tenants. For the same reason, no discourse on agriculture to be preached at tents, because of the difference of soil in the many different parishes from which the people are assembled. So that tent-sermons must either be wholly laid aside ; or the young preachers, and others, must keep in general terms, and recommend agriculture, as they used to recommend, formerly holiness, and now virtue, without any particular directions.

4*thly*, The *Edinburgh* society may be desired to give a premium of five or ten pounds, for the best sermon on each of the above subjects. This will be a way of augmenting stipends, to which I cannot think of any reasonable objection. The landed interest surely could not in honour oppose it. On the contrary, it might be expected, that they would voluntarily augment every minister's stipend, in proportion as his sermons should enable them to augment the rent of their lands.

Since the gentlemen of that laudable and useful society have publicly solicited correspondents to suggest any amendments or alterations that occur to them upon the scheme, I venture further to observe, that the premium for the best discovery in the sciences, which has not been given to any body, ought to have been given to D—— H——, Esq; for his discovery in the science of morals, that *health, cleanliness, taper legs, and broad shoulders*, are capital virtues; and a running
fore

fore an unpardonable crime. This I take to be the most extraordinary discovery of its kind that hath been made in this century. And if the gentleman's modesty prevented his applying to the society, since the thing is well known, he ought not to suffer on that account. Some notice ought also to be taken of him for a discovery in the art of writing for conviction, which he hath practised with so much success, viz. to be sceptical and uncertain upon every point in which the world is generally agreed, and positive and peremptory in such things as never entered into any head but his own.

Leaving these proposals to the consideration of the persons severally interested in them, proceed we now to gratify the expectation of the public, by paying the tribute of praise to the illustrious tragedy of *Douglas,* lately represented upon our own proper theatre, and the author of which is known to be a gentleman, and *public teacher*, of our own proper country. Fame is, by the concurrent testimony of all ages, the reward due to poets; and without it they are less able to subsist in their character of poets, than they can continue their natural life without bread. I will not therefore be so barbarous or unjust, as to refuse the fair and equal claim; but shall do my best; acknowledging, at the same time, that it is far below his merit; and promising, that if, at any time hereafter, I shall find my lungs more vigorous, and fitter for the purpose, I will set the trumpet again to my mouth, and give him still a louder blast.

And here, I am sensible, it is not proper to enter upon the particular beauties of this matchless composition, which is not yet published, left the world should arraign it as partial praise, coming from an intimate friend, perhaps one of that small and select number who

who were admitted behind the scenes. Waiting then till the publication, before we praise the structure of the piece, what I now commend is, the attempt in general, so very uncommon and bold, of introducing upon the stage, a play written by a *minister of the gospel*, and attended by a select band of the same ancient order. What a mortal blow to every enemy of moderation ? Mark ! how the furious bigot stands astonished, his rage repressed with wonder ! And see ! the gloomy enthusiast flies with terror to his cell, upon the exhibition of this new and extraordinary character upon the larger stage of the world! How will these moping and narrow-minded judges, who lately found the stage contrary to law, and vainly dreamed it hurtful to the people, now hide their heads for shame, when they hear this potent advocate rise up and plead the injured cause, and see hoary senators and pious clergy crouding to the theatre? How shall the light of the clergy now shine with redoubled lustre, when they shall be no more overgrown with the rust of singularity and restraint, but polished by collision with the world, and stamped with the very form of virtue, by attending the *instructive stage ?* And how happily shall they give as well as receive improvement, when the mixture of senatorial robes, and sacerdotal vestments, with the gay clothing of these elegant assemblies, shall add severity to sprightliness, and correct the levity of fashion ?

Animated by the inspiring theme, I begin to feel the impulse of prophetic fury. Methinks I see a race of theatrical divines, following the footsteps of this adventrous bard. He having burst the bars of the separating inclosure, and trampled under foot the monster of popular resentment, which stood on guard, behold the emancipated clergy exulting in their liberty,

and

and viewing, with ravifhed eyes, the fcénes of pleafure, for which they have now exchanged their own
melancholy cloifters. O happy period of time, when
virtue and freethinking, having put to flight every religious adverfary, are now in poffeffion of the long
contefted field! O happy actors, and more happy ac-
treffes, who, inftead of being fhunned and contemned
by all except the loofe and diffolute, are now become
the darlings of the clergy, who glory in their commerce with your perfons, and induftrioufly vindicate
your caufe!

I beg the reader's pardon for this impetuofity of ftyle,
into which I have been unwarily hurried by the fubject of my difcourfe. I do indeed think, that the genius of this tragic author hath the power of converting
every thing that touches it into its own nature. It is
known to be of infinite force and fire, difdaining vulgar bounds, and flying the beaten path. What rich
variety of apt epithets, and living metaphor? What
bold and noble fallies of imagination, fpringing not
only to the utmoft verge of probability, but even
touching the very borders of extravagance? And,
from what has juft now happened to myfelf in the celebration of his praife, it is plain, that if I had not
fuddenly drawn the reins, I fhould have been borne,
by ungoverned fancy, into a land of monfters, greater than ever were bred on Mount *Caucafus*, or by the
green banks of the river *Scamander*.

But now let me march with a little more compofure
and recollection, and remember, that I am not in a land
of monfters, but in a land of players; and congratulating the world upon the happy effects of the tranfla-
tion of our author, from the pulpit to the ftage, and
the door now opened for the admiffion of the clergy
to that improving amufement. Thefe effects it is impoffible

poffible for me to enumerate within the compafs of this paper; and therefore, leaving the greateft part of them as the fubject of future animadverfion, let me on-ly obferve, that *D—— H——* Efq; will have no more occafion to fay, as he does in one part of his works, that the calling and office of a minifter is an almoft infurmountable impediment to the practice of virtue. Among other reafons which he gives for this affertion, is the following, That they are obliged to put on the appearance of more fanctity and devotion than it is poffible for any man to poffefs; and this un-avoidable hypocrify debauches the mind, and ruins their integrity. Now, though it may be difficult to determine what is the greateft degree of fanctity and devotion which a man may really poffefs; and though I will allow with *D—— H——*, who doubtlefs hath made the trial, that it is very fmall : yet it can never be affirmed, that our divines who attend the theatre have the appearance of more, becaufe they have not the appearance of any at all.

I was indeed forry to find this remark in my friend *D——d*, which plainly fhows, that the greateft men have not always their wits about them; for it furnifhes a handle to his enemies to renew their charge againft him as a Papift. They will fay, The man has betrayed himfelf : if he was not abroad in perfon when he wrote this, his thoughts muft have been abroad in Ro-man-Catholic countries, prefenting to his imagination the aufterity of the feveral orders of regulars in that religion. As to Proteftant clergy, or thofe of his own country, he could not fo much as form an idea of them, but by experience and feeling. *Reafon could not help him out.* Now, who are the clergy with whom *D—— H——* correfponds, and from whom he muft form a judgment of the reft ? Are they over-
burdened

burdened with apparent fanctity? Their enemies themfelves will not fo much as pretend it. I hope, therefore, that in the next edition he will either wholly leave out this paffage, or at leaft make an honourable exception in favour of the *moderate* clergy of his own dear country, where all things are at prefent going on fo very wondrous well.

I fhall conclude this paper with the following fhort epigram of an anonymous author, and a paraphrafe upon it.

On a little name, which has produced three great heroes to fupport the declining glory of Britain. 1756.

An impious j——e, a wicked fceptic fage,
A ftage-playing prieft; O glorious NAME and AGE!

What is the glory and honour of any ftate or church? Is it not politenefs in the one, and mildnefs and moderation in the other? Do not then thefe three gentlemen promote the glory of this church and na-tion? Is it not our honour to tolerate the two firft? is it not both our honour and happinefs to have pro-duced, nourifhed, and to poffefs the laft?

P. S. Left the interval between my fecond and third paper fhould be longer than I expect, I beg leave to propofe, that, in the lift of premiums by the *Edinburgh* fociety for the year 1757, befides thofe hinted above, may be the following.

To the m——r who leaves his parifh ofteneft and longeft, with very fhort intervals of refidence, and, at the fame time, has made his people fo truly mode-rate, that they neither know, nor inquire, nor care, whether he be at home or abroad, a fum of money e-qual to a fupervifor of excife's travelling-charges.

[Price TWO PENCE.]

23 The Deposition, or Fatal Miscarriage: A Tragedy

This anonymous short play, similar in style to the *Philosopher's Opera*, has been frequently attributed to John Maclaurin. It even deploys a 'Prologue: Spoken at Edinburgh' in mock heroic tone which both mirrors and attacks the style of *Douglas*. Here, the protagonist Poetaster (Home) concludes that in the aftermath of the controversy he will leave the Church, before he is deposed, and make his fortune by means of his pen. However, his lover, Lady Tearsheet, cannot bear the thought of living without a stipend, and leaves him for another. Her actions in this final scene mirror the self-sacrifice of Lady Randolph in *Douglas*, but the lines are manipulated to imply that instead of falling off a cliff, she is falling into another man's bed. Shakespeare's and Otway's ghosts also make an appearance, lamenting that their reputations have been tarnished by comparisons of *Douglas* to their own work.

THE

DEPOSITION,

OR

FATAL MISCARRIAGE:

A

TRAGEDY.

Cantando tu illum? VIRG.

[Price TWO PENCE]

PROLOGUE.

Spoken at EDINBURGH.

*O*FT *has this audience merry humour fhown,*
 And laugh'd at blockheads, blockheads not their own.
This night our fcenes no common laugh demand,
He comes, the blockhead of your native land,
DOUGLAS, *a dunce through all the world renown'd,*
A dunce who roufes like the bagpipe's found.

 Liften attentive to the various tale,
Mark if the author's comic feelings fail.
Sway'd by alternate hopes, alternate fears,
He waits the teft of your congenial fneers.
If they fhall grin, back to the mufe he flies,
And bids your blockheads in fucceffion rife;
Collects the wand'ring wretches as they roam,
DOUGLAS *affures them of a welcome home.*

A

DRAMATIS PERSONÆ.

POETASTER.

ATHEOS,
MORALIS, } Friends to POETASTER.
RABULA,

MODERATOR.

LUCIUS, Enemy to POETASTER.

SHAKESPEAR's Ghoſt.

OTWAY's Ghoſt.

W O M E N.

Lady TEARSHEET.

ANNA.

THE

DEPOSITION:

A

TRAGEDY.

***

ACT I.

A bedchamber.

Enter Lady TEARSHEET *and* POETASTER.

Lady TEARSHEET.

To-morrow's fun fhall ufher in the day,
The great, th' important day, big with the fate
Of POETASTER. Words cannot exprefs
How much I dread th' affembly of your brethren.
In every lane and ftreet the bugbears fwarm ;
In gait and black array moft like they feem
To the forerunners of a funeral.
O my beloved, pacify thofe men,
And footh their bofoms with your fyren tongue.

POETASTER.

I am not *Orpheus*, Lady ;—though I were,
I would not proftitute the power of fong,
To foften ftones, or humanize the brutes.

A 2

399

O GENERAL ASSEMBLY! ne'er will I
Submit to thee, thou many-body'd monster.
Did *Hercules*, when he attack'd the *Hydra*,
Accoft its various heads? Did *Jove* addrefs
Th' enormous giant with a hundred hands?
" Oft have I (when a fimple fchool-boy) read
" Of wondrous deeds by one bold arm atchiev'd ;
" I know no chief that will defy myfelf."
And did I lack fupport, " I've kinfmen near,
" Brothers, that fhrink not from each others fide,
" And fond companions fill my warlike files."

Lady TEARSHEET.

Rebuke, though e'er fo fharp, would not cut deep ;
Sufpenfion would afford thee time to write ;
All day you would compofe your pretty plays,
And all night wanton in thy TEARSHEET's arms.
But, O my love, befeech thefe cruel men,
" By him that dy'd upon the curfed tree,
" And by the bleffed crofs, and King of kings,"
Not to deprive you of your benefice.
By thofe fanatics if thou fhouldft be turn'd
" Out to the mercy of the winter's wind,
" My beautiful! my brave! what wilt thou do?"

POETASTER.

" I'll hear no more ; this melody would make
" Your poet drop his pen, or write burlefques,
Poems and ballads on his own compofures.
Straitway I hie me to *hold dialogues*
With felect friends about to-morrow's combat.
No carking care would I bring to thy bed,
And therefore fhall this night with ATHEOS fleep.
" Lady, farewell ; I leave thee not alone,

       " Yonder

" Yonder comes one will make my abfence light.

[*Exit.*

Enter MORALIS.

" What doft thou mufe on, meditating maid? "

Lady TEARSHEET.

O! fweet MORALIS, *I am fore befet.*
You are not ignorant, how clofe of late
Has been my union with your gen'rous friend.
" Alas! fome months ago I found myfelf
" As women wifh to be who love their lords."

MORALIS.

And why for this fhould Lady TEARSHEET grieve?
" You for a living lover bear your pains,
" And he will blefs you when a man is born."

Lady TEARSHEET.

His brethren (if I fo may call them) threaten
To feize his ftipend, and he marketh not
" Which way the current of their temper fets;
" And therefore he muft be condemn'd to walk,
" Like a guilt-troubled ghoft, his painful rounds,
" And ftarving wander through a fcorning world."

MORALIS.

Nine clergymen him follow'd to the box.
One of the nine was I. Methought, by heav'n,
When I furvey'd him in the midft of us,
We were a fairer fpectacle to fee,
Than the nine mufes, with their prefident
Apollo, though they are divinities,
And we but mortal men. Retire, fair Lady,
And banifh anxious bodings from your thoughts,
" The play of DOUGLAS will protect itfelf."

End of the FIRST ACT.

A C T

A C T II.

A bedchamber.

Curtain draws, and difcovers POETASTER *and* ATHEOS *fleeping.* SHAKESPEAR's *ghoft rifes, with the tragedy of* DOUGLAS *in his hand.*

SO now, thefe barkers at my reputation
  Are fnoring in their kennel—Well, fleep on—
When I defcribe the characters of men,
And paint them as they are, he calls it *barbarifm.*
                              [*pointing to* ATHEOS.
When *Sir John Falftaff* and the *Prince* appear,
'Tis barbarous to make you fo to laugh ;
And when the gentle *Defdemona* dies,
'Tis barbarous to make you fo to weep.
And am I then compar'd to fuch a play-thing?
                              [*fhowing* DOUGLAS,
Are there no ladders wherewithal to fcale
The fort of Fame, but you muft climb to it
                              [*pointing to* POETASTER.
Hoifted upon my fhoulders?—Well, fleep on ;
Yet fhall the fteam of *Styx,* and breath of furies,
Be poppies to thine eyes, thou demi-devil.
                              [*pointing to* ATHEOS.
If *Otway* and myfelf muft yield to thee,
                              [*pointing to* POETASTER.
'Twas true, no dream, that fun and moon defcended,
And made obeifance to the ftripling *Jofeph.* [*vanifhes.*
                              OTWAY's

402

OTWAY's *ghost rises.*

I led a wretched life, and dy'd for hunger,
Had not a cruft of bread to give my ftomach,
Whofe ever-craving, agonizing throes,
Gnaw'd me to death.
Yet did the fame my compofitions gain'd,
Sooth my forlorn fhade ! But thou, inhuman !
Haft been endeavouring to filch that fame,
And rob me of my all. O ! I could weep
With BELVIDERA's or MONIMIA's eyes,
To fee the godlike SHAKESPEAR fo contemn'd,
Myfelf fo difregarded.   [*vanifhes.*

POETASTER *wakens.*

Sleep'ft thou yet, ATHEOS ! then thou haft not dream'd
Of fuch drear fcenes as I've. " Ye minifters
" Of gracious Heav'n, who love the human race !
" Angels and feraphs ! who delight in goodnefs,
" Forfake your fkies, and to his couch defcend ;
" There from his fancy chafe thofe difmal forms
" That haunted me juft now ; his fpirit charm
" With images celeftial, fuch as pleafe
" The blefs'd above upon their golden beds."

ATHEOS *wakens.*

Ha ! what didft thou fay, my POETASTER !
Didft' talk of fweet repofe ? I tafted none.
Two angry ghofts difturb'd my midnight-fleep :
Though pale they were and wan, and in their dead-cloaths
Yet fomething very noble feem'd about them ;
Oft did they frown on me, and oft on thee,
" And ever and anon they vow'd revenge."

POETASTER.

O ! ATHEOS, with thee this night I've fhar'd,

                                        Not

Not only the fame couch, but the fame wo.
I dream'd that my departed fpirit fled
To the infernal regions; there I fought,
And found at length the blefs'd *Elyfian* fields,
Where happy poets dwell. I heard the lyres
Of *Homer* and of *Maro* in fweet concert;
SHAKESPEAR above them all I faw exalted,
An eager-lift'ning croud furrounded him;
To whom he faid, that "all the world's a ftage,
" And all the men and women merely players."
I thought, fure I can fpeak to better purpofe;
And would have ftopp'd him while he fo harangu'd,
Had not fome little ugly goblins feiz'd
And carried me before the three ftern judges,
Whofe nod determines all affairs in hell.
I was arraign'd of being a wretched poet,
One whofe unmanner'd mouth, whene'er it drunk,
Made *Helicon*'s pure font a naufeous puddle.
My judges (befhrew them for it) order'd
My play, my DOUGLAS, forthwith to be funk
In LETHE's ftream, myfelf for ever chain'd,
And link'd with BAYES, to walk that river's banks.

ATHEOS.

Go to, we both have dream'd, that's all the matter:
Some few hours hence, and you muft ftand your trial:
Come, let us then go drefs, and to the pannel.
: Pfhaw! be not difcompos'd. "Departed ghofts
" Are ne'er permitted to review this world."

End of the SECOND ACT.

A C T

A C T III.

The New Church.

The General Assembly sitting.

MODERATOR.

BRethren, you've heard by sev'ral overtures,
How POETASTER, *author of the* DOUGLAS,
(Such is the designation he affects),
For many months was absent from his parish;
Which many months he threw away at *London*
With actors, actresses, and such canaillie,
Hoarding most filthy lucre. Reverend Sirs,
Your sentiments on this behaviour.

RABULA.

Most Reverend Moderator, " rude I am
" In speech and manners: never till this hour
" Stood I in such a presence: yet, dear Sir,
" There's something in my breast which makes me say,
" That POETASTER ne'er will shame the KIRK."
I grant, 'tis new for a *Scotch* clergyman
To write a tragedy; but one that's perfect
Is full as new; and such a play is his.
And had he sinn'd, his youth, his modesty
Would plead most powerfully in his behalf.

B   Let

Let us difmifs him, Sir, and bid him go,
" In peace and fafety to his pleafant home."

LUCIUS.

Moft Reverend Moderator, I am forry
From RABULA to differ ; but far more fo
To give my voice for punifhing a brother :
And yet to me it feems deteftable,
That a *Scotch* minifter, a holy man,
Should thus forego his cloth, and wafte his time,
Seeking the bubble reputation,
Even in the player's mouth ; and, what is worfe,
Seeking an *augmentation* from the ftage.
There was a man whom I remember well,
I will not fay that he was deeply fkill'd
In policy ecclefiaftical,
Of which we now hear much ; yet, as a dove,
Harmlefs was he, though not as ferpents fubtle ;
An honeft man he was, and once our brother :
GILLESPIE was his name ; but, with difgrace,
We did expel him our fociety,
Becaufe he fet his confcience 'gainft the law.
And you will call to mind how POETASTER
At that time thunder'd in your ears DEPOSE.
And is there then no law againft the ftage ?
" Have pity on his youth !" Why, he had none
On poor GILLESPIE's age. This POETASTER
May earn his bread with pleafure on the ftage ;
GILLESPIE could not, would not. 'Tis my thought,
That we fhould ftrip of all his holy things
This author of the DOUGLAS.

MODERATOR.

MODERATOR.

The queſtion then will be, Depoſe or Not?
Clerk, call the rolls.

    [It carries Depoſe; upon which POETASTER *runs*
    out, and the ſcene ſhuts.

Re-enter POETASTER.

Well, I will earn my bread upon the ſtage;
And in the playhouſe ſure there is no danger
Of depoſition. How pleaſant will it be
To act my own performances!

Enter ANNA.

O! POETASTER!

POETASTER.

    " Speak, I can hear of horror."

ANNA.

" Horror indeed!

POETASTER.

    " Lady TEARSHEET!

ANNA.

              " Is yours no more."

My Lady TEARSHEET cannot ſhare your bed
Without your ſtipend; therefore ſhe juſt now
To a new lover yields her beauteous limbs.
" O had you ſeen her laſt deſpairing look!
" Upon the brink ſhe ſtood, and caſt her eyes
" Down on the bed; then lifting up her head
" And her white hands to heav'n, ſeeming to ſay,
" Why am I forc'd to this? ſhe plung'd herſelf
" Into the empty couch."

POETASTER.

POETASTER.
　　　　　　　" I will not vent
" In vain complaints the paffion of my foul.
" Peace in this world I never can enjoy.
Anna, farewel! I am refolv'd t' enlift
Forthwith for the *Weſt Indies* ; there " I'll go
" Straight to the battle, where the man that makes
" Me turn afide, muſt threaten worfe than death."

F　I　N　I　S.

24 Apology for the Writers against the Tragedy of Douglas

The author of this piece, again, often said to have been John Maclaurin, identifies his targets as the Select Society, David Hume and John Home. As with the *Philosopher's Opera*, he asserts that the Select Society has erected a cultural tyranny over the country which 'usurps a kind of aristocratical government over all men and matters of learning'. Hume is depicted as the Coryphaeus of this enterprise, who has trashed the literary capabilities of Shakespeare and Otway to clear a path for an inferior Scottish product – John Home. In the *Apology*, however, Maclaurin engages more directly with the play, attempting to provide more solid critical reasoning as to why he finds the play so objectionable. Among the complaints is his belief that Glenalvon is a shadowy imitation of Iago, and the diction of the play is flawed in several key instances, which he notes. Maclaurin is altogether more generous in this piece than elsewhere, for on several occasions he concedes that *Douglas* possesses areas deserving praise – it is the position which it has been assigned by the Select Society that is his prime grievance.

APOLOGY

FOR

The WRITERS againſt the Tragedy of Douglas.

WITH

Some REMARKS on that Play.

Canſt thou be ſuch a vain miſtaken thing,
To wiſh thy works may make a playhouſe ring
With the unthinking laughter, and poor praiſe,
Of fops and ladies, factious for thy plays?
Then ſend a cunning friend to learn thy doom,
From the ſhrewd judges in the drawing-room.

ROCHESTER.

EDINBURGH:

Printed in the year MDCCLVII.

[Price Two Pence.]

APOLOGY

FOR

The WRITERS againft the Tragedy of Douglas.

IT is at prefent often, and juftly obferved, that the tragedy of *Douglas* has given birth to more burlefque performances, than any occurrence in *Scotland* ever did. Moft of the authors of thefe pieces lurk as unfufpected as they could wifh; but fome of them are known. As the friends of *Douglas* have thought proper to attack its enemies with private backbiting and calumny, and afcribed their writings to the moft ungentlemanly defigns; it is hoped, the public will allow them to explain at fome length their true motives, and juftify their own conduct, by making a few obfervations on that play and its admirers.

It has been faid, That " fpite and envy indu-
" ced us to ridicule this tragedy; and that our
" fole aim was to damp the rifing genius of its
" author." We muft be forgiven to fay, that this infinuation is as falfe as it is injurious. We would have rejoiced to fee a countryman of ours excel in tragedy. We indeed are forry that a *Scotch* clergyman has written a play; but we would have admired the tragedy, had it been good.

A

good, though we thought it blameable in the author to write one; as *Cæfar* liked the treafon, though he hated the traitor.

Some years ago, a few gentlemen in this town affumed the character of being the only judges in all points of literature; they were and ftill are ftyled the *geniufes,* and lately erected what they called a *felect fociety,* which ufurps a kind of ariftocratical government over all men and matters of learning. The firft and fundamental maxim of this dictatorial club is, That a punctilious correctnefs of ftyle is the *fummum bonum* of all compofitions: though the greateft genius fhould fhine throughout a work, yet if in it is found an unguarded expreffion, a flip in fyntax, or a peccadillo in grammar, *ad piper et farras* with it. Hence *Shakefpear* of late is fo much decried, that a noted hiftorian, the *Coryphæus* of this fociety, when difapproving of a wretched fentiment, adds, " What could *Shake-* " *fpear* have faid worfe*?" ADDISON, till thofe gentlemen appeared, was univerfally efteemed as the fineft writer ever *England* produced; but they

Caft him like an ufelefs weed away.

If you believe them, there are ten errors in every page of his *Spectators;* and the above-mentioned author has a copy of them, in which this decalogue of errors in every page is marked with his own hand. They have taken fo great pains to inculcate this doctrine, that now every boy at fchool, if you praife Mr *Addifon,* will perk it

* *David Hume,* Efq; in his hiftory of *Great Britain,* vol. 1. in a note, has thefe words.

in your face, and tell you, that he is not a *cor-rett* writer. Who can, without indignation, behold thefe men thus corrupting the tafte of the country? A punctilious correctnefs, no doubt, is an accomplifhment: but it is no more; nothing is more eafily acquired; every blockhead who has the patience to read over dictionaries, grammars, and fpelling-books, may atchieve it. But to unite fancy with judgment, the fimple with the fublime, and ftrength of expreffion with delicacy of thought, is the birthright of him alone

Quem tu, Melpomene, femel
Nafcentem placido lumine videris.

It would be improper to fpend more time upon a propofition fo plain as this is. Let the reader compare *Voltaire* and *Hume*, with *Shakefpear* and *Addifon*, and give the preference to the former, if he can.

The Reverend author of *Douglas* was a worthy member of this fociety; and his tragedy, long before it appeared in public, was, by this fociety, extolled with all the noife of declamation; and the little merit it has, exaggerated with all the amplifications of bombaft. A famous author whom I have mentioned more than once, faid, in private, that " he would give the *Englifh* 200 years " paft, and 200 years to come, and they would " not be able to produce fuch another tragedy:" and the fame gentleman has publicly told his namefake, that " he poffeffes the true theatrical " genius of *Shakefpear* and *Otway*, refined from " the unhappy barbarifm of the one, and licen-

A   tioufnefs

" tioufnefs of the other *." This author muft be forgiven for thefe rhodomontades; for he frankly owns, that " it is lefs my admiration of " your fine genius, which has engaged me to " make this addrefs to you, than my efteem of " your character, and *my affection to your per-* " *fon*." Love, we all know, is blind; and it would be unpolite to blame *Corydon* for running out extravagantly in the praifes of *Alexis*. Perhaps the fame apology will ferve for another learned gentleman, who averred, that " this was " the beft tragedy in *Englifh* : but indeed, " (added he) this is no great compliment ; for " we have no tragedies in *Englifh*."

What mighty things have not been done by puffing? †

We had feen feveral poems by the author of *Douglas*; which, in the opinion of moft people, were very poor ones; one of them particularly ‡ is perhaps the worft poem 'ever was written in this country by a man of a liberal education: and it feemed not a little paradoxical to us, that this author's mufe, who had mifcarried fo often, fhould have, for her firft perfect birth, an *Herculean* boy. When we faw this play acted, our expectations were fully anfwered. Though the friends of the author had puffed it away as a perfect tragedy, yet the very firft night convinced them, and every body elfe, that it was *crofs'd and divided with ftrange-coloured* abfurdities ; many of which were ftruck out of it then, and more

---

* See the celebrated dedication, p. 4.
† See *Foot*'s *Tea*.
‡ The fubject of it is a building near *Inverary*.

afterwards, when it was re-reformed at *London*; so that, in one sense, this author has shone *more and more unto the perfect day.* The partisans of *Douglas* maintain, that it is the most perfect tragedy ever was written, and infinitely superior to any tragedy of *Shakespear's*. We, on the other hand, admit it to be a tolerable modern tragedy: but we contend, that he who likens this author to *Shakespear*, might as well (to use the words of a correct writer) compare a molehill to *Teneriffe*, or a pond to the ocean *. The play is at length printed; and the public will judge which of the two opinions is most agreeable to truth.

One of the puffers of *Douglas* says in the newspaper, That, in the *Greek* drama, " no subordi-
" nate events are introduced, but what immediate-
" ly tend to the completion of the principal design:
" That a play conducted upon this plan, must want
" the principal requisite to take hold of the minds
" of an *English* assembly of spectators; and these
" observations (he says) explain why *Douglas* has
" not been received with the same warmth with
" which the ingenious dedicator deservedly speaks
" of it." It is not my intention to examine the plot with a scrupulous severity; but I would beg to know, what brings *John of Lorn* into the tragedy of *Douglas*? " Who the devil is this *Lar-*
" *della*? " Does what is said about him *tend to the completion of the principal design?* Every body must see the intention of this; and most people will readily believe, that the success this play has had, is owing, in a great measure, to this absurd

* See the *Essay on taste*, p. 210. of the four late dissertations.

and

and extrinfic epifode. Well might the author fay,

——————*Flattery direct*
Rarely difgufts ; they little know mankind .
Who doubt its operation; 'tis my key,
And opes the wicket of the human heart. *

The beginning of the 2d Act, is, to a plain man, abfolutely unintelligible. In the *dramatis perfonæ*, as reprefented at *Edinburgh*, we find

STRANGER. Mr HEYMAN.

Now, it is certain, that here Mr *Heyman* played the fhepherd, who is not called the ftranger, but the prifoner. In the beginning of this 2d Act, *enter fervants and a ftranger at one door.* Who is this ftranger ? The fervants fay,

This man with outcry wild has call'd us forth,
So fore afraid he cannot fpeak his fears.

A very odd ftranger this ! Like *Shirley* in the *Rehcarfal*, he knows not what to fay, or what to do. When we turn the leaf, we find a third ftranger, who turns out to be *Norval* ; but who the other ftranger may be, is a myftery, to explain which, we ftand in need of a revelation from *David Hume*, Efq; or fome other perfon of as uncommon fenfe. The fcene betwixt Lady *Randolph* and the fhepherd is much admired ; but furely the *reconnoiffance* by jewels is fo hackneyed, that it merits no applaufe. The fcene betwixt

* See *Douglas, p.* 41.

Lord

Lord *Randolph* and *Glenalvon* is poorly executed. The Baron enters saying,

> *'Tis so, by heav'n.*

This, and what follows, shews, that *Glenalvon* had been openly and avowedly persuading and arguing him into jealousy. *Shakespear* has managed in a very different manner. *Iago* utters nothing but what is extorted from him; and the reader is intreated to compare this scene with that in *Othello* upon the same subject; as also the quarrel of *Brutus* and *Cassius*, with that of *Glenalvon* and *Douglas*. It does not clearly appear, how Lord *Randolph* or *Glenalvon* got the assignation into their hands. *Glenalvon* talks of employing a servant; but this he does very obscurely: it is not easy to see how he could use him after he was turned off. This, like all the material business of the play, is transacted behind the scenes.

As to the characters: That of Lady *Randolph* (*alias Barnet*) is tolerably kept up. But her tenderness for her son is irreconcileable with the treatment he met with from her as soon as he was born. She sends him and his nurse, in a dark stormy night, through the *Carron*, when there was all the probability in the world that they would both perish; and the nurse actually did. This conduct was certainly next to child-murder. Nothing can be more absurd than to make her say,

> ——*Had thy fond mother fear'd*
> *The loss of thee*——

And yet immediately to add, that she had no hopes of his being alive; because when she sent him away,

> ——*It was dark December, wind and rain*
> *Had beat all night,* &c.

Her grief is altogether *outré*. It is incredible, that any woman would bewail a husband so long; and it is still more inconceivable, that she should receive no comfort from the embraces of a second. The authors of the *Fatal Marriage* and *Distress'd Mother* have avoided this absurdity. *Isabella* mourns but seven years, and she had many misfortunes to struggle with; and *Andromache* does not continue so long a widow. The author of *Douglas* seems to be sensible, that it was unnatural to make a woman's grief last for eighteen or twenty years; and he endeavours to lay the blame on the *fatal day* which *stirs* her *time-settled sorrow*. But Lord *Randolph* tells her,

> *Seven long years*
> *Are pass'd since we were join'd by sacred ties;*
> *Clouds all the while have hung upon your brow,*
> *Nor broke nor parted by one gleam of joy.*

And she herself says, that, during the interval betwixt *Douglas*'s death and her marriage with Lord *Randolph*,

> ————*Melancholy had congeal'd my blood.*

There is nothing striking in Lord *Randolph*'s character, but his wish that his wife had

> *Pride, anger, vanity*————

Glenalvon is a very bad imitation of *Iago.* It is monftrous to make him over head and ears in love with Lady *Randolph,* whom we *muft* fuppofe to be about forty years of age, and worn out with grief and forrow. When this objection was firft ftarted, the champions for *Douglas* faid, that fhe bore him when fhe was only fourteen years old. " You *may* fuppofe, Sir, what you " pleafe ;" but I hope you will take the Lady's own word for it, that fhe was old. She informs you, that

In the cold bofom of the earth is lodg'd,
Mangled with wounds, the husband of my YOUTH.

And afterwards fhe fays, fhe was in the *autumn* of her years. I humbly think fhe has made it pretty plain now. I have heard thefe gentlemen fay, that there is nothing abfurd in falling in love with an old woman. This makes me begin to confider as ferious, a pamphlet which I hitherto took to be jocular, and to be of its opinion, that there is a propenfity in young men towards old women, which is reftrained by the text, which fays, *Thou fhalt not lie with thy grandmother.* This abfurdity is not to be found either in the *Fatal Marriage* or *Diftrefs'd Mother;* and no body will be furprifed that *Iago* fhould fall in love with *Defdemona.* It is not eafy to tell, why the fhepherd fhould be made to blame himfelf for the unhappy fate of *Douglas.* For, in the *firft* place, he could not reveal to *Douglas* his birth, which he himfelf did not know; and, 2*dly,* Had he been able to do it, yet it was not expedient : For he had all the rea-

B

fon-son in the world to believe, from the situation in which he found the child, that his parents wanted to be quit of him. And the truth is, that had *Douglas*'s birth not been discovered, he might have returned

In peace and safety to his pleasant home.

The character of DOUGLAS is woefully bungled. There is a dreadful noise made about him in the prologue: But, alas!

Quid dignum tanto fert hic promissor hiatu?

The most you can say for him is, that he was in a fair way to have been a hero, but died in apparency.

As to the sentiments, those of Lady *Randolph* are commonly tender; but they flag prodigiously when she discovers herself to her son:

Image of DOUGLAS! *fruit of fatal love,*
All that I owe thy sire I pay to thee.

This is both flat and ridiculous. The love of a husband and of a son are widely different. Any man that considers how long this lady had mourned for her husband, will not think her much in his debt. DOUGLAS takes these words in a gallantish sense, and makes her a very fine compliment on her beauty:

But did my sire surpass the rest of men,
As thou excellest all of womankind?

And she very coquettishly apologises to him for not being handsomer.

The

The following paſſage is quite out of character;

——*My lov'd Lord was call'd*
To fight his father's battles, and with him,
In ſpite of all my tears, would MALCOLM *go.*

Ought not her tears to have been employed to keep her huſband from the battle? Though a multitude of impious ſentiments were expunged, yet many ſtill remain. I ſhall only mention one or two. Lord *Randolph* ſays,

There is a deſtiny in this ſtrange world,
Which oft decrees an undeſerved doom,
Let ſchoolmen tell us why——

When Lady *Randolph* died, ſhe lifted up

——————*her head*
And her white hands to heav'n, ſeeming to ſay,
Why am I forc'd to this?

How different is *Ophelia*'s death! She indeed drowns herſelf, but the exceſs of her grief had bereaved her of her judgment. *Shakeſpear,* poor old *Shakeſpear,* ſays, that when ſhe fell into the water,

Her cloaths ſpread wide,
And, mermaid-like, a while they bore her up;
Which time ſhe chaunted remnants of old lauds,
As one incapable of her diſtreſs.

But Lady *Randolph* dies like a virago who had carefully peruſed the late eſſay on SUICIDE.

The laſt thing to be conſidered is the diction. It has been extolled as ſimple; but, alas! it is

B 2 ſimple

simple to a fault. There is a flaw in the diction of the firſt ſpeech in the play.

——*If departed ghoſts*
Are e'er permitted to review this world.

We who are at preſent in this world, know very well that life

————*can little more ſupply,*
Than juſt to look about us and to die.

But ghoſts have done both already; and if ever they reviſit this world, they certainly do not come out of curioſity, but upon buſineſs of importance. It is eaſy to ſmoke the parſon in the ſtyle of this play; *the King-of kings*, *the bleſſed croſs*, and the frequent prayers make the cloven foot appear rather too often. The following expreſſions are very improper.

I'll give it him refitted *for his maſter,*
Which way the current of your temper ſets.

And there are many ſuch. But the pleaſanteſt paſſage in the whole play is put in the hero's mouth.

May Heav'n inſpire ſome fierce gigantic Dane
To give a bold defiance to our hoſt.
Before he ſpeaks it out, *I will accept.*

This is a very cloſe imitation of the celebrated line in our verſion of the Pſalms:

Be ſilent, *but* ſpeak out.

The

The defcription of the *Bafs* is execrable;

> *The fea-rock immenfe,*
> *Amazing* Bafs, *looks o'er a fertile land.*

though it muſt be confeſſed there is one line in the play,

> *Which ſtands unrival'd in the rolls of fame.*

And it is this,

> *But when the matter match'd his mighty mind.*

" What could *Shakefpear* have faid worfe?" He would not have expreſſed himſelf ſo : for he has ridiculed this *alliteratio* with great drollery, in his *Midfummer night's dream :*

> ——*With blade, with bloody blameful blade,*
> *He bravely broach'd his boiling bloody breaſt.*

And ſo has Mr *Bramſton* in the *Man of taſte.*

> *Nor barb'rous birch e'er bruſh'd my tender bum.*

Upon the whole, we were ſo far from attempting

> *To cruſh down to the ground a lovely plant,*

that we have only endeavoured to trample on a poppy, which would fain paſs for a rofe.

F I N I S.

25 The Philosopher's Opera

John Maclaurin (1734-1796) was one of the most prolific anti-*Douglas* commentators, penning several pieces which undermined both the artistic merit of the play and the cultural ascendancy of its Moderate backers. *The Philosopher's Opera* employed the same literary medium as its target, but recast events to attack Home's abilities as a playwright as well as the philosophical prowess of David Hume, and the Select Society in general. Such burlesques were common in 1757, although most were of questionable quality. Maclaurin's piece takes the form of a three-act play, featuring Satan; Mr Genius – a thinly veiled representation of Hume; Mrs Sarah Presbytery – a 200 year old widow, representing the Scottish Church; Mr Moral Sense – a twisted depiction of the Moderates' moral philosophy ultimately reduced to self-interest, and Jacky, the son of Sarah – playing the role of John Home, a foolish boy who fancies himself as a playwright. The premise of the play sees Satan return to Edinburgh, where under the watchful gaze of the Church of Scotland he had long been absent, until the poison of Mr Genius's philosophizing paved the way for his re-entry. Although delighted with Mr Genius, Satan is himself confused by the absurdity of his writings, questioning whether in fact he is not actually on the side of religion, by promulgating such outlandish theories that no sensible person could believe them. Meanwhile Mr Genius attempts to woo Sarah Presbytery, despite her advanced years. Maclaurin humorously addressed one of the main complaints about *Douglas* in this instance, for Lady Randolph – whom Sarah refers to in the play – is considered to be overly advanced in years to be a suitable object for the affections of Glenalvon. Mr Genius is ultimately successful in winning her hand, owing in no small part to the generous dedication which he bestows upon her son's play.

Maclaurin's dedication to the reader provides some insight into his objections to *Douglas*. He takes exception to Hume's dedication, and in particular to the depiction of Shakespeare and Otway as barbarous and licentious. His anger is not so much centred on the fact that a clergyman has written a play, but rather that it has effectively been declared perfect by his fellow ministers and David Hume. This cultural and nationalistic tyranny, according to Maclaurin, allows plays such as *Douglas* to enjoy overly long runs, whereas plays of genuine art such as *Othello* are wholly ignored.

T H E

P H I L O S O P H E R's

O P E R A.

E tenebris tantis tam clarum extollere lumen
Qui primus potuisti, illustrans commoda vitæ,
Te sequor, O Graiæ gentis decus, inque tuis nunc
Fixa pedum pono pressis vestigia signis.   Lucret.

[Price Four Pence.]

427

DRAMATIS PERSONÆ.

As it ought to be reprefented at *Edinburgh.*

SATAN.	*Mr* Digges.
SULPHUREO, } *Devils.*	*Mr* Ryder.
APOLLYO, }	*Mr* Duncomb.
Mr GENIUS.	*Mr* Love.
Mr MORAL SENSE.	*Mr* Lancafhire.
The Rev. Mr MASK.	*Mr* Heyman.
JACKY.	*Mr* Younger.

W O M E N.

Mrs SARAH PRESBYTERY, } *relict of Mr* John Calvin. }	*Mr* Stamper.
ANNE, *her waiting-woman.*	*Mrs* Davenport.
Mifs SPRIGHTLY.	*Mifs* Ryder.
Mifs WEEPWELL.	*Mrs* Love.
Mifs SOB.	*Mrs* Stamper.
Mifs PITY.	*Mrs* Hopkins.
Mifs BLUBBER.	*Mrs* Salmon.
MOLL KITCHEN.	*Mrs* Ward.

T O

The R E A D E R.

IN the Dramatis Perſonæ *of this opera, there are two cha-*
racters, and but two, which are not imaginary. Be-
fore you pronounce it wrong to point out two men now
living, you would do well to confider the fcurrilous terms
in which they have pointed out two men long fince dead and
gone. Remember the barbariſm of Shakeſpear, *the licen-*
tiouſneſs of Otway, *and that the author of* DOUGLAS *has*
been preferred to both. If (as a late writer will have it)
the uſe of ridicule is "not to inveſtigate known truth, but
" to expoſe known falſehood," it is ſurely as properly em-
ployed againſt the man who avers, that DOUGLAS *is a*
faultleſs play, as it was againſt the hair-brained knight-er-
rant, who maintained Dulcinea del Toboſo *to be the moſt*
beautiful princeſs in the univerſe. As this tragedy was
written by a Scotch *clergyman ; and as it was the firſt*
play he ever had made public, one would have expected,
that he and his friend would have uſhered it into the world,
either with a real or affected modeſty : but, on the contra-
ry, they declared the play to be perfect, and the author to
be endowed with a genius ſuperior to that of Shakeſpear *and*
Otway. *The compariſon which this extravagant encomium*
obliged people to make, has opened the eyes of many who
were at firſt prevailed upon to be partial to the play ; and
induced them to join the impartial men of ſenſe in both king-
doms, who all agree in thinking it a very inſipid perform-
ance : ſo that the author of this tragedy does not a little re-
ſemble the frog in the fable, who, ambitious to become big
as an ox, blew and puffed himſelf up till he burſt.

The author of the few following pages can't agree with
ſome, who think the little time ſpent on ſuch compoſitions as
this

this very ill beſtowed. He can't help numbering the tragedy of DOUGLAS, *and the circumſtances attending it, amongſt the moſt remarkable occurrences that have ever happened in this country. If* Scotch *clergymen may, with impunity, not only write plays, but go to ſee them acted here, and abſent themſelves for months together from their pariſhes, in order to ſolicit their repreſentation at* London, *the religion and manners of this country are entirely changed. If* Shakeſpear *and* Otway *are to be cried down, and the author of* DOUGLAS *ſet up in their ſtead, the taſte of this country is at an end. Religion will (it is hoped) be the care of thoſe who are paid to ſupport it. But the taſte of the country ſeems to be in a deplorable ſituation, being abandoned to a club of gentlemen, who are as unable as they are willing to direct it. As ſome men of learning and character are amongſt them, many people are miſled by their authority; and more, though they deteſt their innovations, yet are afraid to contradict them: hence it was that* DOUGLAS *was acted here laſt winter thirteen times to a numerous audience; but* Othello *(which had not been played here for ſeven years) brought no houſe at all. This ſhews, that the run* DOUGLAS *had here, was owing to the influence of a party: or elſe, that the people who generally compoſe the audience in our theatre, are no more judges of the merit of a play, than the chairmen who carry them to ſee it. It is certainly the duty of every man who regards the honour of his country, to make a ſtand againſt that unhappy barbariſm which the cabal I have already mentioned is endeavouring to eſtabliſh; and as certainly every man who has felt exquiſite pleaſure in reading the works of* Shakeſpear *and* Otway, *makes them but a very ungrateful return, if he tamely looks on while they are hunted down by a ſet of men who owe their title of geniuſes to the courteſy of* Scotland *alone.*

THE

THE

PHILOSOPHER's

OPERA.

ACT I.

A drawing-room.

Curtain draws, and discovers Mrs Sarah Presbytery *sitting in an easy chair ;* Anne *waiting.*

Mrs Pr. AND did Mr *Genius* talk to you in that manner, *Annie?*

An. Indeed the gentleman told me, Madam, that he was desperately in love with you ; that he would be miserable, nay, that he would die, if you refused to put him in possession of your fair person ; and that he was to throw himself at your feet this afternoon.

Mrs Pr. Fie upon the joker ; he has been diverting himself, and playing upon you, *Annie.*

An. O, not at all, Madam ; what should make you think so ?

Mrs Pr. Alas! *Annie,* I am not young now.

An. Young! Madam, what then ? he is not young himself. Young! why, there was Lady *Randolph*; I'm

A   sure.

fure fhe was not young; and yet you fee how the men teafed her, poor lady!

Mrs Pr. Alas, *Annie*, I am now about 200 years of age; but Lady *Randolph* broke her neck before fhe had lived half a century. Go, thou flatterer, thou knoweft he has captivated my heart; this, this only, makes you fpeak fo, and give the name of love to what you know to be waggery.

An. In my confcience, Madam, I believe him to be over head and ears in love with you. Confider, Madam, that kiffing goes by favour. Befides, Mr *Genius*, in his thoughts, words, and actions, has no refemblance to other men; fo that you might be his flame, Madam, though you were as old as *Methufalem.*

Mrs Pr. There is fomething in what you fay, *Annie.* O the lovely *Adonis*, his fhoulders, his legs, his belly! —— But why fhould I attempt to enumerate his charms? every limb of him is briftled with the darts of love; and would to God I had never feen the too amiable porcupine.

AIR I. Can love be controul'd by advice?
The goddefs who fable Night rules,
  From Phœbus *purloins all her light;*
So I make opticians my tools,
  And borrow from glaffes my fight.
Great Genius, *for whofe love this figh,*   [*fighs.*]
  Was furely created for me,
His limbs are fo bulky that I
  Their beauties fans fpectacles fee.

An. Madam, there is the gentleman.
              Enter Mr Genius.
Mr Gen. If Mrs *Anne*, Madam, has delivered that
                                        meffage

meſſage which I begged her to carry from me to your
Ladyſhip, you will not be ſurpriſed, I hope, at this
piece of intruſion.

Mrs Pr. Sir, *Annie* has been telling me of a very
odd converſation ſhe had with you this forenoon; but I
would have you to know, Sir, that I will not be made
a jeſt of by you or any man.

Mr Gen. How you miſtake my intentions! there is
not a man in the world more ſenſible of the great de-
ference and reſpect due to you, Madam, than I am.
jeſt!——be aſſured, Madam, [*kneeling*], that you ſee
at your feet a man who is determined to live or die as
you receive him.

Mrs Pr. Riſe, Mr *Genius*; if you are ſerious, I am
ſorry for you; but I flatter myſelf, you will ſoon perceive the oddity of your paſſion, and the abſurdity of
your choice. The cheek of the town-lady may vie
with the lily, that of the milkmaid with the roſe; but
mine, Sir, can be compared to neither. To uſe my
ſon *Jacky's* words :———" In me thou doſt behold——
" The poor remains of beauty once admir'd." Age has
deadened the glance of my eye, overcaſt my features with
a melancholy languor, and ploughed my forehead into
a multiplicity of wrinkles.

Mr Gen. Pardon me, Madam; age has given to your
eye a philoſophical ſedateneſs, to your features a lan-
guiſhing air, which girls in vain affect; and in what
you call wrinkles, Madam, I ſee the little loves and graces ſporting.

Mrs Pr. O Mr *Genius!*

Mr Gen. Many gentlemen have wiſhed, Madam, for old
wood to burn, old wine to drink, old friends to converſe

A 2   with,

with, and old books to read; but never did I so limit my desires: I have always hoped, that sooner or later I should have an old woman to caress.

Mrs Pr. Incomparable *Genius !* I will not use you with the coquetry of a young huffy; but frankly own that I long have loved you.

Mr Gen. Is it possible? Words are inadequate to my ideas; and this is the only way my lips can express the sentiments of my heart.

[*He endeavours to kiss her ; she struggles, but he prevails.*]

Mrs Pr. Lord ! Sir, you are such another gentleman.

Mr Gen. These breasts, [*putting his hand in her bosom.*]

Mrs Pr. Keep off your hands, naughty gentleman that you are.——Nay now, Mr *Genius*, you grow intolerably rude; I shall be seriously angry with you ;—— you must wait for the grace, Sir.

Mr Gen. Madam, I beg ten thousand pardons, if the violence of my passion has transported me beyond the bounds of decency.—— Yes, Madam, I will wait, and as long as you please; for I am confident, you have more goodness than to make me repent my complaisance.

AIR II. Woe's my heart that we should funder.
If you amuse me with vain hope,
Till Time's unpitying fingers press us,
These my own hands shall knit me up,
And put in practice my own essays.

Mrs Pr. *Imagine not I'll use you so :*
Perhaps my life is everlasting:
But, lovely Genius, well I know,
To the church-yard you fast are hasting.

Let not our interview, Mr *Genius*, end like that of
tw

two youthful lovers, without one word of common fenfe being fpoken by either of us : Do you go to fee my fon's play to-night ?

Mr Gen. I hope for the pleafure of feeing you there, Madam. What makes you afk the queftion ?

Mrs Pr. Why, truly, that I may have an opportunity of expreffing my gratitude. Many of my fons have been greatly obliged to you ; but *Jacky* infinitely.

Mr Gen. O dear Madam !

Mrs Pr. Mr *John Calvin*, my firft hufband, was a very good man ; but he had his oddities ; and notwith-ftanding the affeiction which a woman muft retain for the hufband of her youth, I cannot help thinking you the better reformer of the two. Many of my fons, fome time ago, before they had the honour of your acquaintance, were the moft unlicked cubs ever were whelped : how ftiff was their ftyle ! how ftarch their manner ! how ridiculoufly grave the whole man ! But fince they got into your good company, they have put off the old man entirely : they have acquired a jaunty air, a military fwagger, and a G—d-d—n-me look ; they fwear, they drink, they whore fo handfomely ; ——in fhort, they are metamorphofed fo very much to the better, that I fcarce know them to be my own children

Mr Gen. Your goodnefs, Madam, greatly magnifies my poor fervices.

Mrs Pr. How judicious was that fancy of yours to make *Jacky* write a play ! and how inimitable the dedication with which you introduced it into the world ! To *Jacky* owes both his fame and his fortune, and ought to thank you on his knees for both.

Mr Gen. The young gentleman, Madam, is abundantly

dantly grateful; but I beg you would dwell no longer on this fubject. I wifh it were in my power to do more for him. I muft now leave you, Madam, and join feveral of your fons who are to be at the playhoufe tonight.

Mrs Pr. And I muft away to Lady *Prelacy*, who goes along with me to the fame place. Farewell till fix o'clock. [*Exit.*

Mr Gen. AIR III. A free and an accepted Mafon.
> *Unhappy are you*
> *If a girl you woo;*
> *With rivals you always are fighting:*
> *But I am fecure,*
> *And morally fure,*
> *Old women alone I delight in.*
>
> *Or if you fhou'd wed*
> *A blooming young maid,*
> *You, as at a cuckold, all ftare on.*
> *The lewdeft dragoons*
> *Wou'd fee blood and wounds,*
> *Ere my marriage-bed they wou'd fhare in.*
>
> *And if ye fhall fhew*
> *Ye think my love new,*
> *I'll do fomething ftill more worth feeing:*
> *For novelty's praife,*
> *To make people gaze,*
> *Is the principal end of my being.*
>
> *The bride I now leave,*
> *Has one foot in the grave;*
> *My next fhall be yet more uncommon:*

The

The church-yard I'll seek,
The coffins I'll break,
Till I hug some dead buried old woman. [*Exit.*

Arthur's Seat.

Enter Sulphureo.

What can *Apollyo* mean? he promised to meet me here precisely at three o'clock, and now it is hard upon four. Perhaps he is wandering over this mountain in quest of me. Ho, *Apollyo!* ho! hoa! No *Apollyo* here it seems. What does he keep me waiting for? He is not *Garrick* the player, nor am I a young *Scotch* clergyman come a-beseeching him to act my tragedy; he is not a great man, nor am I an old reverend come a-begging some plurality or other, as a reward for my jobs past, present, and to come. No! we are two devils: and having said so much, I need not add, that we are honest-er fellows than most clergymen.

AIR IV. 'Twas when the seas were roaring.

They constantly are roaring,
From pulpits hung with green,
'Gainst swearing, drinking, whoring,
And ev'ry other sin.
Think not, ye simple hearers,
When thus to you they preach,
That parsons are practisers
Of what their sermons teach.

Their

Their habit now is gaudy;
Like officers they swear;
Their conversation's bawdy:
To stage-plays they repair.
But if we by this nation
Were paid for living well,
We wou'd have the discretion
Our vices to conceal.

Enter Apollyo *at the other end of the stage.*

Ap. Ho, *Sulphureo!* ho! hoa!

Sulph. Here, here.

Ap. O, your servant, Mr *Sulphureo.*

Sulph. I am indeed your servant, Mr *Apollyo*; for I have waited here about an hour for your Honour.

Ap. Why, Sir, such a croud of people from this country came upon us this morning, that *Satan* could not get away from hell till a few minutes ago. So that, good Mr *Sulphureo,* I hope you'll excuse us.

Sulph. O yes, I do. But will you, *Apollyo,* who are one of our secretaries of state, be so good as to inform me why *Satan* is of late turned so negligent of his affairs in this country. I have been his *aid-de-camp* now for some time, yet I never was in this town before: there is a great change in his behaviour to this country; for I am told, about fifty years ago he used to be very often in *Scotland.*

Ap. There he comes, ask himself.

Enter Satan.

Sat. Well, my lads, how goes it? Have you, *Sulphureo,* ordered matters so that every thing be in readiness for my reception?

Sulph. I have, Sir. I saw the Reverend gentleman,
and

and told him that you was to be in *Edinburgh* this after-noon, and would be glad of his company ; he faid he would meet you at five o'clock in Mrs *Kitchen*'s.

Sat. At five, very well. And how do you like the good town of *Edinburgh, Sulphureo?*

Sulph. Good ! call you it ?

AIR V. On ev'ry hill, in ev'ry grove.

In ev'ry ſtreet, in ev'ry lane,
  In ev'ry narrow ſlippery cloſe,
Nothing but filth is to be ſeen;
  In all of them I ſtopt my noſe.
    And ev'ry thing about it ſhows,
    It is a ſpacious little houſe.

'Tis not the clouds of ſmoke alone
  Which mount, when cookmaids dinner dreſs;
But 'tis the manners of the town,
  Which muſt oblige you to confeſs,
    (Forgiving your Sulphureo's *mirth),*
    Auld Reeky is a hell on earth.

Before you came up to us, I was inquiring at *Apollyo* how you came to be fo indifferent about this country ; you'll pardon my prefumption, in begging to know the reafon of this coldneſs, which to me at prefent feems to be mal-adminiſtration.

Sat. In the days of yore, *Sulphureo,* I was almoſt conſtantly in *Scotland,* and obliged to exert all my met-tle. Yet, for all that, I own the oppoſition here fairly got the better of me, and for a confiderable time I had only a ſmall ſelect fociety that ſtuck by me. The miniſters made confcience (as the phrafe was in thofe days) of doing their duty ; the greateſt folks lived foberly ; and indeed all ranks of people were in the moſt deplorable fi-

B   tuation

tuation you can well imagine. I had very near have given
them up altogether: however, I very luckily had the refolution to perfevere; a good many years ago the tables
were turned, and now almoſt the whole nation is my moſt
obedient humble ſervant. I am the more delighted with
this conqueſt, becauſe, of all the countries I have ſub-
dued, this made the moſt obſtinate reſiſtance: but now
the moſt of its inhabitants are more ingenious in my way
than I myſelf can pretend to be.

AIR VI. Nanſey's to the green wood gane.

So when ſome wild deceiving boy
   Aſſaults th' unſpotted virgin,
At firſt the laſs is very coy,
   And long reſiſts his urging.
But after ſhe is fairly won,
   And the foul deed is over,
The wanton gypſy, not half done,
   Out-paramours her lover.

Now, *Sulphureo*, I hope I have ſatisfied you.

Sulph. Perfectly, Sir. I ſee your preſence here is not
at all neceſſary.

Sat. No, it is not: and it was ceremony, not buſineſs,
that brought me here juſt now; for I have all the reaſon
in the world to believe that my people will be too many
for their antagoniſts without my aſſiſtance: but as this
is the third night of the firſt play ever was written by a
Scotch clergyman, I thought the leaſt I could do was to
give my countenance to ſuch a bold attempt to ſerve me

AIR VII. Suſannah.

Good manners would not let me frown
On the young tragic prieſt:

Aij

My company and half a crown
Was all he did requeſt.

Sulph. Ap. *The youthful parſon to refuſe,*
Sure you had not done well;
And to procure him a full houſe
You ſhou'd have empty'd hell.

Sat. There are to be nine clergymen in the playhouſe to-night. Curioſity to ſee people of their character in ſuch a place, would of itſelf ſecure the poet of a good third night; but my emiſſaries have taken care that he ſhall have a full houſe every night his play is acted.

Sulph. I am glad to hear it. Shall I ſhow you the way to Mrs *Kitchen*'s?

Sat. Why, we muſt change our appearance in the firſt place. I think I will aſſume the dreſs of a country-gentleman juſt come from a journey; do you transfigure yourſelves into my footmen. But ſtay, it is but a few minutes after four, we ſhall be too ſoon if we ſet out immediately for Mrs *Kitchen*'s; let us climb to the top of *Arthur's Seat*, the view from it is charming.

AIR VIII.   Over the hills and far away.

Yon mountain's ſummit when I tread,
The proſpect will tranſport my ſight;
Unlike to Moſes, *who ſurvey'd*
The holy land from Piſgah's *height.*

Penſive he ſaw the fruitful plains,
Plains which he never was to ſhare:
All you ſhall ſee to me pertains,
The poſſeſſors my vaſſals are.

End of the FIRST ACT.

B 2   A C T

A C T II.

Enter Maſk.

WHO's there? Bring ſome bottles of claret, and a bowl of punch immediately.

Enter Satan, Sulphureo, *and* Apollyo.

Sat. My dear Mr *Maſk*, I rejoice to ſee you. How does Mrs *Maſk* do, and all your good family?

Mr Maſk. Pretty well, Sir, at your ſervice.

And pray, Sir, when you came from hell,
Our friends there did you leave them well?

Sat. All well. Pray ſit down, Mr *Maſk*. How my heart warms to my good old friend! Fill your glaſs, Mr *Maſk*. Let us drink all our abſent friends. [*They drink*]. Have you had any new books lately, Mr *Maſk?*

Mr Maſk. O, great variety, Sir.

Sat. I aſk for them firſt; becauſe I remember the committee of ways and means, which I had once eſtabliſhed in this country, told me, that new books were commonly my very good friends.

Mr Maſk. Commonly they are ſo. We have only one author of note; but his brain is a very good breeder.

Sat. What is the gentleman's name?

Mr Maſk. Mr Genius is his name. He is the beſt writer againſt Chriſtianity in *Britain*; nay, he gives very broad hints againſt the being of a God.

Sat. Come, drink his health.　　　　[*They drink.*]

AIR

AIR IX. Dear Colin, prevent my warm blushes.

The miser feels exquisite pleasure
   In touching a precious bank-note;
But I wou'd not give for his treasure,
   A leaf which an Atheist wrote.

When that's chang'd, he no doubt may bring home
   Some thousands to hide in his holes;
But this will convey to my kingdom,
   Ten thousand times ten thousand souls.

But hark ye, Mr *Mask,* does he deny my existence?

Mr Mask. O! laughs at it, Sir.

Sat. How very much surprised will he be when he goes to hell! However, I'll have his works reprinted there *typis regiis*; they well deserve it.

Mr Mask. He maintains there is no difference 'twixt right and wrong but what custom has introduced.

Sat. How much am I obliged to the gentleman! Dear Sirs, drink his health again. [*They drink.*]. *Encore,* if you please. Huzza!　　　　[*They drink and huzza!*

Mr Mask. He has broached a great number of such propositions.

Sat. I should be very glad to see him.

Mr Mask. You shall see him very soon.　　　[*Rings.*

      Enter Moll Kitchen.

You know where Mr *Genius* is; tell him I must speak with him here.　　　　　　　　[*Exit* Moll.

Before this philosopher arrives, I will show you another who has a great many disciples. I know he is over a bottle just now in this house.　　　　[*Rings.*

      Enter Moll.

Desire Mr *Moral Sense* to step in here for a few minutes,

nutes, and do you follow him. [*Exit.*] This fellow
pretends to be the moft generous difinterefted man a-
live; though, in reality, there is not a more felfifh dog
on the face of the earth.

Enter Moral Senfe *and* Moll.

Mor. Senfe. O my dear gentlemen, how I love all
and every one of you! I would willingly, moft willingly,
lay down my life, fhed my heart's blood, to ferve you,
my dear, dear, dear Gentlemen.

Sat. Sir, we are very much obliged to you for your
kindnefs. Will you drink a glafs of wine, Sir?

Mor. Senfe. O, with all my heart. I approve of
good wine. Gentlemen, your healths. [*Drinks.*] This
wine is very good. I have an unbounded benevolence
for it. Another glafs, if you pleafe, Sir. [*Drinks.*] O,
Gentlemen, if you knew how much I love you, and your
wine, you would not refufe me a third. [*Drinks.*] Yet
another, Sir, to drink health and happinefs to all mankind. [*Drinks.*] One more.

Mafk. Sir, if you will have patience for a few minutes,
you fhall have your bellyfull; but I beg you would
drink no more, till you have given your opinion upon a
point of fome confequence. What do you think of a
marriage 'twixt me and *Moll* there?

Mor. Senfe. Hui! Hui! Hui! [*fhrieks hideoufly,*]
it fhocks me; I difapprove of it. But I will lie with
her myfelf. [*Coming up to her.*] I will lie with you,
Moll, [*laying hold of her.*]

Sat. Hold! hold, Sir.

Mor. Senfe. I will lie with her; I approve of her.
The סכינה fhines in her face. I will lie with you,
Moll. [*Endeavours to throw her,* Satan *interpofes.*]
What

What do you mean, Sir? My inftinct prompts me to lie with her.

Sat. You impertinent fcoundrel, I'll teach your in-ftinct better manners. [*Kicks him off.*] This is a very odd philofopher, Mr *Mafk.*

Mafk. Very odd, indeed, Sir. It is a rule of his, never to think a moment about what he either fays or does.——There comes Mr *Genius.*

Enter Mr Genius.

Mr *Genius,* your fervant: This, Sir, is Mr *Bevil,* a friend of mine, [*They falute*], who having red your books with great delight, was very curious to fee you face to face.

Mr Gen. You have red my books then, Sir?

Sat. Yes, Sir, with great delight.

Mr Gen. Why, then, Sir, you are convinced, I fuppofe, that there is no God, no devil, no future ftate;——that there is no connection betwixt caufe and ef-fect;——that fuicide is a duty we owe to ourfelves;——adultery a duty we owe to our neighbour;——that the tragedy of DOUGLAS is the beft play ever was written; and that *Shakefpear* and *Otway* were a couple of dunces.——This, I think, is the fum and fubftance of my writings.

Sat. It is, Sir.

AIR X. Leaderhaughs and Yarrow.
Great Hercules, Jove's *darling fon,*
 Was forc'd alone to wander;
And monfters with his club knock down,
 To glut his ftepdame's anger.

Shakefpear

Shakeſpear *and* Otway, *with your pen,*
  Unforc'd you have run thoro' ;
And therefore ſhould be held by men,
  To be the greater hero.

Mr Gen. O, Sir, you do me too much honour. I'm
ſorry, Gentlemen, to leave you ſo ſoon ; but I am engaged to go to the play with a party of clergymen. [*Exit.*

Sat. Mr *Maſk,* I proteſt the play had gone out of
my head. You'll accompany us to the playhouſe, I
ſuppoſe ?

Maſk. Not I, indeed.

Sat. Why ?

Maſk. Why, becauſe your enemies will lay hold of
the proceedings that are to be this night in the play-
houſe, and endeavour to ſtir up a rebellion againſt you.
They will ſoon prepare overtures and libels againſt the
author of this play, and every other miniſter who ſaw it
repreſented. This determines me not to go. I will ſeem
to be rather againſt the author of this play, and his followers ; by theſe means, I ſhall gain the good graces
of the oppoſite party, which will enable me to quaſh
any violent meaſure againſt him.

  AIR XI. O Beſſy Bell and Mary Gray.
The zealous fools will, if they can,
  With depoſition end him ;
But all our party to a man,
  Will vote, Rebuke, ſuſpend him.

Such cenſures will not, I believe,
  His tragic genius ſmother ;
Suſpenſion for one play will give
  Him time to write another.

                                        Sat.

Sat. Thou reafoneft well.

Mafk. 'Tis our only way, Sir; but, *Satan,* what do you think of Mr *Genius ?*

Sat. 'Faith, I don't know well what to think of him. Are you fure he is true blue on our fide ? I confefs, I have fome fufpicion, that he is a fhrewd fellow, endeavouring to convert men to Chriftianity, by writing nonfenfe againft it.

Mafk. You are quite miftaken, Sir : he is reckoned the ableft writer we have; fo able, Sir, that all the good folks fay, when he wrote his books, he had you at his elbow.

Sat. Really, Mr *Mafk,* I think I may fay without vanity, that had I affifted him, he would not have written fo abfurdly. I was very well pleafed to hear him deny the exiftence of a God, and fo forth; but his pofitions about fuicide and adultery will certainly do our caufe no good.

A<small>IR</small> XII. Hooly and fairly.

With hearing his nonfenfe in troth I am weary ;
That nonfenfe will hurt me much, I can affure ye ;
And make many people believe moft fincerely.
O ! gin the lad wad write hooly and fairly,

Hooly and fairly, &c.

[*Exeunt.*

End of the S<small>ECOND</small> A<small>CT</small>.

C

A C T

A C T   III.

A drawing-room.

Enter Mrs Prefbytery, *Mifs* Weepwell, *Mifs* Pity, *Mifs* Sob, *Mifs* Blubber.

Mrs Pr. LADIES, now that you have feen my fon *Jacky*'s play, let me have your opinions on it impartially.

Mifs Weep. I believe, Madam, this company will be very unanimous in voting it to be the beft play ever was written.

Mrs Pr. O, don't flatter me, Ladies.

Mifs Blub. The tears, Madam, you faw fhed in the playhoufe, may convince you, that, without flattery, we are all of Mifs *Weepwell*'s opinion.

Enter Mifs Sprightly.

Mifs Spr. Your fervant, Ladies.

Mrs Pr. My dear Mifs *Sprightly!*

Mifs Weep. Blefs me, child, your eyes are not at all red.

Mifs Spr. What fhould make them fo?

Mifs Weep. Weeping.

Mifs Spr. For what?

Mifs Weep. Was not you at the play?

Mifs Spr. Yes, I was.

Mifs Weep. Have you not then been crying for thefe three hours?

Mifs Spr. Not I.

Mifs Weep. Cruel creature!

Mifs

Mifs Spr. Why cruel, pray?

Mifs Weep. Not to weep for DOUGLAS.

Mifs Spr. What fhould make me weep for him?

Mifs Weep. Not to weep for fuch a hero!

Mifs Spr. What makes you dub him a hero, in all the world?

Mifs Weep. Did not he kill the chief robber?

Mifs Spr. And does that make him a hero?

AIR XIII.

Had DOUGLAS *liv'd on* Englifh *ground,*
Where highwaymen, you know, abound;
And there, by the good-will of Fate,
Some noted robber's brains out beat;
            A warrior's fame,
            Or hero's name,
He in that country ne'er had found.
            The fturdy lad
            Wou'd juft have had
A premium of neat forty pound.

Mifs Weep. You may carp as much as you will, Mifs, at fome particular places of the play; but you will own, no doubt, that, upon the whole, it is the beft play ever was written.

Mifs Spr. Will I fo?

Mifs Weep. Pray, who has written a better?

Mifs Spr. Shakefpear, Otway ———

Mifs Weep. Hold! the very naming of thefe two fellows is enough to make one fick. Sure, child, you have not red Mr *Genius's* dedication.

C 2   *Mifs*

Miſs Spr. Air XIV. Clout the caldron.

In lapdogs, laces, hoops, ſtays, fans,
*   And all your other tackle,*
Howe'er capricious you may be,
*   I care not, or how fickle:*
But yet, for all great Genius *ſays,*
*   I really can't help wiſhing,*
That Shakeſpear, Otway, *and their plays,*
*   May ne'er go out of faſhion.*

                     Fa adrie didle didle, &c.

Miſs Weep. Miſs *Sprightly,* I am not a little ſurpriſed to hear you talk at this rate. Sure neither you nor I can pretend to be ſuch good judges as Mr *Jacky* and Mr *Genius*; and you know very well, what contempt they have for *Shakeſpear* and *Otway.*

Miſs Spr. Jacky *and* Genius, very pretty fellows truly!

Air XV. Gill Morris.

By the remains of Scottiſh *youth,*
*   Who taſte untainted boaſt,*
Let all the paltry works of both
*   To raging flames be toſt.*
This holocauſt alone can ſooth
*   Great* Shakeſpear's *injur'd ghoſt.*

Enter Mr Genius.

Miſs Weep. You are come in good time, Sir. We have had a ſtout battle with Miſs *Sprightly* about the tragedy of Douglas. She has been running it down very warmly.

Mr Gen. I am ſorry to hear it: for ſtill her lips muſt be rubies, and her voice melody, though both be employed againſt the beſt play ever was written.

                                        Mrs

Mrs Pr. [*aside.*] So, fo : this young *Jackanapes* will not only rob the fon of his glory, but the mother of her gallant.

Enter Mr Jacky.

Mifs Weep. O, Mr *Jacky*, your fervant. I give you joy, Sir. [*They all advance, and falute him.*] I give you joy, Sir, that your tragedy has met with that fuccefs which the beft play ever was written deferves. You, Sir, poffefs the true theatric genius of *Shakefpear* ——

Mifs Sob. And *Otway* ——

Mifs Pity. Refined from the unhappy barbarifm of the one ——

Mifs Blub. And licentioufnefs of the other.

Jacky. O Ladies! nay, dear Ladies!

Mrs Pr.   AIR XVI.   Black Jock.

Dear Sir, and dear Ladies, my Jacky *is young,*
And bafhfulnefs hinders the thanks of his tongue,
  For filling his pockets with half-crowns fo white.
He's fenfible 'twas not the mufical laffes,
Who dance, fing, and play on the top of Parnaffus,
  But you who got him the half-crowns fo white.

To thee, noble Genius, *the knee he fhou'd bow ;*
More than to Apollo *to thee does he owe :*
      Shakefpear *fcoffing,*
      Douglas *puffing,*
You fcrew'd mens opinions to fuch a great height,
That they filled his pockets with half-crowns fo white.

Jacky. Dear mother, you have very handfomely expreffed my gratitude, which a foolifh bafhfulnefs would not allow me to do. In return, I muft infift on your giving to Mr *Genius* your hand ; which a bafhfulnefs, ftill more foolifh than mine, will not, I hope, make you refufe.

refuſe. I know you love one another; your marriage to-night will conſummate my happineſs.

Mrs Pr. There, Sir, is my hand; you long have had my heart.

Mr Gen. Madam, I am ſo very ſenſible of the honour you do me, that I here vow and ſwear never more to write eſſays, diſcourſes, hiſtories, diſſertations; but to make your entertainment the ſole ſtudy of my life.

Air XVII. Logan water.

Two hundred years tho' you be old,
And tho' your youthful bloom be fled,
Yet fear not, deareſt, I'll prove cold,
Or loiter when we are in bed.

Mrs Pr. *Two hundred years tho' I be old,*
And tho' my youthful bloom be fled,
Yet fear not, deareſt, I'll prove cold;
I'll be but twenty when in bed.

Miſs Weep. This is the only farce I could have endured to ſee after the tragedy of Douglas. Let us have fiddles, and a dance.

[*They dance.* Satan, Sulphureo, *and* Apollyo *enter*
in their true ſhape, and offer to dance along
with them; but they all run off.

Sat. Ay, why in ſuch a hurry? The devil will not give himſelf the trouble to take the hindmoſt, I aſſure ye; for he is pretty certain to meet with all of you time and place more convenient. Well, my lads, how did you like Douglas?

Sulph. It is a very moving tragedy, Sir; the tears are in my eyes yet.   [*Wiping his eyes.*

Ap. And in mine too.

                                        Sat.

Sat. I agree with Mr *Genius*, in thinking it the beſt play ever was written. I could deſcant upon it all night; but we had better keep our obſervations for *Maſk*, who will by this time be longing much for us, and more for his ſupper. Let us to Mrs *Kitchen*'s, and be merry.

AIR XVIII. Jolly mortals, fill your glaſſes.
Jolly devils, drink I charge ye,
Paſs in ſport the time away;
Bumpers ſwill to all the clergy,
Who or write or ſee a play.

Now I wou'd not give three guilders,
For the ſuperſtitious fry;
You ſhall all be ruling elders,
And the moderator I.

F I N I S.

26 The Infernal Council

Like the *Philosopher's Opera*, this short ballad plays upon the concept of Hume being in league with the devil. Now that the heretical philosophers Hobbes, Spinoza and Bolingbroke are dead, Belzebub calls for a new volunteer on earth, but Lucifer informs him that Hume is already fulfilling the role. Specific allusions are made to Hume's perceived efforts to undermine divine authority in his essays 'Of Suicide' and 'Of the Immortality of the Soul', which although unpublished had managed to find their way into circulation. The piece is supposed to have been written by James Boswell's aunt, Mrs. Webster, the wife of Dr Alexander Webster – the leader of the Popular party – and, as has been indicated, frequently the target of the pro-*Douglas* pamphleteers.

THE INFERNAL COUNCIL,

An excellent new ballad.

To the Tune of, *The devils were brawling*, &c.

GRim BELZEBUB's council affembled of late,
   Where matters important were weigh'd in debate:—
Thus fpoke the ARCH-FIEND,—" What bold *imp* will afcend,
" Our empire on earth to fecure, and extend?
          With a fal, lal, lal, laddle lal, &c.

For *Hervey* and *Young*, and fome more, in ftrange ftyle,
Woo the ears of the *great*, and their *hearts* may beguile:
This attempt on our RIGHTS,—fuch bold *treafon*, we own,
Hath chill'd us with dread, as it fhook our firm *throne.*
          With a fal, lal, &c.

                    " Our

Our friends, *Hobbes*, *Spinofa*, and *Bolingbroke* great,
Who triumph'd in our *caufe*, have now founded *Retreat:*
Wou'd to hell! our *dread arm* had yet fpar'd them a while,
Since our *foes* thus *exult*,—and our *powers* dare *revile.*"
            With a fal, lal, &c.

Amazement and *terror* fufpended each *tongue,*
Til proud LUCIFER rofe, and addrefs'd the *wild throng:*
GREAT LEADER, why dread?—Our worft *fate* is affign'd
What! DEVILS know *terror?—Leave that to mankind!*
            With a fal, lal, &c.

Tho' *thefe champions of hell* have from earth all retir'd,
H—ME aloft bears our *ftandard,* whofe *breaft* I've infpir'd:
Of *talents* fo rare, fo acute, fo profound,
Of fuch *depth,* in your *realms,* there are none to be found.
            With a fal, lal, &c.

His *mind* I have fwell'd with *vain-glory* and *pride;*
Faint emblem his paunch!—tho' fo vaft, and fo wide:
Tho' *wealth* he defpifes, yet, fond of a *name,*
He foars in *new tracts,* to *high glory* and *fame.*
            With a fal, lal, &c.

"

The *laws* of that *Ruler,* whofe *realms* are *on high,*
He boldly fubverts, and has dar'd to defy :
In *his flights how fublime!*—I am charm'd to behold
Our *hero,* furpaffing all *heroes of old.*

          With a fal, lal, &c.

This *maxim* he wifely *refounds* on the *ear*—
Men have nothing to hope, fo have nothing to fear.—
Hence *dagger, ball, poifon,* or *cord*—which you pleafe,
Each *fool* may practife on *himfelf*—and find *eafe."*

          With a fal, lal, &c.

:ceas'd—when in tranfport cry'd BELZIE, " I find
This DAVID *indeed is a man to my mind :*
Shallow politic *fiends* might for ages have try'd
To devife fuch a plan,—and their art been defy'd.

          With a fal, lal, &c.

Directed by H—ME to the *regions of night,*
What *troops* of pale *fpirits* fhall rufh on our *fight!*
To *him* then affign *we* our *delegate fway,*
Who hath *taught* men the *path,* and will foon *lead the way."*

          With a fal, lal, &c.

                      ALL

ALL HELL then refounded with fhouts of *applaufe*
To H—M E, who hath nobly fupported its *caufe*:
Io Pæan to H—M E now their *tranfports* loud tell,
While *Ecko* refponfive—" *Amen*, cries ALL HELL."
With a fal, lal, &c.

F   I   N   I   S.

27 A Prologue to the long expected Tragedy of Douglas *and* 28 An Epilogue to the Tragedy of Douglas, Spoke by the Author

Both of these pieces are examples of the burlesque writings that abounded in the aftermath of the first performance. Both are supposedly published on December 14th, the day of the first performance. Alexander Carlyle, who attended the opening night and was a fervent defender of the play, is spoofed in both the prologue and the epilogue. The prologue cites John Witherspoon's *Ecclesiastical Characteristics*, which was one of the most elegant yet vehement attacks on the Moderate literati. There is also a mention of Sarah Ward, Lady Randolph (Barnet) in the first performance, and her over-familiarity with the clergy who have been attending the rehearsals. The Epilogue addresses the 'great J-g-s of the land', which might well be a reference to legal figures such as the Lords Monboddo and Kames, who both attended the rehearsals of the play.

1756, December 14.

A

PROLOGUE

TO THE

LONG EXPECTED

ᴦRAGEDY of DOUGLAS;

ᴀs it is to be acted this evening at the theatre in the head of the Canongate, Edinburgh.

FORETOLD by * C——ʟᴇ, now the time is come,
    When Scotia bears the palm from Greece and Rome;
When the *learned youth*, wits of the present age,
   ᴊo more need form their taste on the translated page;
When *beaux* and *belles* old Shakespear shall deride,
   ᴀnd *bucks* and *bloods* cast Rochester aside;
When *Levi's sprightly sons* shall quit the chair,
   ᴀnd on the more instructive stage appear;
Successful preachers to the youthful croud,
   ᴛhat all that pleasure is is also good,

* The production referred to will be found in the prologue to Herminius and ᴊpasia, supposed to be wrote by the Reverend Mr C————ʟᴇ.

                                     To

To thee, great H.—M E, thefe happy days we owe,
And fuch the gifts thy D o u g l a s will beftow;
D o u g l a s! who comes a thoufand hearts to chear;
Who wept for * A g i s' death and fate fevere.

Now fhall the Englifh curfe their *Garrick*'s name,
Who banifh'd D o u g l a s far from *Drury-Lane*;
Nor would thy humble earneft pray'r regard,
But void of merit the great work declar'd.

Not fo *fair Ward*, fhe well to churchmen known,
This night in public will thy merit own;
And if fome modeft friends the favour claim,
Place is prepar'd for thefe behind the fcene.

---

* Great were the expectations of the public from this performance of the author which we are told in the *Ecclefiaftical Charaĉterifticr*, carried dramatic poetry to the fummit of perfection; fo that, had it been publifhed, it was believed that never one would have prefumed to have wrote a tragedy after it. But, as that ingenious writer imagined, the knowledge of this effect, and the compaffion thence arifing to future authors, determined the humble and benevolent theatric divine to fupprefs its publication:—and we are told by the advertifement in the Edinburgh Evening Courant, that the fame humble and felf-denied temper had almoft fmothered the prefent production, even after the two journeys the author made to London, and folicitations to Mr Garrick to receive it.

A N

E P I L O G U E

T O T H E

T R A G E D Y of D O U G L A S.

Spoke by the A U T H O R.

SHROUDED in glory, and with praife full blown,
Permit your *Bard* his gratitude to own.

To mine *immortal genius* firft I bow;

And next, *great fquire*, my thanks are paid to you;

By your example and kind precept warn'd,

♭ * heavy moral has my plot deform'd:

Thy fignal too did teach the thoughtlefs croud,

Then fit to weep, and when to clap aloud."

C——LE and C——PLES, all the favourite tribe

Tho on our Zion's top triumphant ride,

* This ought for ever to filence thofe fhallow critics, who have ftated it as an
objection againft this play, that one is at a lofs to know what moral fentiment it is
defigned to infpire.——According to the true fenfe of the word *moral*, as accurately defined by fome late writers, many highly moral fentences might be quoted
in it; fuch as the beautiful adjuration ufed by one of the fpeakers, who is introduced, fwearing, *By him that died on the accurfed tree to fave mankind*;—and the
devout exclamation put in the mouth of another when juft expiring, *I'll rife eternal fire.*

My

463

My thanks receive; nor fear the * bigots frown :
Perfift, and Edin's ftipends are your own.
O happy Edin! who ere long fhall fee
Each pulpit fill'd by fuch bright wits as we.

Permit me next, great J—G—s of the land,
Who grace my audience, and refpect command,
To bow obeifance : What tho' the laws controul
The ftage? you fcorn the antiquated rule.

To yonder box, where fits a humble throng,
Some gratitude and thanks muft fure belong;
They are my flock, from † A—NF—D they come,
And ftand around their paftor as a crown.

How warm my heart to every *beau* and *belle*,
Ere long my mufe to the dull world fhall tell.

To thank thee, *Ward*, furpaffes all my art,
W——N and J——N, bear a friendly part;
For tho' fhe lately died Lord Barnard's wife,
Your prefence foon will quicken her to life.

And now in fame's loud horn each name fhall rife,
Who owns your Bard, and joins his works to prize.——

* This refers to that horrid infult offered by the prefbytery of Edinburgh
Wednefday to wit and genius, by ordering letters to be writ to the different
byteries to which thofe minifters belong, who honoured the playhoufe with
company on this occafion.
† The author fent a number of tickets to his parifhioners, who came in a
to the houfe, and entered fo much into the fpirit of tragedy, that when met i
evening they could fcarce part without blows.

A N

EPILOGUE

T O T H E

TRAGEDY of DOUGLAS,

Spoke by the AUTHOR.

SHROUDED in glory, and with praise full blown,
Permit your *Bard* his gratitude to own.
 To mine *immortal genius* first I bow,
And next, *great squire*, my thanks are paid to you ;
By your example, and kind precept warn'd,
No * heavy moral has my plot deform'd :
Thy signal too did teach the thoughtless crowd,
When fit to weep, and when to clap aloud.

 C——LE and C——PLES, all the favourite tribe
Who on our Zion's top triumphant ride,
My thanks receive ; nor fear the † bigots frown :
Persist, and Edin's stipends are your own.
O happy Edin ! who ere long shall see
Each pulpit fill'd by such bright wits as we.

 Permit me next, great J——G——s of the land,
Who grace my audience, and respect command,
To bow obeisance ; what tho' the laws controul
The stage ? you scorn the antiquated rule.

 To yonder box, where sits a humble throng,
Some gratitude and thanks must sure belong ;
They are my flock, from ‡ A——NF——D they come,
And stand around their pastor as a crown.

 How warm my heart to every *beau* and *belle*,
Ere long my muse to the dull world shall tell.

 To thank thee, *Ward*, surpasses all my art,
W——N and J——N, bear a friendly part ;
For tho' she lately died Lord Barnard's wife,
Your presence soon will quicken her to life.

 And now in fame's loud horn each name shall rise,
Who owns your Bard, and joins his works to prize.——

---

* This ought for ever to silence these shallow critics, who have stated it as an objection
against this play, that one is at a loss to know what moral sentiment it is designed to
inspire.——According to the true sense of the word *moral*, as accurately defined by
some late writers, many highly moral sentences might be quoted from it ; such as the
beautiful adjuration used by one of the speakers, who is introduced swearing *by him
that died on the accursed tree to save mankind* ;—and the devout exclamation put in the
mouth of another when just expiring, *I'll risk eternal fire*.
 † This refers to that horrid insult offered by the presbytery of Edinburgh last Wednesday to wit and genius, by ordering letters to be writ to the different presbyteries to
which these ministers belong who honoured the play-house with their company on this
occasion.
 ‡ The author sent a number of tickets to his parishioners, who came in a body to the
house, and entered so much into the spirit of tragedy, that when met in the evening they
could scarce part without blows.

29 The Apostle to the Theatre his Garland *and* 30 The Second Part of the Apostle to the Theatre His Garland

This light hearted anti-*Douglas* song mocks David Hume for his dedication, but also uses every opportunity to make puns on the names of those ministers who attended the play, for example, pointing out that it was a delight to Couples, Steel and Carlyle, but a 'black sight to White', referring to Thomas Whyte who repented before the Presbytery for going to the play and received a shortened suspension for his penitence. The second part deals more directly with the play itself and the reasons why it does not work as a piece of entertainment. Home's absence from his parish of Athelstanesford is addressed in the last few verses, while specific mention is made of the troubles that Carlyle faced before the Presbytery of Dalkeith.

THE APOSTLE TO THE THEATRE

HIS

GARLAND.

AN EXCELLENT NEW SONG,

To the Tune of, *De'il ſtick the miniſter.*

YE wolves in ſheep's clothing I pray you draw near,
　　Nor lecture, nor ſermon, nor pſalm ſhall ye hear ;
I ſing our *Scotch Shakeſpear,* that promiſing youth,
Whoſe tragedy puts this new ſong in my mouth.

With a fal, lal, lal, &c.

II. That

II.

That DOUGLAS eclipses all other plays, DAVID
Did solemnly swear, as he hop'd to be saved:
A friend of the poet's this oath sharply blam'd,
Your fate, should it share, it would doubly be damn'd.

Fal, lal, &c.

III.

Exalted on high a few clergymen sate,
Where Satan triumphing presided in state;
For the devil's too wise to neglect to go thither
Where two or three in his name are met together.

Fal, lal, &c.

IV.

Dame Barnet's distresses the *beaux* and *belles* feel,
They soft'ned (O wondrous!) a heart tho' of STEEL.
S——L, C—— LE, and C—PLES were lost in delight,
Tho' they prov'd in the end but a black sight to WHITE.

Fal, lal, &c.

V.

But the reverend poet has nothing to fear;
His presbytery never will be so severe:

And

And his flock a good shepherd will reckon him still;
While he gives them a pint, they'll ne'er quarrel his GILL †.

Fal, \lal, &c.

VI.

Dame Barnet's great merit how shall I expres!
Dame Barnet! whom so many lawyers cares;
So fondly cares, that I say without scolding,
Pray think of the laws which abolish *Ward-holding.*

Fal, lal, &c,

VII.

This elegant lady would possibly fail
If she at the bar should attempt to prevail;
But lawyers, and writers, and all men must own still,
She is out of all sight the best *chamber council.*

Fal, lal, &c,

VIII.

She ne'er had consum'd in such tedious sorrow,
Had her second spouse, like the first, been a hero;

And

† GIL MORRICE was an Earl's son.

And hence (to a jeft, if you will, you may turn it)
The lady for Barnet miftakes often ————

Fal, lal, &c.

IX.

Now fhould fome fage critic think this ballad low,
And that it deals too much in a *feu des mots*;
I think fo myfelf, and in other words fay,
Like DOUGLAS it is but a very poor play.

Fal, lal, &c.

F I N I S,

THE
SECOND PART
OF
The APOSTLE to the THEATRE
His GARLAND.

CONTAINING

The Lamentation of a beautiful young Damſel in *Athelſtaneford*.

All which you have for the ſmall and eaſy charge of a Penny.

To the tune of, *Had awa frae me, Donald.*

HAD awa, had awa,
　　Had awa frae me, *Johny*;
The filthy lucre I abhor;
　No tragedies from thee, *Johny*.
　　　　　　　　　　Had awa, &c.
Whae'er ſays that your play will ſend
　Dan *Shakeſpear* to the de'il, *Johny*,
Like the firſt pair before the fall,
　Does not ken guid frae ill, *Johny*.
　　　　　　　　　　Had awa, &c.

Of

Of the great greeting at your play,
  I canna think eneugh, *Johny* ;
For I, and wi' me twa three mae,
  The haill time gauf'd and leugh, *Johny*.
                  Had awa, &c.

Yet am I not hard-hearted, I
  Shed mony a fawt tear, *Johny*,
For Lady *Defdemona*'s death,
  And honeft auld King *Lear*, *Johny*.
                  Had awa, &c.

Your Baron *Randolph* little kent
  'Bout womens doughty deeds, *Johny* ;
Elfe had he fmelt fome chield and's wife
  Had been at loggerheads, *Johny*.
                  Had awa, &c.

The very name o' your fine play
  Gar'd me baith hoot and hifs, *Johny* ;
For *Douglas*, after a' your din,
  A *fticked* hero is, *Johny*.
                  Had awa, &c.

Your namefake does prefer you to
  Shakefpear and *Otway* baith, *Johny* ;
And glad am I he has made this
  Confeffion of his faith, *Johny*.
                  Had awa, &c.

For

For now he feems in a fair way
   The fcripture to receive, *Johny* ;
No more will he fcoff and deride,
   But *miracles* believe, *Johny*.

                            Had awa, &c.

When he's converted, mony ane
   Of this new faint will fay, *Johny*,
He's the firft finner who owes his
   Salvation to a play, *Johny*.

                            Had awa, &c.

If *Shakefpear* (as he vaunteth) you
   In poefy excel, *Johny*,
The only thing you next can do,
   Is to furpafs your fell, *Johny*.

                            Had awa, &c.

Elfe, *muckle Saundie*-like, you maun
   Sit down and weep full fore, *Johny*,
Becaufe no greater bard remains
   For you to go before, *Johny*.

                            Had awa, &c.

A bra bag-wig you'll now hae got,
   And lace upon your cloaths, *Johny* ;
This weel will fuit your fine brown coat,
   That your white filken hofe, *Johny*.

                            Had awa, &c.

                                    Your

Your prefbyt'ry for your return
    Affign'd this month's firft day, *Johny*;
But you have made them *April* fools,
    And ftill at *London* ftay, *Johny*.

                        Had awa, &c.

O! hafte ye, hafte ye to *Dalkeith*,
    Save *Carlile*, your dear friend, *Johny*;
If he's depos'd, of your great gain
    He'll hae a dividend, *Johny*.

                        Had awa, &c.

His depofition, if you think
    Unworthy your regard, *Johny*,
Let not young maidens call you falfe,
    Come down, come down to WARD, *Johny*.

                        Had awa, &c.

Non-refidence in love's a fault,
    Leave *London*'s wild gambols, *Johny*;
Nor treat her body as you do
    Athelftaneford's poor fouls, *Johny*.

                        Had awa, &c.

F I N I S.

31 Douglasiana

This is a small group of five anti-*Douglas* squibs. The first two are songs dealing with the squabbling of the religious factions involved in the controversy, and again allude to the Select Society's interference in the reception of the play. The third part is an epistle from the perspective of the theatre manager West Digges, although all the arguments voiced by him only serve to undermine his position. The fourth is set to the tune of 'Gill Morris' taken to be an inspiration for *Douglas*. It is dedicated to, and refers to the man who 'has been sometimes at Mr Digges's house… but that he had never ate or drunk with Mrs Ward'. That man was Alexander Carlyle, who revealed this when he was called before the Presbytery of Dalkeith to account for his actions. The fifth piece, *An Epistle, to Mr Genius A – st in Edinburgh*, is clearly an attack on David Hume and the company he keeps, including Carlyle, whom the author wishes had been suspended by the Presbytery for his actions.

DOUGLASIANA.

I.

The BATTLE of the MINISTERS.

To be fung over a bowl of punch,

To the tune of, *Down the burn Davie.*

Natis in ufum lætitiæ fcyphis
Pugnare, Thracum eft: tollite barbarum
Morem, verecundumque Bacchum
Sanguineis prohibete rixis.

Hor.

TO me repair, ye martial fons
  Of the church militant;
  Nor powder's fmell, nor noify guns,
  Shall make your courage faint.

Fear not to follow me, my lads,
 Where-e'er my fancy roams;
Thefe lemons are my hand-grenades,
 And kettles are my bombs.

A

This

This eafy-chair in which I loll,
  It is my *feat* of war;
Thefe glaffes which furround the bowl,
  My choiceft troopers are.

My thirft of rum, not fame to quench,
  I laughing bumpers fill;
And hence it is that reeking punch
  Is all the blood I fpill.

Then drink; but all of ye I warn
  'Gainft DOUGLAS not to rail;
This precious moral you fhall learn
  From my true tragic tale.

A brother-clergyman, when o'er
  A punch-bowl fuch as this,
When *J. H.*'s play was talk'd of, fwore
  Nought in it was amifs.

Another, on what he thought faults,
  Began to crack his jokes;
Him, for his mirth, the firft affaults,
  And fo they fell to box.

And boxing, they with hoftile breafts
  Againft each other ftood,
Till of each combatant both fifts
  Were dy'd in *cottage-blood* *.

  * Douglas, p. 34.

The

The fight when they had long maintain'd,
    A third did interpose,
And by good offices reftrain'd
    Their unrelenting blows.

But who the redding-ftrake can mifs?
    A heavy one he got;
Three teeth, three little teeth of his,
    Were driven down his throat.

By the three little teeth he fhed,
    He fhall acquire renown;
Like *John of Lorn* he has bled
    In battles not his own *.

My mufe's word if you won't truft,
    Pray but infpect his mouth;
Spite of the teeth yet left, it muft
    For once declare the truth.

II.

The REVOLUTION.

To the tune of, *A Cobler there was.*

Learned men whilom were under no fetters,
But made what was call'd the republic of letters;

* Douglas, p. 47.

A 2   Republic

Republic of letters! there's now no such thing,
The author of DOUGLAS of poets is king.
> *Derry down, down, &c.*

The poetical crown on his temples was plac'd
By him who is reckon'd the standard of taste:
But amongst us I hope there's not one whose heart
    faints
To tell him with DOUGLAS we are *malecontents*.
> *Derry down, down, &c.*

Who thinks on King James's tyrannical sway,
And candidly reads this I don't know what play,
Will chorus it surely with this Whiggish song,
A poet may write, and a king may do wrong.
> *Derry down, down, &c.*

Of some, I am sorry to say that their plot
Is to make foolish people believe what is not:
From speaking the truth me nothing shall hinder,
Great SHAKESPEAR is King, *J. H.* the *pretender*.
> *Derry down, down, &c.*

I hope your good spirits will not be cast down,
Tho' those hight the GENIUSES on us shou'd frown:
They indeed have thought proper to style themselves
    select;
But, alas! 'tis too plain they're none of the *elect*.
> *Derry down, down, &c.*

III.

III.

An EPISTLE,

From the manager of the theatre,

To the Rev. member of the fynod of *Lothian* and *Tweeddale*, who maintained, in open court, that the profeffion of a player is lawful and honourable; and that the ftage, without any reformation, is the great fupport of religion and virtue.

Ait prætor, Qui in fcænam prodierit, infamis eft.
Pandect. lib. 3. tit. 2. l. 2. § 5.

SOme call you, from their want of tafte,
 The pattern of the true bombaft.
  Such envious critics fcorn;
The grateful bofom of fair WARD
Shall your oration foon reward,
  And *love for love* return.

Each tragedy which ROWE has penn'd,
To be a fermon you maintain'd:
  And who dares to gainfay?
But I would humbly you befeech,
T' inform the public when you preach,
  Each fermon is a play.

        Though

Though young divines may want the trafh,
Yclep'd by trading people *cafh*;
    Yet will I them admit;
The footmens gallery's a place
Fit for thofe who are moneylefs,
    There they on high may fit.

The trick by which *J. H.* off came,
Appear'd as a *beau ftratagem*
    To all impartial eyes :
And fure it evidently proves,
His foes were innocent as doves,
    His friends as ferpents wife.

IV.

The CONFESSION.

Humbly infcribed to the Rev. gentleman who
has owned, " That he has been fometimes
" at Mr *Digges*'s houfe, along with the
" author, and had fome converfation a-
" bout the tragedy; but that he had never
" ate or drunk with Mrs *Ward*, or con-
" verfed with her, further than in agree-
" ing or difagreeing to what was faid a-
        " bout

" bout the play." *Scots Mag. for March,*
p. 160.

To the tune of, *Gill Morris.*

ABout your dialogues with *Ward,*
   What you say may be true :
But will ye tell us, pray, what pass'd
   Betwixt ye in dumb shew.
                 But will ye tell us, &c.

With differences 'bout the play
   Your paper you perplex ;
But did you not fall foul on her
   From difference of sex ?
                 But did you not, &c.

You neither ate nor drunk with her——
   On *Huncamunca* think ;
Who says a maid may want what she
   Can neither eat nor drink *.
                 Who says a maid, &c.

This actress is your better half,
   West Digges your bosom friend :
And shall the sons of holy church
   Refuse to vote, *Suspend?*
                 And shall the sons, &c.

* See *Tom Thumb.*

                          V.

V.

An EPISTLE,

To Mr GENIUS,

A——ſt in *Edinburgh*.

My DEAR SIR,

IT wou'd moſt certainly have been odd,
Had *J——n* been cenſur'd by the ſynod;
For perſonally you before 'em
Appear'd, and plainly *in terrorem*.
I don't mean as a goblin fell,
Who carry'd with you blaſts from hell *.
Nor as a ſpirit good, ('tis giv'n,
You never will bring airs from heav'n).
'Twas neither ſhoulders, legs, nor belly,
The parſons frighted, I can tell ye.
Their ſecret reaſons I o'erheard
From one for wiſdom much rever'd:
" If I ſhould vote, *C——e* ſuſpend,
" Or what is worſe, Depoſe his friend,
" Obſerve the conſequence, with me
" *Genius* will not keep company;
" *Digges* with ſuch a fanatic ſinner
" Will never eat a bit of dinner;
" The actreſs will not lend to me
" Her *body* of divinity.
" And thus by them, with cenſures fretted,
" We'll all be excommunicated."

* Be thou a ſpirit good, or goblin damn'd,
Bring with thee airs from heav'n, or blaſts from hell.
Hamlet.

F I N I S.

32 The First Night's Audience

Another of the more light-hearted anti-*Douglas* works, this ballad colloquially calls Home Jacky, and mockingly alludes to the problems he had with Garrick, not only in staging this play, but also his first drama *Agis*. The Moderate literati and Hume are again the targets for their attendance at the play and their philosophy, but this time Carlyle's behaviour at the play where he was accused of pushing theatre goers is also addressed in the song. These are accusations which Carlyle denied when forced to account for his actions by the Presbytery.

THE FIRST NIGHT's AUDIENCE:

An excellent new ballad.

To the Tune of, *A cobler there was,* &c.

Humbly infcribed to the author of D o u g l a s, a tragedy.

YOur fuccefs, dear JACKY, was great as my wifh,
 The critics may fnarl, and GARRICK cry—Pifh!
Though AGIS they murder'd with envious rage,
Yet could they not hinder your GIL * from the ftage.
   Derry down, down, down, derry down.

Supported by * * * * * *, old *Belzie* himfelf
Could not have prevented your gaining the pelf;
The ladies commanded, to playhoufe all ran,
All happy to follow while thefe led the van.
   Derry down, &c.

---

* The critics obferve, though others cannot find it out, that *Gil Morice,* an old Scottifh fong, is the foundation of the tragedy, from whence the author has taken his fable.

            Glitt'ring

Glitt'ring beaux ne'er beheld such a precious treasure
Of ladies of honour, and ladies of pleasure:
Even j-dg-s of law turn'd judges of wit,
Laugh'd at acts and decisions, and rush'd to the pit *.

    Derry down, &c.

A bumkin there was, and he came from the west,
Who preferr'd to his agent this pressing request,
" This night let's consult, and give ANDREW his fee,
" To-morrow I travel soon as I can see."

    Derry down, &c.

" This night," cries the scriv'ner, " there's no consultation,
" Could it save you from death, or, what's worse, from damnation;
" Our lawyers this night are all gone to the play,
" The *Devil* and *Douglas* have snatch'd them away."

    Derry down, &c.

Hid close in the green-room some clergymen lay,
Good actors themselves too, *their whole life a play;*
C—LYLE with a cudgel, and genius rare,
With aspect as stern as a *Hessian* hussar ;

    Derry down, &c.

 * Here our sonnetteer is mistaken. It should have been the *boxes;* but this
would have spoiled the metre.

          Grave

Grave St—l and fage C---ples; two parfons of note,
And others as dear to the mufe, though forgot.
Learn here, deareft friends of my Jacky, I fay,
Politely to preach, and, if needful, to pray *.

     Derry down, &c.

When the populace dull you to fermon muft call,
Let *Douglas* be quoted inftead of *St Paul.*
I leave to 'Squire David to paint, as he ought,
The poet's fweet art, and th' effect which it wrought;

     Derry down, &c.

How greatly it tickled his fancy to find
The prieft and effayift were much of a mind :
However our Bible-believers may rave,
Self-murder's the dernier refort of the brave—

     Derry down, &c.

The belles were well pleas'd of a marriage to hear;
Though a fham one, it ferv'd tarnifh'd honour to clear:
The beaux were delighted to think of a fcheme
Which hereafter might render the ladies more tame.

     Derry down, &c.

* The unfortunate author of this excellent new fong has not feen the tragedy; but being affured that it was a perfect piece, and contained fpecimens of the
different kinds of oratory, he could not but conclude, that there muft be in it a
pattern for prayer.

                                           But

But the j-dg-s, more wife, were griev'd to behold
What ladies endur'd for mere frailties of old;
While Sopho thus whifper'd amidft the wild din,
All *feeling's deceitful*, for ftill there's no fin.
      Derry down, &c.

Now, Jacky, one word—Had you fwore in plain profe,
Angry zealots might fometime have voted *Depofe*;
'Twas prudent to pour forth your vollies in verfe,
And leave to the players your oaths to rehearfe.
      Derry down, &c.

Well have you deferved the two hundred pounds;
Like the devil in *Milton* you have leap'd o'er all bounds *.
No more can I write, for my paper is done;
You'll live in my numbers, if not in your own.
      Derry down, &c.

* Paradife Loft, *book* 4. *line* 181.

F I N I S.

33a, 33b, 33c The Stage or the Pulpit: A Sermon (Parts 1, 2 & 3)

The sermon is to be sung to the tune of Gill Morice and provides a mocking voice for John Home on the opening night of his play. The first two parts may have been written by John Maclaurin and were published prior to the 29th March 1757, with the third part, differing in tone from the others, appearing on the day of the Edinburgh publication of *Douglas*. It pokes fun at both Home's position as a minister and the physical dimensions of David Hume. By the song's end the playwright forsakes the ministry to seek his fortune in London. The second part is sung after the play's end, and suggests that in keeping with the immorality of the play, Home would take advantage of 'Dame Barnet' (Sarah Ward). And in order to have his play performed in London after Garrick's rejection, he will bribe everyone he needs to. The third part is not an impersonation of Home, but rather a call to judge the play for what it is, and not to praise it because the Moderates have told people to like it.

THE
STAGE or the PULPIT:
A
SERMON.

Sung *

By the Reverend author of *DOUGLAS*,
the firſt night he went to ſee his own play
repreſented.

To the tune of GILL MORICE.

THINK not, my friends, that I'm a prieſt
   Of manners wild and looſe,
Becauſe I leave all holy things
   For this unhallowed houſe.

Without divine aſſiſtance, I
   Shall ſtate the many ills
Which perſecute th' ill-fated man
   Who country pulpit fills.

                      And

---

* Cicero, in like manner, ſung all his orations, but whether to the tune of Gill Morice, or of Chevy Chaſe, is altogether uncertain.

And next the player's happier life
    Exhibite to your view;
Laſt (if your time permits) ſubjoin
    An inference or two.

3

I in my clumſy pulpit ſtuck
    Half man half wood, look'd worſe
Than the fam'd Centaur, for he was
    Half man half gen'rous horſe.

What tho' my *ſhoulders broad* appear,
    And human face divine ?
My *taper leggs*, and *belly long* ‡
    The wooden walls confine.

But *here* I may expatiate free
    O'er all this ſcene of man :
Each limb of mine the fair may ſee,
    And each proportion ſcan.

My church ſhuts out Apollo's beams,
    And lowrs with holy gloom ;
But cluſter'd artificial ſuns
    This gaudy dome illume.

Below me, *there*, a miſcreant ſits,
    The pſalms to ſhriek, not ſing ;
But *here* the *chief muſicians* touch
    The ſiddle's tuneful ſtring.

His

‡ Theſe bodily perfections are the cardinal virtues of a
broad-ſhoulder'd, taper-legg'd modern philoſopher. with whom
our reverend tragedian lives in Chriſtian fellowſhip and
communion.

His true love *there* the clownish fop
    'Twixt sermons treats with ale ;
Here 'twixt the acts with orange sweet
    The *beau* regales the *belle.*

My invitation, *there*, to sup,
    Is giv'n with bits of lead ;
But *here* my *tokens* are white cards
    Adorn'd with glossy red.

Old grey-beards *there*, with yellow wigs,
    My seffion grave compose ;
But *here*, I Stamper, Ward and Diggs
    My youthful elders chose.

Let priefts with unrelenting zeal
    At my *converfion* rage ;
Ye will not blame me tho' I quit
    The pulpit for the ftage.

Againft the ftage fanatic fots
    Throw out their fpite in vain :
Up rife ye heroes of this houfe,
    And guard the facred fcene.

Ye rakes lafcivious, who delight
    To plunder virgin charms,
Support the ftage, which pimps fo well
    For your rapacious arms.

What fair one who beholds the lafs[1]
    With RANGER's dalliance bleft †,

                                      But,

† See the fufpicious hufband.

But, smiling, wishes 'twere her lot
To be so keenly kiss'd.

But when the lusty Bull * appears
The burning blushes glow;
Each maid envies PASIPHAE's fate,
And sighs to be a cow.

Such lewd descriptions, tho' but words,
To facts prepare the way :
Shall canting knaves or whining fools
Rescue the beauteous prey ?

No; let our ladies old and young
In pit and boxes shine ;
And learned ——— club to keep
A ——— house so fine.

Here they, secure behind the scenes,
Their genial heat may cool ;
Nor fear the parson's reprimand,
Or penitential stool ‡.

My London journies cost me dear ;
Somewhat to me afford :
Who gives unto the poor, ye know,
Lends so much to the Lord.

To you much longer would I preach,
But that your time is fled :
At present I shall add no more :
L—— bless what has been said.

* See the orphan.
‡ This piece of church furniture is out of fashion in this polite metropolis; *sed multa manent vestigia ruris.*

THE

STAGE or the PULPIT,

PART II.

Sung by the Reverend Author after the play
was over, but before the curtain fell.

PIT, box and gallery, reftrain
 Your thick heart-breaking fighs :
It grieves me fore to fee you cry ;
 O wipe your gufhing eyes.

I fear my play moves you too much.
 How fad each face appears !
Each box a houfe of mourning is,
 The pit *a vale of tears.*

Dame Barnet has not broke her neck
 By tumbling down the fteep :
She lives, and yet on feather bed
 Shall take the *lover's leap.*

Why fhould I be afham'd atwhat
 Some critics once let fall,
That, like its author, this new play
 No *morals* has at all ?

For I on the *Rehearfal's* plan
 Compof'd this matchlefs play :
Obferve this, and the force of each
 Objection dies away.

Dame Barnet is the mother of
 A youth ftout and robuft :

How

497

How then, some ask, could she when old
    Provoke *Glenalvon*'s lust?

Such snappish fools do not deserve
    Consideration :
They next may ask, how *Prettyman*
    Could wed old wrinkled *Joan* * ?

When the fond mother to her son
    His noble birth reveals †,
Then from the thick'ning plot each breast
    Suspence tormenting feels.

No wonder each spectator then
    The pitying tear lets fall,
When D O U G L A S dreads he shall be thought
    No body's son at all ‡.

Now when my barons bold are slain,
    Ye will not think it wrong
That their last speech and dying words
    Shou'd be somewhat too long.

                             'Tis

---

   * Prince *Prettyman* meeting by chance with old *Joan*
the chandler's widow, and remembering it was she that
first brought him acquainted with *Cloris*, out of a high
point of honour breaks off his match with *Cloris*, and marries old *Joan*. *Rehearsal* in fine.
   † Brave *Prettyman*, it is at length reveal'd
    That he is not thy sire who thee conceal'd.
                       Rehearsal, A. III. S. IV.
   ‡ Was ever son yet brought to this distress,
    To be for being a son made fatherless?
    What oracle this darkness can evince,
    Sometimes a fisher's son, sometimes a prince?
But why is he so mightily troubled to find he is not a
fisherman's son? Phoo! that is not because he has a-mind
to be his son, but for fear he should be thought no body's
son at all. *Rehearsal. ibid.*

'Tis not incongruous they fhou'd talk
  In agonies, tho' lying,
For fweet *Lardella* wrote a fong
  Juft as fhe was a dying *.

With D O U G L A S I to *London* went,
  And made no little racket;
But booby *Garrick* and his crew
  Point-blank refus'd to act it †.

Three hundred pounds of cafh have I
  Got from thefe gen'rous men;
Upon my word I have not feen
  So much the Lord knows when ‡.

No more this ftage fhall *Hamlet*'s ghoft
  Traverfe with haughty pace;
No more fhall the Venetian moor
  Here fhow his footy face;

Old *Shakefpear*, *Otway*, and the reft,
  Muft fly the concert-hall;
My play, like *Aaron*'s ferpent, will
  Devour and fwallow all.

My

---

* This is now a copy of verfes which I make *Lardella* compofe juft as fhe is a dying, with defign to have it pinn'd to her coffin. *Rehearfal*, A. IV. S. I.

† It was I who have written, you muft know, a whole play juft in this very fame ftile; it was never acted yet. How fo? I'gad I can hardly tell you for laughing, (ha, ha, ha) it is fo pleafant a ftory. Ha, ha, ha, what is't? I'gad the players refus'd to act it. Ha, ha, ha, that's impoffible. I'gad they did, Sir, point-blank refus'd it. Fie! that was rude. Rude! ay, I'gad they are the rudeft, uncivileft perfons and all that in the world. *Rehearfal*, A II. S. II.

‡ Here take five guineas for thefe valiant men,
 And there's five more, which makes the fum juft ten;
 We have not feen fo much the Lord knows when.
    Rehearfal, A. V. S. I.

My play, fhou'd any man deride,
    And plague me with his fcoffing,
He may ; but to his coft he'll find
    I know what to think of him †.

And if to blame this faultlefs play
    A God be fo uncivil,
I vow and fwear I'll make that God
    Subfcribe himfelf a devil ‡.

And now ye flaughter'd heroes rife,
    Go off as ye came on,
Th' arch-infidel himfelf believes
    Your refurrection.

---

† When a man tells me fuch a one is a perfon of parts, is he fo? fay I. What do I do, but bring him prefently to fee this play : if he likes it, I know what to think of him; if not, Your moft humble fervant, Sir. *Rehearfal*, A. III. S. I.

‡ See the *Rehearfal*, A. IV. S. II.

T H E

STAGE or the PULPIT.

P A R T III.

It was advertifed in the news-papers, that
the tragedy of DOUGLAS was to be
publifhed this day, being the 29th of
March 1757.

PREPARE, ye Scottifh connoiffeurs,
  To criticife THE PLAY:
This to the pious poet is,
  Of judgment the great day.

But firft attentively perufe
  The dedication,
Which *dainty Davie* has thought fit
  To write to *jumping John.*

At home you undifturb'd may read,
  And judge the poet's caufe;
No ladies, lawyers, and no lords,
  There ftun you with applaufe.

Judge

Judge what it was caus'd manly eyes
 Such heavy fhowers to rain,
If 'twas the actrefs and her art,
 Or cunning of the fcene.

If fuch the manners, fuch the plot,
 And fo fublime the ftyle,
As to make loathing Britons chafe
 Old Shakefpear from their ifle;

You may condemn it; but believe,
 Your wives and daughters too,
Will, after they have read his play,
 Sing, *John come kifs me now.*

To print here and at London does
 The bard's found judgment fhow;
For 'twas a wife precaution, fure,
 T'ave two ftrings to his bow.

Of Douglas the fupporters thus,
 Coloffus-like have fix'd him;
One leg ftands here, another there,
 But nothing is betwixt 'em.

Two hundred pounds here he receiv'd,
 That fum fill'd not his coffer;
But England prov'd to him what once
 To Solomon did Ophir.

Each

Each lord to whom he tickets gave,
    Pull'd out some shining pieces;
The needy author eager said,
    " Whate'er your Honour pleases."

For taking such gratuities,
    Let not the bard be hifs'd,
Remember holy scripture, which
    The *poor in spirit* bless'd.

Ireland will yield him more ; there he
    With *Sheridan* goes halves ;
The land which feeds so many *bulls*,
    Cannot want *golden calves*.

Douglas, this done, a hero's name
    Is well bestow'd on thee,
Who under contribution laid
    Great George's kingdoms three.

This play could lure the money from
    Ev'n French and Spanish spungs ;
'Tis pity our apostles now
    Have not the gift of tongues.

Unmov'd the English audience sat,
    And not a tear was shed ;
But here the most unpitying eyes
    With blubbering were red.

'Tis

'Tis hop'd the Rev'rend author is
    To heaven's kingdom near;
But fure his play at London was
    Not from damnation far.

All men were prefent at this play,
    Who wear or ftar or garter;
The devil's in't, if fuch great folks
    Had not procur'd it quarter.

A more facetious tragedy
    By mortal penn'd was never;
And therefore I fincerely fay,
    O Douglas, live for ever.

On this fam'd tragedy our jefts
    Are pardonable fins,
The Rev'rend bard himfelf at it
    Muft laugh, becaufe he wins.

F   I   N   I   S.

DOUGLAS MATERIAL NOT MODERATE OR POPULAR IN ORIGIN

34 The Irish Parson's Advice concerning the Play-House, or the Reverend Revenge, a Poem

The pseudonym of John M'Debit is used as the author of this short poem which attacks the stage as a symbol of luxury and avarice. As a minister, Home is criticised for spreading this cancer when he should know better. The poem claims that attention would be more profitably focused on the plight of British troops engaged in a war with France, where real blows need to be struck, than on the fake blood-letting that takes place on the stage.

The IRISH PARSON's ADVICE

CONCERNING

The PLAY-HOUSE,

OR

The Reverend REVENGE,

A

POEM.

THE reverend D——s, my Brethren hear,
 Revenge I'll whisper in your Ear,
My Plan is grand, therefore attend
My inspir'd Tale unto the End.

Verily Brethren, ye are Fools,
To tamper thus with Satan's Tools;
Do as I bid, and I'll engage,
You'll drive the Devil from the Stage.

To Cudgel him the common Way,
He'll hold his Ground whate'er you say;
For Pulpit Cant he's not afraid,
He'll burſt and laugh at all that's ſaid.

But my dear Brethren, I ſhall tell
How you may drive him back to Hell;
And knit him there, both Neck and Heel,
Which will pleaſe all the Godly well.

Our Parliament an Act has made,
To glean up all who have no Trade;
Now, by St. Paul, ye underſtand
Plays are not lawful in this Land.

My Brethren, now attend my Voice,
Nor cough, nor ſneer, nor make a Noiſe,
The Godly few will us aſſiſt,
Theſe helliſh Players to reſiſt.

With Conſtables and City Guard,
A choice Band we will have prepar'd,
Our Reverend ſelves upon their Head,
With pious Zeal the Van will lead,

The

The fpiritual Weapons well lay down;
For carnal Ones muft clear the Town,
Of Tragic Sinners bred to Vice,
To Mimickry and Cards and Dice.

Our a'poftate Brother, wicked H————
To Excommunication Doom,
For giving Fuel to the Stage,
Which fhall be burnt, each Line each Page.

The Actors fhall be forc'd to go,
And give the FRENCH a tragic blow ;
No Mimick pufhing will be there,
But real Wounds bleed every where.

While we at Home will fervent pray,
That BRITISH TROOPS may gain the Day ;
Our Tithes in Peace will fwallow o'er,
While Canons Smoak around our Shore.

The Stage Silenc'd, our Rivals gone,
We'll Triumph in the Field alone ;
Plain Texts of Scripture we'll perplex,
With Hyperboles the People vex.

We'll croak and hum, and howl and groan,
Hold forth in hypocritic Tone,
Lecturing long on Myft'ries Deep,
Till the Believers fall a Sleep.

And

And when they from their Sleep awake,
They'll truſt it was all Goſpel ſpake.
To keep up Sound then be your Care,
Nor Value whether Senſe be there.

Finally, Brethren, take good Heart,
Theſe Vagrant Players ſoon ſhall ſmart ;
And when the He-ones are all gone,
W——'s ſly Amours we'll Lecture on.

And bring her ſoon to ſuch Diſgrace,
That ſhe muſt quickly leave this Place ;
The Scheme is good, I add no more ;
May Pulpits Rule as heretofore.

May D——s again to D——— go,
And with him W—— his Midnight Jo ;
This is the Prayer of every Saint,
Noſtræ eccleſiæ militant.

JOHN M'DEBIT.

35 The Finishing Stroke; or, Nothing. A Ballad

The premise of this ballad is that the furore over *Douglas* is little more than a fuss about nothing. According to the writer of this song the talents of Home as a playwright are few, but the Presbytery of Edinburgh managed to make something out of nothing by denouncing his plays so vehemently. Ultimately neither side has gained anything through the arguments they have advanced.

The Finishing Stroke;

O R,

NOTHING.

A BALLAD.

To its own proper Time.

YE Mufes of our modern Wits,

    To whom my Lays belong,

Whofe Name alone my Subject fits,

    For *Nothing* is my Song;

II.

Attend, infpire the meanlefs Lines,

    Like thofe you daily fing,

                         Where

Where *W——r, W——r, C——g* shines,

Or *H——e's* high Praises ring:

III.

Teach me to tell the list'ning Crowd,

    What Wonders *Nothing* wrought;

Nothing made *Agis* fam'd aloud,

    And soon it fell to *nought*.

IV.

'Twas *nought* inspir'd the Reverend Bard,

    Tho' falsly call'd a Muse,

When he once more did labour hard,

    And Mountains bore a Mouse.

V.

Nothing the Reverend Presb'try fir'd,

    To make so great a Phrase;

Nothing

Nothing their pious Lines infpir'd,

But a few doggrel Lays.

VI.

Then on both Sides the Rhymfters wrote,

And *nothing* ftill they fung;

As ancient Sages wifely wrote,

Thus *nought* from *nothing* fprung.

VII.

The Time fhall alfo quickly come,

All this fhall be forgot,

When Men fhall no more talk of *H——e*,

And *Douglas* fink to *nought.*

VIII.

Nought fha'l the Reverend *P——r* ftop,

From's Mufic, and his Dame;

And

And *nought* difturb the chearful Cups,

That *W———r*'s Faith inflame ;

IX.

S———t his *nothings* fpeak in Peace,

His Windows all unbroke,

And *C———g* change his double Face,

And *nought* of it be fpoke.

X.

Thus as the Holy Scripture fays,

Of Duft all Things were made ;

To Duft fhall fall Priefts, Poet's Lays,

In Duft *H———e*'s Lawrels laid.

F I N I S

Short Biographical Details on the People involved in the *Douglas* Controversy

George Anderson (1676/7 – 1756)

Anderson was a Church of Scotland minister, and a staunch opponent of theatrical pursuits. He attacked the poet, Allan Ramsay, for his efforts to rehabilitate the stage in Scotland. Anderson's sermon, *The Use and Abuse of Diversions* (1733), argued that the stage was as depraved as witchcraft, adultery and even murder. Although he had died before the controversy over *Douglas* ignited (five days after the play first appeared in Edinburgh), his work was cited in a number of pamphlets written by the anti-*Douglas* faction.

Anthony Aston (c. 1682 – 1753?)

Aston was an English actor and playwright, who abandoned his job as a legal clerk at the age of fourteen in order to pursue a theatrical career. Although he made his living as a travelling performer, under the stage name of Mat Medley, he informed his friend, Allan Ramsay, that he intended to stay in Edinburgh. Aston attempted to found a company of players in 1726, but was forced out in 1727 by the local council. His position was further undermined when the *Caledonian Mercury* reported on the 15th April 1728 that he had helped to 'entice away' a Mrs Jean Kerr, who happened to be the wife of his son Walter. Aston eventually returned to London.

Alexander Carlyle (1722 – 1805)

Carlyle was the minister at Inveresk in Midlothian from 1748 to 1805, and one of the most prominent members of the Moderate party in the Church of Scotland. He was a lifelong friend of John Home, whom he met at the University of Edinburgh in the 1730s. Carlyle suffered more than any other minister who attended *Douglas*, as the Presbytery of Dalkeith sought to make an example of him because of his lack of contrition. Carlyle eventually escaped punishment for his actions, which he saw as a victory for the Moderates. He wrote a short description of the play entitled: *A Full and True History of the Bloody Tragedy of Douglas* which was designed to encourage people to attend the production. He also anonymously wrote the satire, *An Argument to prove that the Tragedy of Douglas ought to be burnt by the hands of the Hangman*, which was designed to attack the position of the anti-*Douglas* faction, but was frequently taken to be a genuine work of that group.

Patrick Cuming (bap. 1695 – 1776)

Cuming was a Church of Scotland minister attached to the Earl of Ilay's political faction as his ecclesiastical adviser. As a result of Ilay's influence, he became the professor of ecclesiastical history at Edinburgh University. He was the moderator of the general assembly of the Church of Scotland in 1749, 1752 and 1756, but began to lose his influence with the emergence of William Robertson and the Moderates. His rivalry with the Moderates led him to condemn *Douglas*, and attack those Ministers who had attended the play. As a result of these actions, he was nicknamed Dr Turnstile. He was derided, along with Alexander Webster, in the anonymous pamphlet, *A Song or, A Sermon. A New Ballad.*

George Cupples (d. 1798)

Cupples was the minister of Swinton in the Presbytery of Chirnside from 1754 to 1798. He attended the University of Glasgow where he received his MA in 1746. Cupples was a colleague of Alexander Carlyle, and in his autobiography, Carlyle recounts a trip that Cupples, John Home, and himself took into England. Cupples was one of the minsters rebuked by the Presbytery for attending the theatre to see *Douglas.*

West Digges (1725? – 1786)

Digges was an actor and theatre manager in the Canongate during *Douglas's* run in Edinburgh, acting the role of Norval on the stage. Despite, or perhaps because of, the furore surrounding the play, it was a resounding success, and Digges remained as the manager of the theatre for three years. In 1758 he became embroiled in a dispute with the musicians of the theatre over salaries, which resulted in the airing of grievances appearing in six subsequent pamphlets. Since 1752, he had lived with Sarah Ward, the actress who performed the role of Lady Barnet (Randolph) in the original production of *Douglas*. However, when she left him in 1759, the contract both had with the Canongate was broken, and as a result, Digges was dismissed by the owners.

Robert Dundas of Arniston (1713-1787)

Dundas was a judge and politician, and the half-brother of Henry Dundas, who at the time of the *Douglas* controversy was the Lord Advocate of Scotland. Carlyle reported that Dundas 'openly countenanced' opposition to the play, and was himself opposed to its production. In the aftermath of the controversy, when the play's opponents complained that there was no legal act to prevent people from attending the stage, Dundas suggested a compromise that prohibited ministers only. Although this was agreed to by the Moderates, it was ultimately not enforced.

Matthew Dysart (1705 – 1773)

Dysart was the minister of Eccles in the Presbytery of Duns. He attended the University of Glasgow, and was licensed by the Presbytery of Chirnside in

1728. His mother was the daughter of William Sandilands, and when Dysart succeeded to the entailed estate of Coutson he took the name of Sandilands. Dysart was one of the minsters who attended the performance of *Douglas*.

Sir Gilbert Elliot (1722 – 1777)

Sir Gilbert Elliot, the third Baronet of Minto, was a politician, philosopher and poet. He was educated at the University of Edinburgh, and spent a year at the University of Utrecht in 1743. Elliot was a keen classical scholar, who produced a number of poetical works. He was a Member of Parliament for Selkirkshire from 1753 to 1765, and for Roxburghshire from 1765 to 1777. He was also a friend and intimate of the Earl of Bute. Carlyle remarked in his autobiography that although he and several others had offered improvements to Home's play, it was Elliot who had the biggest and most effective influence on its development.

Adam Ferguson (1723 – 1816)

Ferguson was born in Atholl, Perthshire, and was educated at the University of St Andrews. As a speaker of Gaelic he was appointed deputy chaplain of the Black Watch regiment in 1745 although he left that position in 1754 in order to pursue his literary endeavours. He succeeded David Hume as the Keeper of the Faculty of Advocates' Library in 1757, but resigned to become a tutor to the Earl of Bute's family. In 1759 he was appointed professor of natural philosophy at Edinburgh University, and in 1764 transferred to the chair of pneumatics and moral philosophy. Although Ferguson would go on to become one of the prominent figures in the Scottish Enlightenment, when he wrote his defence of *Douglas*, entitled, *The Morality of the Stage Seriously Considered* (1757), he was still a little known clergyman. Nevertheless, his contribution to the debate proved to be the most erudite of the pro-*Douglas* pamphlets.

Andrew Fletcher, Lord Milton (1691/2 – 1766)

Lord Milton was allied to the politically dominant Argathelian faction in Scotland. His ability to provide strong leadership in the aftermath of the Jacobite rebellion found favour with the British government, and cemented his position as a prominent member of the Duke of Argyll's party, which had earlier seen their power diminish following the Porteous riot of 1736. As a key distributer of patronage in the 1750s it was Milton, through the Duke of Argyle, who ultimately sanctioned the performance of *Douglas* to be staged in Edinburgh. Milton even attended the rehearsals of the play.

David Garrick (1717 – 1779)

Garrick was an actor and playwright, and a former pupil of the great lexicographer, Samuel Johnson. As one of the foremost actors of his generation, and the manager of Drury Lane theatre, it was to him that Home sent his drafts of both *Agis* and *Douglas*, hoping to have them performed on the London stage. However, despite pressure from Home's patron, the Earl of Bute, Garrick steadfastly refused to put on *Douglas*, which he believed was totally unfit for the stage. Despite his rejection of Home's dramatic work, the eventual success of *Douglas*, made Garrick became more receptive to his plays. In 1758 he staged *Agis* at Drury Lane, which ran for eleven nights, and in 1760 Garrick himself took the part of Aemilius in Home's, *The Siege of Aquileia*.

John Home (1722 – 1800)

John Home was educated at the University of Edinburgh alongside fellow future clergymen: William Robertson, Hugh Blair, Alexander Carlyle and John Witherspoon. He was the Church of Scotland minister for Athelstaneford in East Lothian, from 1746 to 1757. It was during his tenure there that he composed the tragedy of *Douglas*, having previously failed to get his first play *Agis* (1747) performed on the London stage. As result of the controversy surrounding *Douglas's* performance, Home resigned his position. He was summoned before the Presbytery of Edinburgh to account for his actions, but failed to attend any of the meetings. In 1758 Home became the Earl of Bute's private secretary in London. Encouraged by the success of *Douglas*, Home produced more plays: *The Siege of Aquileia* (1760); *The Fatal Discovery* (1773); and *Alfred* (1778). The lukewarm reception of *Alfred* made it his last offering to the stage.

William Home (d. 1784)

Home was a minister in the Church of Scotland. He was initially made the minister of Polwarth in 1735, a role which he fulfilled until 1758 when he transferred to Fogo, in the Scottish Borders. In later years he was the Chaplain of Edinburgh Castle, although he performed the duty by deputy. According to Alexander Carlyle in his autobiography, he was a cousin to John Home, the author of the tragedy, and was another of the ministers who attended the theatre during the play's initial run, and summoned, as a result, to appear before the Presbytery.

Alexander Hume (d. 1768)

Hume, a minister in the Church of Scotland, became minister of Abbey St Bathans and Strafontain, in the Presbytery of Duns, in 1755. He took over William Home's old Parish of Polwarth in 1758. Hume was educated at Edinburgh University, and along with his fellow minister, James Laurie, wrote a response to the Presbytery of Edinburgh from the Presbytery of Duns, which appeared in the April edition of the *Scots Magazine*, questioning the legitimacy of its Edinburgh counterpart in calling to account clergy who were outside its jurisdiction.

David Hume (1711 – 1776)

Although Hume is today accepted as one of the key philosophers in Western culture, in the eighteenth century it was his reputation as a historian which won him more renown. As a sceptical philosopher he was viewed as a dangerous heretic by the more orthodox members of the Church of Scotland.

Despite his notoriety, he was convivial and good natured, and enjoyed good relations with members of the Moderate party. As a critic of note in his day, his deliberately excessive praise of Home's *Douglas* was calculated to generate maximum publicity for the play, which it succeeded in doing. A great deal of the literature generated in response to the play focuses on Hume's artistic claims for the tragedy. Hume was also concerned that his association with the Moderates, and Home in particular, would provide ammunition to the hardliners in the Church who were incandescent that a minister should have written a play in the first place.

James Laurie (? -?)

Laurie was the minister of Langton in the Presbytery of Duns from 1734 – 1757 at which point he transferred to Hawick. In his youth he attended Edinburgh University, and along with his colleague, Alexander Hume, questioned the right of the Presbytery of Edinburgh to assert its authority over ministers who belonged to different Presbyteries.

John MacLaurin, Lord Dreghorn (1734-1796)

MacLaurin, a judge and author, was the eldest son of the mathematician Colin MacLaurin. After attending Edinburgh University, he chose a career in law over the church. Through the patronage of Henry Dundas, he was made a senator of the college of justice in 1788. His title was taken from his place of residence, Dreghorn Castle, near Edinburgh. In his youth he wrote a number of poetic and comical works including *The Keekiad* and *The Philosopher's Opera* (1757). However, his early works were anonymous, written in his own hand, and initially for private circulation only. These early pieces were excluded in the collection of his works which his son Colin published in 1798. As a consequence of the anonymity of MacLaurin's early poetic efforts, a number of anonymous anti-*Douglas* pamphlets have been subsequently attributed to him because they are composed in a similar style. *The Stage or the Pulpit: A Sermon*, and, *Apology for the Writers against the Tragedy of Douglas*, both fall into this category. MacLaurin did not object to the play on religious grounds; rather, he was opposed to the cultural monopoly – as he saw it – that the Moderates were attempting to exercise over creative production in Scotland.

Thomas Otway (1652 – 1685)

Otway was an English playwright during the Restoration period. His two most famous plays, *The Orphan* (1680), and *Venice Preserved* (1682) continued to be performed well into the nineteenth century. Otway enjoyed a solid reputation during the eighteenth century, but was one of the targets of David Hume in his dedication to *Douglas*, where he claimed that Home's style was free of the 'licentiousness and unhappy barbarism' to be found in the plays of Otway and Shakespeare. His attack resulted in the staunch defence of Otway by critics who were incensed that Hume should venerate the author of *Douglas* so highly.

Francis Scott (bap. 1707 – 1782)

Scott was the minister for the parish of Westruther in the Presbytery of Earlston. He took over the position in 1738 from his father Walter Scott. He was one of the Ministers cited by the Presbytery of Edinburgh for having attended the play in Edinburgh.

Sarah Siddons (1755 – 1831)

Siddons was widely regarded as one of the best actresses of the eighteenth century. She was most renowned for her portrayal of Lady Macbeth, but she also made the part of Lady Randolph very much her own. Following her success in the role of Belvidera in Thomas Otway's *Venice Preserved*, Siddons caught the eye of David Garrick who brought her to his Drury Lane theatre. Although what was intended to be her final performance on that stage was in 1812 as Lady Macbeth, she continued to act until 1819 when she performed for the last time on stage as Lady Randolph, a character of whom she was said to be particularly fond.

John Steele (1711 – 1804)

Steele was the minister of Stair in the Presbytery of Ayr from 1735 to 1804. He attended a performance of *Douglas* in 1756 and was called before the Presbytery to express his regret at having done so. He published his sermons in 1778.

John Stuart, Earl of Bute (1713 – 1792)

John Stuart, 3rd Earl of Bute, was the first Scottish Prime Minister (First Lord of the Treasury) of Britain from 1762 – 1763, and for a time was the most powerful man in Britain. He was the nephew of the 2nd and 3rd Dukes of Argyle, but gained his political power at a British level thanks to his position as tutor to the future George III. Bute was a man of keen literary interests, ultimately becoming the patron of John Home, whom he made his private secretary in 1758. In their correspondence the two frequently discussed the drafts of Home's dramatic works, and Bute often suggested changes and improvements that could be made to the plays. He attempted to use his influence to help Home stage his plays, writing, for example, to Garrick to encourage him to produce *Douglas*. In this endeavour however, he was unsuccessful. Even when Bute lost his status of royal favourite, and drifted into political obscurity, he continued to maintain a warm correspondence with Home.

Sarah Ward (1726/7 – 1771)

Ward was an actress and theatre manager who performed the role of Lady Barnet for the Edinburgh production of *Douglas*. She acted opposite Garrick in *King Lear* at Drury Lane, but came to Edinburgh in 1752 with John Lee, who had recently taken over theatrical management in the city. West Digges was also a member of Lee's players, and it was here that the two began their affair. Ward left to perform on the Dublin stage for three years, before returning to

Edinburgh in 1755. In 1759 Ward left Digges, and departed for Covent Garden where she remained for the next twelve seasons.

Alexander Webster (1707 – 1784)

Webster was a Church of Scotland minister whose wife, Mary Erskine, was the aunt of James Boswell. As a member of Boswell's social circle, Webster often appears in his journal. Webster, a leader of the Popular party, frequently opposed the Moderates, and was vocally critical of ministers attending Home's tragedy. He was elected Moderator of the General Assembly in 1753, and in 1760 was awarded a Doctorate of Divinity (DD) from Edinburgh University. As a man noted for his conviviality, and partiality to claret, he was frequently referred to as Dr Bonum Magnum: a name which the pro-*Douglas* faction often used in their literature. His wife Mary has sometimes been cited as the author of the anti-Hume ballad, *The Infernal Council*.

Thomas Whyte (1717 – 1789)

Whyte was a minister of the Church of Scotland in Liberton in the Presbytery of Edinburgh. He attended the University of Edinburgh, before attaining his licence in 1747. He was one of the ministers called before the Presbytery of Edinburgh on January 12th 1757 to account for his actions in attending the performance of *Douglas*. He defended himself by saying that he was so far from his own parish, that he did not think anyone would recognise him at the Canongate. He was suspended for three weeks for his part in the affair, although this sentence was reduced from six weeks, partly because he showed such contrition for his attendance. Carlyle wrote in his autobiography that his plea was aided by Whyte's claim that he had tried to conceal himself as much as possible when he was there, so that no one would notice him.

John Witherspoon (1723 – 1794)

Witherspoon was a Church of Scotland minister who, in 1768 became the President of the College of New Jersey (Princeton) and was a signatory of the Declaration of Independence in 1776. He was a fellow student at the University of Edinburgh of William Robertson, Hugh Blair, Alexander Carlyle, and John Erskine. As a fierce critic of the Moderates, Witherspoon first assailed them in *Ecclesiastical Characteristics* (1753) which established his position as one of their premier opponents. His work, *A Serious Enquiry into the Nature and Effects of the Stage* (1757), is the most sophisticated response to the pro-*Douglas* apologists.

Timeline of Pamphlet Material

Pamphlet	Date of Publication	Source for publication
Advertisement for Douglas	December 1756	Title page indicates upcoming performance on 14th December 1756
The First Night's Audience	1756?	N/A
A Prologue to the long expected Tragedy of Douglas	Dated December 14th 1756 (Most likely published later)	Date printed on pamphlet
An Epilogue to the Tragedy of Douglas, Spoke by the Author	Dated December 14th 1756 (Most likely published later)	Date printed on pamphlet
A Full and True History of the Bloody Tragedy of Douglas	December 1756 (around 17th/18th)	In his autobiography, Carlyle noted that his piece extended the play's run by two days, so his piece had to be written around four days after the play started
Admonition and Exhortation by the Presbytery of Edinburgh	Dated 5th January, and to be read from pulpits on the 30th. Published in the January edition of the *Scots Magazine*, and then in newspapers from February 2nd	Was published in the January edition of the *Scots Magazine* 1757, with an announcement that it would subsequently be distributed to newspapers

A Letter to the Reverend the Moderator, and the Members of the Presbytery Of Haddingtoun	Beginning of January 1757	The Letter refers to events for the last 'eight or ten days', but the pamphlet's publication date is 1757
Serious Enquiry into the Nature and Effects of the Stage	Sometime in January 1757. Extracts from it were printed in the March 1757 edition of the *Scots Magazine*	The *Scots Magazine* for January 1757 notes it as a new work published in Glasgow for 6d
David Hume's *Dedication*	It was signed on 3rd January 1757, and appeared in editions of Hume's *Four Dissertations* in February 1757. It was reprinted in the June edition of the *Scots Magazine*	Printed in Hume's *Four Dissertations* and the *Scots Magazine* for June 1757
The Moderator Number II	January 1757	Appeared in new works published list in the *Scots Magazine* of January 1757, price 2d
The Deposition, or the Fatal Miscarriage	January 1757	N/A
The Morality of Stage Plays Seriously Considered	January 1757	Appears in the *Scots Magazine's* list of new books for January 1757, price 6d

A Song or, a Sermon. A New Ballad	Dated 29ᵗʰ of January 1757, which was a day before the Admonition was to be read in the pulpits	Date printed on the ballad
An argument to prove that the Tragedy of Douglas ought to be burnt by the hands of the hangman	End of January 1757	In his autobiography (p. 313), Carlyle remarked that the piece was published at the end of the month when he was in Dumfries.
Advertisement	End of January 1757	Refers to the upcoming dates of the 30ᵗʰ and 31ˢᵗ of January, as well as the previously printed pamphlets, *The Moderator*, and, *The Deposition*
The Usefulness of the Edinburgh Theatre Seriously Considered with a Proposal for Rendering it more Beneficial	Published after January 1757	Published after Ferguson's *Morality of Stage Plays Seriously Considered*, because it employs a quote taken from it as its motto
The Apostle to the Theatre his Garland	Published after February 1757	Makes frequent references to Hume's dedication

Some Serious remarks on a late pamphlet , entituled, The Morality of Stage-Plays Seriously Considered	March 1757	Appears in *Scots Magazine's* list of new books for March 1757
An address to the Synod of Lothian and Tweedale concerning Mr Home's Tragedy and Mr Hume's Essays	Must have been published after the London performance of the play on March 14th 1757 as it makes reference to it	The address references the recent London performance, and also cites Witherspoon's pamphlet as a source
The Stage or the Pulpit: A Sermon (parts I, II and III)	March 1757	Alludes to the publication of *Douglas* which the newspapers announced to be March 29th, which is the same date that the third part was written
Apology for the Writers against the Tragedy of Douglas	Late March, early April 1757	*Edinburgh Evening Courant* of April 5th 1757 refers to the recently published 'Apology', price 2d
The Second Part of the Apostle to the Theatre his Garland	Published after March 1757	Makes reference to Home making 'April fools' of the Presbytery of Haddington with his continued refusal to attend their summons

Douglasiana	'The Confession' was published after March 1757	Quotes directly from the March edition of the *Scots Magazine*
The Tragedy of Douglas Analysed	April 1757	Listed in the *Scots Magazine's* new books section for April 1757, priced 6d
The Philosopher's Opera	April 1757	Appears in the new books list for April 1757 in the *Scots Magazine*, priced 4d
A Letter to Mr David Hume	April 1757	Listed in the *Scots Magazine's* new books section for April 1757, priced 6d
The Players Scourge	Published around May 1757	Pamphlet refers to the leniency with which the Synods of Lothian and Tweedale treated those ministers who attended the play
By particular desire of the Reverend members of the G---l As--m — y	May/June 1757	Alludes to a forthcoming date on the 5th of June (day that Home gave a farewell sermon to his ministry at Athelstaneford). Addresses Carlyle's case before the Presbytery which was resolved in his favour on 24th May

The Irish Parson's Advice concerning the Play-House, or the Reverend Revenge, A Poem	1757	Date printed on pamphlet
The Infernal Council	1757	Date printed on pamphlet
Advice to the Writers in Defence of Douglas	1757	Date printed on pamphlet
The Finishing Stroke; or, Nothing. A Ballad	1757	Date printed on pamphlet
Remarks upon the play of Douglas in a letter by a Gentleman to his friend in the Country	N/A	N/A
Votes of the Presbytery of Edinburgh	N/A	N/A
The second part of the Players Scourge	Dated 1768	Date printed on the pamphlet, but possibly a misprint.

Lightning Source UK Ltd.
Milton Keynes UK
UKOW07f1107200715

255483UK00001B/4/P

9 781846 220340